THE AMERICANS
AT D-DAY

Also by John C. McManus

The Deadly Brotherhood:
The American Combat Soldier in World War II

Deadly Sky:
The American Combat Airman in World War II

JOHN C. McMANUS

THE AMERICANS
AT D-DAY

THE AMERICAN EXPERIENCE AT THE NORMANDY INVASION

A TOM DOHERTY ASSOCIATES BOOK
NEW YORK

THE AMERICANS AT D-DAY: THE AMERICAN EXPERIENCE
AT THE NORMANDY INVASION

Copyright © 2004 by John C. McManus

This book is printed on acid-free paper.

All photographs are courtesy of the National Archives and
Records Administration unless otherwise noted.

A Forge Book
Published by Tom Doherty Associates, LLC
175 Fifth Avenue
New York, NY 10010

www.tor.com

Forge® is a registered trademark of Tom Doherty Associates, LLC.

Library of Congress Cataloging-in-Publication Data

McManus, John C., 1965–
    The Americans at D-Day : the American experience at the Normandy
invasion / John McManus.—1st hardcover ed.
        p.   cm.
    "A Tom Doherty Associates book."
    Includes bibliographical references (p. 381) and index (p. 389).
    ISBN 0-765-30743-X
    EAN 978-0765-30743-9
    1. World War, 1939–1945—Campaigns—France—Normandy. 2. United
States—Armed Forces—History—World War, 1939–1945. I. Title.
D756.5.N6M36   2004
940.54'2142—dc22

                                                        2003026398

First Edition: June 2004

Printed in the United States of America

0   9   8   7   6   5   4   3   2   1

For Michael and Mary Jane McManus
With Enduring Gratitude

CONTENTS

Part I: GEARING UP

Part II: THE ASSAULT

LIST OF MAPS

ACKNOWLEDGMENTS

From the earliest I can remember, I have been fascinated with Operation Overlord and the Battle of Normandy. Something about this epic battle has captivated my attention and made me curious to know as much as possible about the fighting. The excellent work of historians such as Forrest Pogue, Stephen Ambrose, Carlo D'Este, Robin Neillands, Gordon Harrison, Martin Blumenson, Max Hastings, and many others only served to stoke my curiosity even more. I have made several visits to Normandy, and each time I go, I come away with a sense of the battle's importance in modern history. Gradually, I have come to believe that Normandy was the harbinger of today's world. Over time, it occurred to me that a fundamental aspect of the battle—the American contribution—had not been written about with the kind of focus, or the kind of depth, it deserves. The rise of the United States as a world power, and the significant impact that U.S. soldiers had on the battle's outcome, is, in my view, the defining aspect of the story of Normandy.

So I decided to embark upon a project that focused exclusively on the American experience in the invasion and the ensuing battle. My hope is that, with this volume and the one that follows, I will have afforded the reader a comprehensive view of the impact the United States had on one of the pivotal battles of World War II.

The research and writing of a book like this was a substantial, time-consuming undertaking. Many dedicated, helpful individuals have made it possible. Doug Brinkley and his staff at the Eisenhower Center in New Orleans welcomed me as one of their own during my visit. They helped me any way they could, gave me tremendous freedom of access, and provided excellent guidance through their remarkable collection of World War II oral histories. Their collection is, in my opinion, among the very best sources of firsthand accounts from American veterans of that war. At the University of Illinois archives, Ellen Swain helped me navigate an extensive collection of documentary material from the 3rd Armored Division. I am thankful for her time and patience. Ronald Marcello, a first-rate oral historian at the University of North Texas, agreed to send me transcripts of several interviews he did with Normandy veterans. His probing, intelligent questions drew many pertinent and important details from these veterans and added to the quality of this book. Christopher Koontz, his assistant, handled the logistics of sending me the transcripts, and I appreciate his efforts. Jay Graybeal, at the United States Army Military History Institute, provided much help in finding good photographs.

The University of Missouri–Rolla, where I teach, is blessed with an excellent interlibrary loan department. In the preparation of this book, I ordered hundreds of books or articles through interlibrary loan. Scott Peterson and several members of the library staff tirelessly processed every request. Often they went out of their way to find rare material for me. Without their efforts, this book would not have been possible.

The History Department at UMR provided me with financial support for my travels. I would like to thank my colleagues in the department for their advice, support, and friendship. Wayne Bledsoe, Jack Ridley, Tseggai Isaac, Pat Huber, Jeff Schramm, Michael Meagher, and Harry Eisenman have contributed their unique perspectives on a range of issues. Special thanks go to Larry Gragg for his cheerful wisdom, Diana Ahmad for giving me information on her uncle, a glider pilot who flew into Normandy on D-Day, and to my mentor, Russ Buhite, for his constant guidance. Each and every day, Russ gives me a larger-than-life role model to emulate. The same can be said of Tom Fleming. I would like to thank him for many years of encouragement and support.

I am grateful to my editors at Forge for their professionalism and good cheer. Brian Callaghan handled many of the unglamorous details of manuscript format, copying, pre-production, and the like, as did Eric Raab. I appreciate their steady guidance. I am grateful to Bob Gleason for his practiced, experienced editorial view. Bob knows the publishing industry inside and out, and he proves it in all of our conversations. In this book, he knew what to change and what to leave in place. I consider myself fortunate to work with him. Along these same lines, thanks go to Ted Chichak, my literary agent. From the start, he believed in this project, shaped it, and helped me bring it to fruition. Thanks, Ted.

My friends and family have had a substantial impact on this book. Ed Laughlin, a close friend who is a veteran of the 82nd Airborne Division, provided me with much good information on his division's experiences in Normandy. Many thanks to Mark Williams, Sean Roarty, Bob Kaemmerlen, Mike Chopp, John Villier, Steve Kutheis, Ron Kurtz, and Dave Cohen for their friendship and their influence on me.

My biggest debt of gratitude goes to my family. My in-laws, Ruth and Nelson Woody, Nancy and Charlie Swartwout, Doug, David, Angee, Tonya, and the kids are all very special people. I am honored to be associated with the Woody family and grateful to all of them for their constant warmth and humor. My brother, Mike, is a fellow military-history enthusiast who is often willing to tolerate my long discourses on my research. I am thankful for his patience and his extensive knowledge of history. I would like to thank my sister, Nancy, her husband, John, and my nieces, Kelly and Erin, for their affection and their tolerance of an uncle/brother/brother-in-law whose mind is often deep in the past. Michael and Mary Jane McManus, my parents, to whom I have dedicated this book, deserve special praise for any success I have had or may have. I hope that this book will serve as an enduring monument of appreciation for everything they have done for me. The last, and largest, debt of gratitude naturally belongs to my loving wife, Nancy. Over the course of many hours, she scoured countless photo archives until she found exactly the right blend of illustrations for this book. In addition, she was a source of constant support and understanding during my seemingly endless hours of research, rumination, and writing. She shares my passion for history and understands me in her own special way. This book is hers as much as it is mine. That being said, any errors are my responsibility and mine alone.

JOHN C. MCMANUS

St. Louis, Missouri
September 1, 2003

THE AMERICANS
AT D-DAY

PROLOGUE

The Battle of Normandy was the pivotal moment of World War II in Europe. It represented Germany's last chance to end the war on any sort of favorable terms. The idea that Germany's eventual fate was sealed from 1942 onward, when it faced the Grand Alliance of Britain, the United States, and the Soviet Union, is, quite simply, wrong. Allied manpower and industrial and material advantages did not guarantee victory. History is replete with examples of lesser powers triumphing over their better armed, fed, and supplied adversaries. The Greek–Persian Wars, the English victory at Agincourt, and the American revolutionary triumph against Britain, the world's most powerful nation in the late eighteenth century, are but a few examples. In the modern era, such stunning upsets as the Israeli triumph in the 1948 War of Independence, the Vietnamese communist victory over French and later American adversaries, as well as the victory of the ragged but dedicated mujahideen over the Soviet Union all proved that logistics alone do not win wars.

Nazi Germany was far more powerful than all of the upset victors I have just mentioned. In fact, one could argue quite convincingly that Adolf Hitler's Germany was the third strongest military power in existence during the bloody twentieth century, behind only the United States and the Soviet Union. What's more, Nazi Germany could only be defeated (and at tremendous cost) when those two eventual superpowers, plus a technologically strong but manpower-poor Britain, concentrated all their efforts on crushing Hitler's empire.

By 1944, Germany had been at war for five long and destructive years. German cities had been reduced to smoldering rubble by American and British bombers. The German Air Force had been eroded into little more than a defensive, fighter reaction force by the demands of the Eastern Front and, especially, the Anglo-American strategic bombing campaign. The German Navy had lost any serious hope of controlling the Atlantic—it had lost too many submarines and crews to Allied convoys or aircraft. Most damaging of all, Germany's single greatest weapon, its army, had been decimated by the Red Army in three of the bloodiest years of fighting in the history of warfare. An incredibly resilient Soviet Union had staved off what looked to be imminent defeat in 1941–42, to instead seize the initiative. The result was a bloody war of attrition that saw the Soviets steadily pushing the Germans westward, even as both sides lost thousands of soldiers every month. In so doing, the Soviets, through an enormity of suffering and sacrifice that still is not completely comprehended in the West, made perhaps the most valuable contribution of any Allied nation in the war—the destruction of the *offensive* capability of the German Army.

Even so, the Soviets by 1944 had not come close to destroying Germany's formidable army. They had only destroyed its ability to conquer the Soviet Union. Joseph Stalin understood this. He knew that even though the Eastern Front war of attrition had turned in his favor, he could not hope to win a decisive victory over Germany without serious help from the West. Pinprick invasions of North Africa and Italy did not constitute the help he needed. Only a cross-Channel invasion of France fit the bill. In 1942, when total defeat was a real possibility for his nation, Stalin had agitated fiercely for this "second front." Two years later, in spite of the fact that his armies had come close to kicking German forces out of Russia, his enthusiasm for a second front had not dimmed. Given his aggressive postwar acquisition of communist-dominated buffer zones designed, undeniably, to diminish Anglo-American power on the European continent, it is difficult to imagine that Stalin would have had much enthusiasm for a second front in 1944 if he was confident that his armies could finish off Hitler's Germany. After all, why welcome the British and Americans back into northern Europe if he didn't have to? Why share the continent with them if the Red Army could conquer Germany on its own?

Stalin, and his cohorts in the West, understood the reality of the war situation in early 1944—that in spite of all the adversity Germany had faced, it could still win the war. German cities may have been destroyed but not its productive capacity. With the possible exception of oil, Germany was producing more war-related matériel in 1944 than ever before. To be sure, the country's manpower resources were stretched perilously thin, but the German Army still possessed enough quality soldiers to hold the line in a two-front war.

The key for the Nazis was to turn this two-front war into a one-front war. That could be accomplished in one of two possible (and admittedly hypothetical) ways. First, the Anglo-Americans could shy away from a true second front. No doubt this would have meant that the western Allies would redouble their futile efforts in the Mediterranean: Italy, Greece, and the Balkans. In this scenario, the Germans could have used the advantageous terrain of southern Europe to forge a stalemate. In all probability, the Allies would have been stopped cold for at least a year, maybe more. Only Germany's Romanian oil supply would have been affected. In the meantime, Hitler could have stripped his "Atlantic Wall" defenses in France and strengthened his own efforts against the Soviet Union, presenting the real possibility of a negotiated end to the conflict in the East, since Stalin would have been embittered by the failure of his allies to open a second front (he never trusted the British and Americans anyway).

In the second hypothetical scenario, the western Allies could attempt to forge a second front and the Germans could defeat it. The consequences of such a defeat would have been enormous. If the Germans repelled an invasion outright or if they succeeded in stalemating Allied forces in Normandy, the Allies, by most accounts, could not have even thought of another assault for at least another year. Quite possibly, Winston Churchill would have fallen from power. Franklin Roosevelt almost certainly would not have been elected to a fourth term in November 1944. These political changes would have put the unconditional-surrender policy of these two leaders in peril. Very probably, the Americans would have shifted their focus to the Pacific. This would have given Nazi Germany precious time to produce technologically advanced weaponry, most notably jet aircraft that could have turned the tide of the European air war. In the meantime, Hitler could have redeployed most of his land forces to the East for one more decisive campaign, the results of which are almost beyond imagination—a Nazi- or communist-dominated Europe, most likely the former.

Thus if 1942 and 1943 marked the turning point of the war in

Europe, 1944 marked the pivot point. By then the Allies had tipped the scales of probability in their favor, but by no means had they achieved an inevitable victory. Only through land victories in 1944 could they win the war against Germany, and those land victories had to come in northern Europe.

There is one overarching reason why 1944 had to be the decisive year of the war in Europe: Any cross-Channel invasion of the continent, and the ensuing campaign, would have to be led by the United States, and, for the first two years of its involvement in the war, America was not prepared for such a leadership role. The British did not have the manpower or firepower to lead this kind of enormous invasion; nor did they have the wherewithal to lead the way in the massive campaign that must surely follow any successful invasion. Only the United States could do this.

Accordingly, the Battle of Normandy serves as a seminal moment in the history of the United States. At Normandy, the United States, by necessity, became a superpower. Only American manpower, airpower, firepower, industrial power, agricultural power, and combat power could make the second front a success. Without question, the victory in Normandy was the product of an Allied effort. But, by the battle's end, over half of Allied manpower was American, and the United States was providing about two-thirds of the logistical support; this was a harbinger for the campaign in northern Europe in 1944–45. The United States had needed two long, and difficult, years to overcome its own unpreparedness for this war, but, in the famous (but erroneously quoted) words of Japanese admiral Isoroku Yamamoto, the United States truly was a "sleeping giant." The summer of 1944 saw America achieve the final transformation from an inward-looking continental power to a military, industrial, economic, and cultural superpower—a world leader. The decisive American contribution to the outcome of Normandy, the pivotal battle in Europe, made that leadership a reality.

This is not to minimize or dismiss the British contribution to the campaign. The valor of British soldiers certainly matched that of American fighting men. But imperial Britain was declining by 1944. The five previous years of war had sapped the strength of the British economy and British military power. What's more, land power had never been the strength of this seafaring empire, and now, in 1944, the mission of defeating Nazi Germany called for overwhelmingly effective land power, something only the United States, among western nations, possessed.

So, a great task—a battle for the future of Europe—lay before the western Allies as 1944 began. The first step in this great task was to successfully invade the coast of northern France. The British and Americans expended enormous resources in planning and carrying out this difficult mission that has generally been dubbed "the D-Day invasion."

Even so, in spite of the enormously complicated nature of the Normandy invasion, *it was only the beginning.* The larger task that had to follow from a successful invasion was the destruction of German combat power in Europe and the resulting elimination of the Nazi regime. Success on D-Day did not, as many historians have intimated, equate with success in inflicting unconditional defeat upon Germany. Field Marshal Erwin Rommel was incorrect in his assertion that the battle would be decided on the day of the invasion. Rommel felt that Germany's only hope of victory was to repel the Allies at the water's edge. If the Germans failed to do so, he argued, then the overwhelming might of Allied logistical superiority would inevitably defeat them. As it turned out, his elaborate beach defenses held off the Allies for, at best, half a day. Yet the ideal defensive terrain of Normandy, plus the tenacity of German defenders, held the Allies in check for most of the summer of 1944. Surely this fact must stand as a damning indictment of Rommel's thesis. D-Day was indeed enormously important, but only for what could go wrong for the Allies—a dismal failure and the earthshaking political consequences—rather than for what could go right—getting ashore and staying there. The former would almost certainly have led to victory for Germany; the latter in no way guaranteed victory for the Allies.

Thus, the Battle of Normandy is the story of the invasion and the fighting that followed. This, of course, is an ambitious chronicle, and, for that reason, this narrative is split into two volumes. This book, *The Americans at D-Day,* will cover the months leading up to D-Day and the great invasion itself, while the second work, *The Americans at Normandy,* will describe the fighting that followed D-Day. Both of these books will, I hope, successfully convey, through many new viewpoints, the vital American role in deciding one of history's great battles. In addition, I hope to join several recent historians in refuting the erroneous view that American soldiers were badly outmatched in valor and expertise by the Germans. The Americans did not win solely through sheer numbers or lavish matériel. More than anything, they prevailed because of innovation, bravery, and resolve. In the end they were better fighters than their adversaries.[1]

It all began with D-Day.

INTRODUCTION
FEBRUARY 1944

General Dwight D. Eisenhower carefully seated himself in a crude wooden chair behind a modest desk, in his austere, cramped office at 47 Grosvenor Square in London. His hands rested on a rectangular desk calendar that he rarely ever used. Just beyond the calendar, a pair of pens, protruding from their brass stand, pointed back at him like missiles. He hardly ever used the pens except when a document required his personal signature. For most everything else, he preferred to work with a pencil. Two black telephones rested just within reach of his right hand.

His mind, as usual, was racing. He was a high-strung, energetic man ("Type A" in the parlance of a later generation), the kind whose work consumed him. Never had this been more true than in the last two months, since he had been named Supreme Commander of the Allied Expeditionary Force that hoped to liberate Europe from the tyranny of Nazi Germany. In that time, he had had to supervise the relocation and transition of his staff from the Mediterranean to England. In late December, his superior, Army Chief of Staff General George C. Marshall, bluntly told him that he must come home for a short rest. In truth, Eisenhower did not want to go home. To be sure, he wanted to see his wife, Mamie, whom he missed terribly, and his son, John, a cadet in his final year at West Point. But Eisenhower's heart was not in the homecoming. He did not think it fair that he go home when so many of his soldiers had to stay overseas for the duration. Plus, the enormous job in front of him kept him from truly enjoying his visit.

Since arriving in England in January, he had dealt with a series of headaches. The invasion plan was inadequate. Lieutenant General Frederick Morgan's staff at COSSAC (Chief Of Staff to the Supreme Allied Commander), which had been planning the invasion of France since early 1943, had done a fine job, but their concepts were limited by Allied inadequacies in shipping and transport. COSSAC envisioned a three-division assault, and Eisenhower knew this limited assault plan was a recipe for disaster. He and his key subordinates, most notably General Bernard Montgomery, had already spent several days reworking the invasion plan to incorporate a five-division assault, augmented by three airborne divisions. But so much still needed to be done. Where would Eisenhower get the needed landing craft for his ambitious plan? He had just spent a couple of days meeting with naval officers on that worrisome issue. Even with adequate landing craft, could the Allies really hope to penetrate Hitler's "Atlantic Wall"? Eisenhower thought so, but he still could not be sure.

London politics were already a problem for Ike (as nearly everyone called him). Prime Minister Winston Churchill was attempting to monopolize his time. Two years before, when Eisenhower came to London with the intent of carrying out a cross-Channel attack in 1942, the two men had forged a friendship. Eisenhower liked and respected Churchill, but the man could be a major gadfly. He was incredibly persistent in pursuit of his pet ideas and projects. These days he was determined to kill Operation Anvil (later Dragoon), an invasion of southern France that would serve as a complementary operation to the main assault, Operation Overlord, in Normandy. Churchill thought Anvil was redundant; far better, he argued, to spend the resources on a redoubled effort in Italy or an invasion of the Balkans. Ike completely disagreed. He knew that in spite of Allied air and naval power, the Germans would enjoy potentially decisive advantages in repelling the invasion. They would outnumber the Allied assault force and could use their best divisions to crush the newly landed troops. Even if the Allies could overcome that daunting challenge, they would need plenty of logistical capacity to support a major campaign in northwest Europe. This meant that they absolutely had to control ports such as Marseilles and Toulon.

Eisenhower knew—could feel it in his achy bones actually—that the biggest argument would have to do with airpower. He strongly felt that he must have control over the formidable Allied strategic air forces during the weeks leading up to the invasion. Not only could these powerful forces destroy German coastal defenses; they could also isolate the battlefield, negating the German advantage of numbers, supply lines, and communications. But the commanders of those air forces, tenaciously and fiercely independent, would not accede to his control, not without a major spat.

He lit a cigarette (one of about eighty he would smoke on this, a typical day), fumbled with his reading glasses, and settled down for some paperwork. He liked to keep his desk clean and organized, as much as that was possible. Sometimes, the weight of his responsibilities could be crushing. He could feel the stress, in his temples, in his shoulders, and in the knee that had been injured playing football nearly thirty years before at West Point. His hair was thin, almost nonexistent, now. His face was drawn. Dark circles had formed under his eyes. He could light up a room with his famous grin, but these days he usually wore a worried expression on his face. Sometimes he fantasized about what life would have been like without this war—a quiet retirement, a fishing pole, anonymity, a small family, and a son of whom he was enormously proud.

But, truthfully, he was right where he wanted to be. A man of great, albeit guarded, ambition, he had prepared himself for this for decades. His mentor, one of the most influential people in his life, General Fox Conner, had convinced him twenty years before that the botched peace of the Treaty of Versailles would one day lead to another war in Europe. So, even in the 1920s, Eisenhower had been one of the few people who anticipated the coming of World War II. Perhaps for that reason, he had stuck with his army career during many low and difficult times, the worst of which were probably the 1930s when he had served as General Douglas MacArthur's chief of staff in Washington and then the Philippines. Ike had never quite gotten over his bitter disappointment at not having had the chance to command troops in combat in World War I. That was in the past, though. This job, this crucial moment in time, the great issues that would be decided by this war, would all make up for that.

He well understood the magnitude of the task ahead. Eisenhower hated Nazism, hated it to the very marrow of his bones. He knew that Nazi Germany must be crushed, mercilessly and completely; only then could a new, peaceful world emerge from the tragic ashes of World War II. He understood that only the United States, among western nations, possessed the power to make that happen. Even so, the United States, rather than exploiting its new position of leadership, must work together with other Allied nations. Eisenhower believed that to his very core. The Allies *must* be united. Without such unity, they would surely fail against so powerful an enemy.

The general nervously stubbed out his cigarette in a rapidly filling ashtray. Immediately he lit another one. As he did so, he perused a cable, for his eyes only, from the Combined Chiefs of Staff, a group of senior-level British and American commanders who jointly planned and supervised the entire war effort. Ike scanned the cable. It was a succinct, eight-point directive formally naming him supreme commander and outlining his responsibilities. His eyes kept returning to the one sentence that summed up their entire directive: "You will enter the continent of Europe and, in conjunction with the other United Nations, undertake operations aimed at the heart of Germany and the destruction of her armed forces."

The rest of the directive, in effect, gave him the necessary power to complete that enormous task. He would not be a figurehead, as he had arguably been in the Mediterranean, nor would he merely concentrate on the political goal of Allied unity while British commanders ran military operations. The directive, in unmistakably clear prose, gave him, in one fell swoop, more military power than any previous general in American history. For the first time all day, Eisenhower smiled. The American in him knew that he and his nation must have this power if the Allies hoped to triumph in the momentous struggles that lay ahead. He set the directive down on his desk. Now the ally in him had to go about the task of making it happen.[1]

PART I

GEARING UP

CHAPTER ONE

THE PLANNING AND PREPARATION

The Germans had four years to fortify their conquered northern Atlantic coast, but they had not, as of early 1944, put that time to good use. For three of those years the Western Front was, to them, a place to refit formations that had been shattered in Russia or a place to station inferior troops not trusted with front-line duty. The Nazi propaganda machine boasted about Germany's "Atlantic Wall," but until the latter part of 1943 the wall was more fantasy than reality. Two things happened in late 1943 that lit a fire under the Germans. First, they began to realize that an Anglo-American invasion of France was a real possibility. Second, they appointed their most prominent commander, Field Marshal Erwin Rommel, the great hero of North Africa, to command in the west.

Rommel toured the beach defenses and came away appalled. In almost every area along the coast, the Germans did not have enough mines, barbed wire, obstacles, pillboxes, cupolas, concrete, guns, or troops to repel the kind of invasion Rommel expected in 1944. He strongly believed that Germany could only win the coming battle by repelling the invasion at the water's edge. The first twenty-four hours would be decisive. If the Germans allowed the Allies a lodgment on the continent, their logistical, manpower, naval, and air superiority would inevitably overwhelm German forces. Only by turning the invasion coast into an impenetrable wall, ironically echoing the Nazi propaganda for which Rommel had little but contempt, could his forces achieve victory. The diminutive, dynamic German commander stood on a French beach one day in early 1944 and pensively told his young aide, Captain Hellmuth Lang, "The war will be won or lost on the beaches. We'll have only one chance to stop the enemy, and that's while he's in the water . . . struggling to get ashore. Believe me, Lang, the first twenty-four hours of the invasion will be decisive . . . for the Allies, as well as Germany, it will be the longest day."[1]

Rommel immediately ordered a dramatic strengthening of the beach defenses. Thousands of slave and local laborers poured millions of tons of concrete and steel emplacements. German engineers sowed millions of mines and beach obstacles. The latter mainly consisted of devices aimed at thwarting landing craft: mine-tipped logs, sharp hedgehogs, concrete tank traps, barbed wire, Belgian gates (steel contraptions designed to snare landing craft), concrete cones, even live shells pointed out to sea. Behind these initial obstacles, his commanders supervised the construction of pillboxes, observation bunkers, communication trenches, guns, and machine-gun nests with interlocking fields of fire. They made brilliant use of terrain. They even took steps to defeat an airborne invasion, denuding local forests to emplace sharpened stakes known as Rommel's asparagus. The asparagus were supposed to tear open gliders or impale descending paratroopers.[2]

The problem for Rommel was that he did not have total control of German forces in the west. He only controlled the armies defending Normandy and Calais. In effect, this meant he was subordinate to one of the German Army's elder statesman—Field Marshal Gerd von Rundstedt, a no-nonsense sixty-nine-year-old who was not afraid to speak bluntly, even to Hitler's retinue. Rundstedt, commander in chief of all German forces in the west, completely disagreed with Rommel. Rundstedt thought that a successful Allied invasion was inevitable. Germany could not hope to be strong everywhere along the coast. Nor could German mechanized formations, which would be desperately needed to repel the Allied Army in France, hope to survive under the muzzles of Allied naval guns. Bitter experiences at Sicily, Salerno, and Anzio had proven the potency of naval gunfire. To neutralize this Allied strength, Rundstedt wanted to concentrate German defenses inland, along defensible terrain, gradually employing powerful reserves in counterattacks, quite similar to the approach the Japanese would later take in such battles as Peleliu and Okinawa.

Hitler's mentality was more in line with Rommel's. The Führer usually wanted to defend every inch of conquered ground. In this case, he did not rule in either commander's favor; instead he divided power between them and maintained operational control over vital armored reserves for himself. In so doing, he ensured a dysfunctional command setup. Consequently, in the coming invasion, while Allied commanders worked together, German commanders often worked at cross-purposes.

One month after General Eisenhower received his momentous directive from the Combined Chiefs of Staff, his plan for Operation Overlord was mostly in place. Thousands of Allied officers and enlisted men had contributed, over the course of two years, to this final plan. Their first task had been to decide where to invade. The Pas de Calais area was, by far, the most desirable. Not only was it closest to England (about twenty miles at its most narrow point), but it also contained several excellent ports necessary for supply of the massive Allied armies. Its beaches were mostly flat and could support the armor and artillery necessary to support the infantry. Beyond the beaches, the terrain of Calais was mostly flat—ideal tank country. A successful lodgment in this area would afford the Allies the chance to head straight east into Belgium and Germany. In short, Calais was the logical, even obvious, place for any invasion of France.

Given their preference, the Allies would certainly have invaded there. Unfortunately, the Germans fully understood the desirability of Calais and stationed their strongest forces there. By the spring of 1944, the powerful 15th Army, containing many of the best armored and infantry forces Germany had in the west, patrolled the area. The Germans expected the Allies to invade at Calais, not just because it was the most desirable invasion site but also because they believed the Allies would need the area's ports.

Indeed, the invasion planners had grappled with the same thorny supply issues. The disastrous Dieppe raid in August 1942 showed the strength, even at that early date, of German port defenses. Even now, two years later, with better trained and prepared assault forces, the Allies knew that such port assaults would be suicidal. To escape such a fate, they had designed, under great secrecy and with tremendous ingenuity, a plan to build artificial harbors of their own. These ports, code-named mulberries, made it possible for the Allies to invade beaches away from heavily defended ports.

In the end, the planners decided on Normandy. Normandy was well within range of Allied air cover, not prohibitively far away from sea bases in southern England, and contained beaches suitable for heavy armor and guns. Its defenses were not quite as strong as those of Calais, and it did feature a couple of attractive ports in Caen and Cherbourg. More than anything, an Allied invasion at Normandy would probably come as a surprise to the Germans, and surprise was of paramount importance. In order to neutralize the inevitable local superiority the Germans would possess in combat power, they must be kept guessing about the invasion's time and location.

To that end, the Allies perpetrated one of the great deception plans of all time—Operation Fortitude. Fortitude was possible because of the success of British intelligence. The British had captured and "turned" every German agent in Britain. These agents provided the Germans with just enough good information to seem valuable, for example, the location of various Allied units or tidbits of gossip about commanders. The agents also fed false, but seemingly desirable, information designed to reinforce the German preconception that the invasion would come at Calais (a preconception the Allies knew about because of their ability to read German message traffic, a process generally known as "Ultra"). The double agents, in their communication with Abwehr controllers in Germany, passed along reams of information about bogus Allied units or intentions. They created the notion that a huge army was forming in England, under the command of General George Patton, whom the Germans considered the best Allied commander. The mission of this "army" (known as the First U.S. Army Group) was to spearhead the main invasion at Calais. Another "army" was to lead a diversionary attack on Norway. The Allies reinforced the agent reports with bogus radio traffic, dummy tanks, and camps. In so doing, they made full use of the American film industry's ability to create excellent props.[3] Fortitude succeeded beyond all reasonable expectations. For the better part of two months after the invasion of Normandy, the Germans held most of the 15th Army in place in expectation of the "real" invasion.

Eisenhower originally toyed with an early May invasion date but was forced to postpone the invasion for a month because of the nagging landing-craft shortages. He finally decided on a June 5 invasion date. This was the first of three days when all necessary conditions for the cross-Channel attack would be in place. Not only would his forces have just enough landing craft by then, but they would also benefit from the low-tide/full-moon combination SHAEF (Supreme Headquarters Allied Expeditionary Forces) planners deemed crucial for a successful invasion. In carrying out the planned daytime assault, the troops needed low-tide conditions to identify, destroy, or evade Rommel's deadly beach obstacles. The paratroopers would make a night drop; they would need the residual light of a full moon to have any chance of coordinating their operations.[4]

The Overlord plan has been related in great detail in many other works and need not be repeated in like detail here. But, as an overview, the following invasion plan had emerged by March: Landings would take place on both the Calvados and Cotentin coastlines of Normandy. On the eastern edge of the Calvados coast, but west of the Orne River, the British and Canadians, augmented by paratroopers, would land on beaches located due north of Caen and Bayeux. First, the British 6th Airborne Division would be dropped near the Orne and Dives Rivers. There they would carry out numerous missions designed to provide flank security and hinder German reinforcements. Most notably, the British paratroopers drew the mission of capturing powerful German fortifications at Merville. These fortifications had the potential to unleash withering fire on the British beaches. The paratroopers were also ordered to capture or destroy various bridges over the Orne.

Shortly after daylight, the main forces would carry out their assault on three beaches. In the east, near the quaint port of Ouistreham, the British 3rd Infantry Division, assisted by British and French commandos, would land at a beach code-named Sword. Just to the west, at Corseulles, the Canadian 3rd Infantry Division, itching for action after years of preparation in England, would seize a beach code-named Juno. The British 50th Infantry Division would assault the westernmost beach, code-named Gold. Once they secured Gold beach and the town of Arromanches, work would begin immediately on the British mulberry, affectionately dubbed "Port Winston" in honor of the prime minister. In totality, British and Canadian forces planned to push inland, seize Caen and adjacent Carpiquet Airfield, cut the St-Lô–Bayeux road, and forge ahead into the inviting plains beyond.

The Americans were responsible for two beaches, one on the Calvados coast and the other on the Cotentin coast. The Calvados landings would take place at Omaha beach, a few miles west of the British beaches, in the vicinity of Colleville-sur-Mer, St-

Laurent, and Vierville-sur-Mer. Assault regiments from the 1st and 29th Infantry Divisions would land at Omaha, straight into the toughest terrain of the entire coast. This six-mile stretch of beach featured very little flat ground, just a steady series of ridges and cliffs ideal for the defender. On the extreme western edge of Omaha, nature had created something else for the defender—an extended bluff that jutted into the sea, flanking the entire span of Omaha beach, as well as the Cotentin landing beaches. This bluff, known as Pointe-du-Hoc, had been heavily fortified by the Germans with 150- and 155mm guns. These artillery pieces could wreak havoc on both American beaches, so a specially trained force of U.S. Army Rangers was assigned the mission of scaling the cliffs and overwhelming the German garrison to eliminate the guns.

On the Cotentin coast, slightly north of the mouth of the Vire River and the Carentan estuary, the U.S. 4th Division and one regiment from the 90th Infantry Division drew the mission of capturing Utah beach, a flat, sandy expanse similar in texture to the British beaches. Utah's flat terrain was inviting to the attackers, but not the ground inland. This was low country, barely above sea level. The Germans had taken advantage of this to flood much of the area inland from Utah beach. The result was an inundated mess of swamps, marshes, and flooded ground just beyond Utah. Infantry might be able to splash through it slowly and arduously, but vehicles could not. The tanks, trucks, self-propelled guns, and personnel carriers on which the mobility of the U.S. Army so depended could only get off the beach over a series of four raised causeways. Those causeways, along with many bridges and crossroads to the west, could only be taken from inland.

This created a mission for the airborne, a growing but still elite component of the U.S. Army. Two airborne divisions, the 82nd and the 101st, would be unleashed along the Cotentin Peninsula, under cover of darkness in the early morning hours of D-Day. Once on the ground, they would secure the bridges and causeways necessary for the 4th and 90th Divisions and their many vehicles to get off the beach. In addition, the paratroopers were supposed to seize locks (to prevent future flooding), destroy bridges that German reinforcements might need, and generally harass any German attempt to move troops in the direction of Utah beach. When the paratroopers linked up with the amphibious forces, their mission was supposed to be finished. Events dictated otherwise, though. The Allied ground forces would be supported by a huge naval and aerial armada. These forces would provide transportation and fire support.

When the American assault forces won control of their beachheads, they would then link up with one another, a tricky process that would be achieved only at substantial cost. The Utah force would then push west, cutting off German troops in the Cotentin, before turning north to capture Cherbourg. From Omaha beach American troops were to push inland and seize St-Lô, the key crossroads town of Normandy. The capture of St-Lô and Cherbourg, along with the linkup of Omaha and Utah beaches, was supposed to then set the stage for an advance beyond Normandy.[5]

All over Britain during that spring of 1944, Allied soldiers, sailors, and airmen prepared to implement this ambitious plan. The American presence in Britain had been steadily growing since 1942. Total U.S. personnel in the United Kingdom had risen from about eighty thousand in 1942 to well over one million in early 1944.[6] American troops, equipment, and supplies were pouring into the country every day.

Among the units earmarked to carry out the pending invasion of Europe, the 29th Infantry Division had been in England the longest. The 29'ers had arrived in Britain in October 1942 and been there ever since. For nearly a year and a half they had endured a litany of training exercises that included, for some of them, grueling Ranger training. Using British Army barracks at Tidworth as their base, they hopscotched around England for an endless series of maneuvers. The soldiers of the division especially hated maneuvers in the Bodmin Moors of southwestern England. The place was eerie, bereft of human habitation, which was, of course, quite unusual for England. Chilly winds constantly swept the land, and it seemed to rain every day. "There's nowhere to go for shelter," one 29'er recalled, "and we lived out in these moors in pup tents and of course when the wind's blowing hard the stakes wouldn't stay in the ground . . . so you'd have to sit up all night, wrap the tent around you, and sit on your helmet to keep from getting your rear end wet. We [would] go out and stay for two or three weeks at a time in this environment." Inevitably they would return to Tidworth wet, miserable, and full of anticipation of a deployment to North Africa or Italy that never came. The 29'ers did not know it, but they were being held back for a special mission—the Omaha beach assault.[7]

The division was a National Guard unit composed mainly of men from Virginia, Maryland, and Pennsylvania. The blue-gray divisional patches they wore on their shoulders symbolized the reunification of North and South after the Civil War. One of the division's infantry regiments, the 116th, traced its lineage back to Stonewall Jackson's brigade, earning for themselves the nickname Stonewallers.

Some of the soldiers had known one another since childhood. They went to school together, played together, ate together, joined the local Guard unit together, and soldiered together in peace and now in war (Company A of the 116th, for instance, contained thirty-eight men from Bedford, Virginia). Felix Branham came from a farm near Charlottesville, Virginia. His father and uncles had fought in World War I. As a boy, Branham listened intently to their tales of war against the Kaiser's army. He soon grew to loathe Germany and everything it stood for, a hatred that hardened even more when the Nazis came to power in Branham's teenage years. When Branham turned eighteen, he immediately joined the local Guard unit: "It was expected in Virginia that young fellows, when they became of age, would join the National Guard, which was also known as the Virginia Militia. I enlisted in 1939 [at age eighteen] and was assigned to Company K, which was also known as the Monticello Guard."[8]

Charles Cawthon was born in Murfreesboro, Tennessee, but he ended up leading troops in the 116th Infantry. Growing up in the shadow of one of the Civil War's most famous battlefields, Cawthon was steeped in the culture of the Confederacy and its soldiers. Cawthon's father, born in the years after the war, became active in organizing veterans' reunions. "The battle was still a presence in the town when I was a boy, its memory revived annually at reunions of the country's Confederate veterans." These meetings of "shrunken and palsied old men who huddled in their gray uniforms under the great oaks at the fairgrounds each spring to hear themselves lauded once again for long-lost battles" made a deep impression on the young Cawthon. He never forgot the smell and feel of these gatherings—the odor of roasting meat, the spring air, and the brotherhood of the veterans. "The reunions pulsed with a vitality and emotion that even a boy . . . could feel and long remember."

In 1940, Cawthon earned a degree from Middle Tennessee State University. After a brief stint at the Murfreesboro newspaper, he moved on to Virginia, finally settling down as the editor of the Charlottesville newspaper. In the meantime, the first ever peacetime draft in the history of the United States became a reality. Young, unattached, and healthy, Cawthon knew his chances of getting drafted were good. He decided to join the Virginia National Guard, specifically H Company of the 116th Infantry, a unit composed largely of men from Martinsville, Virginia. Cawthon had heard that the 116th needed officers, and he wanted to be one of them. He enlisted in H Company with the intention of going directly to Officer Candidate School. He did so in late 1940 and earned a commission. Four years later, on the eve of the invasion, Cawthon was a captain in command of the 2nd Battalion's headquarters company: "Never has the Republic leaned so heavily upon a greener reed, or on one more conscious of his greenness. Otherwise, I was healthy, bookishly inclined, and as yet unaware of a latent paternal feeling for those who came under my care." These leadership qualities would serve Cawthon well at Omaha beach, a place of unimaginable horrors.[9]

Robert Miller, a Baltimore native, was the Army's version of a self-made man. At the urging of his father, Miller joined E Company of the 175th Infantry—a unit composed mainly of Baltimore men—as a private in 1935. "My father observed to me that war in Europe was coming, that the United States would eventually be drawn into it, and that it was advisable for me to experience military training. He was emphatic that to be a soldier was not just to learn to take care of yourself, but to be prepared to lead others." Miller's father could not have been more correct on both points. Young Robert absorbed his dad's wisdom, thrived in E Company, and eventually earned a commission from the ranks in 1940. In 1942, he assumed command of F Company, a unit he led into combat in Normandy.[10]

There were, of course, plenty of old hands like Branham, Cawthon, and Miller in the 29th Division, but the majority of the men who would fight in Normandy had come to the unit after Pearl Harbor. Gilbert Murdoch joined the ill-fated A Company of the 116th in the summer of 1943. Since the company contained a disproportionate number of men from Bedford, Virginia, Murdoch, like many other new men during the months leading up to the invasion, faced the difficult task of being accepted as a new replacement. After all, the old hands had known one another for years. How could a new guy straight from the States hope to crack their brotherhood? Murdoch and hundreds of others found a way, mainly through sharing the misery of tough, monotonous training. "We were trained in what was called assault boat teams. Thirty-two men each, including one officer. The way it was set up, each boat team consisted of a second lieutenant, who was the . . . assault boat team leader, two rifle [squads], a 60mm mortar team, a .30-caliber machine-gun squad with four men, a bazooka team with four men, wire-cutting team with four men, flame-throwing team of two men." Other men handled satchel charges and bangalore torpedoes. In the spring of 1944, A Company endlessly staged mock amphibious assaults.[11]

The commander of the 29th Division, Major General Charles Gerhardt, would not have it any other way. He wanted his soldiers honed to a level of sharpness never before seen in the history of the U.S. Army. He wanted them lean, tough, and aggressive, all the better to maintain momentum in combat. His men must harass the Germans mercilessly—hound them, pound them, chase them, and destroy them. Combat units often take on the personality of their commanders, and this was the way Gerhardt wanted it. He was aggressive, almost hawkish. A 1917 graduate of West Point, Gerhardt was a short, lean, bald man nearing his fiftieth birthday.

He took command of the 29th in July 1943 and immediately went about transforming it into an outfit on the move. Gerhardt knew that his predecessor, Major General Leonard Gerow (promoted now to command of V Corps), had done a fine job of training the 29'ers. The men were physically fit and proficient at their craft. But they were not, in Gerhardt's view, imbued with the proper spirit of battle. Senior officers, particularly regimental and battalion commanders, had not sparked that unique spirit—aggressiveness really—that Gerhardt believed necessary for victory in the battles ahead. Like many Regular Army officers, Gerhardt did not have a high opinion of National Guard officers. He did not think they possessed the same kind of can-do professionalism as regulars.

Not long after assuming command, the general ordered his senior commanders, most of whom were not regulars, to convene at Tavistock Court House, near divisional headquarters. No sooner had his majors, lieutenant colonels, and colonels shown up than he put them through a mock trial, with himself serving as a prosecuting attorney. The senior officers sat in rows in the jury box while Gerhardt stood before them wielding an M-1 Garand rifle. Suddenly he banged the rifle on a table and shouted, "A year from today, one out of every three of you will be dead, and the toll will be higher if senior commanders don't know their stuff!"

Shocked, they stared at him in silence. One by one, he ordered them to "take the stand." Each officer took his turn, sitting uncomfortably in the witness-box as Gerhardt strode around the courtroom firing questions like "Give me the basics of the M-1 rifle" or "How many machine guns in the weapons platoon?" Most of the witnesses stumbled over their words or flushed with a combination of embarrassment and anger. Gerhardt showed them no mercy: "How in hell can you lead your men if you don't know what a private should know?" In the estimation of most onlookers, only the division's senior guardsman and artillery chief, Brigadier General William Sands, held up well under the bizarre interrogation. But Sands was a lawyer in civilian life, so he probably was well used to the kind of tactics Gerhardt employed.[12]

The men soon took to calling their commanding general Uncle Charlie. Day after day, Uncle Charlie could be seen riding around in his jeep, the *Vixen Tor*, supervising training. Gerhardt believed that soldiering meant being in the field, not behind a desk. He thought that commanders should be out preparing their troops, not sitting behind a desk issuing orders. In the months leading up to the invasion, he seemed to be everywhere. "The general's visits to the battalion followed a pattern," Captain Cawthon later wrote, "any part of which could cause extreme discomfort. He would arrive without notice and immediately challenge any and all to marksmanship with the .45 service automatic [pistol]." Only one officer in Cawthon's battalion could beat the general. Once the shooting contest was over, Gerhardt would tour the battalion's training area, watching everything; seemingly nothing escaped his notice. "Any training that he judged to be complicated drew a blast; he demanded simplicity in tactics, a lot of yelling, and much shooting. The division's battle cry, which he originated—'29 Let's Go!'—was a required shout in everything we did."

Some of the soldiers hated Gerhardt and some admired him, but few doubted that he was preparing them as best he could. They also appreciated that Uncle Charlie usually saved his worst recriminations for officers, not enlisted men. This, of course, did not escape the notice of Cawthon and his peers. "Privates, and

NCOs to some extent, did not look on his visits with misgivings, for the word had gotten around that he did not hold them account-able for mistakes. Not so with officers; even the brashest drew mental blanks before a cold, unwavering stare, a volley of ques-tions, and the knowledge that there was no recourse if answers were hesitant or wrong."[13] Lieutenant Colonel John Cooper, com-mander of the division's 110th Field Artillery Battalion, summed up the effect Gerhardt had on his troops: "[He] was a powerful personality, and he stamped it on the division and made it a highly individualistic outfit. He placed his mark upon it so strongly that to understand the division and its spirit, one has to understand Gerhardt."[14]

Ten miles to the southwest of the 29'ers, little more than a short drive over the plains of Salisbury, another division prepared fe-verishly for the upcoming campaign. In Dorset County, along the southern coast of England, sometimes so close to the sea they could smell the salty air, the soldiers of the 1st Infantry Division steeled themselves for yet another battle. From the earliest days of the American war effort in Europe, they had led the way. They fought their way through North Africa, weathering such humili-ating reversals as Kasserine Pass. They hit the beach at a place called Gela in Sicily in the summer of 1943. Shortly after, the Germans unleashed a furious counterattack against the men of the "Big Red One," hoping to push them into the sea. The enemy failed, partially because of the power of naval guns but also be-cause of the resolve of the 1st Division.

The U.S. Army in World War II was an all-encompassing force of millions of citizen soldiers. Even so, the Army's combat divi-sions developed unique identities, almost a kind of culture of their own. This was especially true for outfits, such as the 1st, that had seen a lot of action. The more combat a unit had seen, the more lineage it could boast. The 29th Division might have been a co-hesive unit full of men who had trained together for months or years, but it was, as yet, untested in battle. By contrast, the 1st Division was a Regular Army outfit that had seen extensive action in World War I (earning great plaudits at Cantigny) and now in World War II. The unit had already lost hundreds of men killed and thousands wounded in the bloody battles of 1942 and 1943. The men who made it through those battles evinced the kind of quiet unit pride that came from survival in combat. They thought of themselves as the best, the toughest, the most reliable soldiers in the U.S. Army. They even referred to that army as "the Big Red One and 10 million replacements."

In October 1943, the division loaded aboard ships and returned to England, settling nicely into the little towns of Dorset. Most of the men lived in Nissen huts, crude shelter by civilian standards but luxurious to infantrymen used to living in muddy foxholes for weeks at a time. "Our camp is physically far better than we expected from past experience," First Lieutenant Franklyn Johnson wrote in his diary one chilly night soon after his 18th Infantry Regiment antitank company arrived in Dorset. Johnson, a Rutgers University graduate, had lived through North Africa and Sicily with only a scratch. He and the other veterans soon grew to love England. "No more tents for awhile! Nissen huts form the barracks and company orderly room, while [the] kitchen and mess hall are in an empty barn across from the stone village church." He himself lived in a small house with a few other officers. They enjoyed springy cots and crackling fires that warded off the damp English chill.[15]

The division received an infusion of replacements, and these new men did the best they could to meld with the combat vets. One of the replacements was Private Warren Coffman, the son of a West Virginia coal town barber. Shortly after the 1st Division's arrival in England, Coffman and fifty other replacements joined C Company of the division's 26th Infantry Regiment. The twenty-one-year-old private was thrilled to join this experienced unit. "If I were going to be in the invasion of France, I would rather be with these guys who had been through it twice before. The motto of the 1st Division was, 'No mission too difficult: no sacrifice too great: duty first.' The men of the Big Red One lived by that motto. They worked hard to be the best they could be."

Expecting that the new men would be raw and untutored, Coffman's commanding officer, Captain Allen Ferry, at first decreed that they must be trained as a separate group. But soon he realized that they were quite ready to take their place alongside those men who had survived the Mediterranean campaigns. "Hell, Captain, these men are trained better than we are," one lieutenant told Ferry.

So Private Coffman and the other new men melded in with the rest of the company. "I was pleasantly surprised when I joined the second platoon. Most of the men there were older than the replacements and many of them were Regular Army men who had been in the Army prior to World War II. They didn't treat us as rookies. They were friendly and were glad to see us. In fact, my new squad leader invited me to go down to the local pub with him that first night to have a few beers."

Coffman ended up having many more than just a few beers. "The bar was crowded with both American and British soldiers. They didn't have enough glasses to serve everyone, so we had to wait until someone left, or [find] a glass on the bar when no one was looking. I liked cold American beer but this was warm and bitter. I didn't like it, but the more I drank, the better it tasted. I was having a good time talking and drinking, when I suddenly realized that I was getting very drunk." Coffman decided to leave the bar and ascend the hill that led to his barracks. "I vomited all the way up the hill and was sick all the next day. My squad leader told me later that I consumed about thirteen pints of beer that night. I never drank that way again all the time I was in England."[16]

Private James Lingg also joined the 26th that winter as a replacement. He was assigned to I Company, 3rd Battalion, billeted at Blandford, just northeast of the battalion's headquarters at Dorchester. He and his new buddies found plenty of opportunity for recreation in town. "Down in Blandford were probably some of the happiest times of my Military life. We would grab a bus and be there in about 10 minutes. This was a little town with teashops and nice dances every Saturday night. I am not a dancer so I just enjoyed the music and teashops."[17]

More than tea shops or music, the men were interested in feminine companionship, and they found plenty of it. "A mighty stream of U.S. troops is beginning to roar into England," Lieutenant Johnson wrote. "They noisily fill the pubs, tea shops, souvenir stores, and the hearts of English maidens." Indeed, British women often found the brash, well-paid, well-uniformed, cocksure Yanks irresistible. Private Coffman and his buddies found girlfriends among a British Women's Air Force unit stationed nearby or among the women in town. "I knew of at least one girl who was pregnant when we moved out (not mine). The Company had a generous pass policy. If we were not on duty we could go down town, go to a movie or to a pub."[18] The legendary British lamentation that the Yanks were "overpaid, oversexed, and over here" was never more apropos than for the 1st Division in the winter of 1943–44.

But England was a lot more than fun and games. The 1st Division had a simple philosophy: work hard and play hard. The commanding officer, Major General Clarence Huebner, was one of the most underrated American generals of the war. He had supplanted the popular, flamboyant Terry de la Mesa Allen, a maverick who had led the 1st quite well in North Africa and Sicily. More than anyone else, Allen instilled the uniquely independent spirit that the 1st Division still possessed on the eve of Overlord. He promoted an "us against them" mind-set that ultimately cost him his command. Allen was not a stickler for discipline. He cared little for such things. He cared, instead, about combat performance. His division acquired a reputation for toughness on the front lines and unruliness in the rear. In the end, this "rules don't apply to us" outlook was too much for Allen's superior, General Omar Bradley, to stomach. Mild-mannered and unimaginative, Bradley could not abide a nonconformist like Allen. Bradley sacked him and replaced him with Huebner, a man who had once served in the ranks of the division's 18th Regiment as a private.

In World War I, Huebner had compiled a brilliant combat record in the 18th, leading troops in every capacity from platoon leader to battalion commander. Correspondent Don Whitehead, who would accompany the 1st Division into Normandy, closely observed Huebner before the invasion and judged him to be "one of the finest soldiers and gentlemen I've ever known. He was physically fit and there was an air of confidence about him that I liked. I found that Huebner had a great love for his 1st Division. He knew the job of every man in his division as well or better than the men knew the jobs—because he had once held those jobs himself. The general wanted his division to be the best in the entire Army. It wasn't entirely a matter of personal pride because Huebner knew that the toughest, straightest-shooting division won its objectives with the least loss of life."

Clearly Huebner was a first-rate combat officer, someone who knew how to lead troops in battle. Even so, many veteran 1st Division soldiers had trouble accepting him, mainly because he was replacing the popular Allen. In spite of that challenge, Huebner eventually won the allegiance and respect of his soldiers. He knew when to push them and when not to. What worked in the green 29th Division for Gerhardt did not necessarily work in the veteran 1st for Huebner. Huebner knew that his veteran soldiers already understood what was important and what was not in getting ready for combat. He harped on discipline more than Allen ever did, but mainly in duties that were directly useful in combat such as rifle marksmanship, fire and movement tactics, and combat leadership. "If he was stern in his discipline," Whitehead surmised, "it was because battle casualties have a direct relation to discipline."[19]

As the early months of 1944 unfolded, the division's training intensified. Lieutenant Johnson began to push his antitank platoon especially hard. "Filling every daylight hour between larger maneuvers, we learn and re-learn about night fighting, aircraft and armor identification, street fighting, river crossings, rifle marksmanship, 57 [-mm gun] range practice, radio codes, artillery direction, and hiking sixteen miles in less than four hours."[20]

Soon they started loading up on ships for invasion dress rehearsals. Valentine Miele, an H Company, 16th Infantry Regiment, soldier from Jersey City, joined his outfit in time for the Sicily invasion. "They would walk us to the beach," he recalled, "then we'd walk out to the landing craft, and we'd circle around, then we'd invade England. Then we'd go out again. It was cold up there. Those flat-bottomed boats we had . . . would go up and go down, and the spray would come over. Your field jacket would be icy."[21]

"The ramp of the landing craft would go down and we would pour out on the beach taking whatever cover we could find," Steve Kellman, a replacement in L Company, 16th Infantry, remembered. "The lead men would throw themselves onto the barbed wire so that the rest of us could follow through the barbed wire and whatever obstacles there were. The bangalore torpedo men then would place their bangalore torpedoes where we felt the mine fields were and blow a path for us to approach the pill box. At that point, the man with the satchel charge, who we would give cover to, would place the satchel charge in the aperture and blow the pill box. After the detonation of the satchel charge the flame thrower man would then spray the burning fuel into whatever openings he could find." Kellman's job was to carry an aluminum ladder designed to cross a tank trap. He also moonlighted as a rifle grenadier.[22]

Eventually, the men learned that they would have the lead

role in yet another invasion. Some were devastated. They felt that in return for all their sacrifices in Algeria, Tunisia, and Sicily they were being repaid with a veritable death sentence. Many others, though, took the news with a sense of pride. Sergeant Mike McKinney hailed from Brooklyn. His service with the 1st Division predated the war. He had fought with the 16th Regiment's L Company in North Africa and Sicily. In those campaigns, he had seen plenty of bloodshed, plenty of death, plenty of tragedy. Now he found out that his regiment would lead the 1st Division's assault on France. Like most all of the enlisted men, he did not know where or when; he just knew his outfit had been chosen for the cutting edge. He took the news with a steely equanimity. "It's your job. You're young. You're invincible. Other guys are gonna get killed but not me. You're a fatalist. If a bullet's got my name on it I'm gonna get it; there's nothing I can do about it. Don't worry about it. You develop that kind of attitude. Youth plus fatalism plus faith or trust in a higher power. That kept me in good stead for a long time."[23]

The swaggering 1st Division soldiers murmured rumors to one another that even though the 1st had done more than its share already in this war, General Eisenhower had personally insisted that it lead the invasion because the division was so good. Actually, this was not far from the truth. General Bradley was the highest-ranking American operational commander on D-Day. He commanded the 1st Army, under which every American ground soldier in Normandy would serve on D-Day. Bradley had been a corps commander in the Mediterranean. In the late summer of 1943, when he found out that he would command the 1st Army, he mentally earmarked the 1st Division for the main assault in Normandy. "In quality the 1st was worth the equal of several inexperienced divisions. It had become an almost irreplaceable weapon for the Normandy invasion." Bradley well knew that many of the division's veterans were not eager to lay their lives on the line in yet another amphibious assault. "Although I disliked subjecting the 1st to still another landing, I felt that as a commander I had no other choice. My job was to get ashore, establish a lodgement, and destroy the German. In the accomplishment of that mission there was little room for the niceties of justice. I felt compelled to employ the best troops I had, to minimize the risks, and hoist the odds in our favor in any way that I could." The general had studied the terrain of Omaha beach. He knew that it would be the toughest place to assault. More than anything else, that's why he chose the Big Red One to land there.[24]

For the Utah beach assault, Bradley chose a division that was distinctly different from both the 29th and the 1st. The 4th Infantry Division, a regular outfit, had compiled a distinguished combat record in World War I, but it was, as yet, unblooded in this war. Some of the enlisted soldiers of this unit were prewar regulars, but most had joined after the United States entered the war. By the end of 1943, the division had trained for two solid years, first as a mechanized force and later as a unit specializing in amphibious assaults. Nicknamed the Ivy Division (thanks to the Roman numeral equivalent of four), the 4th deployed to Britain in January 1944. The unit quickly settled into Devon, located in the extreme southwest portion of England. The soldiers admired the picturesque countryside and quaint country lanes of Devon. They also quickly made friends with the locals. Colonel Gerden Johnson, who later authored a fine history of the division's 12th Infantry Regiment, wrote: "The towns in which the regiment was billeted extended a hospitality not to be easily matched. Many lasting friendships were made. During off duty hours men of the 12th explored the shops, toured the towns and surrounding countryside, visited Exeter Cathedral and the Guild Hall. Not many, however, were able to go to London 168 miles to the northeast."

The men of the division lived in British barracks, Nissen huts, or private homes. They soon realized that the burgeoning Allied supply apparatus had selected Devon as a major storage area. Everywhere the 4th Division men went, they saw evidence of the massive buildup—camouflaged dumps of artillery shells, small-arms ammunition, supply crates containing everything from mortar shells to spare parts, vehicles parked fender-to-fender, even searchlights nestled under makeshift tarpaulins. The quality of the food declined from what the men had eaten in the States. Where before they had eaten plenty of fresh meat, vegetables, and eggs, they now subsisted on powdered fare. For recreation, they set up a baseball league, even going so far as to teach some of the locals how to play the world's greatest game.[25]

Like the other two assault divisions, the 4th concentrated much of its training on invasion rehearsals. The men needed to get used to being on ships or in landing craft. They needed to know how to react to getting wet; they needed to understand how best to assault an enemy-held beach. Private Harper Coleman was a machine gunner in H Company of the 8th Infantry, the regiment that would comprise the first wave at Utah beach. Coleman had once aspired to join the Army Air Force, but he tried to enlist when he was underage and his parents would not sign the necessary papers for him. So he ended up getting drafted into the ground forces in October 1942. After a stint in the 83rd Infantry Division, he ended up in the 4th Division. Coleman and the men of H Company carried out three-day invasion exercises in which a premium was placed on transferring from transport ships to Higgins boats. "We would be required to go over the side of the ship on the rope ladders with all equipment. This was quite a task to get into the small LCVP [popularly known as Higgins boats] when the water would be rough. We would land on the beach area and head on in for two or three days, then back to the barracks and in a few days do it all over again."[26]

Challenging as this training could be, the men looked forward to some aspects of it, particularly the Navy's food. Private First Class William Jones was a rifleman/sniper in I Company of the 8th Infantry. He was born in Ivanhoe, Virginia, a town nestled into the foothills of the Appalachian Mountains. When Jones was three, his family moved to Greene County, Tennessee. He worked on the family farm until age fifteen, when he dropped out of school to work at a factory in nearby Kingsport. This factory work helped his family subsist during the desperate days of the Great Depression. When war came, he received a draft notice. Ten days before he left for the Army, he married his sweetheart.

Every time Private First Class Jones and his buddies boarded a ship for invasion rehearsals, they went straight to the galley. "The Navy had a reputation for being well fed. But we were not. We stole all of the white bread that we could off those ships, and camouflaged them in our pack somewhere. It was like eating cake to us. We had been used to that old English brown bread that was hard enough in the first place."[27]

In addition to amphibious training, the Ivy Division soldiers endured plenty of field problems, some of them on the infamous moors that the 29'ers so hated. Usually, the soldiers did not receive advance notice of such field problems. Instead, the officers would order them to pack their equipment, load up on trucks, and move out. This ignorance perfectly simulated the chaotic nature of combat for infantrymen, most of whom rarely had any inkling of their whereabouts or the strategy behind daily orders. But in this case the fog of war caused problems (mostly of his own making) for Corporal Alton Pearson, a soldier in L Company of the 12th Infantry.

Pearson, an efficient, dedicated soldier, had been training hard for many days. His captain looked kindly upon him and issued Pearson, along with several of his buddies, weekend passes. They went to Exeter. "There was a carnival going on in Exeter where we met some girls and we were having a swell time."

Sunday came all too quickly. Pearson was not ready to let go of the revelry and excitement of his weekend with the Exeter girls. He collared the other men. "We are having so much fun, don't you think we should stay another day?"

The other soldiers demurred, intoning about the consequences of being AWOL. But Pearson could tell that, in spite of their reservations, they were looking for an excuse to stay. "This could be the last liberty we will ever have!" That cinched it. They stayed another day.

On Tuesday they finally returned to their company's camp at Budleigh Salterton, only to find everybody gone. They froze in their tracks. Was it the invasion? Had they missed it? They had no idea what to do, but they did know that they were tired from their active weekend. They noticed a few bedrolls, curled up in them, and went to sleep. A few hours later a soldier named Ed Haskew woke them up and told them that the company had gone to the moors for a field problem. The captain had sent Haskew to retrieve Pearson's group. They all hopped on a jeep and drove to the moors. Each of the miscreants speculated as to their fate, especially when the captain did nothing for three days during the field problem.

"I don't believe [he is] going to punish us!" one of them exclaimed hopefully.

Pearson shook his head. "[He] is punishing us now, sweating it out."

Even after they returned to Budleigh Salterton, the captain still let them sweat for another few days. Finally the day of reckoning came. The captain ordered them to report to his office. For several long moments they waited in an anteroom of the resort house the captain was using for his office.

The captain's orderly opened the door and asked, "Who wants to be first?"

Pearson volunteered. He had sweated this out long enough. Now he only wanted to receive his punishment and move on. The captain sat behind his desk as Pearson entered the room, snapped to attention, and gave his best parade ground salute.

"Corporal Pearson reports, sir."

The captain returned the salute. "Corporal Pearson, what do you think of a soldier who has been given special privileges and then lets his company commander down by being AWOL twenty-four hours, thirty minutes, and fifteen seconds?"

"I think it is a hell of a thing to do," Pearson replied.

"What do you think I ought to do with you?" the captain asked.

"Well, sir, you are the captain."

"Well, put me in your place. What would you do with me?"

Pearson gulped. He didn't know what to say. On the one hand, if he suggested some kind of light punishment, the captain might get truly angry, accuse him once again of bad faith, and really let him have it. On the other hand, Pearson did not want to overplay his hand the other way and mention a punishment more severe than whatever the captain already had in mind. Pearson settled on what he thought was a compromise. "I would give you a week of extra duty."

The captain agreed immediately and called his orderly. "Call the others in." When they entered the room he pronounced final judgment. "Corporal Pearson says I should give you one week extra duty."

The other men were not thrilled with Pearson. "They all raised hell with me and said they wouldn't have gotten anything if I hadn't sentenced them." Most likely they were wrong.[28] A couple of months later, in combat, Pearson more than made up for the headaches he had caused his commander.

Not long after Pearson's escapade, his regiment got a new leader. The new man, Colonel Russell "Red" Reeder, was something of a legend in the Army. The son of a soldier, he was literally born into the Army, entering the world just as the reveille cannon boomed at Fort Leavenworth on March 4, 1902. Reeder attended West Point and graduated with more of a flair for athletics than academics. He later coached football at West Point, in addition to serving in a myriad of units throughout the Army. He was best known for his fact-finding visit to the South Pacific. Reeder was a hands-on type of soldier, one who craved action. Instead of confining his studies to the rear areas and the insides of officer's clubs, he continually visited the front lines in the Pacific. There he observed the realities of combat firsthand—the mud, the blood, the disease, the insects, the horrific terrain, and the terrible strain all of those things put on those who did the fighting. He authored a readable, gritty pamphlet of combat lessons learned, which he called *Fighting on Guadalcanal.*

He returned home with a bad case of malaria and the enduring admiration of the army Chief of Staff, General George Marshall, who was quite pleased with *Fighting on Guadalcanal.* When the 12th Infantry's commanding officer, Colonel Harry Henderson, an aging World War I veteran, began to experience health problems during the spring of 1944, Marshall tabbed Reeder to replace him. Reeder did so on April 4, 1944.

Following a whirlwind trip from Washington to Devon, Reeder reported to the 4th Division's commander, Major General Raymond Barton, at his headquarters in Tivington, some fourteen miles north of Exeter. Barton, a straitlaced fifty-five-year-old infantry officer, brusquely welcomed him but began pumping him for information about when and where the invasion would take place. Incredibly enough, even Barton did not know any of this information in early April. He assumed that since Reeder had just come from Marshall's staff, he must know something. "I need to find out when D-Day is, when and where we are going to land. It would help us all in our training if I knew. Do you know?"

Reeder shifted uncomfortably in his seat. He did know but had been pledged to secrecy. "Barton's brown eyes seemed to bore into me. I felt I had to lie. I stared straight ahead. 'No, sir.' I knew General Barton had a big load on his mind, and I suspected that he sensed he had little time to get his division ready for D-Day. Nevertheless his harassed look and the question he asked bothered me."[29] It was a strange moment, for rarely was a regimental commander privy to top-secret information not available to his commanding general.

Reeder jumped right into his new assignment. He liked the personal touch. "In a remarkably short space of time he had met and talked with every officer and enlisted man in the regiment," recalled one officer. "He instilled in them an unshakable faith in themselves . . . and an unsurmountable determination to overcome whatever obstacles might lie ahead. Everyone knew instinctively that here was leadership to be respected."[30] Reeder understood that although enlisted men often want nothing more than to be left alone to do their jobs, they still needed recognition from senior officers. A simple visit from the brass could buck up morale.

General Eisenhower understood that, too. In the months leading up to the invasion, he found time to visit every Allied division, including the 4th Infantry. Alton Pearson never forgot an encounter he had with the supreme commander during his visit. Pearson's company had been split up into platoons, each with a specific mission. The weather was cold and the men were loaded down with full field packs, ammunition, and weapons. As they marched along a country road, Pearson noticed movement up ahead. "A motorcycle and command car approached us with a cluster of stars and a flag in front." Corporal Pearson immediately knew who was in the car. The vehicle stopped and out popped Eisenhower. The men stood at attention while Ike walked among them inspecting. The general sincerely enjoyed these moments when he got to meet and talk with soldiers. He asked each man a question, usually something pertaining to equipment or training. "As I recall he asked me when I had changed socks as the division was having foot trouble from long hiking and heavy loads." Pearson did not record his answer, but he did notice, out of the corner of his eye, Eisenhower's pretty driver, Kay Summersby.[31]

By late April, the division was nearing a state of readiness, after many invasion rehearsals and much tactical training. This was in spite of its participation in the disastrous Exercise Tiger on April 28, an operation that led to the deaths of 749 American soldiers and sailors when German E-boats sank several ships participating in a mock invasion of Slapton Sands, a British west coast beach.

To the north of the camps housing the American amphibious assault divisions, a completely different group of assault troops prepared for the invasion in their own inimitable way. These men cared nothing for invading beaches. Jumping out of airplanes was more their speed. They called themselves paratroopers. In Normandy, they would have a vital mission. The Utah beach invasion could only succeed if these paratroopers could jump into the dark Norman evening, organize themselves behind enemy lines, and secure the vistas from the beach to interior objectives. Needless to say, their task was exceedingly dangerous. Eisenhower's principal aerial commander, Air Marshal Sir Trafford Leigh-Mallory, seriously questioned the wisdom of dropping the paratroopers into the Cotentin Peninsula amid swarms of German reinforcements. In the end, though, Eisenhower and Bradley both insisted that without the airborne drops, the Utah beach invasion was untenable.[32]

Scattered among a series of camps between Bristol in the west and Reading in the east, the soldiers of the 101st Airborne Division were itching for action by the spring of 1944. The division consisted of three inexperienced paratrooper regiments, the 501st, 502nd, and 506th, along with one glider infantry regiment, the 327th. The soldiers may have been green, but they were well prepared. The previous two years had seen them negotiate some of the toughest training ever given to American soldiers. Each of them had volunteered to become a paratrooper. Upon doing so, they entered a world in which little quarter was asked or given.

The 506th, for instance, trained in the heat and humidity of Fort Benning, Georgia. Their training schedule was merciless. They ran everywhere, even to the latrine. On their first day, their training NCOs, sporting gaudy paratrooper jump wings, ordered them to run up and down a 1,000-foot hill called Mount Currahee. Anyone who could not make the six-mile round trip fell out and disappeared. In addition to the constant running, the men did push-ups, pull-ups, knee bends, duckwalks, and practically every other calisthenic the Army could dream up. They also ran an exhausting obstacle course every day. They carried out eleven-mile hikes with no water or food. In fact, anyone who had less than a full canteen at the end of the march received harsh punishment or was washed out of the program altogether. Not surprisingly, most of the volunteers did not make it through this difficult training. Among the 500 officers who volunteered, a mere 148 got their wings. Only 1,800 of 5,300 enlisted volunteers made it.[33]

One of those who made it was Donald Burgett, an eighteen-year-old adventure seeker from Detroit's west side. Burgett had an older brother in the paratroopers and wanted to follow in his footsteps. At the military induction center, Burgett walked past busy navy and army air force recruiters to a lonely airborne recruiter, who had just been turned down by several inductees with absolutely no desire to leap out of airplanes. "Walking over to him, I said that I would like to join the 'Troops, and he looked at me in shocked disbelief—like a salesman who had just made his first sale."

In the summer of 1943, shortly after passing his physical and completing infantry basic training, Burgett traveled to Fort Benning, a place radically different from his native Michigan. A truck dumped Burgett and a small group of volunteers off at the training area. Tall pines, swamps, and sandy soil abounded, and the heat was beyond belief. They stood under a stand of willowy pines, milling around, not quite sure what to do. "One of the best built men I had ever seen, wearing a white T-shirt, jump pants and boots, strode over to us. He had blue eyes set in a handsome tanned face, with shaggy eyebrows and close-cropped hair, both bleached blond by the sun."

The tough-looking man confidently approached the group and noticed a volunteer with his hands in his pockets. "Gimme twenty-five!"

The recruit blinked in surprise. "Twenty-five what?"

"Push-ups. What the hell do you think? Make it right now, or you'll get fifty the next time I tell you."

As the miscreant strained through his push-ups, "the newcomer then introduced himself as one of the cadre, and a sergeant. The cadre sergeants were boss, law and order and second only to God in this camp. At no time was a trooper allowed to sit down, lean against anything or stand in a resting attitude when he was outside the confines of his own barracks."

The sergeant finished his introductory speech on a threatening note: "We're going to be tough on everyone here, and don't expect any sympathy from any of us at any time, because we are going to do everything we can to make you quit the Paratroops."

The next day, the sergeants ran them ragged. "Our feet beat a steady slapping tattoo on the asphalt, and with the sergeant setting the pace, we moved as a single body over the road through the early hours of the morning. After a few . . . miles my body seemed to be operating on its own, my legs driving in a steady rhythm, my chest sucking in and letting out deep lungfuls of air, while I retreated mentally, to an inner corner of my brain to relax in thought."

Burgett noticed some unusual movement ahead of him. "The man in front of me began to weave back and forth a little; this brought me back to reality. In a little while he began to stagger quite a bit. Suddenly he pitched forward on his face and rolled over on his back. The men behind him spread out and ran by on either side while the sergeant yelled for us to keep going and not pay any attention to him. Two more men fell out long before we reached the center of the [drill] field, and the same orders were given. Once in the field we were immediately formed into ranks and began calisthenics starting with side-straddle hops and going the full course to push-ups and other exercises, to cool off after our six-mile run."

Soon the jump training began. Burgett and the others who managed to adapt to the strenuous PT regimen learned how to pack their parachutes, how to leave a plane properly, and how to land properly. All of this training took place on the ground. Then they began jumping from platforms; the first was 8 feet high and the next 40 feet high. The final phase of this segment of the training called for them to parachute from a 250-foot stationary tower. "The troopers put on live parachutes, hooked the opened canopies into large rings or hoops and were hoisted, three at a time, to the top of one of the towers. One at a time they were released, to float to the ground, while an instructor ordered them to slip right, slip left or to make a body turn."

Following the completion of four such jumps, they finished this phase of the training with a night jump from the tower. This experience could be quite disorienting and dangerous, too, because it was easy to get blown into the tower's steel girders, with predictable consequences. "The night was so black that a man at the top of the tower couldn't see the ground, and swinging from the single cable, it was almost impossible to tell which direction the wind was coming from."

When they survived that ordeal, Burgett and the others could now anticipate an end to the training, for the next week they began the real airplane jumps necessary to earn their wings. On the first such jump, Burgett was at the back of his stick (the airborne reference to a squad or planeload of troopers). He watched in fascinated horror as the other men stood up, hooked up their static lines, and prepared to exit the aircraft. A surge of panic came over him. "What the hell am I doing here, I ought to have my head examined." The man in front of him pushed himself through the doorway and out into the air. Burgett was next. "There's still time . . . to sign the quit slip and go to the MPs," he thought.

The thought quickly passed, though. Now his training took over and he lunged from the airplane. "Everything seemed to be moving in slow motion; there was no sensation of falling, not even like that of an elevator ride. Before he could even count to three, as he had been taught, his parachute canopy snapped open. "The opening shock nearly sent me through the bottoms of my boots, and I could feel my cheeks pull out away from my teeth. I opened the risers and looked up; the canopy checked out—no blown panels . . . or snarled lines." Seconds later, the ground loomed below him. "I looked at the horizon, took up what I thought to be a good body position and hit the ground. Pain shot through my whole body sending bright flashes across my eyes, almost blacking me out." He had not landed correctly. Consequently, he had torn a few ligaments in his leg. Burgett had to spend the next ten days healing, even as his buddies completed their jumps and got their wings. In November, he earned his during a night jump. "Standing up, still in my harness, I let out a yell. I had made it. I was a trooper now, a full-fledged paratrooper, and would get my wings. No matter what happened they couldn't take that away from me."[34]

The reward for Burgett and so many thousands of others who completed airborne training was a ticket into combat, amid some of the most dangerous circumstances imaginable. Theirs was one of the most perilous jobs in the Army. Casualties in the upcoming campaign would be high, and the young troopers knew it. But still they persevered and endured the rigors and humiliation of airborne training. Something drove them—perhaps the desire to be part of an elite group, perhaps the recklessness of youth, perhaps personal pride. It varied from man to man, but the inescapable fact was that they had voluntarily endured hell so that they could serve in hell.

In England, the 101st settled into a predictably tough training routine to prepare them for the big jump into France. They engaged in long hikes, including one that saw them cover twenty-five miles in twenty-four hours, with full field equipment. They got used to digging defensive positions, living in foxholes, and dealing with the elements, especially the ubiquitous English rain. They refined their infantry assault tactics and crawled in the mud with live fire over their heads. They learned how to coordinate with the division's artillerymen, a skill crucial to survival in battle. They practiced hand-to-hand combat with knives and bayonets. Glider men learned everything they possibly could about the dangerous contraptions they would ride into action. Of course, the paratroopers never strayed far from their raison d'être—jumping.

They carried out several practice jumps, including a major exercise for VIP witnesses Eisenhower and Churchill in March.[35]

Most of the training was much more mundane than command performances for VIPs. Most of it was standard infantry stuff—misery, privation, hiking, shooting, and toughening up. On a typical field problem exercise, they would scatter themselves into small groups, simulating a combat drop. Their objective was to knock out such targets as coastal defenses or strong points. "After traipsing across great expanses of English countryside, encountering untold hundreds of barbed-wire fences, and stumbling deviously through mud holes, you become hopelessly lost," one trooper recalled. "Then everything went against you, the compass refused to point north, the maps got wet and obliterated, and still the rain came down! But you persisted and eventually you knocked out something, set up a haphazard and hasty line of defense, and bedded down, each person finding his own choice mud hole in which to lie. Then at long last came the dawn. You returned to camp the same way you came down, 'by foot.' Glancing down the line you were of the opinion that everyone had that combat expression, an unshaven face showing extreme weariness and disgust, caked mud from head to foot, and every jump suit looking as though it had come out second best in the ordeal of the fences. You finally dragged your weary body those last few tortuous kilometers, and throwing yourself across the bunk, you said . . . combat can't be that rough! You thought!"

The division generally trained forty-eight hours per week, a schedule that did leave some time for recreation. David Kenyon Webster was a unique trooper. A Harvard English major, he dreamed of being an influential writer. Heavily influenced by the famous British writers of World War I, Webster wanted to experience war and then write about it. He came from a wealthy family with enough connections to secure him a commission and a rear-area job, but he opted to join the paratroopers. He made it through training with the 506th. Later on, he wrote a diary and memoir that serves as a priceless historical record. He described his unit's life in Aldbourne, a quaint village of thatched-roof cottages located about eighty miles west of London: "We got settled enough in town to become steady customers of the three bakers, who slipped us a lardy cake now and then, and to know most of the local inhabitants by sight, if not by name. Gradually the people thawed out and began to speak to us. A few men in the battalion even married Aldbourne girls."

His unit, headquarters company, lived in one-story wooden barracks. The men painted the interior red, white, and blue, even as they acquired radios purchased in nearby Swindon. "Sanitary facilities left much to be desired. Our toilet, an unimposing wooden shanty, housed a pair of stone troughs and two rows of wooden seats on honesty buckets. The toilet paper, when it was present for duty, was coarse brown, very wartime English stuff. That latrine was no place to linger on a cold night. There were five showers for . . . two companies of about 250 men, but this was enough, because nobody was very shower-conscious in the cold climate. Our diet, hitherto rich in such accepted staples as fresh milk, fried eggs, and oranges and apples, suddenly dried up on us, and powdered milk, powdered eggs, dehydrated apricots, and dehydrated potatoes became the order of the day. We looked back on our life in camps in the States as a period of great luxury."[36]

The soldiers frequented local pubs, but when they really wanted to let loose they went to Swindon or London. Passes were relatively easy to get. The young troopers were full of energy, self-confidence, and swagger. When they went to the bigger cities, they intended to do three things: drink heavily, pick up women, and throttle anyone who even looked at them cross-eyed. Private Burgett got roaring drunk one Saturday night and passed out. When he awoke on Sunday morning, he found, to his intense horror, that he was lying on the stage of a community house "just behind a preacher who was blistering out a sermon on the wages of sin. I looked out through heavy-lidded eyes onto a sea of blurry faces." Embarrassed beyond description, he crawled out of there on his hands and knees.[37]

One night a group of troopers got into a big melee with British paratroopers from the 6th Airborne Division. Almost 500 soldiers were involved, and the fight lasted the better part of an hour. Only the arrival of three platoons of American military policemen stopped the fracas. In some ways, trouble of this sort was inevitable. The young Britons and Yanks who volunteered to become paratroopers were adventurous sorts, the kind of men who wish to prove their toughness. Their difficult training taught them to be violent, and it also gave them a great sense of confidence in their ability to take care of themselves. Unit or national pride gave them an excuse to tangle with outsiders. Plus, the American paratroopers were just plain aggressive. "The British were friendly," one American paratrooper later commented, "but we were so young and full of piss and vinegar. I think now so long afterward that perhaps we went out of our way to cause trouble."[38]

Indeed they did, but many more off-duty paratroopers, like Sergeant Robert Webb, were more interested in women than in fighting. Webb was a supply sergeant and his duties afforded him the opportunity to travel to London frequently. In 1942, at the age of nineteen, he had left his job in the stockroom of the Corpus Christi, Texas, Woolworth store to join the Army and, later on, the paratroopers. He had a girlfriend back home, but she was, after all, 3,000 miles away. "Everyone was saying the best place to find fun was Covent Gardens, an opera house, dance emporium and whatever you had in mind. It was said that a soldier could stand out in front and decide what kind of young lady he wanted to go out with and he was almost sure to find her there, every time."

Sergeant Webb went there hoping to find someone who looked a bit like Hedy Lamarr, a popular movie star at the time. He stood in the balcony listening to the music and scanning the crowd below. His eyes wandered to the stage where a dance club from a London suburb was performing. In an instant he spotted the girl he wanted. "She was a perfect double for Hedy Lamarr. Light, white skin, blue eyes, long dark hair and a great smile, terrific figure and every thing pleasing to the eye." When the group finished dancing, he went downstairs and made a beeline for her. "I went up to her and asked her to dance. She smiled and said she had never danced with an American before. She asked me to teach her the shag, jitterbug or whatever we did. I was glad to oblige."

At the end of the evening, he escorted her on the train to her home in Warlingham, outside of London. "That was a long train ride but what the hell, a train ride was a good chance to get to know her." He met her family and they got along well. It was the beginning of an extended relationship. His British girlfriend even visited him several times at his base in Ramsbury. Such liaisons were quite common that spring, at a time when not much was certain except that death could lie ahead.[39]

Eisenhower and Bradley had chosen five divisions to carry out the American portion of the initial assault into France. The vast majority of the soldiers in those divisions had no combat experience, the lone exception being, of course, the Big Red One. But one of the airborne divisions, the 82nd, did contain some experienced combat soldiers. The division had seen combat in both North Africa and Italy. Some of its soldiers, members of the 504th Parachute Infantry Regiment, were still fighting at Anzio. Others, from the 505th Parachute Infantry Regiment, had been redeployed from the Mediterranean to England. There they joined two new paratrooper regiments, the 507th and 508th, along with the 325th Glider Infantry Regiment to form a newly constituted 82nd Airborne Division.

The division rested for a time in Northern Ireland before moving on to the midlands of England in February 1944. The various regiments spread out among the usual barracks, huts, and homes in the Leicester, Nottingham, and Market Harborough areas. The men of the 505th were survivors of bloody battles at Sicily and Salerno. Similar to the veterans of the 1st Division, they spent much of their time indoctrinating newcomers and getting their nerves straightened out.

Lieutenant Jack Isaacs was a Topeka, Kansas, native who joined the Army straight out of high school in 1940. He served stints with the 7th and 3rd Infantry Divisions before earning the chance to attend Officer Candidate School in 1942. He graduated in July of that year and went to infantry school and then jump school. He commanded a platoon in G Company of the 505th during the Mediterranean battles. Casualties ascended him to the position of executive officer. But in England, once his unit received several officer replacements, he was just as happy to go back to being a platoon leader.

In the spring of 1944, he was determined to teach his new men everything he could about survival in combat. "Our training intensified with small-unit and company and battalion field problems, and several practice drops. We knew that the invasion of the continent was imminent and that we would be part of it. We began studying French phrases, most of which didn't stick with us." He and the other officers implemented new jump techniques. "For one thing, in Sicily and Italy we had dropped our mortars and machine guns in bundles, and then we had to find those bundles and assemble the weapon in order to use it. By the time we got ready for the Normandy invasion, we had perfected techniques in which those weapons were actually dropped on the man that was to use them. They were placed in a bag that had a thirty-foot riser which was attached to the man's harness; after his chute was opened and as he approached landing, he let that bag down still attached to him so that it would hit the ground ahead of him and lighten his own weight when he landed." They also developed techniques that allowed men to land with their rifles intact, ready to fire, instead of the folding stock or disassembled weapons that other units sometimes employed.[40]

Just down the road at Nottingham, the 82nd Airborne's fresh-faced newcomers also prepared for war. Operating from a cluster of small bases in and around Nottingham, the 507th and 508th soon became a dominating presence in the area. Day and night, they could be seen training. Captain Roy Creek, commander of the 507th's E Company, made sure that his troopers understood that their mission was special. Creek came from Portales, New Mexico. Several years before, he had earned a degree from New Mexico State University. Now he found himself leading more than 100 tough but unseasoned soldiers. "The training emphasized principles peculiar to airborne units such as speed and initiation of combat immediately upon landing; retention of initiative until the mission is accomplished; recognition of isolation as a normal battlefield condition; readiness of all units to attack and defend in all directions at any time."

Each day Captain Creek stressed improvisation to his men. He knew that once they dived from their airplanes and into combat, little would go according to plan. More than anything he wanted his men to be prepared to "conquer or die." This emphasis served them quite well in the hours after their jump into Normandy.[41]

Like the 507th, the 508th had been training together for the better part of a year. They were also eager to test themselves against the Germans. They lived at a new camp at Wollington Park just outside of Nottingham. "It was a beautiful location with green grass and lots of trees," Private Dwayne Burns, a nineteen-year-old trooper from Fort Worth, Texas, later recalled. "This was enclosed by miles of redbrick fence and iron gates. In the center stood the [Wollington] home. It was a huge four-story building with turrets and lots of ornamental ironwork. By our standard, I guess it could have been called a castle. Behind this were rows of eight-man tents located at one end of the park. Although we were living in tents, it wasn't bad. We had a stove in the middle of the tent, and the floor was paved with concrete stepping-stones."

In spite of continuous training, they found time to explore Nottingham, as well as meet some of its residents. "It was a very modern city, with theaters, good restaurants, fine public buildings. Lots of fish and chips places, and pubs located all over town. The townspeople were very friendly and receptive to Americans, especially the girls. Although we didn't speak exactly the same English, we did make out extremely well. Some made friendships that would last a lifetime. Others would find the girl of their dreams and marry."[42]

Generally they got along well with the British, but being paratroopers, they sometimes could not resist the urge to start trouble. Bud Warnecke, a platoon sergeant in B Company, was drinking in a Nottingham pub one night when a fight broke out. "There were a bunch of British soldiers and a few troopers drinking. A Brit raised his glass and in a loud voice shouted, 'God save the king!' A dumb trooper raised his voice, yelling, 'Fuck the king!' The damnedest fight broke out. I might have been a little crazy but I wasn't a fool. I did not stick around to see how the brawl turned out."[43]

One could argue that such brawls were reasonably good-natured, the product of rivalry, youth, and plenty of excess energy. However, some of the 82nd Airborne's brawling that spring resulted from something much more sinister, something that originated from America's greatest flaw—racism. In the mid–twentieth century, the armed forces were segregated, reflecting civilian life at that time. Moreover, African-Americans were almost entirely prohibited from serving in combat, mainly because military leaders believed the fiction that black men were incapable of serving bravely in combat.

Before the arrival of the All-American division, the only American troops in the midlands of England were African-American units operating in a support role for the Army Air Force. These men had been in the area for many months; they had forged ties of kinship with the locals, including many relationships with British women. Some of the white troopers of the 82nd were none too thrilled about this. Conversely, some of the black support troops were eager to test the toughness of these combat types who wore funny-looking "jump" boots of which they were ostentatiously, enormously proud. Almost immediately violence broke out. "The first night one of our combat units got in there," the 82nd Airborne's outstanding commander, General Matthew Ridgway, recalled, "one of my men was stabbed in a fight with one of these service troops. He didn't die, but the rumor spread among the division that he had, and I knew the situation called for instant and energetic measures to prevent a serious outbreak."

Ridgway oozed army from every pore. Born in 1895 to a distinguished colonel, Ridgway grew up at a succession of army posts. He breathed the fading dust of the closing frontier, as his father's military career had taken the family far and wide in the western United States. Ridgway never considered any other path in life but to be a soldier. He was born to it and took to it magnificently at West Point, graduating in 1917. He was one of the solid coterie of promising officers who stuck with their army careers in the 1920s and 1930s in spite of public scorn and a dearth of promotions. Along the way, he impressed General Marshall. On the eve of World War II, Ridgway was serving on the general's staff. Later Ridgway commanded the 82nd Airborne in its Mediterranean campaigns. He was an excellent leader, a hands-on combat general.

Ridgway understood all too well that he had to take decisive action to quell the racial animosity between his troopers and the service troops. "Immediately, I visited every unit bivouacked in the area. I called the officers together, and laid down the law to them. I told them that the troops who were there when we arrived were wearing the same uniforms we were wearing, they were there under orders of competent authority. They were performing tasks just as essential to the war as the tasks we were performing." To Ridgway, the issue of race might have been one of the great problems American society faced, but "it was not our responsibility to try to settle it three thousand miles from home in the middle of a war. I doubled our MP patrols and personally spent the early hours of the next few evenings riding and walking through the streets to see that my orders were being carried out." His proactive approach worked. The violence ended, if not the animosity.[44]

When the troopers weren't cavorting around Nottingham, they concentrated on practicing night jumps. Private Paul Bouchereau served in the regiment's headquarters company. A native of New Orleans, he joined the paratroopers shortly after graduating from Louisiana State University. One night in late April, Bouchereau and the other men of the 508th loaded up on planes. They had been waiting around for several days hoping for rainy weather to pass. "After about thirty minutes airborne, word was received to return to base. A few minutes after, we deplaned and returned to our quarters in one of the hangars. Several of us found a small radio and tuned in our favorite program, 'The Bitch of Berlin.' "

Bouchereau was talking about "Axis Sally," otherwise known as Margaret Gillars, an American woman who had married a German and, over the years, begun to identify with Germany. Her program was strictly propaganda, bravado aimed at undermining GI morale, but the American soldiers still liked it, mainly because she played popular music. That night the troopers listened to music for about ten minutes before Axis Sally broke in with a short message: "We extend our regrets to the men of the 508th who were to make a practice jump this evening but could not do so because of inclement weather. Come on over, paratroopers; Hitler's panzers are waiting. You will all be killed."

The men stared at the radio in stunned disbelief. How could she know that? Some of them felt a shiver run down their spines. "This message was broadcast less than an hour after the very secret jump was canceled. It was a frightening thing."[45]

Axis Sally undoubtedly got her information from one of the "turned" German agents who provided German intelligence with interesting tidbits that seemed important but were actually of very little value in the long run. Combat soldiers like Bouchereau did not know of any of that kind of cloak-and-dagger intrigue. They only knew that the enemy seemed to know their every move and it spooked them. They could not help wondering if, when the time came to leap into combat, the Germans would be ready and waiting for them.

The Germans certainly knew the Allies were coming, but they did not, as yet, know when and where. Eisenhower aimed to keep it that way.

CHAPTER TWO

THE TRANSPORTATION PLAN

In a way, Ike's aerial offensive, known generally as the transportation plan, was designed as a kind of insurance policy, just in case German intelligence did figure out Allied intentions. The greatest threat to the impending invasion was the possibility that the Germans would make good on the continental superiority of their forces. On the landing beaches, the Allies could be expected to hold an advantage, especially under the guns of their navies and the bombs of their aerial fleets. But, the Germans had an advantage of their own, and it was potentially decisive. They had close to sixty divisions defending northwest Europe. It would take months for the Allies to land and supply armies that large. If the Germans could figure out where the Allies intended to invade and then get their armies to that area, the Allies would be in deep trouble. In Eisenhower's view, the formidable British and American strategic air forces must be used as a weapon to prevent that from happening. In other words, he hoped to isolate the battlefield—deprive the Germans of swift reinforcement, resupply, and sustenance in general.

The Fortitude deception plan was designed to keep them guessing about the time and place of the invasion. But the transportation plan aimed at taking away all possibility of a strong German response to the invasion, regardless of what German intelligence knew. Basically, the plan originated from an analytical paper prepared by Solly Zuckerman, a South African self-made anatomy professor. Zuckerman was a scientific adviser to Ike's deputy, Air Chief Marshal Sir Arthur Tedder. The professor analyzed Allied bombing of railways in Italy and prepared a detailed study of what such a campaign would do in northern Europe. He called for a three-month campaign aimed at paralyzing the French rail system. In this way, the Germans would be deprived of the necessary transportation, and bridges, to move troops to Normandy in reaction to the invasion. Instead, they would be forced to confine their movement to the roads, where they could be savaged by Allied fighter-bombers. Zuckerman's vision was the ideal blueprint for isolating the battlefield. It seemed like an obvious, necessary course of action.[1]

But unfortunately, the situation was not quite that simple. Zuckerman's transportation plan drew a firestorm of opposition and led to the stormiest of pre-invasion debates among the Allied high command. The plan's most influential advocate was Eisenhower. Ike knew that his invading troops would need air supremacy and the isolated battlefield Zuckerman's transportation plan could yield. Although Ike was quite pleased with the Overlord directive he had received from the Combined Chiefs of Staff, he was displeased that it did not give him control of the strategic air forces in the weeks leading up to the invasion. He knew that in order to employ Allied airpower effectively, he needed to have command and control of the planes.

This notion did not sit well with the fiercely independent air commanders. Led by Air Marshal Sir Arthur Harris among the British and Lieutenant General Carl "Tooey" Spaatz among the Americans, these airpower enthusiasts believed they could win the war on their own. Harris commanded all British strategic air forces, while Spaatz held an equivalent command for the Americans. Heavily influenced by the pronunciations of prewar airpower theorists such as Guilio Douhet and Billy Mitchell, they contended that Germany could be defeated solely through a successful strategic air campaign. Heavy bombers could attack and destroy the enemy's very capacity to make war, making ground armies obsolete.

In pursuit of that goal, the air commanders had been steadily bombing Germany for the last three years. Harris's bombers concentrated on nighttime attacks. He was loathe to risk his planes in costly daytime attacks against precision targets. Instead, he sent them over Germany each night with a mandate for "area bombing," which, in effect, meant the wanton destruction of cities and the terrorizing of German civilians. Harris held little sympathy in his heart for the enemy as a people. After all, Germany had bombed British cities earlier in the war, killing thousands of British civilians. Now Britain was simply going its enemy one better. Harris truly believed that if he could unleash enough destruction on Germany, he could break the will of the German people to continue the war. The fact that German bombing of British civilians had merely strengthened their resolve back in 1940–41 did not deter Harris from his beliefs. Night after night, his bomber crewmen took the war to the people of Germany, destroying entire cities, killing and wounding thousands of people, while many more became homeless.

Spaatz and the Americans hoped to achieve aerial victory through more strategic, and slightly more humanitarian, means. They believed that their heavy bombers could fly deep into Germany during the daytime, in order to precision-bomb crucial industries without which Germany could not fight the war. They unleashed raids on Germany's factories, marshaling yards, oil plants, and the like. Of course, the Germans knew all too well the importance of such targets and defended them accordingly, inflicting heavy casualties on the Americans. For two years now, American bomber crews had braved terrifying odds in attempting to carry out the vision of their superiors. They had not destroyed Germany's capacity to resist, but they had seriously eroded the fighting efficiency of the German Air Force.

The airmen, then, believed deeply, almost with a mystical zealousness, that airplanes were the decisive weapon of war. Strategic bombing meant the destruction of infrastructure and the killing of civilians, but ultimately it was still more humanitarian than the massive bloodletting of all-out ground warfare. It would make such costly warfare obsolete, or so the thinking went. Spaatz and Harris, in their views, merely spoke for many others on both sides of the Atlantic. American airpower enthusiasts also had another agenda—an independent air force. If strategic bombing could win the war, then policy makers would have no choice but to create an independent U.S. Air Force instead of maintaining the current situation, in which the Air Force was merely a subordinate branch of the Army.

Men like Spaatz thought of Overlord as unnecessary. They were also quite reluctant to yield control of their aircraft for mere support of ground or naval forces. So when Eisenhower expressed a desire to assume control of Spaatz's planes, the latter reacted like a lioness protecting her cubs. Spaatz was a fine aerial commander, by most accounts a good man with excellent character. In spite of their impending differences, he and Eisenhower got along well. They respected each other. Spaatz understood airpower quite well, but he did not understand much about the war's grand strategy or the true strength of Germany, much less ground warfare. One of Eisenhower's biographers, the late Stephen Ambrose, summed up the difference in outlook between Ike and Tooey: "Spaatz assumed that it would be easy to get ashore and stay there, while Eisenhower did not."[2]

Spaatz, and so many others like him, greatly overestimated the war-winning power of their planes. Airpower was a powerful weapon, but it could not win the war by itself (this has been proven true for almost all modern wars). Spaatz, wedded to the idea that Overlord was unnecessary, even expressed the view to one of Ike's associates in late 1943 that once the weather cleared up in the spring, three months of continuous bombing would bring Germany to its knees. "He said it would be a much better investment to build up forces in Italy to push the Germans across the Po, taking and using airfields as we come to them, thus shortening the bomb run into Germany."[3] A few months later, in a planning conference, Spaatz expressed his views on the kind of grand strategy he would pursue to defeat Germany: "If I were directing strategic operations, I would go into Norway where we have a much greater chance of ground force success and where I believe Sweden would come in with us. Then, with air bases in Sweden, we would attack Germany from four sides (U.K., Italy, Russia and Sweden) simultaneously." He still could not bring himself to terms with Overlord's utility: "Why undertake a highly dubious operation in a hurry when there is a surer way to do it as just outlined? It is better to win the War surely than to undertake an operation which has . . . great risks."[4]

Spaatz had no clue what he was talking about. An invasion of Norway would have been a waste of resources and effort. It would have been like a boxer seeking to land a killing blow by punching his opponent's thigh rather than his chin. The Soviets would not have viewed a Norway junket as the second front they had requested, nor would Sweden have joined the war. Norway would have been a strategic dead end, one with serious weather issues, that would have taken Allied armies further away from ultimate victory. Plain and simple, Germany could only be decisively beaten, and forced into the Allied policy of unconditional surrender, by losing a ground campaign in northwest Europe.

Thankfully, General Marshall understood this and he gave his stamp of approval to Eisenhower in his fight to win command of the air forces in the weeks leading up to Overlord. Marshall's support gave Eisenhower the necessary clout to face down his many opponents over this contentious issue (in addition to Spaatz and Harris, Churchill and his War Cabinet opposed Ike, mainly out of grave doubts about the morality of the transportation plan). The supreme commander ultimately threatened to resign if he did not get his way.

By late March, the issue was decided in his favor, but that did not end the bickering. Spaatz, as a good soldier, had yielded to the inevitability of Ike's control of his planes but now proposed an alteration to the transportation plan. Instead of attacking the railroads and bridges of France, in the process inflicting inevitable civilian casualties, why not target Germany's oil capacity? Spaatz's oil plan proposed an all-out bombing offensive against Germany's oil refineries and storage areas. Certainly, on its merits, the plan made sense, but not as a support mechanism for Overlord. Eisenhower's planners already knew that the Germans had compiled sufficient oil in the occupied countries to function effectively. Using the strategic bombers to attack Germany's oil lifeline was more of a long-range project, since it would not provide much short-term support for Overlord. Depriving Germany of oil was unquestionably a sound approach, but the campaign Spaatz envisioned would have no effect on the outcome of the impending battle.

Eisenhower and Tedder both recognized this shortcoming of Spaatz's oil plan. At a crucial meeting on March 25, the supreme commander politely rebuffed Spaatz's impassioned plea for the implementation of his oil plan. Ike formally decided in favor of the transportation plan and directed Tedder and Leigh-Mallory to ready themselves for SHAEF's impending assumption of aerial command, due to begin in the middle of April. In the interest of harmony, Ike did concede that once he assumed command, approximately 25 percent of the strategic bombers would continue bombing targets, of Harris's and Spaatz's choosing, in Germany. At the same time, Allied airmen would concentrate on crippling not just French transportation but also on destroying the Luftwaffe, a continuing objective.

Now only political opposition persisted, mainly among Churchill's government. The prime minister was deeply concerned about the inevitability of French casualties. In June 1940 he and his War Cabinet had forbidden any aerial attacks that might lead to civilian deaths in occupied countries. Churchill's Ministry of Home Security estimated that Zuckerman's transportation plan would lead to anywhere between 80,000 and 160,000 civilian casualties, mostly in occupied France. Churchill knew that Franco-British relations were delicate. The French were still smarting over a British attack on their North African fleet in the summer of 1940. At that time, the British had acted out of self-preservation. They could not take the slightest chance that the formidable French fleet could end up in German hands. The loss of French life that would surely result from attacks on French railroads, coupled with the eventuality that German propaganda would exaggerate those losses, deeply troubled many in the British government. Foreign Secretary Anthony Eden, a future prime minister, was quick to point out that after the war the British would have to live with the people of continental Europe. Bombing them indiscriminately could poison relations for generations.

Throughout much of April, as Eisenhower prepared to implement the plan, Churchill, during their many conversations, implored him to reconsider. The prime minister thought that the bombings would be "cruel and remorseless" and might very well "smear the good name of the Royal Air Force." Eisenhower finally wrote to the prime minister with a lucid defense of the plan. Ike stressed the point that, in his view, the French were slaves of the Germans. Any effort that could successfully free the French from their bondage was worth doing. "We must never forget that one of the fundamental factors leading to the decision for undertaking Overlord was the conviction that our overpowering air force would make feasible an operation which might otherwise be considered extremely hazardous, if not foolhardy. I think it would be sheer folly to abstain from doing anything that can increase in any measure our chances for success in OVERLORD."[5] This was a brilliant rejoinder. Churchill had, after all, been reluctant for years to engage in a cross-Channel attack because of its risk. He could hardly backpedal now from the use of every weapon in support of an operation he had previously described as prohibitively dangerous. Still, he appealed to Roosevelt to stop or curb the plan. The president refused to interfere.

Before Churchill could redouble his obstructionist tactics, the French undercut him. At the prime minister's suggestion, SHAEF consulted them. Ike's chief of staff, Major General Walter Bedell Smith, spoke with Major General Pierre Koenig, Charles de Gaulle's head of French forces in Britain. Koenig's reply was un-equivocal: "This is war and it must be expected that people will be killed." When informed of the British government's dire pro-jections of French casualties, Koenig did not budge: "We would take twice the anticipated loss to be rid of the Germans." Smith never forgot the earnest but agonized look on Koenig's face when he uttered these statements. "As a Frenchman, he was torn by the additional suffering [the bombings] would cause his people. But, as a soldier, he recognized the vital military part they would play in the liberation of France. I doubt if the expression 'C'est la guerre' was ever used with deeper feeling."[6] With French approval the opponents of the transportation plan now had little other re-course. Churchill continued to wring his hands about it, badgering Ike periodically in the weeks ahead, but the plan went forward.[7] In late April, the bombings began in earnest. The Allies unleashed the full force of their powerful aerial armadas in preparation for the invasion. This meant a mixture of heavy and medium bomb-ers, working in conjunction with fighters.

At La Glacerie, a few miles south of Cherbourg, the Germans had concentrated several gun emplacements. On the morning of April 27, a formation of American B-17 bombers approached La Glacerie from the south. These bombers came from the 91st Bomb Group, based at Bassingbourn, England. In the nose of one of the group's planes, Lieutenant Charles Hudson, a young bombardier flying his sixteenth mission, prepared to assume control of the plane. Hudson huddled against his Norden bomb sight, searching for what aviators called the initial point, or IP. The bomb run began at the IP. The pilot turned over effective control of the plane to the bombardier, who "flew" the aircraft straight into the skies over the target, searching for the best release point. Soon the bomb run started.

Fighting against the plane's buffeting gyrations, Hudson peered through his bomb sight. He fiddled with his oxygen mask. The thing had a tendency to tickle his face, but without it he would fall prey to hypoxia and die at this altitude of over 25,000 feet. His B-17 was not pressurized, so he and the nine other crew-men on this cramped plane had to go on oxygen above 10,000 feet. Plus, it was cold up here, so cold that if you touched your .50-caliber machine gun with an ungloved hand, it could freeze to the gun; so cold that if you didn't make sure to keep your oxygen line free of the saliva from your exhalations, the line could freeze, starving you of oxygen just as surely as if you wore no mask at all. Actually, the nose bubble where the bombardier and navigator sat together in cramped intimacy was probably the warmest place on the plane. The waist gunners had the coldest spot, standing at an open door, braving the whipping winds, straining their eyes looking for enemy fighters.

Today there were none of those, but that didn't mean there was no danger. Lieutenant Hudson heard a faint thumping outside the plane. He glanced at the navigator and they exchanged fearful looks. They both knew that the thumping meant flak and lots of it. The Germans possessed a terrifying coterie of effective antiaircraft guns, most notably the versatile 88mm. The flak bursts increased in their intensity and accuracy. Hudson tried desperately to concentrate. "I strained my eyes for a look at the target, but this is one that I had to throw the towel in on. Our left wing was a cloud of flak puffs, and our number four engine was on fire, but not for long." The pilot shut the engine down, extinguishing the fire, but Hudson could still see the engine smoking ominously.

Desperately, he tried to concentrate on acquiring the target. The damned flak just would not stop, though. It kept getting louder and closer. It was so close that he could see the flash out of the corner of his eye as each shell burst. The sky was full of the residue of these bursts—small, oily black smoke puffs that gave the appearance of splotches on a dalmatian. Still searching for the target, Lieutenant Hudson glanced at the map that rested precariously on the small worktable he and the navigator used.

All of a sudden, Hudson heard a loud bang. "A piece of flak went zipping through the map I was looking at, and another hit Borellis [the navigator] in the back, went through his flak suit, and lodged in his parachute harness." Borellis and Hudson were quite lucky. The shell that had burst so close to their plane sent only low-velocity shrapnel into their compartment. The shrapnel ripped through the map but spent itself in the layers of clothing Borellis wore to ward off the cold.

Seconds later, the booming flak grew even worse. Hudson's plane, one engine already shut down, was now in trouble. He still had not gotten a fix on the target, and the flak had become dangerously thick. Something had to give. He had either to bomb soon or risk getting the plane shredded. The pilot decided to leave the formation. The B-17 turned sharply and headed for the nearby coast. Hudson looked out the window and recoiled. "One of our ships got a direct hit, and dove straight into the ground. My roommate was in this ship."

Sobered by the reality of yet another lost friend, they limped away on one engine. Hudson jettisoned his bombs in the Channel. Finally, they made it home. Upon landing, they inspected their planes. "Every single one of our ships were filled with holes, and several men had been hit, and I didn't even drop on target. This made me feel pretty bad, but it just couldn't be helped."

Hudson and the 91st enjoyed better luck the next day when the group led several others on a mission to hit the airfields in Avord, France. The day was quite clear by European standards. Hudson made a couple of practice runs with his sight as the plane closed in on the IP. This time, he heard no flak outside. "The target was visible from the I.P. and I had a beautiful bomb run. My aiming point was the headquarters building, and my other two groups in trail had hangers on each side." Hudson then had trouble with his sight, so he bombed manually. "We missed the hell out of the aiming point, but we took down the hangers that the other Groups was supposed to hit."

They picked up some flak as they flew away from the target, but nothing serious. Lieutenant Hudson manned his .50-caliber gun, scanning the skies for enemy fighters, not expecting to see anything, since the Luftwaffe had been scarce lately. But all of a sudden, enemy fighters were everywhere. In an instant, they zoomed past Hudson's plane, "I got the chin turret turned around in time to get about a hundred rounds into them." Luckily, the bombers had plenty of escorting P-51 fighters with them. These fighters took care of the enemy planes while the bombers all made it home.[8]

Compared with deep-penetration raids in Germany, the transportation plan missions were safer for the heavy-bomber crews, but casualties still piled up. It could not be otherwise with such a sustained offensive. Frank Vratny was a bombardier in the 487th Bomb Group. On May 11, his unit bombed the railroad marshaling yards at Chaumont, exactly the kind of mission Zuckerman envisioned. Only twenty-four bombers made it to Chaumont. The rest diverted to other targets in eastern France. Consequently, the Germans at Chaumont could concentrate their fire on the small formation of which Vratny's plane was a part.

On the bomb run, a slew of flak bursts riddled Vratny's plane. He heard the bailout bell. His first thought was to salvo his bombs, but the electrical system that controlled the bomb bay doors and the bombs had been knocked out. The plane was losing altitude. Vratny realized he had no choice but to bail out. He fastened his chute and hurled himself through the nose-gear door. He hit the slipstream and tried to get his bearings. A few seconds passed and then his chute opened. He floated down toward the earth, the cool air whipping around him, "On hitting the ground, I hid my chute in a hedgerow, covered it with leaves, then ran for about two miles. I hid in a hedgerow there and watched German patrols walk past me. After dark, I hid out in a pile of hay in a barn."

He hid there until the next evening, but hunger and thirst drove him from hiding, in search of food and water. He made contact with an old man who took him home and fed him. The venerable Frenchman made it clear, though, that the American could not stay there, not with Germans swarming everywhere. The farmer and his wife made Vratny a sandwich gave him a bottle of wine and bid him farewell, "I walked all day and night and the next day a French couple hid me out near their village. They got some civilian clothes for me and contacted the underground." Eventually, he ended up in Paris. When the French underground attempted to spirit him to England, he got caught because a Gestapo agent had infiltrated their group. The Germans sent Vratny to Buchenwald, but he managed to survive the war.[9]

Medium-bomber crewmen did not take the same kind of casualties as crews of the heavies, but their missions were harrowing nonetheless. Medium twin-engine bombers like the B-26 Marauder were a great weapon in the implementation of the transportation plan. They were ideal for bombing at moderate altitudes (usually between 8,000 and 13,000 feet) with precision accuracy, perfect for taking out bridges. The Marauder was fast and quick enough to elude fighter planes.

Of course, the plane did have its drawbacks. Marauder crewmen jokingly called their plane the Flying Prostitute because it had no visible means of support. The B-26's stubby wings and thick fuselage made some wonder how the thing could fly at all. Often the plane's cigar-shaped anatomy produced a critical stall speed at takeoff and landing, hence the sardonic nickname (some even called it the Widowmaker). Once pilots overcame their misgivings about the Marauder (something that usually came with experience), they found it to be an effective, durable aircraft.

Atlanta-born Allen Stephens became a B-26 pilot at the fairly advanced age of twenty-seven in 1943. In early 1944 he and his crew deployed to England. They spent much of the spring months flying support missions for Overlord. The targets varied. One day they would hit coastal guns near Le Havre, another day marshaling yards, bridges, or V-1 rocket sites that housed Hitler's new terror weapons. "We almost always got hit with flak, but we seldom ever saw any fighters at this stage."

The brass wanted to make sure that they did not betray any kind of bombing pattern that might reveal Normandy as the invasion site. In fact, they sought to reinforce the German supposition that the invasion must come at Calais. For every tactical mission flown against targets in Normandy, Allied aircraft carried out two that hit Calais. On May 13, Stephens's 397th Bomb Group flew a mission against coastal guns in Dieppe, home to the disastrous Canadian raid two years earlier.

They approached from the sea. The group was spread out into carefully rehearsed formations. Each plane flew in a tight three-ship flight. Pilots like Stephens made sure to stick very close to the other two planes in the flight. The group consisted of six such flights. As they neared the target, Lieutenant Stephens kept his eyes fixed ahead, following the other flights. Ever so steadily he and the others leveled out their course so that the bombardiers could find aiming points for their bomb sights.

They no sooner did that than they heard and saw the telltale bursts around them. Flak rose up in thick waves, as it always seemed to do during a bomb run. Stephens could just hear it above the din of his plane's engines. It almost sounded like a staccato version of thunder in the distance—*whump, krump, whump!* The experience was terrifying. Stephens knew that at any moment flak could tear his plane to bits. With every passing second, death became a real possibility, a simple matter of mathematical calculations, distance and windage computations, shrapnel velocity, and physics. The German antiaircraft crews, frantically working their guns several thousand feet below, made those calculations and targeted their shells with the help of radar.

Unlike heavy bombers, the mediums could take some evasive action on their bomb run. The heavies, theoretically, could withstand more flak punishment than mediums. Plus, the big planes needed steady flight to enhance accuracy. The mediums could not take as much flak, and they flew lower on their bomb runs, increasing the accuracy of their bombing. As his bombardier prepared to salvo his bombs, Stephens took slight evasive action, "which meant, for example, turning two degrees left, leveling out, turning one degree right, leveling out, two more degrees right, leveling out, and one degree left, and then back on-course toward the aiming point. If we were lucky, we would fool the radar and the gun sights and the flak would burst to our right or left where we would have been without the evasive action."

The evasion was working, at least so far, but the flak still burst uncomfortably close. A kind of steady throb now, it had a sort of rhythm of its own. Stephens could almost get used to it. Almost. The seconds ticked by and still no bombs away. Everyone was impatient now. Almost every airman, except the bombardiers, was thinking, "Drop the bombs and let's get the hell out of here!" Lieutenant Stephens tried to keep his mind free of such impatience. He had found on his previous ten missions that you could not become preoccupied with the flak or you would go crazy wondering if the next burst might kill you.

A few more seconds passed and then he felt the plane lurch upward. "Bombs away!" his bombardier, Lieutenant Francis "Fritz" Carrier, called out. Deadly bombs from the entire 397th Bomb Group fell thousands of feet and exploded, close enough to the Dieppe guns to do them damage. "We hit the target cleanly," Stephens later claimed. As quickly as he could, he turned his plane toward England and followed the other planes home to their base at Rivenhall. At debriefing, Stephens found out that one of the group's navigators had been killed on the mission. Flak fragments had torn through his compartment and smashed into his head, killing him instantly. For the navigator, the fighting was over, but for the rest of his buddies, the Dieppe raid was just another day on the job of fulfilling the goals of the transportation plan.[10]

Lieutenant William Redmond, a B-26 navigator/bombardier in the 387th Bomb Group, kept a diary that spring. Each night, after a mission, he wrote a descriptive entry in the diary, effectively recording a vivid chronicle of the transportation plan. On May 12, his group bombed heavy guns around Cherbourg, *"No flak* surprisingly enough. I lead the low flight of 4 ships and our bombs hit . . . 500 yards from the guns. We all missed the target in the first box of 12 ships." They came back from this mission, gassed up, ate a meal, and took off for a mission to hit guns at Le Havre. "I made a mistake in target identification and dropped on similar installation 3 miles to the south. Once again no flak bothered us. Lead 4 ships hit within 100' of guns to right of target. High flight hit 200 ft. to the left."

A few days later, the 387th went back to Cherbourg. "This time we went after those four 170mm guns with a pathfinder leader [a plane with special navigation equipment]. Our bombs from the second 18 hit to the right of the northernmost gun possibly disabling it. Flak from a 4 gun battery followed us on the way out but we were beyond range." Two days later, it was more of the same. "On this trip we (high flight) hit the southernmost gun on the button. Flak was heavier than the last trip but no hits [were] scored on [our] ships."

A week later, as May neared an end, they began concentrating on railroad bridges. For instance, on May 28 Redmond's group flew a mission to knock out a railroad bridge over the Seine River, northwest of Paris. "Once again I flew in lead 6. Flak was horrible. Our ship was hit twice in the right wing—once in the left wing—twice in the left motor severing the oil line—one big hole in the left aft bomb bay and small crack in the nose near my feet. No ships lost but one crashed in on a flat. No one [was] hurt. [The] bridge was straddled on the west shoreline with bombs." The following day they bombed another Seine bridge. They hit it dead center and watched as the remnants of the bridge tumbled into the river. But the victory came with a price. Redmond was watching the bombs hit their mark when he saw a plane from a sister squadron get hit: "I watched it fall in a tight spin. 3 chutes [were] reported. A gunner was killed by flak. It entered his body between the front and rear of his flak suit. Another ship limped home with a smoking engine. Our ship received one small hole in the right elevator."[11]

As mentioned, the Germans ordinarily did not send their fighters after the Marauders, but sometimes they would attack them if they had been crippled by flak. On May 26, several groups of Marauders bombed German airfields at Chartres. Alfred Freiburger, a twenty-one-year-old native of Fort Wayne, Indiana, was at the controls of one of those planes. Freiburger, his copilot, and his crewmen all enjoyed rum and Cokes, so they dubbed their aircraft *Rum Buggy*. The name, plus a colorful illustration, adorned the plane's nose, "On both sides of the nose of our ship, we painted a big animated bottle of rum standing in a ricksha, cracking a whip over the head of a crew member pulling the ricksha."

Their bomb run at Chartres went very smoothly. They cruised from the IP to the aiming point, where the bombardier disgorged eight 500-pound bombs on the airfield below. Freiburger felt the bombs leave the plane and began to turn his aircraft for home. Then, in an instant, his world changed. "An 88mm shell went thru our right wing tank without exploding, thank goodness, or I wouldn't be here now. Some flak knocked out our left engine, ruptured the main hydraulic lines under my seat, and also hit our tail gunner, Bob Dahlem, in the right arm. Since we were now on one engine, I had to drop out of formation."

They steadily lost altitude. Freiburger called for help from nearby P-51 fighter pilots who were flying top cover for the bombers. The voice of their leader crackled over Freiburger's headphones: "No sweat, buddy. We have you in sight and we will be right down."

Freiburger glanced to his left and saw a German ME-109 swooping in for a pass at his plane. A tremor of fear washed over him. If that fighter got to him before the P-51s, it could shoot him down in a matter of seconds. He called the P-51 leader: "I have a bogie . . . getting ready for the kill."

"No problem, we've got him pegged," the fighter pilot replied.

Now Freiburger and the other bomber crewmen became mere spectators. "Two P-51s came down across my nose and headed straight toward the ME-109. It looked like the ME-109 . . . stopped in midair and did a 180 and tried to get away, but the 51s were right on his tail and shot him down. They came back and did a . . . slow roll in front of me and said, 'Ok, now we'll take you home.' "

They escorted him until the white cliffs of Dover came into sight. "Do you think you can make it from here?"

Freiburger nodded. "Yes, I think I can. Thanks a million."

"No problem, buddy. It's all in a day's work. We'll see you."

Freiburger watched them execute several more victory rolls and tear off for their base. "I never did find out who those pilots were. I sure would have liked to buy them a drink." Freiburger managed to make a safe, albeit challenging, landing at an emergency landing strip. "At the debriefing we were given an extra ration of rotgut whisky and told to take a couple of days off until they could find another airplane for us."[12]

As Freiburger's story indicates, the fighters were lifesavers. They also might have been the most effective weapon the Air Force possessed. The P-47s and P-51s that most American fighter pilots flew by 1944 were wonderfully versatile. They could escort bombers deep into enemy territory or hold their own with enemy aircraft in air-to-air combat. Plus, they could strafe and bomb quite effectively.

The latter type mission was of particular importance to the accomplishment of the Allied goal of isolating Normandy by D-Day. Even as the heavy and medium bombers struck vital targets from altitudes of 10,000 feet and up, the fighters went lower so as to inflict maximum devastation. Bill Dunn was a twenty-seven-year-old fighter pilot, and ace, in the 406th Fighter Group. By the spring of 1944, he had a wealth of experience flying fighter aircraft. He had been a member of the Eagle Squadron, a group of American pilots who joined the Royal Air Force before America's entry into the war. A senior captain, he regularly led flights and perused orders that came down from higher headquarters. "[We] were directed to step up ... armed recce missions. Hunt down and kill everything that moved was the field order—railway trains, trucks, automobiles, river barges, coastal vessels, anything that might support German ground troops—shoot or blow the hell out of it. We were also directed to do a lot of bridge busting, strike heavy flak positions, and knock off flak towers."

These strafing missions were very dangerous for the fighter pilots. They pulled tremendous G forces during their descent. Their planes were durable, but flak could easily shoot them down at such low altitudes. Flying down on the deck could be disorienting under the best of circumstances, but pulling out of a 10,000-foot dive could be quite difficult, especially after absorbing such terrific G forces. Sometimes, the pilots even got killed by the debris from their own ordnance. Captain Dunn especially feared the missions against flak towers. "The enemy gunners were encased in steel-reinforced concrete towers about fifty feet high, with all sorts of automatic weapons pointing, it seemed, in every direction. Since our .50 caliber guns didn't do too much damage to these towers, except knock off a lot of concrete chips, we soon learned to employ our 5-inch HVAR rockets against them. To get a rocket hit we had to get in pretty close because of the rocket's slow velocity and dropping trajectory. To divvy up the flak tower's return fire, we would attack the tower simultaneously from two or three directions. When we were within firing range, we each let go of a pair of rockets. Then we spent the next couple of seconds ducking the other firing aircraft and the rocket bursts. A very tricky business." Nor was the process very precise. Sometimes they mistook water supply towers for flak towers.[13]

Lieutenant Alvin Siegel was very typical of many young American fighter pilots risking their lives on these missions. As a youngster in California, he used to go to the nearest airfield and watch the planes take off. He was fascinated with flying and yearned to one day become an army aviator. When the United States went to war, he got his wish. In May 1944 he flew dozens of sorties for the 358th Fighter Group, including bridge-busting missions. "We would take off in the usual formation, fly over the Channel, and make landfall south of Calais. We would fly down to 12,000 feet. When we spotted the bridge we would pair off. If there was a flight of sixteen the first flight would peel off, dive down and bomb the bridge. They would come back up and circle above us and act as top cover for the next flight. We would continue that way until all four flights dropped their bombs. Usually we carried two 500 pound bombs, one under each wing. There were times when we got a couple of direct hits." Typically, their bombs hit nearby, not perfectly on-target. "Very often we had some very near misses and did a lot of damage . . . and other times we would have a bad day and not do much damage at all."

After each fighter dropped its bombs they would ascend to a safer altitude. "We would climb up to four to six thousand feet and as a group fly back. If the weather was clear we would look for something moving on the ground such as trucks or trains. When you dived at an object you almost couldn't miss. Even if your first shot . . . wasn't perfect you could see the bullets hitting the ground. They would hit in flashes because they were incendiary bullets." The pilots especially shot up any trains or supply trucks they spotted.[14]

Sometimes the fighters did double duty, flying escort for the bombers and then going down to the deck to strafe. The fighter pilots would have much preferred to duel in the skies with enemy fighters, but on these missions they could take out their frustrations on ground targets. One of Captain Dunn's comrades in the 406th Fighter Group was a twenty-one-year-old New Orleans native named Robert O'Neill. Second Lieutenant O'Neill joined the unit in mid-May. He had a year and a half of Louisiana State

University education under his belt and had worked at a shipyard before enlisting as an aviation cadet in 1942.

On May 30 he participated in a duel escort/strafing mission. His unit escorted B-26s to a target in Belgium. The bombers dropped their bombs safely and headed for home. During the bomb run, O'Neill circled above the Marauders, craning his neck, peering intently into the skies, searching for enemy fighters. With the bombing mission accomplished, the fighters headed for the deck. Lieutenant O'Neill followed closely behind his wingman. "We . . . hit the deck and shot at anything that moved! We had a great time, and we did destroy some trains, shot up some flack towers." They buzzed around for several more minutes but ran out of targets and ammo.

That night they watched their gun camera film in order to ascertain how much damage they had done, "One of the pilots took the instructions rather lightly! He had shot up and totally eliminated a large black and white cow! His retort was that it was an enemy cow and was moving!"[15]

Clearly cows had something to fear from the transportation plan, but did the Germans? The short answer is yes. By the end of May, the Luftwaffe had more or less been swept from the skies, but that had been partially accomplished in the months preceding the plan. According to an Air Force historian, the Germans lost 2,262 fighter pilots in the five months before D-Day. In addition, Germany had lost 50 percent of its fighter force.[16] The offensive had an even greater impact on its main target—the transportation network. German rail traffic in northern France had practically ground to a halt. The enemy's transportation ministry claimed in May that "the raids carried out in recent weeks have caused systematic breakdown of all main lines . . . large scale strategic movement of German troops by rail is practically impossible."[17]

The Army's official historian decreed that rail traffic in France "declined 60 percent between 1 March and 6 June." But that statistic does not tell the whole story. The Allied missions mainly paralyzed German rail traffic in northern France, the area in which the invasion was to take place. They left southern France more or less untouched. In total they dropped over 76,000 tons of bombs that drastically affected the rail lines the Germans would need to reinforce their soon-to-be-embattled troops in Normandy. "The bridges were down the length of the Seine from Rouen to Mantes-Gassicourt before D-Day," Forrest Pogue, SHAEF's official historian, later wrote. "Railway traffic dropped sharply between 19 May and 9 June, the index (based on 100 for January and February 1944) falling from 60 to 38, and by mid-July dropping further to 23." In addition, three-quarters of French rail capacity in the northern part of the country had been shut down. The bombings did cause thousands of civilian casualties but nowhere near the dire estimate of 160,000. "Although French collaborationists roused some feelings against the Allies . . . there is no evidence that pro-German sentiment increased sharply because of the transportation attacks." The Air Force's official historian concurred: "The battle against enemy transportation was a splendid success on the eve of D-day. The Allies . . . won their premier objective in the transportation campaign: they were able to build up their forces in Normandy from across the Channel faster than the Germans could reinforce theirs from adjacent areas in France." Even Spaatz later wrote that the transportation plan had "opened the door for the invasion."[18]

The verdict of history should be clear. The plan accomplished exactly what it intended to do. It isolated Normandy on the eve of the invasion and prevented the Germans from sending large-scale reinforcements quickly to the battle area. Most of the German reinforcements making their way to Normandy in the summer of 1944 had to do so the old-fashioned way—by foot and usually at night in order to avoid Allied fighter-bombers. In the end, the political and strategic risks of the plan were more than offset by the tangible results that helped Allied soldiers succeed in getting ashore and staying there.

CHAPTER THREE

THE BRASSY BRIEFING

The setting was quite austere, at least for such a stately gathering of leaders. The auditorium was crescent-shaped, with curved rows of wooden benches that layered, one after the other, to the top of the room. At ground level, a stage—adorned with a huge top-secret colored plaster map of Normandy—commanded the room. Dark gray, almost black, columns supported the high ceiling and the rows of benches. The temperature in this simple amphitheater nearly mirrored the chilly, damp, raw air outside on this cold London day in the middle of May. The moist English chill had a way of penetrating your bones to the very marrow. General Eisenhower knew that all too well by now. He had been in England for four months. He found it amazing that even now, on May 15, in the heart of spring, the place could be so chilly. It wasn't a piercing Siberian type of cold. Rather, it was a damp, dull cold, the kind that came from steady rain and little sunlight.

He sat huddled in an overcoat in an armchair in front of the stage. He watched as the other top Allied commanders took their seats in this cramped amphitheater. They were all here at St. Paul's School in Kensington for the final briefing of the Overlord plan. St. Paul's had been a boys' school before the war. Now it was General Montgomery's headquarters. He had once gone to school here. Ike wondered if Monty ever felt nostalgic wandering the halls of this somber place. No, the prickly little British commander did not seem like the reflective type. Eisenhower fixed his gaze on Montgomery. The hero of El Alamein was outfitted in full khaki battle dress. He was trim and the uniform fit him quite well. He looked like a confident man in full command. Monty kept glancing at his watch and the double doors to the amphitheater. He had issued orders that the hall was to be sealed at 0900 sharp.

As the clock ticked closer to 0900, most of the key leaders of the Allied war effort found their places throughout the room. No one talked much; there was just a dull, expectant murmur. In fact, the room crackled with tension. Many of the commanders knew only their own particular aspect of Overlord. They did not know how the whole plan fit together and they were eager to see if the big picture made sense. Immediately to Ike's right sat the king of England. Next to him was Winston Churchill, cigar firmly in place in his stubby right hand. On Ike's left sat, in order, Tedder, Ramsay, Montgomery, Leigh-Mallory, and Rear Admiral George Creasy of the Royal Navy. It never occurred to Ike that he was the only American in a row of chairs containing only British leaders.

The seating in the room was stratified. The highest-ranking individuals sat closest to the stage. The lowest-ranking personages sat in the upper rows. The second tier included people such as Omar Bradley, Frederick Morgan, Carl Spaatz, and Bedell Smith. Behind them sat various naval task force commanders, British air marshals, assault division commanders, even members of the British War Cabinet.

Montgomery checked his watch again, turned around, and gestured to a pair of imposing American military policemen standing at the doors. They nodded and closed the doors, disappearing from sight. Eisenhower imagined what they must have looked like guarding the doors outside. The burly men wore white holsters and helmets. They both stood well over six feet tall. Even had there been any German spies left in England, they would have thought twice before crossing these military policemen.[1]

Sitting a few rows up from the supreme commander, Rear Admiral Morton Deyo, commander of the naval bombardment force scheduled to shell Utah beach, nervously shifted on the uncomfortable bench. He could see the tension in the body language of the other officers. He stared at the map and wondered how such an elaborate plan could be synchronized. The room was heavy with anticipation. "The proper meshing of so many gears would need nothing less than divine guidance. A failure at one point could throw the whole momentum out of balance and result in chaos. All in that room were aware of the gravity of the elements to be dealt with."[2]

No one more than Eisenhower. He understood that, in part, his job today was to instill complete confidence in the Overlord

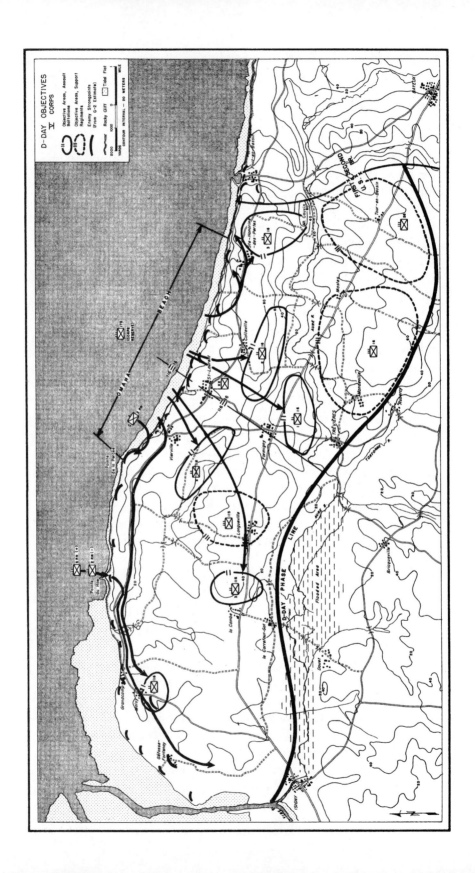

plan among the senior commanders. Once he saw that the doors were shut, he prepared to rise from his seat, only to hear a loud rapping on the doors. All heads turned in surprise toward the doors. The knocking abated for a moment and then began again, even louder than before.

Monty looked annoyed. He had given orders that *no one* was to be allowed in after 0900. Still the knocking continued. "Open the doors," Montgomery commanded the military policemen.

The double doors flew open and in walked General Patton. He unrepentantly strode several rows down to take his seat among the army commanders. A few officers glowered at him for delaying Eisenhower's speech. Ike, however, was used to such mercurial behavior from his best commander but biggest public relations headache.[3] With Patton firmly in place, the supreme commander removed his coat and strode to the center of the stage, right in front of the elaborate map. He gave a brief overview of the Overlord plan and flashed his warm, self-conscious, almost boyish grin.

Admiral Deyo felt a surge of relief sweep over him when he saw the famous Eisenhower grin. "It had been said that his smile was worth twenty divisions. That day it was worth more. Before the warmth of his quiet confidence the mists of doubt dissolved."[4]

Ike spoke for ten minutes, concluding, quite typically, with a message of unity and cooperation. "Here we are on the eve of a great battle. The Force Commanders will brief you on their plans. I would emphasize but one thing. I consider it to be the duty of anyone who sees a flaw in the plan not to hesitate to say so. I have no sympathy with anyone, whatever his station, who will not brook criticism. We are here to get the best possible results and you must make a really cooperative effort."

Ike turned the floor over to Montgomery, who would command all Allied ground forces on D-Day. The dapper British commander was completely in his element. In cool, coherent, articulate fashion he explained each phase of the ground plan. Churchill, perhaps taking Eisenhower's imprecations a bit too seriously, repeatedly interrupted Montgomery, asking questions about strategy or tactics. Montgomery patiently fielded the prime minister's questions, never losing his essential focus in elaborating on the plan. Probably the best aspect of Monty's briefing was his prescription for success: "We have the initiative. Therefore, we must rely on the violence of our assault, our great weight of supporting fire from the sea and the air, the simplicity of our object and a robust mentality. We must blast our way ashore and get a good lodgement before the enemy can bring sufficient reserves up to turn us out. We must gain space rapidly, and peg out claims well inland." He finished on a motivational note: "We shall have to send the soldiers in to this party 'seeing red.' We must get them completely on their toes; having absolute faith in the plan; and embued [*sic*] with infectious optimism and offensive eagerness. Nothing must stop them. This is a perfectly normal operation which is certain of success. If anyone has any doubts in his mind, let him stay behind."[5]

On that note, Montgomery finished, yielding to Ramsay and Leigh-Mallory, Ike's naval and air commanders. Their briefings filled most of the rest of the morning. In the early afternoon, the group broke for lunch, but not before King George closed out the morning with a short, clumsy speech. "With God's help, this great operation will be brought to a successful conclusion," he summarized. In the second row of the hall, Patton cringed. Clearly public speaking was not the king's strong suit. The American general found it "rather painful to watch the efforts he made not to stammer." At lunch, Patton sat opposite Churchill. Oddly enough, the prime minister asked Patton if he remembered him. "Yes, I do," Patton replied. Churchill beamed and ordered Patton a glass of whiskey.[6]

After lunch they resumed their previous places to hear numerous briefings from task force and army commanders, including Bradley, who gave a short talk "[Fort] Benning-style, without notes." In spite of the discomfort of the surroundings and the length of the sessions, no one's attention seemed to wane. Quite possibly, the highlight of the afternoon was a briefing by Major General Elwood "Pete" Quesada, commander of the IX Tactical Air Command. At forty years of age, Quesada was probably the youngest man in the room. Bradley admired him as one of the few air commanders who thought of ground support "as a vast new frontier waiting to be explored."[7]

Indeed, Quesada and his aviators would soon perfect close air support in the Normandy campaign. On this day, he stood before the assembled senior officers and began to speak. An ordinary man might have been intimidated in the presence of so much power and seniority, but not Quesada. He had joined the Army as a private in 1924 and eventually earned a commission and his pilot's wings. He was a stocky, solid man with a full head of thick brown hair and an easy smile. One of his fighter pilots once called him a "good looking devil . . . looks as though he could handle his fists too."[8]

Now Quesada began to explain the American tactical air plan. First the IX Troop Transport Command, consisting of about one thousand C-47s, would shuttle the 82nd and 101st Airborne Divisions to their drop zones during the early-morning hours of D-Day. Next, at daybreak, medium bombers would hit coastal emplacements at Utah beach. Finally, as Quesada discussed the missions his fighters would fly, he swept his pointer airily across the span of Normandy, flashed his winning grin, and said, "We will move like that throughout our progress over the continent of Europe." The audience broke out in good-natured chuckles. These old men, sitting like schoolboys on their hard wooden rows, were looking for a bit of comic relief after a serious day of briefings. Quesada provided it to them.

When the laughter died down, one of the American officers, Major General J. Lawton Collins, commander of the VII Corps that would hit Utah beach, asked, "Pete, how are you going to keep the German Air Force from preventing our landing?"

Quesada didn't miss a beat. "General, there is not going to be any German Air Force there."

That pronouncement set forth a round of subdued snickers. Churchill was intrigued by this confident Yank general. "Ahhh, young man, how can you be so sure?"

Quesada knew that he would not regret his assurances. He knew that Allied planes had decimated the Luftwaffe. He knew that his side would call upon 13,000 aircraft for D-Day. He knew that the German Air Force had no chance to repel the invasion. Only the German Army could do that. He looked at Churchill. "Mr. Prime Minister, because we won't let them be there," Quesada answered, "I am sure of it. There will be no German Air Force over the invasion area."

Churchill hesitated a moment as if pondering whether Quesada was foolishly brash or supremely confident. He made up his mind on the latter. "You are very confident. At least that is a great asset."

There was nothing more to say. Quesada sat down. He was sure that what he said would come to fruition, but he hoped he had not appeared too cocksure.[9]

Late in the day, at about 1600, when all the military commanders had had their say, Churchill, the great orator, finally rose to speak. As was his habit on such occasions, the prime minister absentmindedly grabbed his lapels and held them firmly in his hands. "Gentlemen, I am now hardening on this enterprise. I repeat, I am now hardening toward this enterprise."

Not far away, Eisenhower felt a slight sense of disappointment. All along he had wondered if Churchill really believed in Overlord. True, Churchill had been the original architect of the notion of a cross-Channel attack, but he had shrunk from such an attack in 1942 and 1943, arguing vociferously for operations in the Mediterranean. Even this spring he had sometimes expressed doubts about the invasion, morosely worrying about casualties—French beaches "choked with bodies of the flower of British and American manhood," as the literary-minded prime minister descriptively put it.

Eisenhower interpreted Churchill's opening remarks today as proof that he had not been in favor of the cross-Channel attack until only very recently. Moreover, Eisenhower thought the remarks conveyed a lack of confidence in Overlord. These were misinterpretations on Ike's part. Churchill never meant to convey what Eisenhower thought he meant. At this late stage, the prime minister had worries, not doubts. The British leader spoke for a few more minutes before closing his speech on a somewhat prophetic note: "Let us not expect all to go according to plan. Flexibility of mind will be one of the decisive factors. We must not have another Anzio. Risks must be taken. Rommel cannot afford to concentrate all his forces against Overlord. How does he know we will not launch another Overlord somewhere else? He must keep a strategical reserve."

Churchill finished and sat down. Now it was Ike's turn to adjourn this productive, and unifying, meeting. The supreme commander once again flashed his famous grin. "In half an hour Hitler will have missed his one and only chance of destroying with a single well-aimed bomb the entire high command of the Allied forces."[10]

On that lighthearted note, the meeting ended. The men in the St. Paul's School amphitheater never met like this again. The meeting represented one final, but necessary, step in the launching of the cross-Channel attack. The senior leaders now thoroughly understood the plan, and Overlord took on a momentum of its own. Most of them had confidence that the invasion could succeed. As the generals, admirals, marshals, and politicians went their separate ways on that Monday afternoon in mid-May 1944, a great invasion force sprang to life all over southern England. The senior commanders returned to their headquarters and issued orders— move to the marshaling areas. Overlord was now imminent.

CHAPTER FOUR

FROM THE SAUSAGES TO THE SHIPS

Southern England resembled nothing less than an armed camp. The place teemed with military equipment, weapons, clothing, food, and transport. More than anything else, this normally sleepy sliver of England teemed with soldiers. Expectation permeated the air. British, Canadian, and American soldiers began congregating in special marshaling areas in May 1944. These areas stretched out among the small villages and ports of southern England, forming, on maps, what looked like sausages. Thus most of the soldiers simply began calling them sausages.

Once the soldiers went into their sausages they were sealed off from the outside world. Most lived in pyramidal tents. For security reasons, many civilians in southern England had been evacuated or put under veritable martial law, a controversial political move that Churchill had reluctantly agreed to. Security remained the greatest concern. Anyone who saw the beehivelike activity in and around the sausages could determine that something big was afoot. Moreover, ports along the southern English coast were packed with ships of every description. But an invasion of this magnitude could not possibly happen without leaving some telltale signs. Somehow the Germans missed the buildup or, at least, failed to understand that it meant imminent invasion.

Among the soldiers moving into the sausages, there was mixed opinion as to whether this was the real invasion or just another exercise. Lieutenant Franklyn Johnson, the antitank platoon leader in the 18th Infantry of the 1st Division, felt strongly that this was the real thing. When orders came to move into his unit's sausage, a barbed-wire-enclosed camp at Piddlehinton, Johnson, a fellow officer, and an enlisted driver traveled back to their old billet at Bournemouth to say good-bye to many friends. The three of them dropped into one of their favorite bars, the Old Barn Club, for a few drinks. They found the place full of "last flingers."

Johnson consumed a couple of drinks and was in the middle of singing a farewell song when a drunken major from division headquarters suddenly got in his face. "Stop that singing and get that enlisted man out of here!" the staff officer bellowed, pointing at Johnson's driver.

Johnson was stunned and angered. This was a social occasion, not a duty situation. What difference did it make if officers and enlisted men drank together? Where they were going, they would need plenty of togetherness to survive. So Johnson refused the major's order.

"The fuming red-faced officer repeats his order twice, getting the same negative answer," Johnson wrote in his diary, "whereupon he demands to know my name. He gives me his, Paul Gale ... [We] go on with our merry-making and forget the incident—until morning."

Johnson received a call from General Huebner "wanting to know what the hell I did last night. Gale has sent to him the whole story, adding that I was insubordinate, disrespectful toward a superior officer, drunk, etc. etc." The general ordered Lieutenant Johnson to choose between a court-martial and a fine of $82.50. He chose the latter. "I begin saving shillings to pay the fine, and meanwhile pray to find Gale some night in a dark alley."[1]

Once the invasion troops reached their sausages, their quality of life rose, a sure sign that invasion was imminent. They ate better than at any other time in their military lives. Chuck Hurlbut was with the 299th Combat Engineer Battalion, a unit scheduled to go into Omaha beach with the 1st Infantry Division. At Hurlbut's sausage near Dorchester, the engineers spent a lot of time watching movies and eating whatever they wanted. "Continuous movies, first-rate movies. Food. Unbelievable food. Ice cream. Candy. Cigarettes. Whatever you wanted was there. We took full advantage of it, they were just fattening us up for the kill."[2]

Lieutenant Edward Jones, a reconnaissance platoon leader with the 29th Division, went into a sausage on the outskirts of Liskeard. He and his men relished the feasts they were served. They would go through the chow line and take whatever they pleased, even as the cooks encouraged them to come back for seconds. "The food was just the very best, the finest that any of us had seen or eaten since we had left the U.S.—white bread, ice cream, steaks, chicken—all the really fine food that many of us had dreamed of for so long." Like Hurlbut and the engineers, Jones and his recon troopers sardonically referred to their tasty fare as the "last meals for the condemned." Unfortunately, this was all too true "for so many fine men who would be dead in the next few days."[3]

Farther to the west, near Plymouth, where the 4th Division was bivouacked, another Jones, Private First Class William, from Kingsport, Tennessee, was not content simply to enjoy regulation-issue food, delicious though it may have been. One of his buddies, an ex–professional boxer, routinely visited his tent taking orders for food he managed to pilfer from the cook's stocks. "He was one of the roughest characters I've ever met. And one of the nicest. Anything we wanted: canned peaches, pineapple, anything you can imagine . . . he would come back with it before the night was over. He'd raid the supply houses every night. We had been starved for that kind of thing for a long time and he supplied all our needs while we were there." The boxer brought them more canned goods than they could ever consume. When they left their sausage and moved on to their ships, each man still had several cans of food stored under his cot.[4]

For some men, the food was too much of a good thing. At a sausage near the port of Weymouth, Lieutenant James Eikner, a thirty-year-old Mississippian and 1935 graduate of Blackburn University, began to feel very sick one night after a dinner of thick, hot dog–like "wieners." Soon he began to vomit. So did many others. In fact, Eikner's unit, the 2nd Ranger Battalion, was inundated with food poisoning from the wieners.

The men of this unit were the cream of the infantry crop. Veterans of a training regimen even more intense than airborne training, they would have the toughest D-Day mission. Their job was to scale a sheer cliff, roughly six stories high, and capture six heavy guns at Pointe-du-Hoc, the cove that flanked Omaha and Utah beaches.

Eikner and the other Rangers were superbly conditioned, aggressive assault troops, but they were no match for the bacteria that felled them: "We were all laid low and put a lot of concern in our minds whether we could go ahead with our mission. Some of us thought that perhaps this was an act of sabotage of some kind." It wasn't. They were simply unlucky enough to be served tainted meat. The food poisoning ordeal, terrible as it was, lasted about a day or two. Then it ran its course and the Rangers regained their enthusiasm for the task ahead.[5]

As the days unfolded in late May 1944, the soldiers of the amphibious assault forces, some 175,000 men, busied themselves as best they could. The men were full of pent-up energy. They spent their time cleaning weapons, waterproofing vehicles, hiking, drilling, and packing and unpacking their newly issued invasion vests with necessary equipment. Still it wasn't enough. They had plenty of free time and a lot of nervous energy. Tempers were on edge. Fistfights were common. Arguments were even more common.

Sports proved to be a good outlet. Corporal Gale Beccue, a twenty-one-year-old Minnesotan in E Company of the 5th Ranger Battalion, played a lot of softball. His unit was slated to assault the western sector of Omaha beach and link up with the 2nd Rangers at Pointe-du-Hoc, a tough assignment indeed. In the days leading up to the invasion, he and his buddies tried to keep a regular game going at their sausage near Weymouth. The games were fun, but the surroundings made it difficult to forget the war. "The camp we were in was surrounded by fencing with machine-gun towers on each corner manned by British troops. Even when we were playing softball, we had to signal the tower if we had to go close to the fence to retrieve the ball. We spent most of our free time playing ball or throwing knives at playing cards tacked on trees. We couldn't write or receive any mail, so there wasn't much [else] to do."[6]

The prodigious, almost onerous, anticipation manifested itself in other ways, too. Gallows humor was quite common. Felix Branham, the veteran guardsman from the 116th Infantry, constantly ribbed one his buddies, named Ferrari, because he routinely carried money and valuables. "He carried a big wad of money, $700 or $800, and he had a beautiful ring. I would say, 'Ferrari, when you hit that beach and you fall, man, I'm going to be getting your wallet out.' And another guy would say, 'Yep, I'm going to have that ring of yours.' And we sat around and thought about that, never thinking it would happen. But what else did we have to talk about?"[7]

Practically nothing, except perhaps rumors, the gossip of military life. Lieutenant Johnson scribbled in his diary that as he and his men sat day after day in their sausage "most of our time is spent in bull sessions. Inevitably the conversation veers around to conjecture as to when the attack will begin. Every announcement of a meeting sets off speculation, and the mess hall buzzes with, 'I heard over at the C.P. . . . ,' or 'Now, here's the straight dope . . .' We thought that we'd be on our way weeks ago, and we have planned and discussed it so long that . . . the novelty has worn off."[8]

Besides softball playing, there was little for the 5th Rangers to do at Weymouth but wait. Twenty-two-year-old First Lieutenant Stan Askin was the battalion's assistant operations officer. He and many other Rangers spent plenty of time in the entertainment tent. "The weather was hot. Some of us sat sweltering in a large tent, stripped to the waist, watching Mickey Rooney and Judy Garland in 'Girl Crazy' for the tenth time." When they weren't watching movies, they did some last-minute training on the ladders they would use to scale Pointe-du-Hoc: "Two converted DUKWS [amphibious vehicles] were parked in an open field with their ladders extended far into the sky and fastened together to form an inverted 'V.' We were lined up single file and had to climb the first shaky ladder, step across very gingerly at the top, and descend on the other. One or two men froze momentarily in the mid-journey, but eventually everybody made it."[9]

No more than a couple miles away, in a stifling wooded marshaling area near Weymouth, the 5th Engineer Special Brigade sat waiting for the word to board ships. These specially trained engineers had been assigned this mission in response to the millions of mines and obstacles Rommel's labor force had deployed along the beaches. Allied intelligence had gradually, over the last few months, detected the heightening presence of the mines and obstacles. Engineers now comprised nearly one-quarter of the troops going into Normandy on D-Day. One of them was Private George "Jeff" Boocks. He watched in amazement as new haircuts and facial hair fashions swept through his company. "Some soldiers began to sprout goatees or neatly trimmed beards. Handle bar mustaches were being carefully groomed. To find a man with an ordinary hair cut was almost a novelty. Most fellows just had their hair completely shorn. But individualities cropped out. Some came up with just a strip of hair down the center like the Mohawk Indians, some with a cross cut in their hair, others had their initials or designs cut in their locks."[10]

Clearly the atmosphere was permissive among the engineers.

Not so for armored units like the 70th Tank Battalion, a veteran unit that would go ashore in special amphibious "duplex drive" tanks at Utah beach. Captain John Ahearn, commander of the battalion's C Company, had led tankers in North Africa and Sicily. Even in the sausages, Ahearn was feverishly trying to integrate his veterans with his replacements. Plus, he had received new tank dozers, designed to breach minefields, and now had to quickly train his people how to operate the contraptions. Thus he had no patience for a ridiculous order that came across his desk one afternoon: The men were to take down their pinup pictures of Hollywood stars like Betty Grable, because someone thought them too much of a distraction. How amazing! "That one really pissed me off, but I stayed cool about it and let it pass, which it did."[11]

Bizarre as that no pinup order was, one of Colonel Red Reeder's experiences might have been even odder. One day, Reeder was busy attending to a myriad of details pertaining to his 12th Infantry's Utah beach assault when a scholarly-looking major came to see him.

"I am the division psychiatrist. Just arrived from the States. General Barton sent me to you."

Reeder was confused. "The what?"

"Psychiatrist. I have checked the other two regiments of the division and now I'm to spend three days with yours. A check on mental health."

The colonel had no idea what Barton's motive for this impromptu psychiatric examination might be. What if he found an entire regiment of mentally ill soldiers? Would he decide to scrub the mission and send them all home? The whole thing was laughable. However, Reeder had been in the Army long enough to know how to handle strange situations like this one. Bemused but not flustered, he had only one request for the psychiatrist: "I don't care what you do, Doctor, but I want you to tell me what you find before you return to General Barton."

The doctor agreed. Three days later he came back with his report. Everyone was clean except for one oversize mortar man ("six feet four and built proportionately") in H Company whom the doctor deemed "a psychopath. This man has the personality of a five-year-old child. You cannot be sure that he will do his part in a fight." The doctor took his leave and reported to the general.

In the meantime, Colonel Reeder consulted the commanding officer of the H Company "psychopath." The company commander shrugged off the psychiatrist's report: "He gets along fine, a big harmless dummy—never bothers anyone. Strong as an ox—strongest man we have. His job is to carry 81-millimeter ammunition, and he enjoys it." The only time the man ever experienced problems was when he got a letter from home; "then he always cries like a baby."

Reeder had no sooner returned to his office when General Barton summoned him. The general had heard about a supposed psychopath with the intelligence of a five-year-old who would not fight. "Why hasn't he been gotten rid of?"

"Because his captain thinks he can do the job," Reeder replied.

Barton was not pleased. "Reeder, I am holding you *personally responsible* that this psycho . . . does his job when he hits the beach."

Reeder saluted and left. He was puzzled and perhaps a bit disgusted by Barton's behavior. "I made up my mind to disregard the order. There would not be time on the beach to worry about the H Company giant." The colonel never heard anything else about the man, so he assumed that he did fine. It is virtually incomprehensible that, on the eve of the most momentous invasion in history, General Barton found time to be concerned with the mental health of one of his ammunition carriers. Clearly the stress and the uncertainty of what lay ahead had gotten to Barton.[12]

While the stress produced anxiety in some, others struggled with depression. Chuck Hurlbut had not yet been in combat, nor had most of the soldiers of the 299th Engineers, but many of them still thought of their task as a suicide mission. Obviously no one wanted to die, but these young men were forced to struggle with the stark possibility that they could be dead in a matter of days. A deep gloom set in among some of them. "They wouldn't sleep. You could tell by looking at them, that they had a hopeless feeling." In all honesty, Hurlbut felt the same way, but he could not bring himself to show it. Instead he tried to perk up his comrades: "Hey, it's not that bad. Come on." They would shake their heads and express doubt. "I think what I was doing was relieving my own anxieties, getting them out of me. But I was just as scared and anxious as they were."[13]

The stifling security of the sausages, so necessary to maintain the secrets of Overlord, did not do much to quell anxiety. If anything, the security made anxiety even worse. Private Vincent

Schlotterbeck, a member of the 5th Engineer Special Brigade, did not like the dark, moody, oppressive atmosphere of his unit's sausage. "The month that we spent there was a miserable one. Although it was May, there was a heavy frost almost every morning, and during the day the sun never reached us because the forest was so dense that it was impossible for the sun's rays to filter through." Armed guards made sure that they did not tread under any openings in the forest: "We could not enter these because of the danger of disturbing the landscape, thus making it possible for the enemy to spot our location through aerial photography. For the same reason, no fires were permitted."[14]

Some men felt like caged animals. A few even tried to escape from the confines of the sausages, usually in search of women or liquor. Captain Charles Murphy was the commander of A Company of the 1st Division's 1st Engineers. One night he found out that two of his sergeants had gone AWOL. One of them was his first sergeant. Somehow, they had gotten out of the compound, but military police had then apprehended them. "Well, I was mad enough to bite nails. Here were two of my senior NCO's that I really depended on. They had gotten to know lots of the girls in Charmouth and we were there for quite a while, six months I guess. These girls had come all the way down from Charmouth to see these boys and they went AWOL." Captain Murphy had no room in his heart for this renegade love story. "I busted them, and I made my first sergeant . . . my runner." Murphy relished doing so, because he knew that he himself was going in just after the first wave, presumably at the most dangerous moment in the invasion. He told his ex–first sergeant, "You have just signed your death warrant. I don't think we stand a chance." Murphy made the other sergeant a runner for one of his platoon leaders. As it turned out, Murphy was correct. His former first sergeant did get killed right at his side on D-Day.[15]

Elsewhere in the 1st Division's sausage, Allen Towne, a veteran medic in the 18th Infantry, witnessed something quite unsettling. One of his platoon's new men came over to talk with him. At first, they had a normal conversation. Within moments, though, the conversation became decidedly abnormal. "At first he was rambling on about his family. Then he went on to say, 'I have seen the light. Everything is alright. We have nothing to worry about. God is with us.' He began talking incoherently and every so often would say, 'I have seen the light.' After a short time, he was shouting and had to be restrained. We quickly got him out of the area and sent him to a hospital. He was our first casualty in the Normandy invasion!" Needless to say, the new man's breakdown did not abet the mental state of his fellow replacements.[16]

Captain Charles Cawthon, commander of Headquarters Company of the 2nd Battalion, 116th Infantry Regiment, an inexperienced unit going ashore at Omaha beach on D-Day morning, found out that one of his men had disobeyed a direct order. This refusal had earned the man a spot in the stockade, under armed guard. Cawthon's battalion commander, Major Sidney Bingham, told him to straighten the man out, "as there was no time for such foolishness." Cawthon was surprised at the man's behavior because he had always known him to be a good soldier. In talking to the man, Cawthon discovered that he was simply struggling with the irrationality and insanity of war. He wondered why there had to be so much in the way of "lives, effort, and materiel being projected across the English Channel to destroy lives, effort and materiel arrayed on its other side." Cawthon nodded his understanding. He had wondered the same thing but never doubted, for a moment that it had to be done. He told the man that he did not have all the answers, only that others were relying on him to do his job when the time came, "He seemed relieved at having gotten his feelings across and said that he did not want to let his squad down and would like to go back and do his best. I was happy to have the problem resolved."[17]

Nor were veterans immune to such problems. Captain Ahearn, the company commander in the 70th Tank Battalion, was stunned and troubled by an incident with a man he thought of as dependable. "One of the men . . . who was an excellent driver . . . reported ill. I had been told that he was probably not ill but was trying to get out of this thing. I was told he was in the medical tent, and I went down to drag this guy out. I told him how much I needed him, that he was a good man who could not be easily replaced. He said he was ill with some respiratory ailment, which I thought didn't sound terribly serious." The man eventually did leave his sickbed and participate in the invasion, but the incident still troubled Ahearn.[18]

As May dwindled away, most men had the opposite problem. They were more than eager to go, perhaps too eager. They had been training seemingly forever; now they simply wanted to get on with the thing and get it over with. At first, when they went into the sausages, the vast majority of the soldiers did not know the secrets of Overlord (they were not "bigots" in the top-secret terminology of SHAEF). Finally, the brass gave the go-ahead to brief the soldiers on their respective missions. All over southern England, the troops who would be asked to carry out the invasion finally gained access to top-secret planning tents or rooms that had previously been off-limits to all but the "bigoted" few.

The troops had been speculating and guessing for months. Now they crowded into the top-secret areas, eager to be privy to one of history's greatest secrets. Lieutenant Johnson stared in fascination at a massive amount of information that bombarded the senses. "The Secret Room's walls are hung with maps, charts and sketches of Omaha Beach and gully E-1, which is our exit from the sand. Recent photos outline the steep and bare cliffs along our sector of Omaha, Easy Red; diagrams clearly show us what units will proceed shoreward in which tides and landing craft." Graphic, up-to-date photographs showed enemy defenses in detail. "Tables along the wall hold the latest G-2 and daily enemy situation reports. What stands in the center of the room, however, commands all attention: the ten-foot rubber scale model of the coast and approximately twenty-five miles of inland territory. This possesses detail in color down to individual trees and fences." Johnson's men studied the model with curious absorption.[19]

At a sausage in Cornwall, Sergeant Forrest Pogue watched as the various platoons of K Company, 175th Infantry, 29th Division, got briefed on the invasion. The Kentucky-born, thirty-one-year-old Pogue was a well-trained observer. He had a Ph.D. in European history and had taught college before the war. Now he was serving as a combat historian. Shortly before, he had been assigned to V Corps. His job was to circulate among the troops, interview them about their experiences, and record their stories for the official record. Those duties brought him to the 175th Regiment at this historic moment.

As part of his job, the bespectacled, balding Pogue had been allowed, a few weeks earlier, to study the Overlord plan in detail, so he was "bigoted" right down to knowing the actual date of the invasion. Even so, he enjoyed watching the men cluster around photographs or models to learn about their impending mission. "They listened closely to the story of D-Day as it was outlined, still not clear as to the overall plan. As the plan was unfolded and as the platoon and squad leaders learned their specific mission on the beach, the men showed greater animation than I was to see at any other time during the invasion. With the growing grins that one sees on the faces of listeners who anticipate the denounce- ment of a risqué joke, the men showed their pleasure at the pros- pect of getting the attack started. 'Jesus,' one of them remarked, 'now we can get started on the way home.' Most of them had been waiting two years for this invasion. There was little talk of Nazi monsters. Instead, they were simply happy to embark on a mission that would hasten the end of the war and, if all went well, the return trip home."[20]

Following that company-level briefing, the men of the 175th listened to briefings from their field grade officers. General Eisen- hower liked to say that plans were everything until the battle be- gan. Then they were nothing. The 175th Regiment's beloved commander, Colonel Paul "Pop" Goode, took this advice to heart when he briefed his soldiers on the regiment's role in the Nor- mandy assault. They would go in with follow-up waves, after the division's 116th and 115th Regiments got ashore. As Goode spoke, he referred to the detailed plan and orders he and his staff had prepared. Then he paused a moment. Somewhere in the anony- mous mass of listening soldiers, Private Joseph Bria of H Company curiously watched the colonel during his moment of hesitation. "He held up the regiment's invasion orders, which were as thick as a metropolitan city telephone directory, 'Here it is, men. Study it; learn it,' and with a dramatic flourish, he dropped the orders to the floor with a resounding crash."

The colonel turned his head, glanced at the orders, and faced his men: "All the complicated facts amount to one thing: Get off the boat; keep moving, no matter what. Get off the beach no mat- ter how confused the situation." Bria and the other soldiers heartily approved of this sage advice. They and other 29'ers found it quite useful when they went ashore.[21]

A few miles away, in the 116th Infantry's sausage, Gil Mur- doch, the replacement who had slowly gained acceptance in A Company, now sat intently studying reconnaissance photographs of his unit's beach area. They were scheduled to hit Dog Green beach, Omaha, with the first wave at H-Hour. Their mission was to capture the Vierville beach exit, then turn west to link up with the Rangers at Pointe-du-Hoc. Murdoch had never been in com- bat, but he could tell from the photographs in front of him that the mission would be very rough. "The beach . . . had cliffs of about 170–200 feet high. The beach itself consisted of stone called shingle, which was the tidele [*sic*] shelf at high-water line. At the cliff there was a seawall . . . made out of concrete, about 12 feet high, rounded at the top so that nothing, certainly not a grapple on a line, could catch on the other side. In the water itself, they had . . . Belgian gates, which were . . . about 8–10 feet high, 12 feet long. They had angled logs with mines on top facing seaward so that the underpart of the landing craft would hit the mine and explode. They had hedgehogs which were three crossed steel rails which in some cases had mines on top. Ashore there were mines and barbed wire." Murdoch looked away from the photos. He hardly wanted to imagine what the job of assaulting such formidable defenses could entail. But a slightly queasy feeling in his stomach told him that soon he and the other men of A Company would find out.[22]

Due to the very nature of their mission, the Rangers needed an extensive briefing. All along, these adventurous men knew that their training would lead them to the very cutting edge of combat. They knew that their D-Day mission would most likely entail scaling cliffs or assaulting strongly fortified positions. In the 2nd Rangers, the men of Companies D, E, and F, plus headquarters troops, found out that on D-Day they would do both. One of them was Technical Sergeant Owen "Leroy" Brown, a communications specialist. Brown was a midwesterner, the son of a World War I veteran who had struggled to support a large family during the depression. Immediately after Pearl Harbor, Brown volunteered for the Marines, but they were not impressed with his physical condition, so they put him on a waiting list. He grew impatient and volunteered for the Air Force. They accepted him, but when Brown got called up, he found he had been assigned to the infantry. He was angry at first but eventually made the most of it, by volunteering for the Rangers and making it through the rigorous training.

Now Brown and his buddies listened to an extensive briefing on Pointe-du-Hoc. "We had miniature plaster layouts of the French coast, giving the location of beaches, cliffs, and the German defenses. They showed us pillboxes, barbed wire, mine fields, underwater obstacles. They even told us the composition of the [enemy] soldiers. There was supposed to be a cadre of Germans with Polish, Russian, and Hungarian men . . . fighting with the Germans. My assignment was to land on the beach with five communications vehicles: two wire jeeps, two radio jeeps . . . and one three-quarter-ton truck with wire, switchboards, and radio repair equipment."

Immediately following the briefing, Sergeant Brown lodged a complaint with his superior, Lieutenant Eikner, the Mississippian who headed up the 2nd Ranger's communications section. Brown "requested to go [up] the cliffs." The sergeant was completely unenthusiastic about staying down on the beach while his fellow Rangers scaled Pointe-du-Hoc and captured the guns. Brown wanted to be in on the action. Eikner shook his head. "[He] informed me that he was running the show, and I would go where I was assigned, and that was it."

Brown was disappointed, but he understood. A day or two after the briefing, he began to feel pain and his face swelled up. At first, he thought the problem might go away, but it didn't. He had an abscessed front tooth and there was no way to hide that kind of affliction. Eikner sent Brown to Weymouth to see an army dentist. The dentist took one look at Brown and told him he would have to "stay in the hospital until the swelling went down. I told him I couldn't do that because I had an invasion to go on. I asked if he could pull the tooth. He told me he could pull it, but he couldn't deaden the jaw."

Sergeant Brown didn't hesitate for a moment. "Pull it." The doctor shrugged and complied. Waves of pain engulfed Brown. "As he pulled the tooth, his nurse stepped behind the chair to watch me. I sat for maybe thirty seconds, and then got up and started to walk to the door. After three steps, I suggested they open the windows because I got lightheaded. The nurse pulled out the smelling salts until I recovered." Brown went through the invasion and the entire campaign in Europe without front teeth.[23]

In the briefings, the soldiers of Overlord were told everything but the date of the invasion. The "bigots" still held on to that last secret and would until nearly the very moment when the fleets left port. Finally, after all the preparation and briefing, the amphibious assault troops received orders between June 1 and June 3 to leave the sausages and board ships. They were issued new equipment, including gas-impregnated clothing that itched terribly and stank to high heaven. They also received special invasion vests to carry the massive loads of personal equipment, (grenades, packs, ammo, and the like) they needed once they hit the shore.

When this massive army began to move to its ports of embarkation, it soon jammed the small roads of southern England. Soldiers, trucks, and equipment were everywhere. Private Boocks and his engineer unit spent nearly three days hiking along a narrow road to Weymouth. "It seemed like the whole Army was moving. Some troops were going in our direction and others moved in the opposite direction. Someone said the movements had been to confuse the enemy, and we all heartily wished that they were as confused as we were." When Boocks and the engineers finally reached Weymouth, British civilians lined the streets telling the Americans to "give the bloody Jerrys 'ell. We assured them we would."[24]

At each port of embarkation, this scene repeated itself. British civilians were keenly observing troop movements, hoping for some sign that the invasion was at hand. When they saw soldiers boarding ships, they knew exactly what that meant. At Weymouth, the 5th Rangers clomped through the streets, their brogan-style boots thumping dully on the concrete. Lieutenant Jay Mehaffey, a platoon leader in C Company, glanced at his men and the civilians lining the street. The atmosphere was hushed. "The men were quiet as they struggled under their loads of equipment with none of the usual horseplay. English civilians were silent, too, as they stood in small groups and watched us move to the boats. One woman was saying, 'God bless you,' as our men moved past."[25]

At Plymouth, where the 4th Infantry Division was now boarding ships, the crowds were a bit more animated. Somewhere in the mass of invasion-bound soldiers, Private First Class William Jones shuffled along, struggling against the weight of his ammo, rifle, and equipment. "The townspeople were all lined up along the sidewalks, something they had never done before, so . . . they knew that we were going for the real thing this time. They would say, 'Good luck, boys,' and all that stuff. That was unusual because it hadn't happened before."[26]

Elsewhere in the harbor area at Plymouth, the soldiers of the 12th Infantry walked single-file to their ships. These men would follow Private First Class Jones's 8th Infantry into Utah beach. The scene was really quite dramatic, at least for those who cared to think about such things. England had waited four long years for this moment. The young Americans who were now jostling their way onto ships had left their homes and families to reclaim Europe from a monstrous tyranny. The case could be made that the battle they were about to fight would be the most important in history. Certainly many of the civilians and soldiers at Plymouth that day thought of the invasion in those terms. First Lieutenant Paul Massa was one of them. He could not force such thoughts from his mind as he steadily marched to the 12th Infantry's ships that day. Massa was an artillery observer who had been specially trained to coordinate with the Navy on D-Day. He commanded a small observer group consisting of a naval officer and eight soldiers. Massa's task as the primary observer would be highly important: "My job was to stay with the rifle companies and visually direct naval gunfire." Now, in Plymouth, Massa thoughtfully watched as hundreds of soldiers boarded ships while British civilians bade them a fond farewell. The lieutenant felt a mixture of emotions welling up inside of him. "I'll never forget the feeling I had that morning as we marched down to the harbor. I felt the power and strength of the seemingly endless line of our men, moving in a column of twos down the long winding road."[27]

By June 4, the amphibious forces had loaded aboard their ships. They were like a cocked fist waiting for the signal to surge forward with a mighty punch. For now, the soldier-laden ships remained in place, waiting for the order to put to sea.

Farther to the north, from Devon to the midlands, in tented clusters around the numerous airfields of England, the airborne troops experienced the same kind of incarcerated life as the amphibious forces. As June began, the paratroopers and glider soldiers who would lead American ground forces into France finally made their way to various airfields. Similar to the sausages in southern England, their bivouac areas were sealed off with barbed wire and armed guards. Once a trooper went into his airfield marshaling area, he was not supposed to leave. Soldiers like Private David Kenyon Webster spent several days feasting on great food and living a life of luxury after so many months of a spartan existence. Webster and the other troopers in Headquarters Company, 3rd Battalion, 506th Parachute Infantry, could hardly believe their treatment when they got off a train and settled into pyramidal tents near an Exeter airfield in southwestern England. "The food situation was incredible. Friendly, obliging Air Corps KP's loaded our tin dishes like garbage scows. It was a beautiful load: white bread (our first overseas), great gobs of melting butter, marmalade (from an open keg swarming with yellow jackets, but who cares?), rice pudding and cream, all the coffee you could drink."

Webster and his buddies helped themselves to seconds of this fine meal. Afterward they were sitting talking and smoking when someone stuck his head in the mess tent "and shouted something about a movie in fifteen minutes." They could hardly believe their ears. White bread and movies? All on the same day? Happily enough, it was true.

They trooped over to the base theater, close to the runways. The whole regiment sat in the theater waiting for the film to start. "The atmosphere was more like a cruise to Bermuda or a high-school graduation party than a prelude to invasion. Friends shouted to friends in other companies and battalions. Officers visited back and forth. Colonel Sink [the regimental commander] stood benignly up front like a headmaster, smiling at his boys, or people, as he called us."[28]

The next day, in a scene repeated at every airborne marshaling area, they listened to a detailed briefing on their role in Operation Overlord. The whole process was nearly identical to the briefings for the seaborne assault troops, except that the 82nd Airborne Division troopers learned that their drop zone had been moved to the east in response to recent intelligence reports. "The 82nd Airborne Division was to land on both sides of the Merderet River," General James Gavin, the division's second in command, later wrote. "It was then to . . . secure the general area of Neuville-au-Plain, Ste-Mère-Eglise, Chef-du-Pont, Etienville, Amfreville. It was to destroy crossings over the Douve . . . and then to be prepared to advance to the west." The mission of the 101st remained unchanged. It would drop to the north and east of the 82nd, with the job of securing causeways from Utah beach, destroying gun positions, harassing German reinforcements, and capturing important locks and bridges.[29]

General Gavin, affectionately known to his men as "Slim Jim" or "Jumpin' Jim," was already something of a legend in the ranks of the airborne. He had commanded the 505th Parachute Infantry during its jump into Sicily and then, three months later, Salerno. Both times the West Point–trained Gavin had jumped with his men into battle. His outstanding combat performance earned him a promotion to brigadier general at the tender age of thirty-five. Now, on the eve of Normandy he served as General Ridgway's second in command in the 82nd Airborne. Once again, Gavin planned to lead the jump himself (some liked to refer to him as the highest-ranking platoon leader in the U.S. Army).[30]

He was a frenetic bundle of energy, a formidable commander with a deep sense of integrity. In the marshaling areas of the 82nd Airborne, the general seemed to be everywhere. Private Dwayne Burns, the nineteen-year-old Fort Worth native, found this out firsthand when he and a buddy tried to sneak out of their F Company, 508th Parachute Infantry, bivouac near an airfield in Saltby. Private Burns and his friend embarked on this unauthorized escapade because they were antsy. They wanted to go to town and have a few drinks, maybe find some girls. To their pleasant surprise, they had no trouble slipping through the barbed wire surrounding their camp. "We walked along the road, and we were just getting into town. We thought we were doing all right. But about that time, a jeep pulled up beside us and an officer sitting in the back asked what we were doing off-base." Burns and his buddy didn't know what to say. "We gave him a wild story, but . . . I don't think he bought it."

The officer smirked. "What company are you from?"

"F Company, sir," they replied.

"Will you do me a favor?" the mysterious officer asked.

"Yes, sir."

"You go back to the field and tell Captain Flanders [F Company commander] that no one is to be off-base for any reason."

The two miscreants readily agreed. "We saluted and watched as he drove away." Relieved that they had not gotten into deep trouble, they started walking back to base.

"Burns, do you know who that was?" his buddy asked.

Burns shook his head. "No, I couldn't see him."

The other man smiled. "That was Jumping Jim Gavin."

Needless to say, Burns never forgot his encounter with Gavin. Burns also, of course, made no effort to tell his captain that he had been AWOL. "We hadn't made it to town, but we gave it a good try."[31] Burns, like so many others, went back to the tension of waiting for the word to gear up, board a plane, and jump into combat.

The airborne soldiers had enjoyed ideal weather the first couple days in the marshaling areas, but now a steady rain began to beat down. At Uppottery, in Devon, Private Burgett of the 506th spent much time sitting on his cot, under the shelter of a heavy canvas tent, waiting for the loading order. "Rain . . . was coming down so hard that a trooper standing in it could hardly see the front sight of his rifle. The strong musty odor of tent canvas became stifling with the heavy humidity of the warm rain-laden June day." The only light in the tent came from a bare lightbulb hanging from the tent's center post. Burgett watched in the half-light as his tent mates prepared for a jump they expected to carry out that very night. "Some of the men were burning small piles of paper on the dirt floor, then smearing the cooled ashes on their hands and faces to blacken them for the coming night jump." The smoke from the fires threatened to overpower them. They had tears running from their eyes and snot from their noses. They quickly finished blackening their faces and stamped out the fire. "We lay there talking and joking with each other and wondering what combat would really be like." In the distance they could hear one of their buddies playing "San Antonio" on an acoustic guitar. When would they get the order to board their planes? they wondered. What was the holdup? For now, they could only sit, wait, and wonder.[32]

Young Burgett and the other troopers had no idea of the incredible drama playing out to their east, at Portsmouth. For the invasion to be launched as planned, three conditions needed to be in place: First, the tides had to be low, so that Rommel's mines and obstacles would be readily visible to coxswains who controlled the landing craft that carried assault troops to their beaches. Second, the airborne needed a full moon to provide some semblance of light to guide their night drop. Third, everyone needed reasonably good weather—airmen needed to see their targets, sailors needed calm seas, and soldiers needed low winds to go ashore or jump from airplanes. Only three days in early June, the fifth through the seventh, offered these ideal conditions. General Eisenhower had settled on June 5 as the tentative invasion date. He knew that meteorologists could readily predict the tides and the moon, but the weather was another story altogether. If the weather got bad, he could always postpone and have two immediate replacement dates from which to choose.

In early June, General Eisenhower seemed to be getting the kind of mild weather on which his invasion depended. As late as June 3, he cabled General Marshall: "Weather prospects so far as sea conditions are concerned are rather favorable. From air viewpoint the forecasts are not yet firm but we have almost an even chance of having pretty fair conditions. In any event I should say that only marked deterioration beyond that now expected would disarrange our plans."[33]

Ike had no sooner sent the cable when the "marked deterioration" he mentioned to Marshall became a nightmarish reality. Truthfully, this new headache was the last thing the supreme commander needed. For several days now, he had been dealing with a slew of problems that ate away at his time and his resolve. Leigh-Mallory, who had never been keen on the U.S. airborne mission, visited Ike on May 29 to express his fears that the airborne could take casualties as high as 75 percent. He urged Ike to call the whole thing off. Eisenhower carefully pondered the whole thing— he knew that his decision could mean life or death to thousands— before consulting with Bradley, who urged him to continue with the mission. He knew that Bradley was right. The Utah beach landings made no sense without the airborne drops. Moreover, the Allies needed the Utah beach landings to secure the flanks of those troops who would land on the Calvados coast, not to mention the need for the supply port of Cherbourg. The airborne drop would proceed as planned.

Ike was spending most of his time now at his advance command post (CP) in the woods near Southwick House north of Portsmouth. True to form, he chose to live in a modest trailer rather than in the expansive Southwick House, a mansion dating back to the eighteenth century. The trailer contained a small bedroom, a shower, a toilet, a tiny sitting room, an observation deck, and a desk with three telephones, one connected to 10 Downing Street, one to the War Department, and the other to SHAEF. A small number of paperback Westerns were scattered on a night table next to his bed. He read them to relieve the stress of his responsibilities. Next to the books he had placed pictures of his wife, Mamie, and his son, John. Ike's immediate staff spread out in tents and trailers throughout the woods, so as to escape detection from the air.

Several times he had worried that the Overlord plan was compromised. Two of his senior officers, who ought to have known better, publicly discussed secrets about the time and place of the invasion. The worst incident happened in late April. It involved one of Ike's classmates, Major General Henry Miller, commander of the 9th Air Force Service Command. Over dinner at Claridge's, Miller had a few drinks and, within earshot of many civilians, complained of supply difficulties. Showing a stunning lack of common sense, Miller remarked that his troubles would be over by June 15, since the invasion would take place before that time. Someone immediately reported the incident to Eisenhower. Steaming with indignant anger at his old friend, the supreme commander reviewed the facts of Miller's case and decided to send him home. Effective immediately, he relieved Miller of command and even reduced him to his permanent rank of colonel.

Miller wrote to Ike protesting his innocence and requesting to be allowed to maintain his wartime rank of major general. Eisenhower wrote back with a polite but firm rejection: "I know of nothing that causes me more real distress than to be faced with the necessity of sitting as a judge in cases involving military offenses by officers of character and of good record, particularly when they are old and warm friends. In fact, it was because of your long record of efficient service that I felt justified in recommending only administrative rather than more drastic procedure in your case."[34] Miller went home to a quiet, albeit ignominious, retirement.

Another time, a sergeant had, innocently as it turned out, sent a sheaf of top-secret Overlord documents to his sister in Chicago. The bulky package burst open at the post office, in full view of about a dozen postal employees. Postal supervisors immediately called the FBI. Intelligence agents thoroughly questioned the employees, the sister, and the sergeant but found no nefarious motives.

By the far the most perplexing, and troubling, incident involved the daily crossword puzzle of the London *Daily Telegraph*. Over the course of May, the top-secret code words *Mulberry, Utah, Omaha, Neptune,* and *Overlord* had appeared in various editions. The appearance of one or two of these could be written off as coincidence but not all five and in so short a period of time. Could a German spy be using the puzzle to communicate information about the invasion? The British intelligence service, MI5, eventually interrogated the puzzle's unassuming creator, fifty-four-year-old Leonard Skidmore Dawe. Dawe was a physics teacher who lived in Leatherhead, Surrey, just south of London. The agents questioned him at length but came to the conclusion that Dawe was not a spy. In the end, they wrote the whole thing up to coincidence. Only in recent years has the full truth come to light. Dawe routinely asked his students to provide him with words for his puzzles. One of those pupils revealed that he had heard the code words while hanging around nearby camps listening to soldiers' conversations. He then passed the words on to the unwitting Dawe.[35] In spite of these gaffes, the Germans still did not know the date and place of the invasion, although they did know it was imminent. Eisenhower obviously would have been quite relieved to know the level of German ignorance, but at this point, in early June, he could not be sure.

To make matters worse for Ike, Churchill and de Gaulle added to his headaches. The prime minister visited one day and childishly insisted on going along with the invasion armada. Eisenhower told Churchill that in doing so he would add immeasurably to his worries as supreme commander. Churchill still insisted. Eisenhower knew he could not stop the pugnacious Englishman. Soon, though, the king found out about Churchill's intentions. The king declared that if Churchill was going, he must go, too. The prime minister knew this was unthinkable and backed down, a bit petulantly but decisively nonetheless. Later, de Gaulle threw a fit over the fact that, once the invasion began, Eisenhower would be the supreme authority in France. The difficult Frenchman refused to make a broadcast in support of the invasion unless he himself was recognized as the supreme authority. Only on the evening of D-Day did de Gaulle agree to broadcast, and even then he did not necessarily recognize Ike's authority.[36]

Now, at 2130 on June 3, a Saturday, Eisenhower learned that his rosy weather assumptions were not coming to pass. He left his trailer and got into his staff car. Kay Summersby drove him a mile to Southwick House, where he and his high-level commanders met with Group Captain J. M. Stagg, SHAEF's chief meteorologist. Admiral Ramsay had been using Southwick House as his headquarters. The commanders—most prominently Ramsay, Leigh-Mallory, Tedder, Montgomery, and Smith—met in the mess room of the mansion. The room was large, with partially empty oak bookcases lining the walls. A large table, smothered with a green baize tablecloth and surrounded by easy chairs, sat in the middle of the room. Double blackout curtains concealed the windows. Not far from the table, two comfortable couches sat invitingly near the walls.

Eisenhower had recently gotten into the habit of meeting twice daily with his commanders and Stagg. Ike thought of the twenty-eight-year-old Stagg as a "dour but canny" Scot. He had grown used to Stagg, and the minute he and his two principal associates (Instructor Commander John Fleming of the Royal Navy along with Lieutenant Colonel Donald Yates of the Army Air Force) walked into the room, Ike could see that Stagg was distressed.

The supreme commander's heart sank. Yesterday Stagg had warned him that the high-pressure front of the last few days might soon give way to several low-pressure fronts that would create serious storms in the Channel. Stagg faced the commanders and cut immediately to the chase: "Gentlemen, the fears my colleagues and I had yesterday . . . have been confirmed." Having begun with that gloomy preamble, Stagg launched into his grim forecast. He expected rough seas, high winds, and storms in the Channel on June 5.

When Stagg finished, Eisenhower turned to each of his operational commanders—Ramsay, Leigh-Mallory, and Montgomery—and asked for their opinions. Ramsay thought that the naval forces could probably put the troops ashore but would have no resupply or follow-up capacity. Leigh-Mallory bluntly said that his airmen could not possibly see their targets in such conditions. Only Monty, concerned about the consequences of postponement, favored going ahead with the invasion on June 5. "I'm ready," he said.

Eisenhower nodded his understanding. He felt sure that he must tentatively postpone the invasion for at least a day, but one other possibility occurred to him. The general knew that sometimes Stagg and his colleagues disagreed on their forecasts.

He asked Stagg, "Is there unanimity among the weathermen on what you have just presented?"

Stagg did not hesitate for a moment: "Yes, sir."

That cinched it. Ike ordered the postponement. The meeting broke up, but the group would meet again the next morning at 0415, at which time Eisenhower would make the final decision on postponement. In the meantime, some ships would remain at sea.

He went back to his trailer and slept fitfully, if at all, that night. He could not stop worrying about the weather. The ships, bobbing around in the Channel, crammed with seasick soldiers, could still be called back, but time was running out.

At precisely 0415 on June 4 the weather meeting convened. Stagg shook his head. Nothing about the forecast had changed. Eisenhower was disappointed but not surprised: "In that case, gentlemen, it looks to me as if we must confirm the provisional decision we made at the last meeting. Are there any dissentient votes?" There were none. Overlord was officially on hold.[37]

At about that same time, Lieutenant Stephen Freeland, commanding officer of a tiny LCC (Landing Craft Control), stood on the deck of his craft and wished for little else but to be warm, dry, or both. Freeland had fifteen men under his charge. The job of this small, decidedly unglamorous boat was traffic control. The LCC measured only fifty-six feet long and thirteen feet wide. Its only armament consisted of three twin-mounted .50-caliber machine guns. Belowdecks the crew had crammed a radar set, a gyrocompass, three radio transmitters, and two fathometers. All in all, the intrepid little craft looked like an undersize PT boat. On this windy morning, Freeland's LCC was just to the rear and starboard of a long column of landing craft sailing for Utah beach.

Maintaining one's footing on the slippery deck could be a challenge. Water sprayed everywhere as the angry sea pitched and sloshed the LCC about. Out of the corner of his eye Lieutenant Freeland noticed movement coming from belowdecks. A green-faced gunner's mate, looking sick and thoroughly miserable, hoisted himself onto the deck. He glanced at his skipper: "Sleeping down there is damn rugged duty." Freeland could not disagree.

Still they plodded onward. It seemed as if they could not keep from burrowing squarely into each wave. The wind was picking up now, making the seas even rougher. Freeland felt physically exhausted, as if someone had beaten him up. Someone handed him a message from a radio signal that had just come through: "Post Mike One." Freeland knew exactly what that meant. Overlord had been postponed. He and his crew were to return to Portland-Weymouth immediately.

He peered into the morning mist, looking for some indication that the seemingly endless convoy had gotten the message. Fifteen minutes passed. Another postponement message arrived. Half an hour passed. Still the convoy of landing craft continued on its heading for France. Lieutenant Freeland frowned in anxious confusion. "I was a little worried." Freeland signaled Lieutenant Jim White in a neighboring LCC in the port column. "He replied that he hadn't heard any message. That had me really bothered until we got another signal from [him] saying that their radio hadn't been working in the first place."

Even so, the convoy continued unabated. With every passing moment Freeland grew increasingly worried. He kept his signalman busy communicating with adjacent vessels. "Ships of the screen would come within range of our blinker, and, of course, we'd pass along the message to them. They always acknowledged, but maybe they didn't get what we said. After all, rolling, pitching, squirming as we were, our signalman had to be a combination of chimpanzee and acrobat to flash messages anywhere near the ship he was sending to."

At last, after two hours of this uncertainty, the convoy turned back and headed for England. "It was a long wet haul against wind and tide, with rain squalls . . . but eventually by six in the afternoon, we entered the delightful calm waters of the canal which forms Weymouth Harbor. There we tied up, ate and grabbed some sleep."[38]

As Freeland's experiences indicate, the recall order was not accomplished without some problems. By the very nature of their job, minesweepers were the vanguard of the invasion armada. One unit of sweepers closed to within thirty-five miles of the French coast before receiving the recall order. Freeland did not know it, but his convoy only got the word when destroyers and Royal Navy seaplanes were scrambled to intercept it. By 2200 on June 4, all of the ships had finally made it back to port. The crews of the ships caught some sleep, took on some supplies, and dealt with restless, seasick soldiers.[39]

CHAPTER FIVE

IKE'S DECISION AND THE AIRBORNE MARSHALING AREAS

Confusion also reigned in many of the airborne marshaling areas. During the afternoon of the fourth, the storm began to rage throughout the marshaling areas and airfields containing the assault forces. Private Burgett was still lying on his bunk, listening to the rain, waiting for something to happen, when a runner poked his head into the tent! "This is it. Let's go."

Burgett and his tent mates looked at one another in surprise. The driving rain had led them to expect a postponement. They stumbled and slipped their way through the mud until they reached the concrete runways of Uppottery. "Feeling like a bunch of half-drowned rats, we started to get ready. I was trying to get the wet parachute harness fastened while water ran into my eyes, off my nose and down my neck." Before long a jeep pulled up and skidded to a halt, splashing the soldiers with muddy water. The driver told them about the postponement. Burgett and the others "just stood there not knowing whether to feel relieved or mad, because we knew that we would have to go through the same thing again." They went back to their tents, dried off as best they could, and went to sleep.[1]

At Saltby, Private Ed Boccafogli's B Company, 508th Parachute Infantry, 82nd Airborne, actually boarded planes in anticipation of a combat jump. "We circled around for about a half hour . . . and then the crew chief said it's being cancelled because of the storm. Christ, it's like a man going into a ring. He's gonna fight now for his life or death. You could hardly breathe. It was a complete letdown, because you're keyed up." In a somber mood, the troops went back to their tents. That night lightning struck the tent next door to Boccafogli's and collapsed it.[2]

Boccafogli and his comrades were obviously disappointed with the postponement. They had prepared themselves mentally to face death and most of them did not want to go through that mental preparation again. In Private Webster's 506th the reaction was quite different. He was lying on his cot, waiting for word to don his gear and march to his plane, when he heard a strange noise. "A mighty shouting filled the air. Men whooped and hollered and gave the rebel yell. The joyous sound swept over the marshaling area like a tidal wave. Yelling and laughing like idiots, we leaped from our cots, incoherent with joy, and danced wildly on the sod floor. Men ran from tent to tent shaking hands and slapping backs and screaming at the top of their lungs. The reprieve had come to the death house."[3]

The reprieve could not last forever, though. At least Eisenhower hoped that it wouldn't. All day long on the fourth, even as young soldiers like Burgett and Webster sweated out the future, Eisenhower worried his way through the day. In his trailer he could hear the winds whipping around, but still the rain had not come. This gave him hope that perhaps the storm would not hit the Channel. He alternated between brooding in his trailer and aimlessly pacing outside. He smoked cigarette after cigarette. He peered at the skies as if attempting to will the storm away. For a few minutes he took a walk with Merrill "Red" Mueller, a veteran NBC newsman. Ike barely spoke. "It was almost as if he had forgotten that I was with him," Mueller later recalled. The newsman could see that the general was deeply preoccupied, so he refrained from asking any intrusive questions. When they returned to Ike's trailer, he said good-bye and went inside. Mueller watched him and formed the impression that he was "bowed down with worry . . . as though each of the four stars on either shoulder weighed a ton."[4]

Eisenhower commanded the most powerful force the world, to that point, had ever seen. But at this moment he was helpless, a prisoner of the weather. By the time he drove to Southwick House for dinner and his 2130 weather briefing, the storms had begun to hit Portsmouth. Winds, along with horizontal sheets of rain, pounded against the windows and French doors of the house. The very notion that an invasion could be launched in the midst of this storm seemed ludicrous. When Eisenhower strode into the meeting room, everyone was waiting for him. In all, there were twelve senior officers present. Montgomery wore his usual baggy corduroys and sweater, while Ramsay looked very proper in a blue-and-gold Royal Navy dress uniform. These two men and the others were standing around in clusters, talking in low, worried voices. Ike looked at them with a hint of his famous grin and sat down at the table. Everyone else got comfortable around the table or on the couches. Many of them sipped from cups of coffee.

Presently Stagg strode in amid a kind of hush among the somber officers. All eyes rested on the young Scot as he began his momentous report. In effect, his forecast would be the main determinant in Ike's decision whether to launch the invasion on June 6 or postpone it until mid-June, when the required ideal conditions would once again present themselves.

Stagg had the barest hint of a smile on his weary face. "I think we have found a gleam of hope for you, sir," he told Eisenhower. "The mass of weather fronts coming in from the Atlantic is moving faster than we anticipated. We predict there will be rather fair conditions beginning late on June 5 and lasting until the next morning, June 6, with a drop in wind velocity and some break in the clouds. Ceiling—about 3,000 [feet]." In the recollection of General Kenneth Strong, SHAEF's intelligence chief, a cheer involuntarily erupted from the officers. "You never heard middle-aged men cheer like that."

When the cheers died down, the commanders began firing serious questions at Stagg: How confident was he in his forecast? What would the seas be like on the sixth? How about the wind? How many hours would the good weather last? At one point, Tedder asked Stagg to predict the actual Channel weather at the moment of the invasion. Stagg deliberated for several long moments: "To answer that question would make me a guesser, not a meteorologist."

Just in case Ike was tempted to postpone the decision until the morning weather conference, Ramsay stressed that if the invasion was to be launched on June 6, the orders must be given within half an hour. If not, then Admiral Alan Kirk's Omaha beach invasion force could not make it to their beaches in time for H-Hour. Basically, Eisenhower's decision boiled down to choosing between a risky June 6 assault and an extremely unpalatable two-week postponement of the whole operation.

Realizing this, he stood up and began pacing the room, chin on his chest, hands clasped behind his back, weighing the options. In turn, he asked each of his commanders for their frank opinion.

Leigh-Mallory urged postponement. He thought the flying conditions on D-Day would be below the acceptable minimum.

Eisenhower stopped pacing for a moment, looked at Bedell Smith, and asked, "What do you think?"

Smith pondered for a second, mulling over exactly what a postponement would mean. "It meant an almost insoluble problem of what to do with the thousands of troops in the ships," he later wrote. "It was almost impossible to keep them closed in for two weeks, yet to let them out of the beach areas would almost certainly convey information to the Germans about our attack." Smith also worried about the dozens of press correspondents who had been briefed on Overlord. If they filed no dispatches for two weeks, suspicions would inevitably arise. He stared back at Eisenhower: "It's a helluva gamble, but it's the best possible gamble."

Ike nodded and resumed pacing. "What do you think?" he asked Tedder.

The British airman thought that going would be "chancy." He urged postponement.

Eisenhower nodded his understanding and paced some more. "Do you see any reason for not going Tuesday?" he asked Montgomery.

The ground commander's reply was succinct and decisive. "I would say—go!"

Only Ike could decide now. He paced a bit more, stopped, and said, "The question is just how long you can hang this operation on the end of a limb and let it hang there?" The question was rhetorical. The supreme commander was thinking out loud. He paused a few more moments before continuing. Outside, the storm raged malevolently, rattling the French doors with growing intensity. Inside, one lonely American weighed a decision that could alter the course of history. Rarely does history provide such seminal moments. At last, he spoke: "I am quite positive that the order must be given. I don't like it, but there it is. I don't see how we can possibly do anything else."

Within moments the commanders scurried out of the room to issue their orders. Tuesday, June 6, was to be D-Day. They would meet again at 0330 on June 5, at which time the invasion fleet could still be recalled if Stagg was wrong and a two-week postponement was necessary. At the 0330 meeting Stagg would provide another briefing. If his forecast still held true, Overlord would proceed.

Eisenhower left Southwick House and drove through the

storm back to his trailer. He caught a few hours of sleep, but the buffeting winds awakened him. They were shaking his trailer. He worried that Stagg's forecast might be wrong. According to his prediction, the storm should be out of the area by now. Ike dressed, left his trailer, and hunched in the backseat of his car while Kay Summersby drove him back to Southwick House.

The general felt groggy and sluggish, but a cup of steaming hot coffee helped clear the cobwebs. Once again the group of senior officers took their places throughout the room. A moment later, Stagg walked in with a "ghost of a smile" on his face, Smith later recalled. "Well, I'll give you some good news," the Scot said to Eisenhower. Stagg was now even more certain that the weather would clear by June 6. The only trouble was that another storm front would set in by June 7. This presented the possibility that the assault waves could get ashore but be stranded there as bad weather impeded follow-up waves and naval support.

Once again, Eisenhower had to contemplate enormous risks and make a binding decision that could affect the future of the world. He stood up and paced, just like the night before, and asked his commanders for their opinions. Ramsay worried that spotting for naval gunfire would be difficult, but he favored going. Tedder still preferred postponement, as did the cautious Leigh-Mallory. Monty and Smith still wanted to go.

Everything that could be said had been said. It was now time to decide on the fate of Overlord. The supreme commander paced some more and ruminated. He could not stop thinking about all those young men, crammed aboard ships or waiting around at airfields. Soon they would be asked to risk their lives at his behest. He owed it to them to make a responsible, sensible decision. "Goodness knows, those fellows meant a lot to me," Ike later said, "but these are decisions that have to be made when you're in a war. You say to yourself, 'I'm going to do something that will be to my country's advantage for the least cost.' You can't say without any cost. You know you're going to lose some of them, and it's very, very difficult."

A few feet away from Eisenhower, Smith studied his boss intently. It seemed to him that Eisenhower looked forlorn. In nearly thirty years of military service, Smith had never truly "realized before the loneliness and isolation of a commander at a time when such a momentous decision has to be taken, with full knowledge that failure or success rests on his judgement alone."

Roughly a minute passed as Ike silently deliberated over the fate of Overlord. Finally, he faced the group, looked up, and said, "OK, let's go!" As had happened the night before, a cheer erupted from the men who would command Overlord. In a matter of seconds, they excitedly cleared the room to disseminate Eisenhower's orders. Eisenhower found himself standing alone in the room, wondering if he had just done the right thing: "That's the most terrible time for a senior commander. He has done all that he can do, all the planning and so on. There's nothing more that he can do."[5]

As Ike hinted, from this point on the success of the invasion depended upon the young men who would soon assault Hitler's fortress Europe. Throughout the morning and afternoon of the fifth, the airborne troopers killed time at their airfields, waiting for the order to board their planes.

The easy life of the previous week had given way to nearly unbearable tension. "There was no laughter, no singing, no shouting," Private Webster wrote. "The most inveterate gambler couldn't get a crap game started. A deadening stillness hung in the warm, sweet air."[6] At Folkingham, in the English midlands, Private Tom Porcella, H Company, 508th Parachute Infantry, 82nd Airborne, waited grimly with his buddies. Porcella was a twenty-year-old from Long Island, New York. He had joined the paratroopers in late 1942. Now his mind was racing as he lay on his cot with nothing to do but wait for orders: "Do I have enough training for combat? I wonder how the hell I'll react under fire. Will I be too scared to carry out [orders]?" He pondered the troubling contrast between the Ten Commandments' prohibition against killing and everything he'd been trained to do. The idea of killing someone face-to-face terrified him: "I wonder how I would feel if I killed a man in cold blood?"

Porcella shook his head and looked around. Everyone was quiet, intense, wound tight. They were probably contemplating similar troubling questions. "The tension was building up in all of us. Boy, I'm telling you, if you put a match near any of the guys, they were so uneasy and keyed up, I think the match would have exploded."[7]

The inevitable fights and arguments broke out. Usually they came to nothing, but in one instance Sergeant Russell Schwenk of F Company, 506th Parachute Infantry, 101st Airborne, remembered some damage being done: "One of our privates was beaten severely by several members of the company for showing invasion currency to the cooks."

At Exeter, the tension caused the troopers of 3rd Battalion, 506th, to do something a bit more humorous, and embarrassing, but damaging just the same. Late in the afternoon on June 5, they sat in a hangar and watched a movie about the bombing of enemy cities. During a scene in which bombs were being dropped on the enemy cities, the troopers heard a hissing sound along with a great crash in the darkness behind them. "Everyone immediately thought there was real bombing going on overhead," Private First Class Clair Mathiason recalled, "and in one great movement everyone started for the doors and outside. Chairs were knocked over. By the time everyone was outside and realized that there was no attack, we had suffered our first casualties of the war. There were a couple of boys hurt in the mad rush to get out and as I remember two had broken legs." What had caused the hissing and the crashing? A fire extinguisher had been knocked down and activated. At the same time it got knocked over, it crashed into a chair, which promptly toppled over with a great clatter. The battalion commander, Lieutenant Colonel Robert Wolverton, gave his men a real tongue-lashing at being so easily shaken up.[8]

Some tried to alleviate the tension with last-minute preparations. They cleaned their weapons, checked equipment repeatedly, or practiced donning their jumpsuits. Of the six parachute regiments jumping into Normandy, five had not seen combat (one of the two glider assault regiments, the 325th, was experienced). In those five parachute regiments, many troopers whipped up a sense of bravado by blackening their faces or shaving their heads. The experienced troopers of the 505th disdained such practices as, at best, useless symbolism or, at worst, false, rookie histrionics. The new troopers either did not know or did not care what the salty 505th thought of their grooming rituals. Some soldiers shaved their hair into patterns and painted their faces, in conscious imitation of what they believed Native Americans had done in an earlier age. Others merely applied ashes or greasepaint to their faces and hands in an effort to blacken them so they would not reflect moonlight. In Private Burns's F Company, 508th, the ritual ran the gamut: "We blacked out faces with burnt cork. Some of the guys cut their hair Mohawk style. Some shaved it all off. Each trooper was going into combat in whatever style suited him best. I left mine in a crew cut."

When they finished, they went to a nearby hangar for a special treat. Red Cross workers, mostly young women, were handing out coffee and doughnuts. Burns gave one of them a jar of candy he knew he could not take with him on the jump. She took it gratefully and fixed him with a solemn stare. "She thanked me as big tears ran down both cheeks. Some job of cheering us up she was doing."[9]

Minute after minute, hour after hour, the time to face death drew closer. Afternoon turned into early evening and the airborne troopers ate a final meal. Actually, some were too nervous to eat. Even many of those who did eat could not enjoy it as they had before. They knew that within hours they would be in combat, fighting for their lives. Few things could be more conducive to reflection.

In the hangar of an airfield in the midlands, Staff Sergeant Bob Brewer, A Company, 508th Parachute Infantry, penned, like so many others around England that night, one last letter to his father. "In the near future I'll be thinking a lot about my family life and boyhood days, and shall try to be all that you and Mother would want me to be. My regards and love to everyone." Brewer survived the jump but was captured five days after D-Day.[10]

Some could not escape the terrifying, depressing feeling that they were witnessing their last sunset. Not far away from where Sergeant Brewer sat writing to his father, Private Boccafogli, the B Company, 508th, trooper who was so disappointed at the previous day's postponement, noticed one of his buddies, Private Johnny Daum, standing outside his tent, "like a statue, looking into space." The skinny, towheaded Daum barely looked a day over sixteen. Boccafogli had never known him to act so morose. He was a few years older than Daum and thought of him as a little brother. He walked over to him. "Hey, Johnny, what's the matter?"

Daum hardly even replied. He just stood there in a kind of stupor. Boccafogli was really concerned now. "What the hell's the matter with you?"

Daum finally replied in a matter-of-fact tone, "I'm gonna die tomorrow."

Boccafogli tried to cheer him up: "Ahh, come on. Some of us will, some of us won't, but you ain't gonna be one."

Daum could not be dissuaded. He insisted on the imminence of his death. Eerily enough, he was right. He got killed on D-Day. Boccafogli never forgot him. "These things stay with you the rest of your life."[11]

Private Porcella had a similar experience with one of his friends. As the interminable moments of waiting unfolded, Porcella felt less and less like talking to anybody. Soon, though, Private Harold Wilbur sidled up to him. Wilbur clearly had something on his mind. Porcella knew that, one week before, Wilbur's fiancée had broken up with him and declared her intention to marry someone else. She sent him a Dear John letter with all the photos and mementos they had compiled over the years. In a particularly cruel flourish, she even sent him a picture of the man she was planning to marry.

Wilbur had been understandably subdued ever since. Now, as he sat next to Porcella, he was downright gloomy. "Let me ask you a question," he said to Porcella.

"Go ahead. Shoot. What is it?"

"Are you nervous? Are you scared?" Wilbur asked.

Porcella thought it was a silly question. "Yeah, I'm nervous. I'm scared. What the hell do you think, I'm somebody different? I'm as keyed up as everybody else."

Wilbur looked closely at Porcella. "You know, Tom, I don't think I'm going to make it."

Porcella was quite troubled with his friend's fatalism. "Why do you talk like that?"

"I don't know. Everything has been going wrong."[12]

Predictably, Wilbur did not make it. There is no way to know just how many troopers confessed to premonitions of death that emotional evening or how many of them ended up getting killed, but there were enough stories like Daum's and Wilbur's to make one wonder if some of those who died in the invasion experienced some kind of innate sense of foreshadowing.

Still the clock ticked inexorably forward, beyond the afternoon and into the evening hours. The soldiers of the airborne armada received orders to suit up, move to the flight line, and be ready to go. At Exeter, Private Webster gulped hard and donned his equipment. He wriggled into his woolen long johns, olive drab (OD) shirt, trousers, and the smelly, stifling gas-impregnated jumpsuit.

Then he buckled on his musette bag, and his cartridge belt complete with his canteen, a bayonet, a trench knife, a first-aid packet, and a pair of wire cutters, "Hot, itchy, stiff, and extremely confined, I broke my rifle down with trembling fingers and put its three pieces into the padded canvas case that would be buckled under my reserve chute."

Private Webster and the others lined up and prepared to march to the airfield's hangars to receive ammunition and parachutes. To the studious, Ivy League–educated Webster, the whole thing was beginning to feel all too real. He knew now that there was no way out. They were going. Some of them would die. He began to regret joining the airborne. A stream of terrified thoughts ran through his brain: "What a lousy way to leave the world. Nobody to say good-bye. No friends or relatives at the bedside. How quiet it is—and godforsaken lonely." He could not help but feel sorry for himself. "Nobody gives a damn for us, nobody cares. We'll fight their war, and they'll all make money and get good jobs and gripe about the butter shortage and chisel on the gas ration."

Moment by moment, Webster started to feel more surly and cynical. In near total silence, lined up four abreast, he and the other Screaming Eagles marched to the hangar. The scene at the hangar was one of motion and purpose. Black-faced soldiers tore open ammunition boxes and handed out the contents to neat lines of waiting troopers. Shouts and instructions echoed off the metal roof of the hangar. A rigger worked his way down Webster's line, handing out parachutes and helping the troopers put them on. The man could be heard nervously saying over and over how much he wanted to go with them: "I told the colonel I wanted to go. The hell with flying resupply! I didn't join this goddamn outfit to be a messenger boy. I want to jump. Colonel said I had to stay here and fly the ammo over. Fuck resupply! If I can get a chute, I'm going." Webster was not impressed with the rigger's monologue. He looked at the man resentfully and thought, "You jerk! You goddamn jerk."

A few minutes later, Webster and the other troopers boarded trucks that took them to their planes. Their lieutenant lined them up in jumping order and they lay down on the grass to wait for the inevitable order to board the planes. "The enthusiasm that had led me to join the paratroopers and the challenge that had kept me going were gone forever. In their place I felt numbness, a blank, heavy all-filling numbness." Men constantly got up to relieve nervous bladders.

Bored and sullen, Webster took a look at the mimeographed sheet containing Eisenhower's famous Overlord order, the one that began with the statement: "You are about to embark on the great crusade." Eisenhower truly did think of this enterprise in those terms. He understood all too well what the tyranny of Nazi Germany really meant. The cynical Webster was unmoved, though. He was disgusted with the clichés and high-minded prose. He crumpled up the paper and threw it away; then, thinking that it might make a good souvenir, he retrieved it.

One of his buddies, an ammo bearer, said defensively, "It's from Eisenhower."

Private Webster could not have cared less, "God, those generals. They don't talk our language. There isn't a one of them that knows why we're here. Do you know why we're here?"

The other man shrugged. He did not want to hear Webster's diatribe, but Webster didn't care. He voiced his opinion anyway: "We're here because the outfit's here. This crap has nothing to do with it. If we fight, it's because the outfit's fighting . . . not because we're a bunch of knights on a goddamn crusade. This war doesn't mean a thing to me beyond this outfit. Piss on SHAEF!"

The other soldier could only shake his head and sigh. They settled into silence, looking west, waiting for the sun to set on this English summer night (a sunset that did not occur until close to 2200). As they waited, they shivered in the encroaching chill of evening; or maybe it was out of fear. Webster was not sure which.[13]

Webster's cynicism reflected the kind of focused mind-set the soldiers had to have on the eve of battle, but his broader dismissal of the war's aims was dead wrong. Eisenhower was correct. This was a crusade, one that would change the course of history for the better. Most of the soldiers waiting around tarmacs and hangars that evening sensed the electricity of the moment. Certainly their commanders did. All over the airborne marshaling areas, officers gave rousing pep talks to their troopers. The mood was supercharged, almost like a modern incarnation of what Shakespeare must have envisioned when he wrote Henry V's famous pre-Agincourt band of brothers speech in the play *Henry V*.

At Fulbeck, Captain Roy Creek, the New Mexico native who commanded E Company, 507th Parachute Infantry, gathered his men around him in an informal semicircle. The captain looked at his men with affection. Their curious, eager, blackened faces stared back at him. "We have worked long and hard for this moment. Collectively and individually, you are the best fighting men in the world. At this time tomorrow, we will be on our first objective and we will have made our first contribution toward winning the most fearful war the world has ever known. We won't all be there. Some of us will fall along the way. And as men fall, there will be doubling of effort for those who stand. God bless you."[14]

At Cottesmore, where the 505th Parachute Infantry prepared for yet another combat jump, General Gavin stood on the hood of a jeep and talked to the soldiers. One of those soldiers, Sergeant Charles Lieberth, a platoon sergeant and demolitions specialist in the headquarters company of the 1st Battalion, listened intently as the general spoke. "Some of us were real veterans going all the way back to Fort Benning. And his opening remark, with a big smile, was, 'Here we go again.' He talked a little bit about . . . North Africa, the jump in Sicily, the jump in Italy and so on. [He] told us what to expect. That we were going to meet a fierce enemy, well entrenched. And that he knew . . . we would come up to the measure of the mark and he wished us well."[15]

Probably the most moving of all the many speeches that night was made by the commander of the 3rd Battalion, 506th Parachute Infantry, Lieutenant Colonel Wolverton. Just before marching to their planes, the colonel called his battalion together. The men stood in an orchard on either side of an earthen hedgerow that fenced the orchard from nearby fields. Wolverton stood atop the hedgerow and studied his men for a few moments, as if trying to remember every face. He knew this was a culminating moment. Most of the men in front of him had been civilians a year or two before. Intense training and camaraderie had molded them together into a formidable fighting force—a group eager for battle, confident, tough, and completely dedicated to one another. He was so proud of these men—truly he loved them—but he knew that soon the moment would come when he must risk destroying those he loved. Such was the reality of command in wartime. In a few hours, everything would change. Men would be killed, wounded, or captured. A few would shirk or break down mentally. Most would do their duty to the best of their ability, while praying to survive. The colonel could not even be sure of his own fate.

Wolverton had arranged for a couple of soldiers to don German uniforms, so that the troopers could visualize and recognize their enemies when they got to Normandy: "Get used to this image, he is the enemy and he wants to kill us." The colonel showed the men some of the nuances of the German uniform and then dismissed the two "Germans" amid good-natured laughs. The models had no sooner jumped off the hedgerow than another man hopped onto the hedgerow next to Wolverton. This man was clad in full jump equipment similar to the hundreds of troopers standing in loose columns around the orchard. Robert Webb, the supply sergeant in headquarters company who some weeks before had found an English girlfriend resembling Hedy Lamarr, immediately recognized the man standing next to the colonel. "It was Valloue the cook. He had tears in his eyes. He had never made a parachute jump." At thirty-six years of age, he was the oldest man in the battalion. Wolverton pointed at the cook: "This is courage." Valloue had come to him and told him that "he could not see his boys go into combat without him. He had to go." A wave of emotion swept over Webb and the other troopers. "Nearly all of us came apart. Most of us loved him like an uncle."

The cook jumped off the tiny hedgerow and got back into ranks, and the expression on Wolverton's face turned deadly serious as he prepared to give his own version of a pep talk. The buzz over Valloue died down and silence reigned. The colonel was blessed with a fine speaking voice, one that projected quite well: "Men, you know that I'm not a religious man but I want you to pray with me now. I want you to get down on your knees and don't look down but look up to God . . . with open eyes as we pray while asking him for his blessing and help on what we are about to do."

In a flurry of motion, the troopers sank to their knees. Only the sound of clinking pieces of equipment could be heard. Wolverton saw that his men had settled into kneeling positions. He himself was now kneeling on the hedgerow. His head was raised, looking straight up into the darkening sky. "God almighty! In a few short hours we will be in battle with the enemy." Wolverton's baritone voice echoed around the orchard. "We do not join battle afraid. We do not ask favors or indulgence, but ask that if you will, use us as your instruments for the right and an aid to returning peace to the world. We do not know or seek what our fate will be. We ask only this, that if die we must, we die as men would die, without complaining, without pleading, and safe in the feeling that we have done our best for what we believed was right. Oh Lord! Protect our loved ones and be near us in the fire ahead, and be with us now as we each pray to you."

For two minutes, the troopers of 3rd Battalion, 506th Parachute Infantry, silently prayed, each in his own way, each to his own God. At last Wolverton bellowed, "Move out!" They stood and marched solemnly to the airfield "without a dry eye in the whole 760 men," according to Sergeant Webb. One other trooper stole a last look at Wolverton, a man he revered. "Most men in this battalion, as well as myself, will never forget him as he knelt on top of that hedgerow and prayed. He could not have been more trusted and loved by the men in this battalion had he been the father of each one. I believe any of us would have followed him through hell, had he asked it."

The distance to the airfield was about a mile; this was an exhausting march given the tremendous load of equipment carried by most troopers. They received a welcome hour's rest before the order to board planes came down.[16]

At this point, even as many of the troopers of the 101st Airborne spent their last moments waiting to board their planes, they welcomed a distinguished visitor—Eisenhower. Of the many compelling moments of that emotional invasion eve, this incident ranks near the top. Ike had spent the day in restless anticipation. The fact that the storm had gone away by sunrise did much to improve his mood. He played several games of checkers with his naval aide and confidant, Captain Harry Butcher. In one game, Butcher cornered Ike with two kings left to only one for Eisenhower, but the supreme commander rebounded to jump one of Butcher's kings and get a draw. According to historian Stephen Ambrose, Ike thought the outcome of the game "was a good omen." At lunch Ike and Butcher traded political yarns. Afterward the general wrote his famous failure message (which, luckily, never had to be utilized) and briefed correspondents on the upcoming invasion.

That afternoon he continually found himself thinking about the airborne troopers. Could Leigh-Mallory be right? Were these units really going to take 75 percent casualties? If so, these losses would be on Eisenhower's head, because he had personally ordered their mission to proceed in the face of grave doubts. By evening, the supreme commander could not stand it any longer.

He had to go see these men, look into their faces, or it would haunt him forever if Leigh-Mallory was right.

The general, Butcher, and a few other members of the staff took a ninety-minute ride from Portsmouth to the nearest airfields, Greenham Common (502nd Parachute Infantry) and Welford (501st Parachute Infantry). At both airfields, Ike, without any fanfare or preamble, simply got out of his car and walked among the troops. Preoccupied with last-minute preparations, some of the black-faced troopers did not notice him, but most did. They would spot him, do a double take, and say to one another, "Hey, there's Ike," or, "I'll be damned. It's really him."

At Welford, First Lieutenant LeGrand "Legs" Johnson, commanding officer of F Company, 502nd, met Eisenhower in somewhat ignominious fashion. The lieutenant was in his tent, sitting on his bottom bunk, honing a jump knife. All of a sudden, "Ike walked into my tent. I jumped up, crashing my poor head against the upper bunk, and damn near knocked myself out. The gash required several stitches to close." Eisenhower told the bloodied lieutenant, "I've done all I can. Now it is up to you."

Mainly, Ike moved among the soldiers, flashing his warm smile, saying such things as, "If you see a plane overhead tomorrow, it'll be ours," or, "Good luck to you, soldier." Corporal Kermit Latta, a divisional artilleryman, was lying under the wing of his stick's plane, contemplating the white invasion stripes (common to all 13,000 Overlord aircraft) that had been painted on its wings, when he heard his jump master bellow, "Attention!"

The soldiers quickly stood and snapped to attention. Corporal Latta could see Eisenhower moving down the line of soldiers, seemingly talking to each one. Ike stopped in front of the man standing next to Latta. "While he spoke to the man beside me I was struck by the terrific burden of decision and responsibility on his face."

Eisenhower asked the man next to Latta a question: "What is your job, soldier?"

"Ammunition bearer, sir."

"Where is your home?"

"Pennsylvania, sir."

Ike smiled. "Did you get those shoulders working in a coal mine?"

"Yes, sir."

"Good luck to you tonight, soldier," the general said, and he moved on to the next stick.

Eisenhower had brought a small group of reporters and photographers with him, and they recorded some of his encounters with the soldiers that night, most notably that with Lieutenant Wallace Strobel, a platoon leader in the 502nd at Greenham Common. In one of the war's most famous photographs, the supreme commander, clad in his famous "Eisenhower jacket," talks with Strobel, who has his helmet on, his face blacked out, and a placard bearing the number 23 (signifying his status as jump master of plane #23) draped around his neck. Ike asked the young lieutenant for his name and his home state.

"Strobel, sir. Michigan."

"Oh yes, Michigan. Great fishing there. I like it. Are you ready for tonight?"

Strobel replied in the affirmative. He said he had been well prepared, well briefed, and that he thought the mission should not be too much of a problem. Someone in the crowd around them called out, "Now quit worrying, General! We'll take care of this thing for you!"

That soldier and many others sensed that Eisenhower might ostensibly have been there to raise their morale, but in reality, it was the exact opposite. He was now powerless. Everything was up to those heavily burdened, menacing-looking soldiers standing around their planes, cheering Eisenhower. He drew strength from them.

Indeed, Eisenhower asked Private First Class Dan McBride of F Company, "Are you scared?"

"No, sir!" McBride replied firmly.

"Well, I am!" Eisenhower rejoined, amid gales of jocular laughter.[17]

Around 2230, even as Ike was still chatting with the soldiers, the engines of the C-47s roared to life. Seconds later, the commanding voices of jump masters could be heard ordering the soldiers to board their planes.

Miles to the north, at Folkingham, Private Porcella was waiting in a hangar with dozens of other soldiers when he heard the order to go. "There was silence throughout the entire hangar. Then all of a sudden . . . there was a tremendous roar." The tension that had permeated the 508th was gone in an instant, like air escaping from a balloon. "Everybody was hollering, 'Geronimo! Give 'em hell! Let's go! Come on!' I could truthfully say that the morale of the men at that time was very high. I think we were ready to take on the Germans. The noise in that hangar . . . was just deafening." Immediately the hangar turned into a beehive of activity. "We all started to help each other, buddied-up. We helped each other put the equipment on. Everything had to be just right. We couldn't afford to make any mistakes."[18]

Porcella could not have been more correct about mistakes. They could be fatal. Sergeant Lieberth, the demolitions specialist in the 1st Battalion, 505th, saw this firsthand in his platoon as it loaded aboard its planes. Lieberth was completely loaded down with dynamite sticks, fuses, blasting caps, and plastic explosives. "The guys were kidding me that if the Krauts hit me on the way down . . . I would blow up like a Fourth of July explosion." Lieberth and another soldier were helping each other with their parachutes when they heard a "tremendous explosion. I dropped my parachute and I ran around to the tail of the plane. And here the other plane that was part of our complement was burning and guys were on the ground screaming like hell." Sergeant Lieberth ran back to his own plane, grabbed a fire extinguisher, and began spraying the burning aircraft. He knew that if the fire spread to the plane's gas tanks, more men would lose their lives. "The pilot and copilot somehow got out of the plane and they helped with their fire extinguishers. We put out the fire. There were about twelve troopers on the ground seriously wounded, three of them already dead."

Lieberth quickly figured out what had happened. Another demolition man had some Composition C plastic explosive (quite combustible when combined with a blasting cap) in a leg pocket. "When he tightened his leg strap, he tightened it right over this plastic grenade and it let loose and exploded." Sergeant Lieberth stood and surveyed the grisly results of this accident. "It blew him up. His head was there and his leg was over here. He was a mess. Pete Vaughn had part of his neck blown out. He was dead."

Lieberth spotted a good friend, who had a dazed look on his face. "One of my oldest buddies . . . walked up to me and said, 'Look, Sarge.'" The man raised his hands from his belly. "His guts rolled out."

The sergeant was horrified. "Christ, Eddie." He pushed Eddie's guts back into his abdomen, took Eddie's hands, placed them there to hold the guts in place, and said, "Now hold them tight; the medics will be here soon and you will be sent to the hospital." None of this mattered. Eddie died that night. Greatly chastened, Lieberth and the other survivors boarded their planes and waited to take off.[19]

At Barkston Heath, Sergeant Edward Barnes, a wire chief in the 507th Parachute Infantry, prepared for the ordeal of climbing into his plane. "I wore a wool shirt and wool pants under my jumpsuit, as I figured it would be cool at night [in Normandy]." In his musette bag, strapped to his back, underneath his parachute, he carried "extra socks, mess kit, insecticide, powder, candy bar, and plenty of cigarettes and a gammon grenade [antitank mine]." From his musette bag harness he had "a grenade hanging, one on each side." In addition to a rubberized black case containing a gas mask and more candy, he carried a "folding stock .30-caliber carbine, and about sixty rounds of ammunition. We were issued K rations for three days." The coup de grâce was a "sixty-pound switchboard strapped across the front of my thighs."

Barnes, like so many other paratroopers, needed help to get into his plane. He "climbed in and with a little push from the crew chief [of the aircraft], I was able to make it up the ladder, as I could not climb because of the switchboard strapped across my legs. Most of the men tried to be jovial, including myself, but you could feel the atmosphere was a little subdued."[20]

At Uppottery, Private Burgett carried a similar load, but one tailored to his job as a rifleman. In addition to the usual array of food and clothing, he carried nearly 700 rounds of ammunition for his rifle, which he broke down into three parts and stashed in a canvas case attached to his reserve chute at his midsection. He also carried various fighting knives, morphine syrettes, and grenades. When he finally fastened everything in place, he found that he could not connect his bellyband. To do so, he needed help from two airmen, "I told one of them to stand on my back while the other fastened the bellyband, after which I found it impossible to even get to my knees. The two men lifted me bodily, and with much boosting and grunting shoved me up into the plane, where I pulled myself along the floor and with the aid of the crew chief got into a bucket seat." The pilot of the plane read Eisenhower's invasion message (the one that had so irritated Private Webster) over the intercom. Burgett listened carefully but was not all that moved. "A canteen cup of whiskey would have been more appreciated," he thought.

Burgett and the men around him now took their airsickness pills, a mysterious aspect of the story of the airborne jump into Normandy. No one is entirely sure who had the idea to push these pills on the troops. Airsickness had never been a serious problem during training or previous combat jumps. All the pills succeeded in doing on this night was making the troopers sleepy. Also, some of the paratroopers had strapped British-style leg bags to themselves, another Overlord debut and failure. The Americans had never used such bags. These bags, attached to twenty-foot-long ropes, mostly broke loose upon the shock of chutes opening, rarely to be found on the ground.[21]

Soon the roar of the revving engines threatened to drown out conversation. At his airfield, General Ridgway stood in the doorway of his plane and took a last look at England. As a senior officer, he was not quite as burdened down with equipment as the average trooper. Ridgway admired the green beauty of the English midlands. He had been in battle before, but this would be his first combat jump. He was a military professional, but that did not mean he did not experience the fears common to any mortal man. Each night in the marshaling area, he had struggled with those fears. "In the darkness after you have gone to bed, when you are not the commander, with stars on your shoulders, but just one man, alone with your God in the dark, your thoughts inevitably turn inward, and out of whatever resources of the spirit you possess, you prepare yourself as best you may for whatever tests may lie ahead."

A devout Christian, Ridgway found comfort in the story of Jesus Christ's pre-crucifixion ordeal at the Garden of Gethsemane. "I . . . felt that if He could face with calmness of soul the great suffering He knew was to be His fate, then I surely could endure any lesser ordeal of the flesh or spirit that might be awaiting me."

Now, as General Ridgway turned away from England and shuffled into the plane, he could only think of an epitaph he had seen carved into a soldier's memorial in Edinburgh a few weeks before: "If it be Life that waits, I shall live forever unconquered; if Death, I shall die at last, strong in my pride and free." As he buckled himself into his hard bucket seat, the general felt a quiet serenity creep over him. "I was ready to accept whatever was to come. The mood of the men around me seemed equally tranquil."[22]

Moments later his C-47 took off, followed by hundreds more of the 52nd Troop Carrier Wing carrying thousands of 82nd

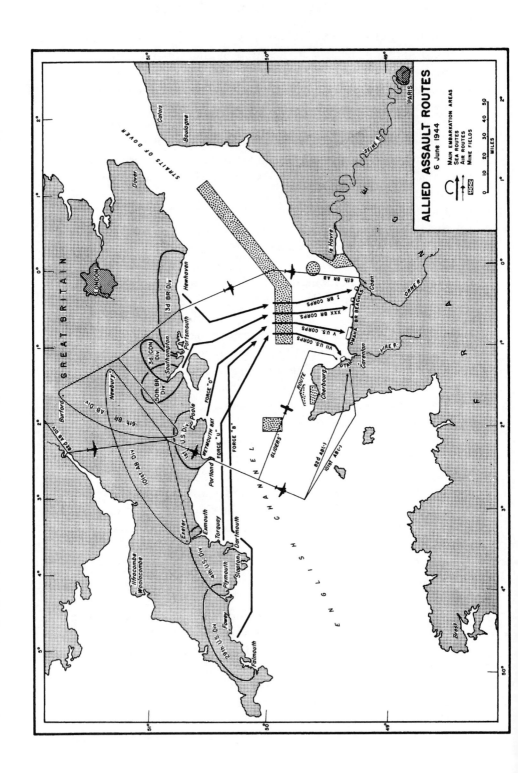

ALLIED ASSAULT ROUTES
6 June 1944

MAIN EMBARKATION AREAS
SEA ROUTES
AIR ROUTES
MINE FIELDS

0 10 20 30 40 50
MILES

Airborne troopers from numerous fields in the midlands. The same was true for the 101st Airborne. The transport crews had received their final briefing at 2000, at which they learned everything they needed to know about the mission: navigation, winds, weather, beacons, drop zones, radar, and radio aids (strict radio silence), even what to do if forced to ditch in the Channel. "I saw how flushed and bright-eyed everybody looked—tense but not jittery," Sergeant Marty Wolfe, a radio operator in the 436th Troop Carrier Group, recalled. His unit would carry troopers from the 1st Battalion, 502nd, into Normandy. Wolfe and the other aviators left the briefing and went directly to their planes. "The troopers, sitting on the runway near the plane door, looked sullen and resentful, and made a couple of bitter cracks to [the crew chief] and me. We didn't blame them."[23]

But there was little time now for such bitterness. Fortress Europe beckoned. Technical Sergeant George Koskimaki, a literary-minded Michigan native, was the personal radio operator for the commander of the 101st Airborne Division, Brigadier General Maxwell Taylor. Koskimaki's group got the order to load up just as Eisenhower had begun to chat with them. "A colonel from Eisenhower's party gave me a helpful boost into the plane. I moved into the darkened interior and took my seat in the fifth jump position near the door."

The young radioman looked out the door and witnessed Eisenhower and Taylor saying their farewells. Taylor was a forty-three-year-old West Point graduate who had once served as the artillery commander of the 82nd Airborne Division. He had received plaudits for a clandestine mission to Rome, as Ike's envoy, in the late summer of 1943 when Pietro Badoglio's Italian government engaged in secret armistice negotiations with Eisenhower. The youthful Taylor had assumed command of the 101st just a few months before when the division's creator and the avowed father of American airborne forces, Major General William Lee, had suffered a heart attack. In fact, when General Taylor had given his own pep talks to the division's troops during the previous week, he had asked his men to shout General Lee's name as they jumped tonight.

Taylor would get his second star a few days after D-Day. Ike held him in high esteem. The two had eaten dinner together earlier this evening before Eisenhower's impromptu tour of the Screaming Eagles' airfields. Now, as the two men parted, the supreme commander did not know that Taylor was withholding something from him. While playing squash with one of his officers a few days before, Taylor had pulled a tendon in his leg. Since then, he had barely been able to walk on the leg. Tonight, it took all of Taylor's considerable willpower to keep from betraying any sign of the injured leg to his commander. The airborne commander wanted nothing to interfere with his participation in the coming battle.

Taylor could tell that the supreme commander had been impressed with his men, particularly those who had adopted a bizarre appearance by painting their faces and shaving their heads. As the two commanders strode toward Taylor's plane, Eisenhower leaned over and whispered, "They might not scare the Germans, but they would certainly scare me." Taylor chuckled.

They stopped at the door of the plane. Eisenhower grinned and extended his hand: "Good luck."

"Thank you, sir." The men in General Taylor's stick helped him don his equipment and make it into the plane. The general smiled and took a seat. He patted his leg bag. Inside he had managed to spirit away a bottle of Irish whiskey to disseminate among his men at the right moment.

Eisenhower moved on to other planes to say last-minute goodbyes. Private Walter Turk had just settled into his seat when "Ike stuck his head in the door of our plane as we waited to taxi out onto the runway. He wished us luck."

Once the planes started moving, Eisenhower walked toward the control tower to watch them take off. On his way, he spotted a diminutive private who was about to board a plane. To Eisenhower, the man looked "more equipment than soldier." The supreme commander called out, "Good luck!" The little soldier snapped off a salute and Ike returned it. At that the private turned to the east and called out, "Look out, Hitler. Here we come!"

Ike took his place atop the control tower. One by one, the planes hurtled down the runway and lifted off, circling the airfield as they waited for others to become airborne. Ike and his group watched until the last plane left the runway and roared into the crisp night.

Standing next to the supreme commander, Kay Summersby could see tears welling up in his eyes. He started for the car, but as he did, she heard him say something barely audible: "Well, it's on."[24]

PART II

THE ASSAULT

CHAPTER SIX

CROSSING THE CHANNEL

N aval power made the invasion possible. The Allies possessed plenty of it. The Germans did not. Following the postponement, a breathtaking armada of ships, large and small, geared up once again and put to sea on June 5. There were thousands of ships doing a dizzying variety of jobs—submarines whose mission was to guide the C-47s that carried airborne troopers, tiny patrol craft acting as traffic cops, destroyer escorts hunting for enemy submarines, destroyers doing the same but mostly preparing to lend gunfire support on the invasion beaches, powerful, stately cruisers and battleships whose ordnance equaled that of heavy bombers, minesweepers clearing the way for the entire force, and, most numerous of all, specialized transport craft such as the Landing Craft Tank (LCT), the Landing Ship Tank (LST), the Landing Craft Infantry (LCI), and rhino ferries carrying everything from ammunition to soldiers. Hundreds of these amphibious ships carried most of the invasion force. The rest sailed in more traditional transport ships like the *Samuel Chase* or the *Charles Carroll.*

The armada sallied forth from ports all over southern England, rendezvoused south of the Isle of Wight, and headed straight for the coastline of Normandy. To make it there unscathed, they needed to pierce minefields the Germans had sown in the middle of the Channel. Some 255 minesweepers—the unsung heroes of Overlord—led the way. They swept five major channels through the mine belt, one for each invasion beach.

Most of the sweepers were British, but a few American ships, like the USS *Swift,* helped accomplish this dangerous task. Some of the mines were visible on the surface. Others were chained to the bottom of the ocean, programmed to detonate when a ship passed overhead. The most dangerous were free-floating magnetic mines attracted to the hull of a ship. The *Swift*'s communication officer, Lieutenant Edward Dunton, a native of Mason City, Iowa, served as officer of the deck on this night as the *Swift* sailed through the cold Channel waters. He watched closely as the *Swift*'s special wire cutters severed the moorings of the enemy mines. Crewmen then shot at the mines until they exploded harmlessly. "We streamed our sweeping gear to sweep moored mines."

Once they had punctured the minefield in the middle of the Channel, the work was by no means over. In some ways it was just beginning. The sweepers had to make sure that the bombardment ships could take up station unmolested off the Normandy shores. "We swept the fire support channel . . . the channel leading to the fire support area where the battleships, cruisers, and destroyers were to be stationed and in which they were to maneuver while bombarding Utah beach."[1] When they were certain they had cleared an area of mines, they dropped lighted buoys to guide the ships that would soon follow. This was very dangerous work. One undetected mine could blow this 220-foot vessel apart. On this night, the USS *Osprey* had already touched off a mine and sunk. Several other Allied ships met with a similar fate in the days ahead. Mines were, in reality, the only significant German naval defense against Overlord. Allied sweepers did a magnificent job of clearing the way for the invasion fleet, but in the days and weeks ahead mines remained a real danger in the coastal waters.

Behind the minesweepers came the LCTs, followed by the bombardment ships, then the LCIs, the LSTs, the LCCs (Landing Craft Control), the rhino ferries, and the small, auxiliary ships. The whole armada was a stunning display of naval might such as the world had rarely witnessed. In the cloudy moonlight of this night, there appeared to be so many ships that seemingly, if one wished, one could hopscotch from ship to ship all the way to the coast of France.

Aboard those ships, embarking now on Eisenhower's "great crusade," thousands of individual dramas unfolded. Frank Feduik, a pharmacist's mate on board LST-338, stood on the deck of his awkward but utilitarian vessel and squinted to see British sub chasers hunt for U-boats. "Boy, it was dark. But we made sure we always had [them] in sight because they protected us from submarines. Every LST carried a big [barrage] balloon [shaped like a small blimp] to keep German planes from coming in low and strafing us." The balloons were designed to discourage low-level strafing from enemy planes, but Feduik shook his head in amusement at the sight of them. "We thought [they were] a joke because it was like announcing to the world, 'Here we are under this big dirigible.' "[2]

The sailors might have laughed over the ungraceful barrage balloons, but they knew that what lay ahead was serious indeed. Reality set in for Edward Duffy, a twenty-three-year-old fire controlman from Brooklyn, when the captain of his ship, the destroyer USS *Shubrick*, addressed the crew as the ship sliced through the waves on this night. The very fact that he was making a speech was unusual. In Duffy's experience, only the officer of the day spoke over the PA system, not the captain. But now Duffy heard his captain's crisp, low voice echo over the sound system. "He announced that we were about to begin the biggest military operation in the history of the human race. He instructed us to shave all beards, shower, and dress in clean clothes. For us that meant dungarees. The reason we were told to do this is that there is less chance of serious infection to wounds if we wear clean clothes and have shaved faces. That was a sobering thought."[3]

Not far away from the *Shubrick* in the line of ships, Rear Admiral Morton Deyo, the naval officer who had been so impressed with Eisenhower three weeks earlier at the St. Paul's briefing, stood on the bridge of the cruiser *Tuscaloosa*. Deyo commanded the bombardment group that would soften Utah beach for the 4th Division. This powerful ship dwarfed many of the landing craft and destroyers within Deyo's sight. From time to time he raised his binoculars and surveyed the choppy seas. Here on the *Tuscaloosa* everything was stable, even comfortable, but Deyo knew that conditions had to be quite miserable aboard the LCTs ahead. The admiral could tangibly feel a sense of anticipation on the subdued bridge. "Our flag bridge is dead quiet. On the forecastle and upper deck where the crew are now at battle stations, voices are hushed. One seems to feel the presence of millions of men. The atmosphere is alive with the spirits of men. One is aware of a sort of quiet exaltation. We begin ticking off the lighted buoys (so well placed by our sweepers) red to starboard, green to port. One thinks of those minesweeping squadrons far ahead, numerous and tough, moving unprotected save for a few destroyers, into the dangerous waters. With exact navigation, working in the darkness . . . these stout sailors have cleared numerous and intricate channels, hundreds of miles of them."[4]

A few hundred yards away, in the same line of warships, Lieutenant John Blackburn, an antiaircraft gunnery officer aboard the cruiser USS *Quincy*, went belowdecks for one last "cup of wardroom coffee and a nervous half-smoked cigarette." The mood in the wardroom was electric. "Everyone was talking in excited, low voices. Conversation was difficult because no one was listening to the talker's words. It was as if we all had our ears cocked awaiting the alarm of battle stations, which . . . would indicate that we were under attack."

Blackburn finished his coffee and left the wardroom. He went topside and ascended a ladder to his station, in sky control, high above the bridge. His job was to direct antiaircraft fire in the event of an attack by enemy planes. The lieutenant fully expected those planes to arrive at any moment. Surely the Luftwaffe has to be out there somewhere, he thought. In sky control, he enjoyed a terrific view. "The ships ahead of us were warily feeling their way along the channel that had been swept of mines. Every fifteen or twenty minutes we would pass a small green lighted marker buoy close aboard to starboard. The red ones on the port side were given much wider berth. Our swept channel was supposed to have been eight hundred yards wide."

Much to Blackburn's surprise, enemy planes never materialized. He spent the crossing listening to excited communications among the ships trying to find the way that had been marked by the buoys. If they went even slightly off-course, they could lead the fleet back into the minefield. Luckily, that did not happen.

Blackburn's birdlike perch contrasted sharply with a group of sailors far below him, deep in the bowels of the *Quincy*, in one of the ship's four boiler rooms. Within the claustrophobic confines of this sweaty, stifling area, sixteen sailors provided the necessary power to keep the cruiser running smoothly. One of them was Seaman Michael Brienze, a baby-faced nineteen-year-old from Hawthorne, New Jersey. His boiler room was located well below the waterline. The sailors in this grim room kept themselves fortified with pot after pot of steaming coffee. When the caffeine and adrenaline wore off, Brienze and the other sailors "slept in the boiler room in the buldges (where the piping ran) on part of a bed of rags we had down there. The hatches on the doors were about a foot thick and dogged (closed) down. We also had an escape hatch. Only one man at a time could go up the ladder." When they got hungry, they sent someone up that ladder to the galley for franks and beans.

All night long, they monitored their intricate web of pipes and pumps. "One man checked the water on the water glass . . . one fireman on the headphones, one fireman taking care of five burners on saturated side 600 pounds steam, and another fireman taking care of five burners on superheat side 850 [degrees]. As the feed increased, the fireman would have to put more burners in. He would increase the air at his valve, and it led to the blower, and he'd open up more and give us more air, as we lit more burners." One man constantly checked pressure gauges, compressors, and temperature indicators. If the ship hit a mine or if the boilers overheated, the sailors could be trapped and scalded to death. Brienze and the others tried not to think about that.[5]

Lieutenant Blackburn on the *Quincy* was not the only who expected a Luftwaffe appearance. Throughout the armada, gunners prepared for the possibility of an enemy aerial attack. Aboard the destroyer USS *Harding,* James Jones and several other sailors readied their 20mm gun. "All paint and burnable material was thrown over the side. All fire hoses were broken out, all damage repair equipment broken out; extra projectiles were piled in handling rooms and hoists filled with powder and all watertight doors closed and dogged tightly." Jones arranged his ammunition exactly the way he wanted it. "I broke out 20mm magazines for my gun besides eight of them in my ready box. I loaded my gun [and] all other 20mm did the same. The 40mm guns put a dip in the loading tray so all they had to do was press the firing pedal."[6]

As mentioned, conditions aboard the bombardment ships—cruisers, battleships, destroyers—were reasonably comfortable, since they were large enough to deal with the rough seas of the Channel. The same could not be said for the smaller, less forgiving LCTs, LSTs, LCIs, and patrol craft. The mere task of staying in line and maintaining course could be a great challenge for these vessels in the face of high winds and buffeting seas. Lieutenant Stanley Bodell, the skipper of one LCT, had an extremely difficult time maintaining control of his craft. "We were located in one of the inside columns and spent our entire time trying to keep station." The British craft behind Bodell's LCT could go twice as fast, but it could not reverse itself. "We would pound along, the whole boat bending and buckling; then the one ahead would slow down. We would go into full reverse to keep from riding its stern, then the Britisher would start to climb ours. To avoid collision we would go full speed ahead with full right rudder." This merely created a new problem, as they repeatedly came close to colliding with ships of another column. Sometimes they came as close as five feet from hitting them.[7]

This kind of perilous sailing created nightmarish circumstances for many of those men who were crammed aboard the transport craft. On one LCT, Seaman Second Class John Talton, a member of Naval Combat Demolition Unit 44, sat on the port side hanging on to a cable that held several tanks in place. Wind and spray whipped everywhere. Talton's unit was specially trained to go into the beaches with the initial assault waves to clear paths through German obstacles, but at this moment, as he fought seasickness, he could not have cared less. "The speed of the LCT was such that it seemed to start up a wave & slide off the side. The roll & slide of the LCT caused the water depth on the deck to vary from 2–5 feet. The rock & roll, decks awash . . . rains and sea sickness eleminated [sic] the need for food & the scene, from my position on the deck, was . . . men, helmets, vomit & all unlashed equipment rolling back & forth in a sickening soupy mixture, untended and left to the luck of the roll."[8]

Obviously, the LCTs were not designed for comfort. They were made to carry tanks or other cargo safely over the span of relatively short distances. They were 105 feet long, flat-bottomed, with a landing ramp and makeshift crew quarters on the stern. They had no running water except for that provided by a hand pump. There were only two toilets aboard, both hand-operated: one for the crew (fifteen enlisted men and two officers) in the stern and one for the soldiers in the forward compartment.

No wonder that the men aboard these contraptions experienced such awful conditions as they crossed the Channel. Aboard LCT-271, twenty-year-old Seaman Robert Evans of Muskegon, Michigan, could not help but feel sorry for the nauseous 1st Division soldiers strewn all over the crude deck. These poor men looked like they would rather be anywhere else. "All the Army guys were half-sick, vomiting, just praying to get off that landing craft. Our troops were tired. They hadn't had any sleep. We were up all night." In the wheelhouse, Evans had spent most of the night at the controls of LCT-271. He wore full Navy battle gear—helmet, two life jackets, foul-weather equipment. Still, he felt cold and queasy. The cook had been at his battle station all night, so no one had eaten anything. One of the soldiers worked up enough strength to make his way across the slippery deck, ascend his way into the wheelhouse, and ask Evans if he could use the galley to make pancakes. "Hell, yes, go ahead." The soldier did a fine job. He and Evans ate their fill and they ended up feeling much better.[9]

Conditions were not much better on the transport ships carrying assault units like the 2nd Ranger Battalion. The hardy Rangers had been felled by food poisoning a week earlier. Now some of them gave way to seasickness produced by the monotonous bucking of ships like HMS *Prince Charles*. Half of the battalion, Companies A through C, along with part of headquarters, was crammed aboard this old ship. "We were all downstairs in the hold, officers and enlisted men alike," Lieutenant Gerald Heaney recalled. "We were very crowded, the sea was rough, and a lot of people became ill. I personally was woozy and really couldn't eat. In fact, I purposely refrained from doing so, so I wouldn't get sick to my stomach."[10]

In anticipation of this problem, the troops were issued seasickness pills, but similar to the airsickness pills given to the paratroopers, these pills created more problems than they solved. Aboard LST-512, Lieutenant Edward Jones, the 115th Infantry reconnaissance officer, noticed that "all personnel were taking seasickness prevention tablets. They made you woozy and sleepy. I finally gave them up after a day or so. I concluded I would rather arrive a little seasick than to go ashore three-quarters asleep and ineffective. With seasickness the symptoms go away once you are on dry land anyway."[11]

Most troops came to the same conclusion. Miserable though they were, they knew that battle readiness trumped the temporary misery of seasickness. August Thomas, a coxswain aboard LCT-633, could hear nauseous 4th Division soldiers quietly talking of the battle that lay ahead. "Stillness fell, and in soft voices you could hear different groups discussing what they thought the dawn would bring and how they would fare in all of this."[12]

It is fair to say that every man aboard those ships wondered the same thing. Each man dealt, in his own way, with the possible imminence of death. Not surprisingly, many turned to religion. Private Samuel Ricker, B Company, 4th Engineer Combat Battalion, sat on the deck of an LST bound for Utah beach. Ricker's unit was assigned as engineering support for the 12th Infantry, 4th Division, assault troops going ashore at Utah. A chaplain had given Ricker a pocket-sized armed forces Bible. The Tennessee-born Ricker leafed through the Bible and found himself returning time and again to Psalms 23. Over and over he read, and whispered to himself, the cryptic verses: "The Lord is my shepherd, I shall lack nothing. He makes me lie down in green pastures, he leads me beside quiet waters, he restores my soul. He guides me in paths of righteousness for his name's sake. Even though I walk through the valley of the shadow of death, I will fear no evil, for you are with me, your rod and your staff, they comfort me. You prepare a table before me in the presence of my enemies. Surely goodness and love will follow me all the days of my life, and I will dwell in the house of the Lord forever." These verses helped him control his considerable fear.[13]

Others turned to more public expressions of devotion. Captain Richard Fahey, a doctor in the 60th Medical Battalion, a unit that would soon go ashore at Omaha beach, attended a Catholic absolution service. In contrast to the one-on-one confessions normally prevalent in the Catholic Church, this was a general absolution. They gathered on deck and listened to their priest. "I went aboard deck and accepted general absolution, knowing full well that it was just what I needed, but I was concerned all the while about what was going to happen to all those Protestants, Jews, and atheists that did not have this privilege extended to them."[14]

He need not have worried. Most chaplains offered general services, geared toward all denominations and beliefs. Aboard the transport ship *Thomas Jefferson*, Captain Charles Cawthon of the 116th Infantry listened to his regimental chaplain, Reverend Charles Reed, speak over the steady drone of the ship's engines. Cawthon studied the men around him, standing impassively, thinking their own private thoughts, as Reed conducted his service. "There were probably more than the usual number of private prayers launched that night as the realization grew that this was not another exercise, and that at dawn metal would be flying both ways. Friends gravitated together; I noted no bravado." Cawthon took in the whole service before retreating belowdecks to his bunk and a copy of *Collier's* magazine.[15]

Many other soldiers and sailors concentrated on other things to cope with the uncertainty so typical on this eve of battle. In his bunk aboard the Utah beach–bound destroyer USS *Fitch*, Ensign

Richard Bowman scribbled a final letter to his parents describing the mood of the crew: "The men are restless and worried and afraid of the immediate future but not markedly so. Just in a few nervous ways like excessive letter-writing, card playing, reading and rumor spreading. We are making last minute preparations and trying thro [sic] drills and planning to anticipate every conceivable casualty or request for ships performance. We are confident, coldly calculative and ready for the worst."[16]

Staff Sergeant Harry Bare, a squad leader in F Company, 116th Infantry, sat in the crammed hold of a transport ship and contemplated the fact that he and his men would soon comprise the first wave to assault the Dog Red sector of Omaha beach. "We didn't sleep much that night. In the rough Channel, a lot of the men were seasick, and some just remained quiet, deep in thought. How does one explain their feelings at a time like this? I really didn't know what to expect, any more than anyone else. Some were just sitting there, some were checking their equipment, and some were just plain sick. No one seemed to want to talk too much."[17]

Inevitably card and dice games, especially among the soldiers, sprang from this nearly unbearable tension. Money meant little to men who might soon be dead. Gambling provided a way to burn off some nervous energy in the company of friends. Aboard the USS *Bayfield*, command vessel of Force U (the Utah beach task force), Private Jack McQuiston of the 1st Engineer Special Brigade spent the entire night gambling with his buddies. "We played cards, shot craps, and swapped stories. Very few of the men slept. I know I didn't. I had butterflies in my stomach all night long."[18] Seaman Second Class Buddy Shellenberger, standing on the slippery deck of LST-373, watched in fascination as a group of soldiers played endless card games. The Wrightsville, Pennsylvania, native had a birthday coming up. In one week he would turn seventeen. The teenage Shellenberger had never seen this kind of gambling. "All they did was sit around and play cards. I mean, they were playing for big stakes, shooting craps and everything. I think they ... sensed 'the big thing' ... was coming up, so they didn't care too much about money." Shellenberger wandered around in search of a friendly face from home. "After I got my duties done, I just walked around and talked to these people, trying to find somebody from Lancaster ... or Columbia or somewhere close."[19]

Aboard a cramped transport ship sailing inexorably toward Omaha beach, Sergeant Mike McKinney sat in on a crap game for an hour or two. McKinney knew exactly what to expect on D-Day. He had been through combat with his L Company, 16th Infantry, 1st Division, in the Mediterranean. He soon tired of the raucous crap game and retired to his tiny bunk. "They were about a foot or two apart, wire mesh, and they were four or five high. You couldn't sit up in the thing; you could get forward and slide in. It was not conducive to sleeping, but you could doze. I think most of us stayed awake during the night." The salty McKinney used the time to inspect every last piece of equipment, especially his brand-new invasion vest. He knew he was setting an example for all the new soldiers in his platoon who looked up to him as the platoon's second in command. "We had some new guys that were probably a lot more nervous than we were, but I guess our calmness helped to assuage them a little bit and make them feel a little better. I like to think so, anyhow."[20]

On a transport ship in Force U, the soldiers of Private William Jones's I Company, 8th Infantry, distracted themselves from their impending Utah beach assault by turning their uniforms into impromptu billboards. "We nearly all had something painted on our field jackets. Usually the name of our state or something. Of course I had Tennessee on mine." Private Jones strode around the ship proudly displaying his newly emblazoned jacket.

As he stood at the rail watching the other ships of the armada, a man saw his jacket and sidled up to him. "What part of Tennessee are you from?"

Jones thought the voice was familiar. "I looked around and it was a friend of mine who lived a few miles down the road from me. Well, I was really glad to see that old boy; his name was Thurman Charlton. He was in the Coast Guard . . . a coxswain on one of the landing craft." They talked for several moments about home and then Charlton turned serious: "If you don't make it, is there anything you want me to tell the people at home?"

Private Jones felt like spouting a bit of bravado. "Just tell them that we went down swinging."[21]

As the ships closed in on the Norman coast, most did not feel such bravado. Instead they quietly went about their business, waited for the word to move out, and hoped for the best. Many, like Captain John Ahearn, commander of C Company, 70th Tank Battalion, spent some introspective moments on their own. "I went below deck and tried to sleep but I couldn't, so I pulled out a little book I had been intending to read about my home city, *A*

Tree Grows in Brooklyn. I read it in three or four hours but never could go to sleep."[22]

Even as he turned the pages of that famous book, Ahearn could hear, ever so faintly, the sound of aircraft engines high above. All over the expanse of Force U and Force O (Omaha), sailors and soldiers raised their heads and looked skyward at thousands of shadowy planes. Overhead, an enormous aerial fleet— the one carrying the airborne vanguard of the invasion of Europe— rumbled inexorably south. In the desperation of the approaching fight, these brave paratroopers, glider men, and aviators were about to lead the way.

CHAPTER SEVEN

THE AIRBORNE RIDE OVER

Truthfully, they looked a bit like wild men. Underneath several layers of uniforms, equipment, weapons, helmet, and face paint, each airborne trooper lost his individual identity. Maybe that's the way it was supposed to be. They were all part of one team now with one aim—the accomplishment of a difficult mission. Individual agendas had no place here; only survival and success mattered. When Sergeant Robert Webb of the 506th settled into his bucket seat aboard a C-47 at Exeter, he glanced around and actually found it difficult to determine who was who. "The inside of the plane was eerie with all our faces painted with camouflage paint. We had to look hard to recognize each other."[1]

At Folkingham in the English midlands, Lieutenant Colonel Wesley Leeper, an air force officer, stood and watched, with a deep, emotional respect, as airborne troopers from the 508th Parachute Infantry prepared to leave, "Never have I seen a finer group of physical specimens. I cannot say they were 'good-looking' from a sense of beauty, for actually they looked almost 'horrible' as we stood there and watched them prepare for take-off. Their faces were blacked, and their steel helmets were covered with green nets, into which had been fastened bits of green foliage. They looked like some savages I had seen in the films! Fastened to their person was more equipment than I thought it possible for one man to carry. I must say that at that moment I was indeed proud to call myself an American . . . to know that I came from a country which produced men like these." Colonel Leeper marveled at the intrepid, quiet courage of these youthful troopers. "Here was a group of young men—the flower of America—many of them, no doubt, about to face a horrible death, yet they laughed and joked about what they were going to do 'when they got home.' "[2]

One of those troopers was Private Porcella, the New Yorker whose friend had earlier confided expectations of death to him. As Porcella plopped into his seat aboard his stick's plane, the aircraft's friendly crew chief began checking on the soldiers, dispensing advice. "Listen, you guys, when you go out the door . . . make sure you have your line hook in your left hand. OK?"

"OK, Sarge, we'll do that," the troopers hollered back.

The crew chief then started to make conversation: "Hey, where are you troopers from?"

Naturally, the answers varied. "Most of us replied with the name of our home state," Porcella recalled. "He insisted that Kentucky was the best state in the Union. We all laughed and gave the guy hell. I told him I thought Long Island was a better place than Kentucky anytime."[3]

Another 508th trooper, Private Dwayne Burns, had a decidedly less friendly experience with the crew of his plane. "I found my seat and it had a flak vest lying on it. I said, 'Hey, this is great! I can use all of the protection I can get!' So, I folded it and sat on it. Before long the pilot came back looking around and wanted to know who was sitting on his flak vest. He said that he wasn't going to take off without it. I reluctantly pulled out the vest and handed it over. The pilot gave me a dirty look, but didn't say anything, just turned around and went back up front."[4]

The transportation of these two great airborne divisions required over 800 aircraft. When they fired up their engines in preparation for takeoff, waves of noise engulfed the airfields of middle and southern England. One by one, as the final moments of June 5 ticked into eternity, the planes revved their engines and waited for their turn to take off. Aboard one of those planes—belonging to the 441st Troop Carrier Group at Merryfield—a nineteen-year-old crew chief named Charles Bortzfield popped his head out of the open door of his idling C-47. Bortzfield was a graduate of a New York vocational high school. He loved anything mechanical, especially engines. Now he watched as a line of C-47s, adorned with flashy new invasion stripes, slowly taxied for takeoff. "Hundreds of the propellers spun furiously as they awaited the go signal. The signal came and two abreast the C-47s roared down the runway, then another two, then another; finally it was our turn." Sergeant Bortzfield assumed his normal takeoff position between the pilot and copilot. "[The pilot] pushed the throttle full forward. We were rolling, tail up; we were airborne. The air was a little rough at this point from all the prop wash from the planes up front ahead of us. We'd dipped a wing once in a while, mushed a little bit, but finally we leveled out... [into] a formation... nine planes wide, three v-groups across."[5] Formations were tight; planes flew within 100 feet of one another.

Heavily laden down with troopers, fuel, and equipment, the planes lurched awkwardly into the air, prompting sighs of relief or howls of exuberance from thousands. At Uppottery, when Private Burgett's C-47 left the runway, he hollered, "Flap your wings, you big-assed bird!" He and many others in his stick found the seats of the plane too uncomfortable, so they knelt on the floor, leaned back, and tried to rest. Burgett was amused later to read a reporter's contention that they had knelt in prayer during the ride into combat. "Actually, it was just a comfortable way to ride."[6]

At every airfield, each serial of planes circled until all planes had gotten into proper formation. Only then did they head south. Those who sat near the open door of their C-47s (usually jump masters or men with low jump numbers in their sticks) beheld an incredible aerial armada in the clear skies over England that night. "I could hardly see the sky for planes," reported Sergeant Thomas Buff, of 101st Airborne headquarters. "There just was not room for more." On General Taylor's plane, Technical Sergeant George Koskimaki, his radioman, could not take his eyes off the dizzying number of planes he saw outside the door, "Wing lights were on and it was a beautiful spectacle to behold through the open doorway." Visibility was terrific. "The night was beautiful," Private First Class James "Pee Wee" Martin, G Company, 506th, recalled. "There were a few stratus clouds drifting by here and there. The moon silhouetted the planes around us... the fiery exhaust of our engines reminded me strangely of a blast furnace."[7] To Private Joe Bressler of the 508th it seemed that "there were so many planes ... you could almost walk across them."[8]

As the voyage unfolded, many of the troopers fought the onset of drowsiness from the airsickness pills. Hundreds of men fell asleep. On a C-47 carrying part of E Company, 506th Parachute Infantry, First Lieutenant Richard "Dick" Winters tried to fight off sleep and nervousness by singing with his men. "I had to stay awake so I'd be able to think and react quickly. But those pills seemed to slow down feelings of emotion. The song was soon lost in the roar of the motors. I fell to making a last prayer. It was a long, hard, and sincere prayer that never really did end for I just continued to think and pray during the rest of the ride."

On another E Company plane, even a lighthearted joke by one of the men could not pierce the reverie. "Do any of you bastards want to buy a good wrist watch?" Private Wayne "Skinny" Sisk bellowed above the din. Everyone laughed, but soon the group fell into a thoughtful silence.[9]

The same held true on most all of the planes. Engine noise precluded meaningful conversation. Most troopers who had not fallen victim to the pills were left alone with the privacy of their own thoughts and fears. Clarence Hughart of H Company, 507th, stole a look at his lieutenant and saw that he was "white as a ghost."[10] Private Paul Bouchereau, riding in the serial carrying the headquarters element of the 508th Parachute Infantry, welcomed the engine noise and eerie darkness. He and some others were "afraid the fear would show on our faces. Each of us wished to keep our emotions to ourselves."[11]

Some tried to fight that fear in unusual ways. In a plane carrying a stick from E Company, 502nd Parachute Infantry, Private Lud Lubutka, a soldier in Lieutenant Wallace Strobel's platoon, could not resist the allure of a crude form of liquid courage. One of Lubutka's buddies, Private Albert Jones, looked at him and said, "Lud, do you want a drink?"

Lubutka, a native of Ford City, Pennsylvania, shot a dubious glance at Jones. He did not believe that his buddy had smuggled alcohol aboard the plane. As if anticipating Lubutka's skepticism, Jones whipped out a bottle of Aqua Velva (the aftershave contained a small quantity of alcohol). As Lubutka watched, Jones took a big gulp from the bottle.

"You're crazy!" Lubutka said.

Jones leaned over and offered the bottle to Lubutka. "Jones, if you're crazy, I'm crazy, too." He grabbed the bottle and took a healthy swig. In the short term, the Aqua Velva calmed Lubutka, but later, when he jumped into Normandy, he puked it up during his descent.[12]

Aboard many of the planes, men sat in contemplative silence, smoking or dozing. Sergeant Buff felt like he was in the reception room of a dentist's office. Buff could feel fear within himself, but he kept it under control. "Inwardly, without even knowing it, I was fighting to remain unruffled." He kept thinking, "I'm lucky as hell to be mixed up in this affair. I am glad to be along; honored to be a member of the Division which will be the first to land in France." Each time those thoughts went through his mind, he wondered just "how much truth" they contained and decided that it was "open to question."[13]

Private Burns's mind raced as his plane flew inexorably toward France. He looked around at the men in his stick, the best friends he had ever known. Their blackened young faces betrayed little in the way of emotion. They sat in awkward clusters along the walls of the plane, equipment at their feet. How many of them would be dead in two hours? Burns prayed not to screw up and decided that he was too young for this war business. Soon his thoughts turned to a friend in another plane. "I wonder if we will ever see each other again. Chances are very slim that both of us will make it. I sure don't want the job of going to see his family when this war is over and telling them how sorry I am that John didn't make it. And I sure don't want him having to go looking up my family." Burns thought about his mother and father and how they would react to the news of D-Day.[14]

Miles ahead of Burns, George Koskimaki busied himself by wondering what each of his family members back home would be doing tonight at the exact moment he jumped into Normandy. He stared straight ahead and thought about the time difference between Normandy and Michigan. By Koskimaki's calculations, he would jump at 8:00 p.m. Michigan time. "This meant Dad would be fast asleep on the couch in the living room with the radio going full blast. Mom would be mending socks for my ambitious hard hiking younger brothers who wore out their socks faster than she could replace or repair them on their numerous fishing trips. Sister Milly would be with her girl friend Betty listening to the latest records. The boys would be in the backyard tinkering with their version of a World War II hotrod known as the 'Blue Beetle'— that was all they could do with gasoline being rationed." In the dark, as Koskimaki gyrated to the increasingly familiar rhythm of the plane, a tiny smile crossed his face. "I thought of a particular girl friend in Detroit who would set her students straight on the importance of this date when she met them in her classroom on the morrow."[15]

Aboard a plane carrying a stick from F Company, 505th Parachute Infantry, Private First Class R. R. Hughart sat and wondered what in hell he was doing here. Before the war, the Valparaiso, Indiana, native had worked in a steel mill in nearby Gary. He joined the Army after Pearl Harbor, volunteered for the paratroopers, and ended up fighting with them in Sicily, where a German machine-gun bullet had smashed into his arm during some particularly fierce fighting. Now Hughart was fully healed and heading into combat once more. "How come you got yourself into this?" he wondered. "This is your third combat jump and it could sure be your last one." The twenty-three-year-old knew it would "only be a matter of time . . . before my odds run out." Every other veteran of the 505th, spread out in dozens of planes around Hughart's, probably thought the same thing.[16]

Such thoughts led to nervousness, and nervousness for some troopers meant loose bowels. The C-47 was equipped with a small toilet at the rear of the plane, but the heavily laden paratroopers found it very difficult to wedge in there. Aboard one of the planes carrying the 82nd Airborne Division headquarters, General Matthew Ridgway watched in bemused silence as some of the men got up to relieve themselves. "Now and then a paratrooper would rise, lumber heavily to the little bathroom in the tail of the plane, find he could not push through the narrow doorway in his bulky gear, and come back, mumbling his profane opinion of the designers of the C-47 airplane. Soon the crew chief passed a bucket around, but this did not entirely solve our problem. A man strapped and buckled into full combat gear finds it extremely difficult to reach certain essential portions of his anatomy, and his efforts are not made easier by the fact that his comrades are watching him, jeering derisively and offering gratuitous advice."[17]

By now the planes were well over the Channel. Their flight path took them directly over the invasion fleet. In an effort to evade German radar, the airborne serials had dropped down to an altitude of about five hundred feet, thus affording the troopers a great view of the fleet. On Private David Kenyon Webster's plane, the crew chief alerted his lieutenant to the view. The officer rose from his seat, waddled to the door, looked out, nodded, and smiled. "Look, men, look! It's the fleet!" he shouted.

Webster turned stiffly, "like a rusty robot," to a tiny window behind him and caught a quick glance. He emitted an involuntary gasp, "Man, oh man." The sight nearly overwhelmed him. "Five hundred feet below, spread out for miles on the moonlit sea, were scores and scores of landing barges, destroyers, cruisers, and attack transports. They were bearing the infantry slowly . . . like a flood of lava, to a dawn assault on the shingle shore of Normandy."

Webster saw a lamp blinking from a ship. Seconds later the wingtip lights of his plane flashed off, as did the blue lights in the pilot's passageways. Webster stared at one of his buddies in the "racketing, vibrating, oil-reeking, vomit-scented darkness" and exclaimed, "Isn't it great? Those guys are going in!" His buddy couldn't hear him and Webster did not feel like repeating himself.[18]

On one of the planes carrying the 326th Airborne Engineers of the 101st Airborne Division, a young machine gunner, Private First Class Chuck Storeby, watched the fleet below and felt like a giant. "Looking down on the invasion fleet below us . . . they looked like hundreds and hundreds of ships floating in a bathtub. It was a sight I will not forget."[19] As the 508th overflew the fleet, Private Bressler wondered "how we could lose with this many ships. Everyone in the plane gave a cheer."[20]

Not long after they passed over the fleet, the planes turned to the southeast, straight for the western coast of Normandy. This course took them just north of the German-occupied Channel Islands, the only British soil that fell under German control in the war years. The Germans had the equivalent of one understrength infantry division on the islands, mainly on Guernsey and Jersey. Some of those soldiers manned antiaircraft guns or machine guns and started shooting at the C-47s of the two American airborne divisions, but the fire was ineffective and out of range. To troopers like Private Porcella, though, the fire was a sobering precursor of what was to come. "I looked out the window and you could see the stuff, the flashes . . . of the artillery shells. You could see the shells bursting outside the plane and off in the distance you could see the machine-gun fire, in the distance, flares. I could feel a chill come over me."[21]

When the serials made landfall on the western coast of Normandy, they flew into clouds that served to scatter formations and confuse pilots. Lieutenant Roger Airgood, sitting in the right-hand copilot seat of a C-47 that was carrying troopers from the 502nd Parachute Infantry, 101st Airborne, was concentrating on keeping the next plane in formation visible. "I flew from the right hand seat . . . I could see the exhaust stack glow and the phantom outline of the plane. We maintained our position flying as tight a formation as possible. When entering an unexpected cloud bank we continued on without any appreciable difference in visibility."[22] Airgood and the others flew on as best they could, dipping in and out of cloud banks, scanning with quick glances for landmarks below.

At nearly the same time, back in England, the tail end of the airborne armada, the glider serials, prepared for takeoff. The six regiments of paratroopers jumping tonight were taking some of the necessary weapons and equipment with them that they would need in the days ahead. They were to jump with leg bags or bundles containing such things as mortars, bazookas, heavy machine guns, radios, ammo, rations, and medical supplies. Still, once on the ground, the troopers would be little more than light infantry, unable to sustain themselves for any appreciable length of time. They desperately needed the vital support that only heavy vehicles and weapons could provide. That's where the gliders came into the picture. These unwieldy wood-and-metal contraptions carried the jeeps, artillery pieces, antitank guns, and supplies that the paratroopers would so badly need in combat. They also carried reinforcing infantry.

There were two common types of gliders—the British Horsa (better payload) and the American Waco (better maneuverability). American glider pilots flew both types into Normandy. The glider was fastened by a twenty-foot nylon tow cable to a C-47. For communication with the tow pilots the glider pilots wrapped phone cord around the tow cable. The glider pilots were an obscure group of black sheep within the glamorous pilot ranks of the Army Air Force, but they deserved more acclaim because their job was quite dangerous. Once the towing C-47 had flown their gliders over the drop zone, they were cast free; the glider pilots then flew their little aircraft, fighting winds and disorientation, until they could find a suitable landing spot. In anticipation that the Allies would employ gliders, Rommel had ordered many French fields to be flooded with water or studded with the wooden stakes called Rommel's asparagus.

Now, with the clock edging toward twenty minutes after midnight on this momentous day, June 6, C-47 tow-plane pilots of the 434th Troop Carrier Group, at Aldermaston, revved their engines in preparation for takeoff. Behind the tow planes, the glider pilots and soldiers (from the 101st Airborne) listened to the deafening roar of the engines and steeled themselves for the whirlwind experience of leaving the strictures of earth. There were fifty-three planes in all. In the pilot's seat of one of them, Glider 50, Flight Officer George "Pete" Buckley listened to the engines and apprehensively waited for his tow plane to start moving. He could just barely hear light rain tapping against the canvas skin of his glider. As usual, the canvas smelled strangely like bananas. The roar of 106 C-47 engines grew steadier by the moment. "The muffled noise and throbbing from their motors spread around the field like a distant, approaching thunderstorm, and contributed to our uneasiness." Behind Buckley and his copilot, Flight Officer Bill Bruner, a three-man antitank crew from the 101st Airborne sat crammed in corners around their weapon, a 57mm gun, plus ammunition, a camouflage net, and boxes of supplies.

Buckley knew that these men were depending on him to get them safely onto French soil. He could not escape thinking that "in roughly three and a half hours I might be dead." He tried to force such thoughts from his mind, but it was quite difficult. "It was a very sobering moment, and I wondered why I had been so foolish as to volunteer for this job. When I first went into the glider program, nobody had ever explained to me how gliders were going to be used." Buckley's mind might have been racing, but he tried to keep his face impassive.

Other men in the line of gliders were struggling with the same dread of death. Seven planes ahead of Buckley, in Glider 42, Lieutenant Irwin Morales and his copilot, Lieutenant Thomas Ahmad, surveyed each other with deep apprehension. "Right before the takeoff," Morales recalled, "Ahmad and I made a pact. If I got killed, he would visit my folks, and if he were, I'd go to his parents' home." Seconds later, they took off. Such pacts were actually quite common up and down the line of planes that night.

Almost all of the planes were safely airborne by now. Buckley's plane, at the tail of the column, was one of the last to take off. "Our tow ship gunned its engines and started down the runway through a light rain shower and into the black of night. As the wheels of the glider left the ground, someone in the back yelled, 'Look out, Hitler, here we come!' This helped break the ice for a moment, after which no one said a word as I trimmed the glider for the long flight ahead. For the next three and one half hours, we would be alone with our thoughts and fears. It wasn't too bad for me, because I was flying the glider. But the airborne men in back and Bill Bruner, with nothing to do, must have been going through hell with their thoughts."[23]

Flight Officer Buckley kept his eyes on the bluish engine flame of the tow plane. He fought the turbulence produced by so many propellers and worked to keep his glider centered properly (above and behind the tow plane). He and the other gliders comprised the tail end of the airborne assault force. Far ahead of him, already on the ground, the lead portion of the assault force was going about its assigned task. These men, the first to touch French soil, called themselves pathfinders.

CHAPTER EIGHT

THE NIGHT DROP

In theory, the pathfinders had a simple job: jump into the drop zones first and mark them with lights and radar beacons, so that the follow-up forces could easily find the drop zones in the inky night. In practice, the job proved to be quite difficult.

Each American airborne division featured a force of about 120 trained pathfinders, broken up into eleven sticks. Planners had earmarked drop zones for each parachute infantry regiment. They were as follows: the 505th in Drop Zone O near Ste-Mère-Eglise, the 507th in Drop Zone T west of the Merderet River near La Fière, the 508th at Drop Zone N, also west of the Merderet, the 502nd, along with the 377th Parachute Field Artillery Battalion, at Drop Zone A, just west of Utah beach at St-Martin-de-Varreville, the 501st west of Ste-Marie-du-Mont at Drop Zone C, and the 506th at Drop Zone D in the vicinity of St-Côme-du-Mont. Three sticks were supposed to jump into each paratrooper drop zone. The remaining two sticks had the task of marking the glider landing fields. Each stick was commanded by an officer who jumped with an SCR-536 radio designed to help him communicate with other pathfinder officers. Two pathfinders per stick jumped with special Eureka radar sets that sent out signals for the lead aircraft carrying the main airborne force. Four men carried special halifane lights to mark the drop zone. The rest of the stick provided security.

The pathfinders left airfields in the English midlands at about 2130 on June 5, an hour before the main force. These pathfinder troopers knew they would be the first into Nazi-occupied France.

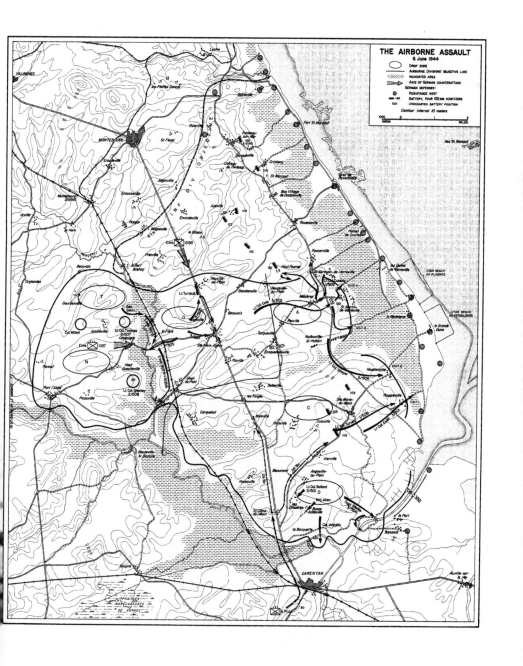

THE AIRBORNE ASSAULT
6 June 1944

DROP ZONE
AIRBORNE DIVISIONS' OBJECTIVE LINE
INUNDATED AREA
AXIS OF GERMAN COUNTERATTACK
GERMAN DEFENSES:
RESISTANCE NEST
BATTERY, FOUR 152MM HOWITZERS
UNOCCUPIED BATTERY POSITION
Contour interval 10 meters

1000 0   1
YARDS
0   1 2
MILES

No friends would await them, only foes. For the first hour on the ground, before the follow-up serials disgorged thousands of American paratroopers to reinforce them, some 250 intrepid pathfinders would find themselves facing the entire might of the German Army in Normandy. They could only hope to achieve the surprise so necessary for completion of their mission.

Around midnight, the aircraft carrying the pathfinders closed in on the western coast of Normandy. Aboard one of them, Corporal Joe Haller, a 101st Airborne pathfinder, could feel his bladder filling up, practically by the second. Before taking off at North Witham Airfield, he had fought off nervousness with the help of numerous cups of coffee. Now he was paying the price. Haller awkwardly stood and staggered a few steps. The normal buffeting and lurching of the C-47 kept him from walking a straight line. Haller knew that he could not possibly fit into the tiny bathroom at the rear of the plane, so he chose the next best option—the door. He stood in the windy door, unzipped his trousers, and urinated. Immediately the wind blew the urine back in his face and all over several troopers sitting by the door. Horrified, they cursed at him. Haller calmly finished and said, "You guys are gonna have a lot more to worry about than a little *pee!*"[1]

Haller's plane and many others soon ran into cloud cover and flak over Normandy. The combination of these two obstacles dispersed them. In a harbinger of what was to come, only about one-third of the pathfinders dropped in the right place. The rest scattered in the vicinity of their zones.

Frank Brumbaugh, an 82nd Airborne pathfinder, was supposed to jump at Chef-du-Pont and set up his Eureka radar set. He normally weighed a diminutive 137 pounds, but with all of his equipment fastened to his person, including the 65-pound radar set, he figured he weighed 315 pounds. When the pilot of his C-47 turned on the green light, Brumbaugh waddled to the door with the others, pushed himself through it, and hoped for the best, "I watched all of the shell bursts in the air around me, and I watched one stream of tracers which looked like it was going to come directly at me." Bullets clipped his chute and punctured three of his shroud lines. "In an obviously futile, but normal, gesture I spread my legs wide and grabbed with both hands my groin, as if to protect myself." It didn't matter. The bullets still came closer. "Machine-gun bullets traced up the inside of one leg, missed my groin, traced down inside of the other leg, splitting my pants on the insides of both legs, and dropped both free Red Cross cartons of Pall Mall cigarettes to the soil of France."

A second or two later, he "landed extremely hard with all of this weight." He pulled out his knife, cut his way out of his chute, assembled his rifle, grabbed his radar transmitter, and took it to the middle of the field in which he had landed. "I stripped its cover, put the antennae together, plugged it in, and turned it on. This was a few minutes after midnight, early morning on June 6." Brumbaugh and another trooper stayed there several hours but never saw or heard any other planes. At sunrise, Brumbaugh and his partner began to wonder where they were. They spotted a signpost that indicated they were more than five miles east of Chef-du-Pont, hopelessly far away from their intended drop zone.[2]

The commander of the 101st Airborne pathfinders, Captain Frank Lillyman (generally credited with being the first Allied soldier to land in France), also landed away from his intended drop zone. Lillyman's stick, along with two others in adjacent planes, ended up near St-Germain-de-Varreville, a mile north of Drop Zone A, the area they were supposed to mark for the 502nd. As was his custom, the captain had jumped with an unlit cigar clenched in his teeth. He quickly assembled several of his men in the dark, quiet night. "After the landing we met at the church in St-Germain-de-Varreville and traveled through fields to the northwest where we set up lights as markers, along with installation of other special equipment in trees."

Lillyman's orders were to avoid contact with the enemy, but as he and his men went about their tasks, a German machine gun opened fire. The gun kept harassing them with intermittent bursts. "This was annoying and I finally sent two men to convince the Krauts of the 'errors of their ways.' Soon, I heard a grenade go off with a 'whumpf,' and then everything was lovely and quiet."

Later, in searching a farmhouse, they encountered a Frenchman smoking a pipe. "He was standing in the doorway. He jerked his thumb toward the stairs and said, 'Boche.' We caught the German, in a nice pair of white pajamas, in bed. We disposed of him and expropriated the bottle of champagne beside the bed."

Other pathfinders flew into thick German flak. First Sergeant Charles Malley was part of a stick assigned to jump at Hiesville to mark Drop Zone C for the 501st. But he and his stick never got there. Instead, as they flew eastward looking for the proper drop zone, German fire tore into their aircraft. "Bullets were whizzing through the fuselage like bees chasing a 'honey-robbin' bear." Malley heard the bailout bell ringing. He looked out the door and saw one of the engines burning. The plane's crew chief shouted, "Clear the ship!" The paratroopers knew they were too low to jump and they stayed put.

The copilot ordered everything overboard. The plane was going in. Hurriedly the troopers and air force crew threw all the heavy equipment out of the plane. Now they were over the Channel. Steadily the plane lost altitude as the pilot fought to maintain control. Everyone clustered into the front of the plane and donned their Mae West life vests in preparation for a water landing. The pilot fired a red flare. First Sergeant Malley could make out the angry sea, closer and closer by the second: "The channel was running high that night, but the pilot did one helluva job. He brought her in on top of one of the waves, dragged tail, and flopped her in."

They inflated dinghies, but these were not designed to hold this many men. "We were mostly in the water just hanging on the lifeline around it," pathfinder Richard Wright, another man in Malley's stick, recalled, "and taking turns as to who was hanging on." They splashed around for about thirty minutes until a British destroyer picked them up. First Sergeant Malley was thrilled to see them. "I have a great warm feeling in my heart for the English. They fished us out of the briny depths; gave us grog, and extended such hospitality as was available on D-Day at very early morning (0100)." When they got back to England, the British imprisoned them until they could verify their identities as American soldiers.

Another plane in Malley's formation successfully dropped its pathfinders near the intended drop zone. These troopers were able to partially set up their equipment and mark a zone within a quarter-mile of what the planners intended. Not far away, at Landing Zone E, the 101st Airborne glider landing zone near Hiesville (destination for pilots Buckley, Morales, Ahmad et al.), the pathfinders did a fine job, right under the noses of the Germans. Richard Lisk, a T/5 communications specialist—the majority of the pathfinders were trained in communications—landed awkwardly and broke a foot. He lay alone in a ditch while his comrades prepared the landing zone. To his great consternation, he heard the clomping of hobnailed boots. "I held my breath as German soldiers passed by. As they passed within arm's reach, they kicked dirt in my face." Lisk managed to keep absolutely still and the German soldiers never knew he was there. In the morning, a medic gave him a shot of morphine, enabling him to walk to his regiment's headquarters.[3]

In summary, the pathfinders, thanks mainly to flak, navigational errors, German resistance, and nighttime confusion, only partially accomplished their mission of illuminating the drop zones for the main force. They did the best they could under difficult circumstances, but it was not enough. The majority of troopers who jumped into Normandy in the early-morning hours of D-Day did so without the guidance of the pathfinders.

It could even be argued that the pathfinders alerted many Germans to the presence of Allied paratroopers. When the serials of both American airborne divisions approached their drop zones in the Cotentin Peninsula just after 0100, they ran into a hailstorm of flak and small-arms fire. This enemy resistance wreaked havoc on the integrity of the airborne drops.

Consequently, the crews of the transport planes found themselves flying into flak-filled skies, a peril for which they were neither trained nor prepared. This happened in every serial. No sooner had Sergeant Joseph Terebessy's C-47 dropped its paratroopers over Ste-Mère-Eglise than a hunk of flak scored a direct hit on one of their engines. The engine quickly caught fire, but the pilots shut it down. Now they had to fly back to England on their only remaining engine. They managed to limp their way over the Channel, but when the pilots prepared the plane for landing, they found that the plane "didn't have any hydraulic fluid. So the flaps wouldn't come down."

Sergeant Terebessy and the others sat and wondered what they should do. Finally someone piped up, "Let's pour water into the hydraulic lines." The idea sounded good, so "we all got our canteens out and poured water into the hydraulic system. We got the flaps down about halfway, and they quit. We were getting closer to the base and wondered how we were going to get the gear down; we were out of water."

Again they silently contemplated what to do, until someone suggested, "Let's urinate into the canteens and pour that into the hydraulic system." They waited until they were on final approach and then employed their makeshift hydraulic fluid. "It worked; the gear came down. We landed."[4]

The aviators of the 81st Troop Carrier Squadron, carrying soldiers from the 1st Battalion, 502nd Parachute Infantry, ran into a hailstorm of flak as they approached Drop Zone A. The pilots in the lead planes were doing everything they could to fly a straight course and spot the areas marked by the pathfinders, but it was no use. All they could see was flak, tracers, and the faint outline of land below. They understood that they were only in the general vicinity of the drop zone but knew they had to give the order to jump, sooner rather than later.

Before long, individual planes began to take evasive action. Sergeant Marty Wolfe, a radio operator, could see them out of his window in the back of his C-47. "They dove and twisted under the upcoming arc of tracer bullets." Wolfe knew that inside those planes troopers were hooked up to their static lines, struggling to remain standing, knocking over "barf buckets," and slipping in a drool-stained cesspool of vomit.

In a nearby plane, Sergeant Ben Obermark, a crew chief, stared at the beautiful but deadly tracers as they shot skyward, "Watching the tracers come up at us made the hairs on the back of my neck feel as though they were standing straight up." Obermark, a mere spectator now, took in the whole terrible scene aboard the plane. "The rattle of flak fragments against our plane; the sight of flak and tracers above us, some seeming right on the mark for planes in front of us; the absolute stark terror in some paratroopers' eyes, their vomiting into helmets and forgetting to empty these helmets out."

What had once been neatly assorted formations soon degenerated into the aviation equivalent of every man for himself, as pilots took evasive action. In doing so, they nearly collided with one another. One of those pilots, Don Skrdla, had a terrifying close call. "One of our squadron's planes was taking such wild evasive action that he almost drove me into the ground. And that so-and-so wasn't even part of my flight—which shows how big a piece of sky he was using up! It took every bit of my strength and know-how, plus that of co-pilot Doug Mauldin, to prevent a collision." To make matters worse, when Skrdla turned on the green light for the Screaming Eagle troopers to jump, an equipment bundle became wedged in the door. Skrdla had to fly over the Channel, turn back, find the drop zone again, and brave the killer flak for the equivalent of two more passes before crew chief Dick Nice finally pried the bundle loose so that the troopers could jump.[5]

Aboard a nearby plane carrying troopers from F Company of the 502nd, Lieutenant LeGrand "Legs" Johnson, the young officer who had bumped his head when Eisenhower entered his tent, also experienced serious problems with equipment bundles. As jump master of his plane, Johnson was standing in the door, scanning the ground for any landmark that might indicate the drop zone. Flak exploded everywhere, but he tried to ignore it. Inwardly he was seething. At his feet lay six bulky bundles of antitank mines weighing nearly 400 pounds. Originally, the bundles were going to be dropped from the belly of the plane, relieving Johnson and his men from the responsibility of pushing them out the door. But the day before, someone had gotten the bright idea of putting radar equipment, instead of the antitank bundles, in the belly of the plane. Lieutenant Johnson protested vociferously, but to no avail.

Now, as he stood waiting for the green light, he wondered how in the world he was going to wedge these awkward bundles out the door. Johnson also had another headache in the form of an inexperienced naval forward observer, whose SCR-300 radio was so bulky it could barely fit through the door. Jumping with the radio would have been a real challenge for even the most experienced jumper, much less an officer not accustomed to this kind of mission.

The green light flashed. Johnson and the first few members of his stick sprang into action. "We had to manhandle those bundles out the door with those static lines draped all through our arms and shoulders and everything else, and we finally got rid of them. I don't know where the hell they are, to this day. And then we had to wrestle the navy guy out the door and had to push him, and he had the radio on about a thirty-foot line, and the bundle went out, and he went out immediately after it; and I hollered to the guys, and out we went." As Johnson descended, he could see German antiaircraft fire lock in on the naval observer. "I could see the tracers just eating through his canopy, so I . . . slipped my parachute as much as I could to get as far away from that particular location as I could."[6]

Even as Johnson was dealing with his problems, Second Lieutenant Bernard McKearney, a platoon leader in E Company of the

502nd, watched the tracers and, like so many other Americans that night, thought of the Fourth of July. The whole spectacle seemed beautiful to him, almost unreal, but then reality intruded on his reverie. "One burst clipped us in the wing. The plane lurched and nearly threw me out of the door. The men's faces were grim and tight. I tried to relax them by kidding a little. Then the green light, and I shouted, 'Let's go, girls!' and I piled out. The air was crisscrossed with tracers."[7]

The reception was similarly hot for the other two regiments of the 101st Airborne, especially the 506th, a unit that saw its first two battalions badly scattered from St-Marcouf to Vierville-au-Plain, while its third dropped accurately but right on top of German defenders near St-Côme-du-Mont. This 3rd Battalion of the 506th was the unit that Lieutenant Colonel Wolverton had led so eloquently in prayer just a few hours before.

Among them was Sergeant Robert Webb. As he stood waiting to jump, he became aware of the frightening accuracy of German antiaircraft guns, "I saw a bright flash and the plane next to us nosed over with all the troopers spilling out. I didn't see any chutes opening. Then another plane just blew up. This was getting serious. The tracer fire was really coming up, red and green. The green was from machine gun fire and the red was from 20mm cannon."

Not far away, in another C-47, another 3rd Battalion trooper could hardly believe the volume of fire. "They must have had every gun in France turned on us. The explosive shells and machine gun bullets were red, orange, and yellow, and were as thick as rain, only going up instead of down. There was no hesitation on anyone's part in going out of the door, although none of us expected to reach the ground alive. When I cleared the door, the plane was bucking like a crazy horse and the tracers were so thick it looked like a wall of flame."

On the descent, Sergeant Webb attracted the interest of a 20mm gunner, but the German missed. The sergeant landed right in the middle of the flooded Douve River, whose waters turned out to be a bigger peril than the enemy gunner. Webb had anticipated this and inflated his Mae West, but it did no good. If anything, the Mae West made things worse by catching on his harness and inflating too close to his throat, "I couldn't get my head up because that damn Mae West was under the back edge of my helmet. I had to swim to be able to breathe a little." This wasn't working. Webb began to swallow water and fight for air: "I was going to drown. Still fighting harder than ever to stay afloat, it seemed like a losing battle. The water was filling my parachute and pulling me downstream. My English leg pack with . . . radio and batteries became a perfect sea anchor, holding me back." He contemplated giving up. "I prayed to God! 'Don't let this mission fail, don't let all these people die for naught. Keep us in your grace. Take my life now and make it count for your sake.'" When all seemed lost, Webb caught hold of a branch and hung on until one of his comrades pulled him out of the water.[8]

The flak almost killed Sergeant Robert "Rook" Rader before he even left his plane. Immediately after the order came to stand up and hook up, he was amazed to see that "a shell passed through the metal bucket seat where I had been seated. The jump light was shot off from its position near the door."

Rader was very lucky. In many cases, the enemy shrapnel hit vulnerable troopers as they waited to jump. In a plane carrying part of G Company, 506th, Private Gordon Walthall could hear the macabre sound of spent shrapnel clattering against the skin of his C-47. "We heard what seemed to be gravel rattling against the tail of the plane. The craft rocked heavily and then the noise got louder, like balloons bursting. All of a sudden, one of the boys on the other side of the plane pitched forward on the floor. He had a hole through his helmet."

Sergeant Louis Truax and several other men came very close to the same fate. Truax was at the end of the stick and thus one of the last to exit his plane. The lead men were in the process of jumping and Truax was trotting down the aisle, waiting for his turn, when "suddenly the plane was hit in the left wing by flak. The wing went straight up. My left shoulder crashed into a window." Truax was carrying about one hundred pounds of equipment, including a sniper rifle, so he was amazed that the window did not break. "The pilot was fighting to right the plane. When he succeeded, I was appalled at the view which greeted me—I was the only one standing. Four men lay in a tangled heap on the floor. I realized it was almost impossible for them to stand up with their equipment loads."

The hopelessly tangled survivors had no choice now but to get out of the plane any way they could. "One man dived out the door head first. I stepped over the top of two men. The closest man to the door crawled out head first. I grabbed the ammo belt in the center of the man I thought next and gave him a heave out nose first. The next man made it crawling on his own power." Sergeant Truax reached up and pulled the salvo switch to release machine-gun and mortar bundles in the plane's belly. "Then I dived out." In checking later, Truax found that the first man landed near Ste-Mère-Eglise while he, the last man, landed just inland from Utah beach, a distance of four miles.[9]

Private Bill Oatman, a twenty-year-old rifleman in B Company, 506th, was one of the lucky ones on his plane. Just as he jumped, all hell broke loose. "Our plane was hit and the wing was on fire. We were so low that when my chute opened I swung twice and hit the ground. I know that all the men didn't get out."[10]

The story of flak, chaos, and misdrops was much the same for the 82nd Airborne. One regiment, the 505th, dropped near its as-signed zone in and around Ste-Mère-Eglise. The other two regi-ments, the 507th and the 508th, ended up scattered along the flooded expanse of the Merderet River. Some sticks from these regiments even ended up getting dropped near Valognes, Mon-tebourg, and Cherbourg.

Dan Furlong, a sergeant in H Company, 508th, had no idea where he was as his plane overflew the Cotentin Peninsula. He only knew that he wanted out of his plane—fast. "You could see the shells coming up. They looked like roman candles. And when they hit, it would sound like someone threw a keg of nails against the side of the airplane. They would rip a hole through it. We were hit three times. The first shell hit the wing. It took about three feet off of the tip of the wing. The next one hit right along-side the door and took the light panel off. And then the next one went through the floor, and it blew a hole about two feet across the floor and then hit the ceiling and exploded in the plane."

The shell killed three men and wounded four others. "There was so much confusion in there . . .'cause there was smoke and static lines and parachutes all over inside that airplane." Furlong's lieutenant kept waiting for the green light to come on, but Furlong screamed at him to go now. "The pilot was telling us to jump because the pilot knew the lights were gone anyway. I was scream-ing . . . to go and was pushing, so they finally got the message and went."[11]

In another plane carrying 508th troopers, rifleman Harold Canyon, son of Finnish emigrants, was also fortunate to escape injury. "Tracers went up all over the place. Our plane was hit hard up front. We got the order to stand up and hook up. Just as I approached the door, the top of the plane opened up and the right wing began to dip, the start of the death spiral. It took every bit of strength I could muster to get out that door. Instead of stepping out, I rolled out over the threshold."[12]

Somewhere over the swollen Merderet, the planes carrying F Company, 508th, wandered around the sky, in an effort to avoid the thickening ground fire. Aboard one of them, Private Burns stood waiting for the order to jump. As he watched his comrades vomit on the floor or struggle to stay on their feet, he could only wonder, "Oh dear God, will any of us get out of this alive?"

The flak seemed to get heavier by the second, hitting the plane from all sides. "The noise is awesome: the roar of the engines, flak hitting the wings and fuselage and everyone yelling, 'Let's go!' I can see tracers sweeping by in a graceful slow motion arc. Flak is knocking holes in the wings and I pray that none comes up through the bottom of the ships where I'm standing."

At last, the order came to jump. Burns and the others readily complied. They were supposed to jump from 600 feet, but they descended from perhaps twice that height. Everything seemed to quiet down as Private Burns slowly descended to earth. "I land in a long narrow field with two anti-glider poles in it. I hit hard and roll over on my back, tangled in my shroud lines. I'm all alone. It's very quiet. I've landed on good solid ground." Frightened out of his wits but still functioning, Burns managed to rendezvous with several other comrades (mainly by passwords whispered in the night), and they set off in search of their objectives.[13]

In one way, Burns was lucky. He landed on dry ground. Many others in his division did not. A total of thirty-six soldiers from the 82nd drowned in the floodwaters of the Cotentin that night.[14] This was exactly what the Germans intended when they opened up the locks at Carentan at high tide and closed them at low tide in order to flood potential drop zones for paratroopers. Because grass began to grow through the water, American photo-intelligence analysts had misjudged the water's depth in the environs of the Merderet and the Douve. They thought the water was only ankle- or shin-high when in fact it was often much deeper, sometimes chest-high or even over the heads of the soldiers.

Lieutenant Ralph DeWeese, a platoon leader in H Company, 508th, came very close to being one of the many All-Americans who fell victim to these dark, murky floodwaters. He descended through thick enemy fire. "The flak and machine gun fire was so heavy I believe you could have walked down on it. Some men were hit and never had a chance to get out of their chutes. Others had their canopies on fire due to the fire of tracer bullets. Much to my surprise I looked down and all I could see was water."

DeWeese landed with a splash in chest-high water. His equipment and chute quickly dragged him below the waterline. He could not seem to keep his head above the water. "The chute dragged me for about three hundred yards. Several times I thought it was no use and decided to open my mouth and drown. Each time the wind would slack up and I'd get a chance to put my head up out of the water and catch a breath." This happened several times until finally Lieutenant DeWeese, barely alive at this point, summoned his last reserves of strength. "With the last bit of energy I had I reached down and pulled out my trench knife." He cut himself free of the parachute. "What a relief it was to get away from that chute. Bullets were singing over my head from machine guns and rifles, but it didn't bother me because at that point I didn't care." Shivering and gasping for air, the lieutenant rested for nearly two hours in the water. "I was still panting like a dog that had run for about ten miles."[15]

Hardly any of the 508th sticks landed within the confines of Drop Zone N. Private Ed Boccafogli's B Company got scattered in an orchard. When he saw the green light, Boccafogli did not really jump out of the plane. "I fell out. I slipped on vomit. Some guys were throwing up, from nerves, and as we pivoted out my feet went out from under me, and I went upside down. Then as I'm coming down I hear crackling through the air. Bullets were going through the parachute. I could hear crack-crack." When he landed he was "hung up on a tree about a foot off the ground." He quickly cut himself down from the tree and bolted for the cover of a nearby hedgerow.[16]

Like so many other paratroopers that night, Private Webster landed all alone in shallow water, far away from his drop zone, angry as could be at the Air Force for the whole debacle. "Lost and lonely, wrestling with the greatest fear of my life, I stood bewildered in the middle of a vast lake and looked for help." He shivered and began to cry. "A flare burst over the water several hundred yards away. I bowed my head and waited for . . . bullets to hit me like a baseball bat, but there were no bullets."

Relieved, Webster pulled himself together and tried to wade

out of the swamp. He was hoping to find Hébert, his unit's objective, but he had no luck. He could not help feeling a great sense of disgust. "Suddenly, the whole thing struck me as ludicrous: all the preparation and briefings, all the maps and sand tables, and for what? Why had they bothered? For all the good they did, the army might as well have yanked us out of a pub and dumped us off helter-skelter to find our own way to the Germans. Instead of a regiment of over fifteen hundred men carefully assembled on a well-defined drop zone, D-Day was one man alone in an old swamp that the Air Corps said didn't even exist. The angry clatter of a plan gone wrong filled the air."[17]

It is fair to say that thousands of other troopers felt the exact same way as Webster. Many of them blamed the Air Force for their predicament. In response to the flak, the pilots often took evasive action, negating the kind of jump conditions on which the paratroopers so heavily depended. Instead of jumping from the ideal height of 600 feet, from planes flying close to stall speed and in tight formations so that sticks could assemble quickly on the ground, the C-47 crews mostly dropped their troopers from low altitude, at great speeds, while carrying out evasive maneuvers. This meant that the paratroopers experienced a tremendous opening shock (from the speed of the planes) as their parachutes deployed or that they descended from too high into water or enemy guns. A few troopers even got carelessly dropped into the ocean, where they drowned. Some got dropped from way too low. Their chutes barely had time to open before they hit the ground. Private Burgett, after landing safely from 300 feet, swore that he saw another plane disgorge its troopers from an even lower altitude, with terrible consequences. "I saw vague, shadowy figures plunging downward. Their chutes were pulling out of their pack trays and just starting to unfurl when they hit the ground. They made a sound like large ripe pumpkins being thrown down to burst against the ground."

Burgett blamed the pilot of the C-47 for this tragedy. "That son of a bitch of a pilot," I swore to myself, "he's hedgehopping and killing a bunch of troopers just to save his own ass. I hope he gets shot down in the Channel and drowns real slow."[18]

Few paratroopers expressed sentiments so murderous against those who flew them into combat, but they did, in general, blame the Air Force for the busted night drop. This view has generally prevailed among D-Day historians, but perhaps it needs some revision.[19] It is certainly true that the C-47 pilots defied strict orders to avoid evasive maneuvers, but the aviators were given these instructions as a result of the planners' belief that German flak batteries in Normandy had largely been destroyed in the weeks leading up to D-Day. The intelligence officers who briefed the troop-carrier groups on the eve of D-Day sincerely believed that flak would not be an issue for their crews.

In other words, they expected a smooth, orderly drop with little opposition. Instead, the exact opposite happened. The flak and machine-gun fire arcing up from unseen positions all over Normandy proved to be accurate and devastating. In the face of that kind of deadly peril, could the fliers—mortal men after all—really have been expected to fly at low speed and low altitude in straight lines with no evasive maneuvers? They were flying very vulnerable aircraft. The C-47 was thin-skinned, slow, with no armor and no self-sealing fuel tanks. At the kind of altitude and speed necessary for an ideal drop, the C-47s made perfect targets for the thick enemy fire. The pilots of these planes did what any sane, mortal men would have done in their place. They tried to avoid suicidal danger. Flying in a straight line through such deadly flak was the aviation equivalent of paratroopers making a frontal attack on an entrenched machine-gun nest. To be sure, many of the pilots probably were thinking of their own safety first in taking evasive action. But, in all likelihood, many of them understood that their paratroopers would be just as dead if their plane blew up from flak as if the troopers were buffeted or scattered from a misdrop at undesirable altitudes and airspeed. In the desperation of the moment, they chose the better of two unpalatable options.

The ultimate cause of this fiasco was not the cowardice of transport pilots but intelligence and operational failures. Allied intelligence analysts chose to believe that they had destroyed German flak capacity in Normandy, a tragically erroneous assumption. As a result of that flawed assumption, they sent the vulnerable C-47s into enemy skies protected by fighter planes but no pre-drop bombardment of enemy positions. They did this in the hopes of achieving surprise for the paratroopers on their drop. The Germans were certainly confused as to the objective and character of the airborne drops, but the paratroopers did not yield enough significant dividends from surprise to validate the strategy. Once planes disgorged their troopers, enemy gunners were alerted to their presence and began shooting at them.

In retrospect, the airborne drop could have been better protected by more efficient use of strategic bombing forces in the hours leading up to the drop. If heavy bombers had preceded the airborne serials and dropped their ordnance on known flak or troop concentrations, they might have seriously reduced the amount of fire the C-47s took as they approached their drop zones, thus resulting in a smoother drop. But those planes could not be everywhere at once, and the planners earmarked most of them for use (ineffectively, as it turned out) against beach targets ahead of the amphibious forces. The failure to use some of those planes to suppress German flak at Normandy was the real root cause of the misdrop, not cowardice or errors on the part of transport pilots.

The gliders also experienced serious problems. Three hours after the paratroopers jumped from their embattled C-47s, the tow planes and gliders of the 434th Troop Carrier Group flew inexorably toward Landing Zone E near Hiesville. They were at 600 feet now, preparing for the final approach to this landing zone that the 101st Airborne's pathfinders had so competently marked. At the controls of *The Fighting Falcon No. 2*, the lead glider, Lieutenant Colonel Michael Murphy, a stunt flyer in his prewar life, scanned the ground for landmarks. Murphy, the senior American glider pilot in Europe, had deep misgivings about this entire mission, mainly because there had been so many major changes in so short a period of time. Initially, he and his men were ordered to fly into Normandy at first light, in British Horsas. He spent a considerable amount of time and effort training his people to fly in these unfamiliar wooden contraptions. Then, scarcely a week before D-Day, his orders changed. Now he and his men were to fly in Wacos at night. Frustrated and angry, Murphy protested this at a planning meeting of troop-carrier and airborne commanders that included General Montgomery. The tiny enclosed fields of Normandy would make for a very difficult target at night. Murphy expected a 50 percent loss of men and matériel. Montgomery was unmoved. He stood up, slapped the table, and exclaimed, "We'll have to suffer it!"

In addition to this, someone had recently welded armor plating to the cargo compartment floor to protect Murphy's high-ranking passenger, Brigadier General Don Pratt, the deputy division commander of the 101st Airborne. Neither Pratt nor Murphy knew anything about this until it was too late. *The Fighting Falcon No. 2* was carrying only Pratt, his aide, Murphy, his copilot, and Pratt's jeep, but the extra weight of the armor caused overload problems. "It was like trying to fly a freight train," Murphy later commented.

So the die was cast for Murphy and his aviators. Like so many other Americans on this night, they would simply have to make the best of a bad situation. Murphy kept alternating between keeping an eye on his tow plane and the ground, "The moon was shining down through scattered clouds and you could see the tree line and the shapes of the fields." All at once, German antiaircraft batteries opened up. Murphy was transfixed by the colorful spectacle of enemy firepower. "I remember watching the tracers making pretty patterns in the dark and thinking of fireworks. Occasionally a bullet would ricochet off the jeep or hit our wings."[20]

Not far off Murphy's right wing, Lieutenant Vic Warriner tried to hold his glider steady. He was carrying Captain Charles Van Gorder and Major Albert Crandall along with their medical team and supplies. Warriner noticed fire on the ground. "We could see several fires burning that we thought had been ignited by the pathfinder crews. Wrong! They were bonfires built by the Germans on top of flak towers to help them stay warm on a chilly night. We encountered heavy machine gun fire." The fire was mostly inaccurate, but at one point Warriner thought his glider had been hit. "The controls suddenly were very stiff and unresponsive." Not to worry. His copilot had mistakenly taken the controls. "He grinned sheepishly and let go of the wheel."

Approximately forty planes back in the formation, Lieutenant Irwin Morales fearfully watched the enemy tracers. "Jesus! The flak and tracers became so thick that I don't know how the hell we [got] through it."[21]

Others, like Flight Officer Pete Buckley, at the rear of the serial in Glider 50, had the same reaction. As he sat at the controls of his glider, he could feel the icy fingers of terror creeping up his spine. "It looked like fluid streams of tracer bullets and explosions in every direction. It seemed so thick that I could not see how it would be possible to get through it unscathed. One feels completely alone up there while every German in Europe zeros in on just you." Buckley pulled his arms in and his knees together. He wanted to make himself as small of a target as possible. He even squeezed the cheeks of his rear end as close together as possible: "I probably could have cracked walnuts from the pressure I was exerting."[22]

Still the planes flew on, dodging the flak the best they could. Captain Van Gorder was struck by the cool resolve his pilot, Lieutenant Warriner, seemed to show in the face of such deadly peril. "We held our course in the face of all this explosive activity, which I thought showed great bravery. At one time, a German 88mm gun fired almost straight up at us, just missing, but the blast sent our glider high in the air. Fortunately we were pulled back in line by the tow rope."

In the cramped compartment of a nearby glider, Lieutenant William Padrick, an artilleryman, peered through a window and saw the withering enemy fire. The whole spectacle looked like "beautiful, yet frightening orange balls of fire coming up through the air and arching off in a curve." He felt a keen sense of admiration for the C-47 pilots in the tow planes. "Always the fire was directed at the tow ship ahead, with its exhausts belching bright blue flames."[23]

They had now flown through this fire for about ten minutes, but it seemed like ten hours. They had spread out into two columns and descended to about four hundred feet. To everyone's immense relief, Lieutenant Colonel Murphy spotted the landing zone. He could see the green lights, in a T formation, that the pathfinders had placed in the landing zone. He could also see some prominent geographic features. "I spotted the railroad track that was only one-half mile from our field, so I said, 'So long' to the towplane and away we went." The inside of the glider was noisy with the sound of the wind, but Murphy could hear German machine guns. He lined his glider up on the landing zone. "The field ... was almost a thousand feet long but completely surrounded by fifty-foot trees. It looked easy because a fully loaded Waco can be stopped in two hundred feet."

It was anything but easy. In fact, for most of the glider men, the danger was just beginning. Very few, if any, had been hit by the ground fire. The trees, ditches, and hedgerows of the landing zone, combined with wet grass, proved to be the greatest peril. Murphy set his glider down on the marked field, but thanks to the wet grass, he could not get his craft to stop. "We slid for over eight hundred feet on the wet grass and smashed into trees at fifty miles an hour." The glider hit the trees with terrific force, emitting a sickening crunching sound as the frame crumpled; the crash actually shook the ground, too.

Roughly forty yards away, Lieutenant Warriner struggled to land his glider safely. "We actually brushed the tops of the trees as we went in. We touched down almost immediately, and I put the glider up on its skids and applied full brakes. Instead of slowing down, we were gaining speed. As we hurtled through a herd of terrorized dairy cattle, I could see . . . the end of the field coming fast. Luckily, we slowed up enough so the crash was only minimal." A poplar tree tore through the cockpit, right between Warriner and his copilot, but only left a few scratches on Warriner.

When Flight Officer Buckley received the signal to cut loose (a green light shining in the astrodome of the tow plane), every fiber of his being wanted to stay put. "I'm sure I wasn't the only one who felt this way on that night. It was dark; everything but the kitchen sink was coming up at us from the Germans below, and that tow rope . . . was my umbilical cord." Buckley wanted to stay fastened to his tow plane, go back to England and safety, but he knew he couldn't. He released the tow rope, executed a 360-degree turn, and made his way through the darkness, at close to stalling speed. The first few gliders had wiped out the T lights when they landed, so Buckley could not find the landing zone. "I knew the ground was down there, but I couldn't see it. And all the time, the flak and tracers are still coming up." Out of the corner of his eye, he spotted a field. "With a prayer on my lips, and a very tight pucker string, I straightened out my glide path and headed in." He landed smoothly and thought he was out of danger until suddenly "there was a tremendous, bone-jarring crash, accompanied by loud splintering and tearing noises." The glider had hit a deep ditch, probably dug by the Germans. "The floor split open and we skidded to a halt in a field on the other side. For a split second, we sat in stunned silence."

Buckley and the others breathed a sigh of relief. No one was hurt. They spent half an hour digging the glider's nose out of the mud, so that they could extract the 57mm gun they were carrying. When they finished, a German flare went off, lighting up the whole area. Only now did Buckley's group see that they had landed right next to the glider that carried the jeep to transport their antitank gun.

Perilous but fortunate landings were common. T/5 Johnny

Walker, a signalman riding in a glider near Buckley's, also had a close call. "Our glider brushed a tree top and slipped sharply into a small field. I held my breath and waited for the impending crash. As the pilot applied the brakes, the tail section rose sharply threatening to slip over. Gradually, it settled down as the glider came to a halt." Walker, like most of the other men of the Chicago mission, emerged unscathed.

Murphy's group probably suffered the worst fate. When their Waco smashed into the tree, the force of the crash sent General Pratt's jeep careening forward. Pratt was sitting on a parachute (just in case the armor plating did not provide enough protection) in the front seat of the jeep. Pratt was not a tall man, but since he was sitting on the parachute, his head caught one of the upper girders, breaking his neck, killing him instantly. At the same time, the jeep rammed forward and crushed the copilot.

Captain Van Gorder, safely evacuated from Warriner's glider, could sense that Murphy and the others had to be in bad shape. Van Gorder saw German tanks on the other side of a hedgerow, but the presence of the enemy did not deter him from rushing to Murphy's glider. The general's aide, Lieutenant John L. May, had somehow emerged from the crash uninjured. He had set up a security detachment of troopers around the glider but had not gone in. Van Gorder found Murphy lying a short distance from the glider, and the colonel was in bad shape. Murphy would have been crushed by the jeep, like his copilot, except that he had been thrown sideways, partially out the window. "My body up to the belt was outside the glider with my legs still tangled in the twisted steel tubing," Murphy recalled. "When I let myself down to the ground, I just fell because my legs were broken." Van Gorder examined him and saw that he had compound fractures of the femur in both legs. At first, the doctor doubted he would survive, but somehow he managed to stabilize him and Murphy lived.

A few minutes later, Van Gorder investigated the glider to make sure Pratt and the copilot were dead. "I found the General sitting in the front seat of his jeep with his head bent forward on his chest and no pulse. The co-pilot registered no pulse either. He had taken the brunt of the force in his position." Pratt was the first general, on either side, to die in the Battle of Normandy.[24]

A few of the gliders went way off-course, landing far behind German lines. One of them was piloted by Lieutenant Morales, who had made the solemn pact with his copilot, Lieutenant Ahmad. They ended up in a swamp seven miles south of Carentan. Morales, Ahmad, and their glider soldiers hooked up with an isolated band of paratroopers and fought a hopeless battle against superior forces. During the fight, Morales and Ahmad got separated. The last time Morales saw his friend, he was manning a position with several paratroopers. Morales was able to find a boat and paddle it through the swamps around Carentan until he found friendly forces. Ahmad was never seen again, but Morales found his grave near Carentan after the war. Morales could never bring himself to visit Ahmad's parents.[25]

A glider piloted by Flight Officer Alfred Sapa also landed near Carentan, in a water-filled ditch that the Germans had probably dug to snare gliders. The landing was a bit rough, but no one was hurt. Sapa and the others got out of the glider and started to move as far away from it as possible. "We crossed the ditch and came to a stop about 150–200 feet from the ditch. We received a lot of small [-arms] fire. German soldiers were dug in on one side of the ditch. We came to a stop on the other side. Many were killed by rifle and mortar fire. My copilot was wounded pretty badly. I, too, was wounded, but could navigate. We fought off the Germans until we were [overrun] by them and what was left of [us] was taken prisoner." They moved him to St-Lô, then to Alençon, and eventually to Germany, where he spent the rest of the war.[26]

In all, only six gliders of the Chicago mission landed in the proper area (Landing Zone E where Murphy and Warriner set down). Most of the others landed in various fields within a half-mile of Landing Zone E. They suffered twenty nine casualties but provided six antitank guns, along with much-needed vehicles and communications equipment, to the 101st Airborne Division by late morning on D-Day.[27]

Approximately one hour behind the Chicago mission, the serial carrying the 82nd Airborne's glider reinforcements (code-named the Detroit mission) made landfall on the western coast of the Cotentin. This serial consisted of fifty-two Wacos and their tow planes. The Wacos carried sixteen antitank guns, twenty-two jeeps, and ten tons of supplies. They were supposed to land just northwest of Ste-Mère-Eglise in the drop zone of the 505th Parachute Infantry. However, cloud cover, along with enemy fire, dispersed the formation into individual groups of planes, clinging together, with pilots frantically searching for drop zones in the murky grayness below. Most of the gliders cut loose over the wrong place. Some disappeared forever. The majority ended up scattered anywhere from the Merderet River to the environs of Ste-Mère-Eglise.

All semblance of order disappeared. What had once been a cohesive formation degenerated into an aerial mob of tow planes searching the clouds for an opening. In one of those planes, Second Lieutenant Richard Denison, a navigator in the 437th Troop Carrier Group, saw his pilot flash the green astrodome light "back to the glider pilot, telling him that he was to cut off. Our pilot... chose not to do so. And from what we could see below us, I would certainly not blame him for not wanting to cut off; the flak was coming up. For every tracer that came by, we knew that there was a large bunch of bullets, shells going by, that we did not see."

Denison's C-47 pilot made a 360-degree turn, at low speed, low altitude, and approached the same area again. Denison knew that time was running out. The glider had to cast free. "This time, he had no choice, for if he did not cut off from the tow plane, we would disconnect him from [it]. The glider pilot simply knew he had no choice. He cut off. This was in the vicinity of Ste-Mère-Eglise." Denison's crew had no time to watch their glider descend. The pilot increased their speed to 220 miles per hour, descended to the deck, and zoomed for the Channel. "A tree loomed up ahead of us, and I yelled so loud, 'Watch out for the tree!' that I was hoarse all the way back to England."[28]

Flight Officer John Lang, a glider pilot in the 437th, cast free of his tow plane somewhere over the Carentan–Cherbourg railroad, just east of the Merderet. His glider was carrying white phosphorous shells, along with his copilot and six infantrymen. Lang glided as slowly as he could until he saw a field that he figured was about six hundred feet long. He could see trees around the field and a ditch fencerow bordering one side. He just did make it over the trees and set the aircraft down "slow enough so that I didn't have to put the glider on a skid and [we] coasted to the ditch fence row on the other side of the field." He and the other men unloaded their cargo and eventually met up with a group of 82nd Airborne troopers.

Vic Allegretti was part of a 57mm gun crew. As his glider cut loose, all was quiet for a moment. Then he and his buddies heard ground fire and whooshing wind. "We were all quiet and sweating. We just missed a large bridge over the Merderet River [probably La Fière]. The pilot did his very best as he made a complete circle to slow down and land wherever he could. There was no such thing as the right place." They landed fairly softly. "When daybreak came . . . we could see we had been very lucky. The next field over was . . . mined. Germans were all around us, but none of us were injured. We took the gun and jeep out immediately up at a crossroads. Around us lay a lot of dead cows, very smelly, plenty of mortar and machine gun fire. Also there were some bodies of paratroopers and glidermen who crashed into trees and hedgerows. The medics were very busy."

In the 82nd Airborne's Detroit mission on D-Day morning, twenty-two of the gliders were destroyed (mostly by hedgerows, swamps, or trees, not ground fire). Only a dozen did not suffer some sort of significant damage. Three men were killed and twenty-three wounded. Half the jeeps were destroyed or could not be extracted from wrecked, swamped gliders. Eight of the antitank guns survived to influence the fighting along the Merderet and in the Ste-Mère-Eglise area. The glider landings were, to be sure, a dangerous fiasco, but they helped provide the lightly armed paratroopers with some measure of fire support, mobility, and resupply on a day when they would badly need it.[29]

CHAPTER NINE

THE CUTTING EDGE OF COURAGE: THE ALL-AMERICANS AND SCREAMING EAGLES ON D-DAY

Ste-Mère-Eglise was one of the most important objectives for U.S. paratroopers on D-Day. The quaint crossroads town had to be taken in order to prevent German reinforcements from getting to Utah beach. The 3rd Battalion of the 505th Parachute Infantry drew the assignment of taking the town, but as it turned out, a diverse mixture of troopers—some of them even from the 101st Airborne—fought to capture the town.[1] An understrength company of German service troops garrisoned Ste-Mère-Eglise. Some of these soldiers, and many of the town's residents, had been awakened by the sound of antiaircraft fire to the north and south of town. A tracer round strayed into a building located in the town square immediately opposite the town's main feature—a church that dated back to the eleventh century. The tracer cooked off hay inside the building (owned by Madame Julin Pommier) and the whole structure caught fire. The mayor of Ste-Mère-Eglise, Alexandre Renaud, along with several German soldiers, supervised a bucket brigade to put the fire out.

At 0115, they were concentrating on putting out the fire, even as German tracers continued to light up the skies, when the first American paratroopers began to drop right into the town. Overhead, in one of the planes, Private Ken Russell, a seventeen-year-old native of Maryville, Tennessee, stood waiting to jump. The young private saw tracers whip past his plane. Russell was a replacement soldier whose youth precluded him from understanding the full magnitude of what he was about to experience. A few days earlier, he had battled a fever that threatened to keep him from participating in this jump. He had lobbied fiercely for inclusion.

He had looked forward to the invasion of Europe for better than four years now. He could not stand the idea of missing it. On the flight over tonight, he realized that if he had not dropped out of school to join the Army, he would be graduating with his high school class right at this very moment.

Instead of striding across a stage to accept a diploma, he jumped into the fiery maelstrom above Ste-Mère-Eglise. His parachute opened with callous, spine-straightening shock. Russell looked down. "Oh Lord, they are jumping us into hell," he thought. Below him, he could see the fire fiercely burning in the town. The fire lit up the whole night sky around him, as did German bullets. "I knew we were in trouble, and it was so horrifying." All of a sudden, Russell heard an explosion nearby. A German bullet scored a direct hit on a trooper, detonating his gammon grenade. "He just exploded. There was nothing but a chute. He was blown away. I have never seen anything like that and hope I never see anything like it again."

Seconds later, he saw something even worse. One of his buddies let out an anguished scream. Russell's eyes bulged as he watched the trooper descend into the burning building. "He cried once and then was gone." Flames voraciously consumed the unfortunate trooper. Now Russell could feel himself getting pulled toward the fire. "The heat drew the nylon chutes toward the fire, and the air to feed the fire was actually drawing us into it. I had to work my risers hard to keep from going in, too." Three other members of his stick (Privates H. T. Bryant and Ladislaw Tlapa and Lieutenant Harold Cadish) got hung up on telephone poles and machine-gunned: "It was like they were crucified there."

Private Russell successfully avoided the burning building, but he felt a bullet crease his hand. Seconds later, he landed on the roof of the church. His suspension lines caught on a promontory and snared him. Russell hung helplessly from the roof. Approximately thirty feet above him, another 505th trooper, Private John Steele, of *Longest Day* fame, hung perilously from the steeple.

Immediately below him Russell saw a deadly struggle unfold. Another man in his stick, Sergeant John Ray, landed in the square, directly beneath Russell and Steele. Ray's feet had barely touched the ground when a redheaded German soldier ran up to him and shot the sergeant in the stomach. Ray grunted and went down. In a horrifying instant, the German soldier turned away from Ray and looked upward, right at Russell. Terror shot through the young

Tennesseean. Caught on this damnable promontory, he was a helpless target. Just as the German began to raise his rifle, Russell heard a single pistol shot. The back of the German soldier's head exploded. Ray, in his dying moments, had unsheathed his .45 revolver and shot the enemy soldier dead. "There is no doubt in my mind he saved my life that night," Russell asserted.

Russell cut himself free, plunged about twenty feet to the square (breaking two ribs and wrenching his back), and ran for cover as bullets ricocheted around him. He could hear the chattering sound of a German flak battery somewhere close by. Running like a madman, he found the battery just south of town. He yanked a grenade from his harness, pulled the pin, flipped the spoon, and heaved the grenade into the darkness. "I covered my ears. I knew what would happen." The grenade exploded. "It jarred the ground a good distance away. The Germans didn't have time to pick it up and throw it back to me. They were too interested in shooting paratroopers."[2]

Machine gunner Ray Aeibischer's F Company, 506th Parachute Infantry, stick got misdropped in Ste-Mère-Eglise. This was miles away from the intended drop zone. Private Aeibischer's opening shock was so sharp that most all of his equipment, stored in one of the infamous leg bags, plummeted to earth, never to be seen again. He landed "with a thud" in the square near the church. He now had only a trench knife and a canteen with which to defend himself. The church bells were ringing loudly, but he could hear machine-gun fire coming from across the square. He tried to take refuge in the church but found the doors locked. Using a high cement wall behind the church as cover, he crawled around in search of other Americans. Along the way, he saw Ray's body.

Now, in the moonlight, Aeibischer saw what looked to be an American. "I could see the silhouette of his shoulders, and the familiar outline of his helmet. Without making a sound, I crawled to within three or four feet of this man. I first tried the cricket which each man had been issued to use in lieu of password or identification. The cricket I had didn't work, apparently broken or mashed, so I whispered the password, my knife in hand, ready to plunge into this person's body. He quickly turned around, facing me . . . bringing his rifle into firing position." Luckily, the man restrained from firing and gave the correct reply. "For this we were both much relieved."[3]

Another misdropped Screaming Eagle, Sergeant Carwood Lipton, E Company, 506th, landed heavily in somebody's walled-in backyard. Like Aeibischer, Lipton had lost his leg pack, containing his tommy gun, ammo, rations, and antitank mines. He took a few moments to regroup. He could see and hear planes roaring overhead, but they did not seem to follow any particular pattern. No one stirred in the backyard where he stood, nor in its adjacent house. "I was quite calm and I very deliberately unbuckled my chest strap and loosened my belly band and the leg straps and stood up and took stock of where I was."

Armed with only a trench knife, grenades, and several blocks of TNT, he skulked around the town, trying to find out where he was. Light from the fire reflected off the clouds, creating some residual illumination. Sergeant Lipton used that light to read a road sign that said: STE-MERE-EGLISE. He later fell into an abandoned German antiaircraft position before linking up with members of his unit and a few 82nd Airborne troopers.[4]

Lipton was fortunate to land in a quiet section of town. Many of the 505th troopers like R. R. Hughart, the veteran who wondered if this would be his final combat jump, landed right in the middle of the town, where the fighting was fiercest. Hughart was floating to the ground, right in the middle of Ste-Mère-Eglise, when an equipment bundle, full of antitank mines, exploded immediately beneath him. The explosion blew him sideways. "I landed on the side of a large pile of dirt in someone's backyard and busted my left ankle." He could do little else but try to lay low.[5]

Private James Eads landed squarely in a manure pile—a smelly but soft landing. A few streets away he could see the reflection of the burning building and hear shooting and yelling. He was snickering softly at his manure landing when he saw movement to his right front. "Three men in a line about ten feet apart came running towards me, the first one about a hundred feet away." He could see that these three men were Germans. "Oh hell—out of the frying pan, into a latrine, now this," he thought. His tommy gun was still strapped to his chest, so he reached for his .45, strapped more accessibly to his right thigh. "I thumbed back the hammer and started firing. The third man fell right at my feet. I heaved a huge sigh of relief and tried . . . to get up."

As he did so, a German machine gun opened up on him from about seventy-five yards away. "I could hear the rounds buzzing and snapping . . . into ground all around me." He dived for cover and began to fiddle with his tommy gun. He heard a loud *boom!* Now he could still hear shooting and yelling, but the machine gun had stopped firing. "A trooper whom I didn't know crawled up, and I could have kissed him for just being one of us. His first words were, 'I got those over-anxious Kraut machine gunners with a grenade, but it blew off my helmet and I can't find it.' " A sour look crossed the other trooper's face. "Holy Cow—you stink!"[6]

The shooting soon died down in Ste-Mère-Eglise. Eads, his newfound friend, and dozens of other airborne troopers hovered around the fringes of town, looking for landmarks, trying to find their units, or waiting for orders. In the meantime, the fire was extinguished and the remnants of the German garrison, incomprehensibly, went back to bed.

For their laziness some of them earned eternal slumber. A dire threat to their mortality was crystallizing just outside of town. In the meadows around Ste-Mère-Eglise, Lieutenant Colonel Edward Krause, commander of the 3rd Battalion, 505th, succeeded in organizing the equivalent of two companies of his soldiers by 0400. Guided by a drunken but friendly Frenchman, this stealthy force infiltrated unhindered into the town just before dawn. Krause ordered some of his men to break off and set up roadblocks along the six approaches to the town. The rest filtered right down the town's main street. "We moved quickly, filing past the darkened houses that lined the street," Sergeant Ronald Snyder of G Company recalled. Here and there small groups searched the building, rousing the snoring Germans. They killed eleven enemy and captured thirty others.

Private Howard Melvin of I Company wandered into a German motor park adjacent to the church. There he saw some of the remnants of the brief but violent battle that had been fought there a few hours before. He saw dead American paratroopers (who he believed were from the 101st) dangling from the trees. "There were about four or five. This other trooper . . . and I . . . came around the church and stopped short because we saw a dead German laying right by the door." This was probably the redheaded German whom Sergeant Ray killed.

Private John Fitzgerald, a 502nd Parachute Infantry trooper who arrived in town around the same time with a mixed group of troopers, never forgot the sight of a dead 82nd Airborne trooper. "He had occupied a German foxhole and made it his personal

Alamo. In a half circle around the hole lay the bodies of nine German soldiers. His ammunition bandoleers were still on his shoulders, but empty of all the M-1 clips. Cartridge cases littered the ground. His rifle stock was broken in two, its splinters adding to the debris." Fitzgerald looked at his dog tags. "The name read Martin V. Hersh. I wrote the name down in a small prayer book I carried." Fitzgerald, an Irish Catholic kid from New York, hoped to someday meet someone who knew the valiant Hersh. "I never did."[7]

Private Hughart, who had managed to hobble into the town for medical care, watched as soldiers retrieved the body of the man whom Private Russell had seen land in the burning building during the night. Hughart watched soldiers go into the still smoldering, ruined building and remove "what was left of him, on a long plank. He was burnt up so bad that he broke in two."[8]

By the time the sun rose, Ste-Mère-Eglise was firmly in American hands. Thanks to the addition of elements of Lieutenant Colonel Benjamin Vandervoort's 2nd Battalion, Colonel Krause now had a force of some three hundred soldiers holding the town. In addition, he had cut the main communications link between Cherbourg and Caen, along with the N-13, the only major road between those two largest of all Norman towns.

The question now was whether the Americans could hold the town against the inevitable German counterattacks. Krause and Vandervoort deployed most of their troops at or near roadblocks at the edges of town. Two companies, E and I, acted as a mobile reserve. Vandervoort before arriving in Ste-Mère-Eglise had originally set out for Neuville-au-Plain, a small hamlet one mile north of Ste-Mère-Eglise, before joining Krause. On a hunch, Vandervoort (confined to a glider-delivered jeep now because of a broken ankle suffered on the drop) detached one platoon from his D Company and sent it north to defend Neuville-au-Plain. Events would prove this decision to be fortuitous.

The first enemy attack came at 0930, at the southern edge of Ste-Mère-Eglise. The Germans preceded their attack with preparatory machine-gun and mortar fire. Two companies of infantry, supported by three light tanks and two self-propelled guns, drove north against the roadblocks (consisting of antitank mines and dug-in soldiers) Krause had emplaced.

On the N-13, the lead scouts of this enemy force drove cattle ahead of them for cover. In an outpost position near the road, Private Dominick de Tullio took in the whole bizarre scene. He leaped from his hole and guided the cattle into a field by waving his field jacket. Even as he herded the cattle, de Tullio pitched a grenade at the Germans, killing one, wounding another, and stampeding the remaining cattle.

At the edge of town, Lieutenant Colonel Krause watched all this and noticed German soldiers fanning out beyond the road, in an effort to flank de Tullio's position and infiltrate the town. Krause immediately ordered reinforcements to deploy in the buildings between roadblocks. These Americans opened fire on the Germans, hitting a few, and the German attack began to stall. The enemy was now content to trade shots from a distance. For his trouble Krause took some mortar fragments in his lower right leg.

The enemy attack had been stopped, but the withering accurate enemy mortar fire continued. The rounds screamed in mercilessly, sending fragments and shards of masonry flying in every direction. An American 81mm mortar team under Lieutenant William Wilson tried to respond in kind, but they could not locate the German positions. The Frenchman had told Lieutenant Colonel Krause that the Germans had an entire battalion camped south of town. Krause knew that he had just seen part of that battalion during the attack. A little more than a mile south of Ste-Mère-Eglise, a slight rise overlooked the road. The Americans called this rise Hill 20. The many hedgerows and trees between Krause's position and Hill 20 prevented him from seeing enemy positions on Hill 20, but his instincts told him that the German mortars had to be there. When he saw several enemy trucks moving in the direction of the hill, he decided that the enemy mortars were certainly there. He ordered I Company, about ninety men strong, to swing wide right of the road, double back, and take the hill.

The commander of this unit, Captain Harold Swingler, assembled his troops and led them along the dizzying span of hedgerows and miniridges just west of town. With Swingler accompanying the point element, the company, in staggered rows of alert, taut soldiers, zigzagged from cover to cover. "It cost time," one officer recalled. "Worse yet, we lost sense of distance and direction. Almost two hours after the start, we were back . . . next to the main road one mile south of town. That was far short of the goal. We discovered too late that we were approaching on a line which put us directly in front of the mortars we were supposed to be out-flanking. It was like a kick in the groin."[9]

All at once, the enemy mortars zeroed in on them. To make matters worse, German machine gunners and riflemen unleashed a deadly volley of fire from somewhere in the right rear. Bullets tore through Captain Swingler's body, killing him instantly. Several other men went down. The I Company troopers dived for the cover of ditches and embankments. One of the pinned-down troopers, Sergeant Bill Dunfee, could not understand why his captain had placed himself with the point troops, in a terribly vulnerable position. "For some reason, he was out with the point, where he shouldn't have been. I believe that he didn't think there were any Germans between us and Fauville [another name for the position on Hill 20]." The company remained pinned down for about an hour. Sergeant Dunfee maintained that the officers were arguing over who should now assume command: "My understanding is that the ranking platoon leader didn't want to take over. So another one did."[10]

Under scattered enemy fire, the company eventually withdrew back to Ste-Mère-Eglise. At times, the German fire intensified, as Private Bill Tucker, a machine gunner, found out. "The musette bag on my back stuck above the drainage ditch on the side of the road. Jesus, there were bullets going through it. So we got by this hole . . . and the damn machine-gun receiver fell in. I couldn't get it out. The guy behind me was screaming, 'Get moving or I'm dead!' So I had to leave it there."[11]

Only one good thing came out of this ill-fated attack: It helped convince the Germans that Hill 20 was indefensible, because they believed the Americans were present in great strength in Ste-Mère-Eglise. The German battalion eventually left its positions and slipped west to the Merderet.

Immediately to the north of Neuville-au-Plain, Lieutenant Turnbull and forty other American soldiers waited for any sign of the enemy. When they were sure he was out of earshot, Turnbull's men affectionately called him Chief because of his Cherokee heritage. These soldiers of D Company, 505th, were deployed behind hedgerows in orchards and oat fields on either side of the N-13. They were the extreme northern outpost for the American forces holding Ste-Mère-Eglise, roughly a mile and a half to the south.

At around 1300 they saw two long columns of men walking

down N-13, approaching from the north. Turnbull and his men studied them carefully but could not tell if they were friend or foe. Just then, Vandervoort arrived in his jeep, towing a 57mm antitank gun. As several soldiers deployed the gun in an ideal position along an intersection, Vandervoort, Turnbull, and the others continued to watch the approaching column. They saw what appeared to be GIs waving an orange flag, a recognition signal used by Americans at this point in the Normandy campaign. Just then, a Frenchman on a bicycle pedaled up to them and told them in English that American paratroopers were bringing in a group of German POWs. Vandervoort wanted to believe him but grew suspicious when he noticed two tracked vehicles at the end of the column. He knew that no American tracked vehicles could be coming from that direction.

A few more moments passed during which the colonel grew even more skeptical. He ordered Turnbull's machine gunners to fire a burst in the direction of the column. Immediately the "POWs" scrambled into ditches and returned fire. The collaborationist Frenchman rode away furiously before anyone could catch him. The battle was on. Mortar fire began to fall on Turnbull's positions. The two tracked vehicles, self-propelled guns, as it turned out, slowly advanced under cover of smoke canisters. They were only 500 yards away. One of them fired. The round blew up among a bazooka team Turnbull had deployed in a building at the northern edge of Neuville-au-Plain. These men were shredded, killed instantly. Another round singed the antitank gun, driving the crew to the safety of nearby buildings. Vandervoort hollered at them to get back on their gun. They obeyed, fired at one of the SPs, and blew it up.

The victory was short-lived, though. The enemy column consisted of nearly 200 soldiers from the well-trained 91st Airlanding Division. Under cover of intense mortar fire that kept Turnbull's people hugging their hedgerows, the Germans began to fan out along both flanks. Slowly they worked their way close to the American positions. Mortar shells kept exploding among the Americans, inflicting casualties, mainly shrapnel wounds to the extremities.

Seeing that Turnbull's platoon was greatly outnumbered and in deep trouble, Vandervoort hobbled back to his jeep and went back to Ste-Mère-Eglise to send help to the embattled D Company survivors. Meanwhile, Turnbull's men fought on for several hours. Near 1600, they began taking sniper fire from buildings in

Neuville. One of the men turned to look at the houses and, in so doing, was shot and killed. When the fire slackened enough for quick glimpses beyond the hedgerows, the Americans could see German infantrymen crawling in ditches on their flanks, only sixty yards away. The lieutenant was down to twenty-three effectives now.

Sensing that soon his men would be surrounded, he knew the situation was becoming more desperate by the minute. For a brief moment he contemplated charging the enemy soldiers, but one of his men, Private Julius Sebastain, talked him out of it: "We're not quite cut off yet. There's a chance we can get out. And that's what we ought to do."

Lieutenant Turnbull looked at the rest of his men. "Tell me what you want to do."

They agreed with Sebastain.

"We'll have to leave the wounded," Turnbull said.

His medic, Corporal James Kelly, grimly said, "I'll stay here with the wounded and surrender them if I can keep from getting killed."

Turnbull nodded. Three other men, Sergeant Robert Niland, Corporal Ray Smithson, and Sebastain, offered to cover the withdrawal. "I talked you into this withdrawal," Sebastain said bravely, "so I stay here and cover Kelly and the others with my BAR." The lieutenant agreed. The bravery of these men was astounding. He only hoped that somehow, someway, they would survive this mess.

"For Christ's sake, let's go!" someone screamed.

They rose as one, sixteen men in all, and rushed methodically, deliberately, out of Neuville and all the way to Ste-Mère-Eglise. The Germans captured all but one of those who had been left behind. The other man, Sergeant Niland, was killed by German small-arms fire as he rushed from one position to another. He fell dead, right on top of Kelly the medic. Kelly spent one night as a POW, while the wounded were evacuated to a German hospital in Cherbourg. American soldiers liberated them one month later when they captured the town. Niland's death, along with the concurrent deaths of two of his brothers (one of whom turned out to be alive but in Japanese captivity), served as the inspiration for the film *Saving Private Ryan*. The "only" surviving brother, Fritz, was a member of the 501st Parachute Infantry. He made it through

Lieutenant Thomas Ahmad bidding farewell to a friend just minutes before taking off on D-Day eve. Ahmad's glider crashed somewhere near Carentan, and he was killed while fighting with an isolated group of paratroopers. *Courtesy of Diana Ahmad*

General Dwight D. Eisenhower, shown here in one of the war's most famous photos, visiting troops from the 502d Parachute Infantry Regiment, 101st Airborne Division, at Greenham Common on June 5, 1944, the eve of D-Day. In the foreground (with the "23" placard around his neck) is Lieutenant Wallace Strobel. The number indicates that Strobel was his plane's jump master.

General Dwight D. Eisenhower, Supreme
Allied Commander, at headquarters for the
European theater of operations, February
1, 1945. He was wearing the five-star cluster of the newly created rank of General of
the Army.

Field Marshal Erwin Rommel. He strongly believed Germany's only chance of victory was to stop
the Allies at the waterline.

American generals, 1945. *Seated (left to right):* William H. Simpson, George S. Patton, Jr., Carl Spaatz, Dwight D. Eisenhower, Omar Bradley, Courtney H. Hodges, and Leonard T. Gerow. *Standing (left to right):* Ralph F. Stearley, Hoyt S. Vanderberg, Walter Bedell Smith, Otto P. Weyland, and Richard E. Nugent.

Two American paratroopers making their final preparations before take-off on June 5, 1944. Most paratroopers jumped with 70–100 pounds of equipment strapped to their bodies.

On the evening of June 5, 1944, General Eisenhower visited paratroopers of the 101st Airborne Division before they took off for Normandy.

Medium bombers of the 9th Air Force struck Pointe-du-Hoc on June 4, 1944—the beginning of two days of intensive bombardment and naval shelling leading up to the D-Day assault. *U.S. Air Force / National Archives and Records Administration*

A B-26 Marauder flying above Utah Beach on D-Day morning. Medium bombers like this one did significant damage to German defenses.

The face of the enemy. This German soldier is well armed with a *panzerfaust*, several grenades, and a rifle.

A B-24 Liberator on a bombing mission above the Plain of Caen.

One of the guns that First Sergeant Len Lomell and Staff Sergeant Jack Kuhn discovered a mile inland from Pointe-du-Hoc.

Smoke streaming from a landing craft hit by machine-gun fire as it was approaching Omaha Beach, D-Day. *U.S. Coast Guard / National Archives and Records Administration*

A soaked first-wave boat team, probably from the 1st Division, approaching Omaha Beach. Their lieutenant, standing by the ramp, with a vertical mark on his helmet, peeked at what might lie ahead.

The USS *Arkansas* opening fire on the coast of Normandy.

Landing craft heading for Easy Red sector, Omaha Beach.

Landing virtually unopposed, men of the U.S. 4th Division wading ashore at Victor sector.

The 4th Division gained a foothold on Utah Beach. Amphibious "DD" tanks were lined up at the water's edge. *U.S. War Department / National Archives and Records Administration*

American soldiers landing on the coast of France under heavy Nazi machine-gun fire, shown just as they left the ramp of a Coast Guard landing boat.

Crossed rifles in the sand were a comrade's tribute to this American soldier who sprang ashore from a landing barge and died at the barricades of Western Europe.

An American soldier lying dead on the sands of Utah Beach. Behind him, his comrades pushed inland.

An injured soldier seeking refuge at the foot of the bluff of Omaha Beach.

A headquarters area at Uncle Red sector. More and more men, equipment, and supplies were landing from the ships and craft such as those shown at low tide in the background. *U.S. Signal Corps / National Archives and Records Administration*

Graves registration teams identified and buried the dead at Omaha Beach.

A landing craft crowded with wounded soldiers. The medics saved hundreds of lives on D-Day.

GIs from the 4th Division, supported by a Sherman from the 70th Tank Battalion, advancing along a marshy causeway near Utah Beach. Control of the causeways was the key to success of the American landing at Utah.

Paratroopers attempting to flush out a sniper hiding in the church tower in Ste-Mère-Eglise. This is very close to where Private Ken Russell had his near-fatal encounter with a red-headed German soldier.

Local Cotentin farmers meeting paratroopers from the 101st Airborne Division.

German prisoners at Utah Beach, June 6, 1944.

A Sherman tank made from inflatable rubber. "Tanks" like this one were a major component of the Fortitude deception effort.

A Horsa glider lying flipped onto its back at landing zone "C," where it had attempted to land in support of 101st Airborne Division paratroopers on the evening of D-Day. Some of the many troops killed in the crash are laid out in the grass. *U.S. Signal Corps / National Archives and Records Administration*

A pockmarked bunker that was repeatedly hit by shells from the bombardment fleet.

Another look at the partial, bombardment-induced collapse of the cliffs of Pointe-du-Hoc.

Colonel James Rudder's headquarters on the edge of the cliff. Note the German POWs in the background.

In the town square of Ste-Marie-du-Mont, paratroopers of the 101st Airborne Division enjoying a lighthearted moment during the uncertain early hours of D-Day. *U.S. Signal Corps / National Archives and Records Administration*

A group of paratroopers in the French village of St-Marcouf near Utah Beach, June 8, 1944. *U.S. Army Military History Institute*

Louis Lisko at Pointe-du-Hoc after the June 6 invasion. *U.S. Army Military History Institute*

Norman D. Cota. *U.S. Army Military History Institute*

Matthew B. Ridgway. *U.S. Army Military History Institute*

Charles H. Gerhardt. *U.S. Army Military History Institute*

James M. Gavin. *U.S. Army Military History Institute*

Clarence Huebner. *U.S. Army Military History Institute*

Maxwell D. Taylor. *U.S. Army Military History Institute*

J. Lawton (Lightnin' Joe) Collins. *U.S. Army Military History Institute*

Russell P. Reeder *(right)*. *U.S. Army Military History Institute*

4th Infantry Division, 8th U.S. Infantry. *U.S. Army Military History Institute*

the Battle of Normandy and was later sent home, despite his protests.

Turnbull's men escaped, in part, because of a group of helpers they never saw. The E Company relief force Vandervoort sent to Neuville arrived at about the exact moment when Turnbull's forces were retreating. Incredibly, the two groups of Americans did not initially see each other. Sergeant Otis Sampson, a mortar squad leader who had seen extensive action in Italy, helped drop withering mortar fire on the advancing German soldiers. This kept them at bay as Turnbull's soldiers escaped. Sergeant Sampson had no love for the Germans. When he could, he liked to sneak up close to them and blister them with .45-caliber Thompson fire. "I liked to see exactly who I was shooting at and to let them see me. It was like a contest, to prove I was better than the Krauts. They pissed me off with their talk about the Master Race."

On this day, Sampson had to be satisfied to kill from a distance. Riflemen and BAR men laid down a strong base of fire while Sampson and another soldier repeatedly fired and displaced their 60mm mortar. "Just over the hill, the Jerries were crossing the lane one at a time, on the run. I timed the interval and when I thought another would cross over, the tube was fed a round. As planned, when Jerry was in the center of the lane, the shell hit, right to the fraction of a second." Sergeant Sampson could see Germans getting hit, but he did not know how much damage he was inflicting. "So far we had not lost a man. The fight had been short and heavy."

Sampson's mortar, along with effective small-arms fire, blunted the momentum of the German advance. The E Company soldiers broke off contact and headed for Ste-Mère-Eglise. Soon they made contact with Turnbull's retreating force. "I brought up the rear with Lieutenant Turnbull and we talked. He was strong . . . well liked."

Behind them they could hear the sound of guttural voices. The Germans were yelling at them, taunting them. "It reminded me of an unfinished ballgame and they were yelling at us to come back and finish it; they were really trying to draw fire, to find out where we were. We withdrew in a casual way, as one would after a day's work."[12]

Another small group, under the command of First Lieutenant Charles Sammon, also helped keep the route open for the remnants of Turnbull's platoon. Sammon commanded a light machine-gun platoon in Vandervoort's headquarters company. Just before first light, the colonel ordered Sammon to deploy his troops in a position roughly a mile northeast of Ste-Mère-Eglise, just east of N-13. Sammon had three machine guns and supporting riflemen.

All was quiet at his position until the daylight hours. Lieutenant Sammon and his runner were in the process of checking on Sammon's first machine-gun position when he discovered that it had been infiltrated by enemy soldiers. They were nearly killed by a "long burst from . . . a German machine gun and one or two machine pistols. The bullets hit the dirt at our feet and the two of us hit the ditch beside the road."

They were thoroughly pinned down. Sammon felt completely helpless. He could do nothing to help his soldiers. He was frightened, but more than that, he was angry at having been outsmarted by the Germans. Eventually he and his runner crawled, flat on their bellies, out of the ditch and back in the direction of their original position. When they got there, they found mass confusion, so Sammon set about the task of restoring order. "I managed to round up the remnants of my platoon and set up one machine gun to keep firing at the German position so they wouldn't attempt to advance any further." He also ordered several of his riflemen and rifle grenadiers to keep up a steady stream of fire at the Germans while his mortar set up and opened fire. "With the grenades and mortar shells falling into their position the Germans had no choice but to move out." Sammon and his men picked about half of them off as they retreated.

German artillery shells began to drop near Sammon's position, but still he hoped to close with the enemy force and destroy it. "We were so pinned down by artillery fire that I was unable to find anyone to go with me." Sammon tried to charge them himself, but he failed to do any damage. He lay quietly behind an embankment wondering what to do next. All at once, a lieutenant from the airborne engineers materialized and offered to help. "We scrambled up the embankment so I could show him what to do. As we cautiously poked our heads up over the top a machine gun cut loose from the German ditch, we both slid back down the embankment. When the firing stopped I got up but he didn't, so I rolled him over. He was shot right through the head."

Sammon grabbed a couple of grenades, scrambled over the

embankment, tossed them into the German positions, and hurried back over the embankment. He heard two explosions but not much else. When he chanced a look, he saw a white flag poking out of the German ditch. A German doctor came out in the open and, in perfect English, proposed surrendering. Two or three of the dead engineering lieutenant's men had joined Sammon now. They wanted to shoot the Germans, but Sammon ordered them to accept the surrender. It never happened. Instead, while Sammon and his small group waited for the Germans to come back with their wounded, German artillery began raining down on their position near the embankment. "It was obvious that the Doctor's surrender was all part of a very clever German plot."

Sammon went back to his platoon's original position, found the rest of his men, and led yet another attack that broke German resistance. Making liberal use of grenades, the battle-weary Americans closed in on the enemy-occupied ditch. "Those that were not killed by the grenades got up to run and were cut down by machine gun fire from our main positions. There were about 15 dead and wounded Germans lying about the position."[13]

They rounded up about ten prisoners, along with whatever wounded they could carry, and went back to Ste-Mère-Eglise. The stubborn, resilient performance of these 505th troopers, along with Turnbull's D Company platoon and the E Company soldiers, helped save Ste-Mère-Eglise for the Americans. In tandem, these soldiers held the northern approaches to the town, while the main group warded off yet another German counterattack on the south side of Ste-Mère-Eglise. This guaranteed that German reinforcements could not use the town as a gateway to counterattack Utah beach on D-Day.

It also meant that those 82nd Airborne troopers who had landed farther to the west, in the marshes of the Merderet, were not cut off. Their mission was to seize and hold two vital causeways over the flooded Merderet—one at Chef-du-Pont and the other a mile and a half north at La Fière. Infantry soldiers could wade, with great discomfort, across the marshy Merderet, but not vehicles. German vehicles moving east toward Ste-Mère-Eglise and the invasion beaches would need to use these causeways. The same held true for American vehicles rumbling up from Utah beach and moving in the opposite direction, west across the river. So the fighting in this sector amounted to a bloody contest for control of the causeways.

General Gavin jumped with the 508th and, like so many troopers from that regiment and the adjacent 507th, landed in shallow swamp water west of the Merderet. He spent his first few hours in France organizing troopers and trying to find out just where he was. As it turned out, he and the others were northwest of La Fière. German fire, seemingly coming from everywhere, immobilized Gavin's growing force. Most of the troopers were content to hunker down behind hedgerows and wait for the enemy shooting to slacken. Gavin made repeated futile attempts to get them moving or, at least, shooting back.

The general soon learned of the existence of a 57mm antitank gun wedged into a crashed glider in the swamp, little more than a quarter-mile away from his position. "I sent a patrol, led by Lieutenant Thomas Graham, a veteran of the 505th, to get it. The Germans knew it was there and increased their fire into the area."[14]

Following a short hike, Lieutenant Graham and a few other troopers attempted to wade out to the glider, all the while taking fire. They steadily sloshed through the water and reached the glider. "We could not raise the front end. It was wedged into mud and grass. The occupants apparently had gotten out through the side of the glider." They tried several times to lift the nose of the glider, something they had to do to free the gun. Nothing worked. Exhausted, wet, and more than a bit jumpy from the German fire, they reported their failure to the general. He decided to abandon the effort to retrieve the gun.[15]

By now, he knew his position was quite unfavorable. He had hoped to advance on La Fière from the western edge of the Merderet, but he knew that German opposition was too intense and his tactical situation poor. Instead, Gavin gave the reluctant order to abandon the current position (along with many of the wounded whom he hoped to recover later), cross to the east side of the Merderet, and advance on La Fière from the north.

The sun had risen, bathing the Americans in the half-light of dawn. As the troopers, rifles held high, plunged into the water, the Germans could see them through the foggy mist that rose just above the water. "We must have covered an area several hundred yards across," Gavin later wrote, "with troopers 15 to 25 yards apart, holding their rifles and sometimes their equipment over their heads as they went into the marsh. Soon we were almost shoulder-deep and the going was exceedingly difficult. The grass wrapped itself around our legs and seemed to pull us down. By then the Germans . . . were firing at individuals. Occasionally troopers would be hit and go down."

Lieutenant Graham, wading several yards behind the general, could see bullets kicking up water all around them, "and sometimes you heard them go overhead, but you never knew how close. I had cramps in both of my legs. I didn't know whether I could make the next step, and I believe others felt the same." Gavin inspired him to keep going. "The general was out in front, and when you have someone like that leading, you know you're going to make it." They finally made it across the Merderet to a raised railroad embankment. Gavin and his force, consisting of about three hundred troopers, turned south and headed for La Fière.[16]

As they closed in on the town, they made contact with other Americans, from the 1st Battalion, 505th, who were fighting their way toward the same objective. In fact, the assignment of this unit was to capture the La Fière causeway. Their drop had been, by Overlord standards, quite orderly, and they were now in the process of accomplishing their mission. They were led by A Company, under the command of a redheaded Boston Irishman, First Lieutenant John "Red Dog" Dolan. Dolan's A Company had landed on its intended drop zone. Within an hour, he had gathered up all of his equipment bundles and 90 percent of his soldiers.

Now, just after daylight, his men were deployed along a dirt road on the eastern edges of La Fière. "Hedgerows were on either side of this road; and beyond it in the direction of the bridge, was an open, flat field, about 100 yards deep and about 75 yards wide." Those fields, a farmyard really, were dominated by a small collection of stone buildings, just east of the bridge. The buildings were known as Le Manoir. When Dolan's lead troops, led by Lieutenant James Presnell, closed to within 300 yards of Le Manoir, they began taking machine-gun fire. Immediately Dolan's company took cover in the ditches alongside the dirt road. Dolan ordered his mortar squads to pepper the buildings. They did so, but with little effect.

Lieutenant Dolan knew that the buildings had to be dealt with—they commanded every approach to the bridge. There was no getting around them. He had to order some of his men out to capture those buildings. He ordered Lieutenant Donald Coxon to send several of his men forward. German small-arms fire continued pouring out of the buildings, spattering along the road and ditches. The lieutenant was a courageous officer who understood the first rule of military leadership—never ask your men to do anything that you yourself are not willing to do. "Well, sir, if I must send someone out into that, I'll go myself," he said.

Coxon and one of his scouts began crawling alongside whatever cover they could find along the road. They had gone about one hundred yards when a German machine gun opened up. Immediately the bullets scythed through the scout, killing him instantly. Then Coxon got hit. He turned around and had started crawling in Dolan's direction when another bullet caught him flush in the abdomen, tearing open the lining of his stomach. In a matter of minutes, he bled to death, dusty and alone, by the side of a little French road. Coxon's second in command, Lieutenant Robert McLaughlin, took over the platoon. He and his radio operator tried to crawl forward. Suddenly a sniper's bullet smashed into the radio operator. Lieutenant McLaughlin tried to render first aid. With a loud crack, the sniper's rifle opened up again. A bullet slashed Mclaughlin's thigh, ripping through his stomach and buttocks. The Americans in the ditches fired back at the unseen enemy.

Dolan was now joined by the battalion executive officer, Major James McGinity. Dolan and the major could not sit still and watch anyone else get killed. "With Major McGinity and myself leading," Dolan wrote, "a few men holding and returning frontal fire, the platoon flanked to the left." They moved along a high, thick hedgerow that they hoped would provide cover. Dolan was trotting a few paces behind the major. "When we had traveled about two-thirds of the way up to the hedgerow, they opened up on us with rifles, and at least two machine pistols. I returned fire with my Thompson Sub-Machine Gun at a point where I could see leaves in the hedgerow fluttering."

In the next instant, Dolan saw the major drop like a sack of wheat, as a shot from a sniper tore through his brain, blowing out pieces of skull. Before the sniper could take a shot at Dolan, the Irishman sprayed the hedgerow with his Thompson. "As luck would have it, there was a German foxhole to my left which I jumped into and from where I continued to fire." The fire was effective. He got the enemy sniper full in the face.

At this spot, Dolan was close to McLaughlin. Still under heavy fire, he crawled to McLaughlin and tried to drag him back to the foxhole. "Don't move me!" McLaughlin, writhing in pain, cried. Dolan felt speckles of rain beating on his neck. Small droplets pelted softly, mixing with the blood from McLaughlin's wounds. Dolan crawled back to his foxhole, retrieved his raincoat, and covered up McLaughlin, who bled to death in a matter of moments. Dolan's company was effectively pinned down and remained so for at least an hour. In just a few minutes he had lost ten killed and twenty-one wounded. He stayed put and dispatched a runner to look for a patrol, under Second Lieutenant William Oakley, he had sent out earlier.

Unbeknownst to Dolan, Oakley's group was having better luck taking Le Manoir. They had managed to swing around behind Le Manoir undetected until they were between the bridge and the buildings. The lieutenant told several members of the patrol to cover his platoon sergeant, Oscar Queen, and him as they rushed the first building. Just as they did so, a German charged them firing a machine pistol. The two Americans opened fire with their rifles, killing the charging German and two others nearby. The Americans caught their collective breath behind a stone wall and then kept going, right into the rear of the machine-gun position that had raked Dolan's men. In the meantime, another group, mostly comprised of 507th troopers under the command of Captain Ben Schwartzwalder (coach of the Syracuse football team after the war), began attacking from the other direction. The Germans were effectively surrounded. They showed a white flag. When an American private stepped from cover to receive the surrender, a German shot and killed him. Amazingly, the Americans did not slaughter the cornered German force. Instead, they captured the remnants of an understrength infantry platoon that had, through an odd coincidence, appropriated the houses (owned by Monsieur Louis Leroux) the night before. The Americans had been unable to coordinate their attack on this key objective. Consequently, a single German platoon had held off a force ten times its size for several hours. Even so, the Americans now controlled the eastern end of La Fière causeway.[17]

About midmorning of D-Day, another group, mainly composed of 507th troopers, briefly held Cauquigny, the little town at the opposite end of the causeway. The scattered drop of the nighttime hours, combined with a rash of radio problems, meant that American airborne forces operated in small groups, with practically no coordination. A force of about eighty troopers under Lieutenant Colonel Charles Timmes took Cauquigny, a tiny hamlet consisting mostly of a church and a graveyard. Timmes left a twelve-man squad under Lieutenant Lewis Levy to garrison Cauquigny while the rest of his group headed for Amfreville, another D-Day objective. Unfortunately for Timmes, he found that Amfreville was too strongly defended to be taken by a force of this size. He and his men ended up dug in, stymied, in an orchard north of the village.

Nor was luck with Levy's men. His small force had been reinforced by a mixed group under the command of Lieutenant Joseph Kormylo. They dug in behind the walls of the graveyard and sited their machine guns to command a road that led into the village and to the bridge over the Merderet. Levy's soldiers had no sooner finished K-ration lunches (supplemented by milk and cider from the locals) than they heard the sound of approaching vehicles. Strangely, a German ambulance, flying a Red Cross flag, briefly appeared and then left just as quickly.

An instant later, shells, probably fired from German light tanks, began to land in the graveyard. Levy shouted a warning to his men to expect an attack and ran along the shelter of hedgerow next to the road. The Americans could hear the tanks approaching. They were Renault tanks that the Germans had captured from the French four years earlier. German infantry accompanied them. Fighting like a madman, Levy pitched grenades over the hedgerow. Several other Americans poured fire down the road. They could see the lieutenant, bleeding from the shoulder, "laughing like a maniac." He ran back to the churchyard. The enemy tanks were visible now. To oppose them, the Americans had only gammon grenades. The German tanks paused a few moments while the commander of the lead tank scanned the American positions.

No more than a few feet away, lying unseen on a slope of ground that overlooked the lead German tank, nineteen-year-old Sergeant David Waters was hastily assembling his gammon grenade. Waters was a code clerk in the 507th regimental headquarters. All morning he had been wandering alone in search of other Americans. Just minutes before, farther up the road, he had found the bodies of five 82nd Airborne troopers who had been killed (maybe by this group of Germans) as they set up a machine gun. "They died in the position they were firing from. There were also many dead Krauts." This macabre sight had nearly shattered Waters. He opened his mouth to scream, but nothing came out. "My body was shaking from head to toe. I was sure I wouldn't be alive by sunset. Never ever in my life had I felt such horrible fear." The only thing that kept Sergeant Waters going was the memory of his intense airborne training. He knew that he was expected to be scared but that he had to overcome that fear, "to do your job carrying your fear."

Now, as he assembled his gammon grenade, Sergeant Waters focused on revenge. The grenade "consisted of a black bag with a plastic cap and a hole in the bottom with the elastic sewn in." Waters removed the cap, inserted the detonator, and carefully screwed the cap back on the bag, arming the grenade.

Below him, the German tank commander, still completely oblivious to the presence of Waters, continued to eyeball the Americans in the churchyard. Waters unscrewed the cap and prepared to throw the grenade. "My brain was clicking along at 90 miles per hour. It was as though all the fear had changed to a... cold calculating frame of mind knowing what I had to do. The whole process took maybe about a minute and a half."

Waters rose up to throw the grenade. The German noticed the movement and looked up, but too late. The gammon grenade flew straight down the tank commander's open turret. "The tank opened up like a can of sardines." The explosion combusted the tank immediately. Searing flames consumed the tank as Waters scrambled away.

At the graveyard, the other Americans were amazed at the sight of the lead tank blowing up. They could not see Waters, nor did they know him. To them, the tank appeared to mysteriously blow up, but this inspired one of the soldiers, Private Orlin Stewart, and another man to run forward and pitch several gammon grenades at the other tanks. Simultaneously the other soldiers opened up with rifles and BARs. The tanks blew up and the Americans were tempted to think they had blunted this German attack, but dozens more infantry and another tank suddenly appeared from around the bend. Their fire drove the Americans back to the church. Levy and the other officers knew they could not hold out any longer. They had used up their gammon grenades and they were clearly outnumbered. The surviving Americans sprinted out of the town, eventually joining up with Timmes's force. They had made a brave stand, but they could not hold Cauquigny.[18]

A mile to the south, American soldiers were fighting hard for possession of the causeway at Chef-du-Pont. Once the fight at Le Manoir had been successfully concluded, General Gavin teamed up with Lieutenant Colonel Edwin Ostberg of the 507th and took a force of about one hundred men south along the railroad track in hopes of capturing the Chef-du-Pont causeway.

They ran into some enemy resistance as they approached the railroad station on the outskirts of Chef-du-Pont. "A train began to move from the railroad station," Gavin recalled. "There were German troops aboard and they fired at us and then scattered." The general quickly sent his troops after the train and the station. One of those troops, Private Paul Bouchereau, the New Orleans Cajun, charged forward with the others. "The Germans were taken completely by surprise and all were killed or wounded. We set fire to a few boxcars and blew up a locomotive." The Americans searched the train. Gavin was surprised to see that the boxcars were filled with empty bottles and aromatic Norman cheese.[19]

The Yanks pushed forward into the town, heading southeast, in the direction of the bridge. All at once, German fire rained down on them from several buildings. Four Americans were hit. This slowed the advance to a veritable crawl as the troopers systematically searched the town, building by building. But the Germans had no intention of staying put to be hunted down like rats. They knew that the town had no value. It was the bridge that mattered. Enemy soldiers, in cohesive groups, sprinted to prepared positions along the causeway. They were supported by comrades who fired at the Americans from a collection of buildings located on an island in the middle of the flooded Merderet.

It took the Americans two hours to clear Chef-du-Pont and finally turn their attention to the bridge. At the eastern edge of the bridge, the situation was fluid. Individual Germans hunkered down in holes and took potshots at the Americans. Then the shooting quieted for a couple minutes. All at once, a German rose up and shouted something. The Americans were not sure what the enemy soldier was doing. A trooper shot him and the German toppled over, dead in an instant. The same thing happened to another German a minute later. In his classic book, *Night Drop*, S. L. A. Marshall asserted that the German soldiers were trying to surrender but were foolishly gunned down by jumpy American troopers. Marshall argued that those trigger-happy troopers ended any hope that the Germans might surrender the bridge without further resistance. This, he believed, condemned the American force to a tough all-day fight for the crucial objective.

But Captain Roy Creek, the E Company, 507th, commander who had briefed his men so directly and eloquently back at Full-beck, did not see it that way. He and his men were near the bridge, right in the thick of this fighting. Creek saw the whole incident firsthand, from only a few yards away. "I would defy anyone to make a split-second judgment on what to do when an enemy soldier jumps up out of a foxhole five to twenty feet from you in the heat of heavy firing on both sides and in your own very first fight for your life. I support the action taken by our troops. To this day, years later, I don't know if the enemy was trying to surrender or not. In my opinion, any enemy shot during this attack, as close and intense as it was, had waited too long to surrender. He was committed, as the attacker was, to a fight for survival."

Perhaps the whole tragedy can simply be filed under the "fog of war" category. Whatever the truth of what happened that day at Chef-du-Pont, the objective still needed to be taken. Lieutenant Colonel Ostberg believed quick action was necessary. He ordered Creek and the others to charge. As he rose from cover, Creek saw Ostberg himself leading the wild run for the bridge. "Speed seemed to be the answer. We knew the bridge must be taken before the Germans could organize their defense, so we made a semiorganized dash for it. Two officers reached the bridge and were both shot, one toppling off the bridge and into the water, the other falling on the eastern approach. The officer toppling into the river was Colonel Ostberg. He was rescued shortly afterward by two soldiers of the 507th and lived to fight again. The other officer was dead."

Obviously, the bridge could not be taken with a quick dash. The job would require more tactical planning. The Americans found cover on the edges of Chef-du-Pont while officers like Creek decided what to do. "For practical purposes, the only approach to the bridge was the one we had chosen through Chef-du-Pont. The approaches from the west were not approaches in a military sense. They were causeways, long and straight and completely flooded on both sides. Germans were dug in on the shoulders of both sides of the road occupying foxholes dispersed at intervals of about ten yards for a long stretch leading to the bridge and beyond."

Another seventy-five troopers under the command of Lieutenant Colonel Arthur Maloney reinforced the pinned-down Americans. Maloney and Creek led yet another attempt for the bridge. The best the Americans could do was crawl, under fire, into the German holes at the eastern edge of the bridge. To do this they made liberal use of grenades, throwing them into any hole they saw. With this done, they plopped into the holes and, mustering all their strength, threw the holes' dead occupants out into the mud. German fire from the island and the western section of the causeway was deadly, though. Any trooper who raised his head risked getting his brains blown out. German artillery and sniper fire continued to harass the Americans, but they kept control of the eastern edge of the causeway while the Germans held the west.

The battle had stalemated and remained that way for a couple of hours. In the meantime, General Gavin, believing that the Chef-du-Pont causeway had been secured, ordered Maloney's men to leave the town and head for La Fière so that they could help with a crisis there (more on that later). This left only thirty-four lonely, battered men under Creek's command to hang on to an objective that they did not really control.

During this vigil, the captain and his troops experienced a litany of emotional highs and lows. No sooner had Maloney's people left than intense German artillery fire began to fall on the American foxholes at Chef-du-Pont. Seemingly every shell inflicted casualties. Creek himself came very close to getting hit. He was circulating among his men, checking on each position, when a flurry of shells caught him out in the open. "I spotted a very small brick sentry house just short of the bridge on our side. I made a dash for it and went inside and found a still burning enemy soldier, victim of a white phosphorous grenade. The house only had room for one man standing. So it became crowded with my arrival and the other guy in there wasn't going anywhere. This coupled with the fact that the smoke and stench from the burning man caused me to make a quick decision that I would rather take my chances out in the open."

Creek survived the shelling, but many of his soldiers did not. Before long, he was down to twenty men who were still able to fight. As if this weren't bad enough, one of his observers, nestled into the upper floor of a creamery that overlooked the bridge, reported the sight of a German company, massing for an attack.

Luckily for Creek's tiny force, this German unit was headed for Ste-Mère-Eglise, not Chef-du-Pont.

Still, the captain did not know how much longer he could hold out. He was underwhelmed when an officer, sent by Gavin, appeared at his side and told him the general wanted him to "hold at all costs. It was pretty obvious that it couldn't cost too much. At the same time, it was doubtful we could hold something we didn't have." Creek sent the officer back to Gavin with a request for reinforcements.

Then, in a scene reminiscent of Hollywood, C-47s appeared overhead. The planes dropped bundles of weapons and ammunition, right on top of Creek's position. Creek was now able to set up a 60mm mortar position and return fire on the Germans. "Within 30 minutes, the officer who had previously delivered the hold at all costs message returned with 100 men and a 57mm gun which was pulled into position on our side of the bridge." The gun silenced the German artillery piece that had caused so many casualties.

Thus reinforced, Creek now went on the attack. During another one of his reconnaissance forays, he had found a narrow finger of terrain that enfiladed the enemy positions on the causeway. Creek moved a squad to this sliver of land and it proved an ideal place for sniping. When the captain determined that the Germans had been softened sufficiently, he gave the order to assault. "On a prearranged signal, all fires lifted and ten men and one officer stormed the bridge and went into position on the western approach to guard the causeway. Five Germans made a run for it down the deathtrap causeway and were immediately shot down. That did it. The battle was over. The bridge was ours and we knew we could hold it."[20]

The D-Day afternoon fight at La Fière turned out to be every bit as desperate. By that time, several small groups of Americans were deployed along the eastern edge of the Merderet, in or near La Fière. The principal group holding the eastern portion of the causeway was still Lieutenant Dolan's A Company. Dolan ordered them to dig in as best they could. "Down at the bridge now was most of Company 'A,' about one platoon of Company 'B,' a platoon of the Division Engineers (mission to blow the bridge if necessary), about half of Battalion Headquarters Company with mortars [and] machine gun sections and several stray men from other regiments." In addition, Dolan could now call on the services of a

57mm gun he had emplaced at a suitable point along the road. The gun crew had an excellent field of fire against anything that came across the causeway.

In foxholes on the muddy causeway, close to the actual bridge, Dolan had bazooka teams in place. "The two Company 'A' bazookas were dug in to the left and right of the bridge. They were . . . dug in below the level of the road, so that in order to fire, they had to get out of their foxholes."[21]

In one of those foxholes, Private Marcus Heim, one of Dolan's A Company men, prepared grimly for the possibility that German armor might attack across the causeway. Heim shared the foxhole with Private Lenold Peterson, a willowy Swede who spoke only rudimentary English. Heim was the loader. Peterson was the gunner. The two of them had to stand to see the causeway, peeking at it like children peering over a windowsill. Peterson, Heim, and several others moved around the area near their holes, preparing the terrain for battle. "There was a concrete telephone pole in front of us," Heim recalled. "We carried antitank mines and bazooka rockets from the landing area. These mines were placed across the causeway about 50 or 60 feet on the other side of the bridge. There was a broken down German truck by the Manor House, which we pushed and dragged across the bridge and placed it across the causeway. All that afternoon the Germans kept shelling our position." Heim and the other soldiers heard rumors that the Germans would soon counterattack.

Not long after this rumor buzzed through Dolan's command, his men heard engines and rumbling coming from the other side of the causeway, in the vicinity of Cauquigny. West of the Merderet, just around the bend of the road leading to the bridge, three German tanks (probably Renaults) and dozens of infantry were on the move. They closed in on the Americans who were deployed around the bridge. Dolan, operating from a foxhole on the edge of La Fière, gave the order to open fire. "When the lead tank was about 40 or 50 yards away from the bridge, the two Company 'A' bazooka teams got up just like clock work to the edge of the road. They were under the heaviest small arms fire from the other side of the causeway, and from the cannon and machine gun fire from the tanks."

At his forward position, probably no more than thirty yards away from the lead tank, Private Heim saw the tank grind to a halt. The tank commander popped open the hatch to inspect the mines and the truck that Heim and the others had placed near the bridge. Somewhere to the left, an American .30-caliber machine gun opened fire, spewing a staccato stream of bullets that smashed into the German tank commander. Spurting blood from many wounds, he slumped lifelessly in the turret. Heim and Peterson were squatting behind the telephone pole, trying to line up the sights of their bazooka through a tangled jumble of tree branches.

Heim loaded the 2.36-inch rocket into the back of the bazooka, armed it, and patted Peterson on the shoulder. Peterson pulled the trigger, and the rocket left the bazooka with a whoosh. "The first tank was hit, started to turn sideways and at the same time was swinging the turret around and firing at us," Private Heim related. He and Peterson displaced as the enemy tank fired. "We had just moved forward around the cement telephone pole when a German shell hit it and we had to jump out of the way to avoid being hit as it was falling."

Bullets kicked up dust around them. They found a new position, calmly reloaded, fired, and hit the tank again. The enemy tank burst into flames, roasting the crew inside. Dolan watched it all unfold and could hardly believe that the withering enemy fire missed his brave men. "To this day, I'll never be able to explain why [they] were not killed. They fired and reloaded with the precision of well-oiled machinery. Watching them made it [easy] to believe that this was nothing but a routine drill."

The other crew, Privates John Bolderson and Gordon Pryne, was doing just as much damage. They fired and displaced, hitting the second tank several times, setting it afire. The antitank gun crew, about one hundred yards to the rear, was busy firing at the third tank, but Heim and Peterson were in their own world. They had no idea what was happening anywhere but the ten yards in front of them. German infantry had taken cover in the ditches and behind the burning tanks. They fired their rifles and machine pistols at the bazooka men. The Americans kept dodging the enemy bullets while trying to line up a shot on the third tank. "Peterson and I were almost out of rockets, and the third tank was still moving." They started screaming for more bazooka ammunition, but they thought that no one heard them. Actually, the 1st Battalion's commander, Major Frederick Kellam, heard them quite clearly. He scooped up a bag of rockets and, accompanied by the battalion operations officer, Captain Dale Royden, sprinted for their position. They didn't make it. "When they were within 15 or 20 yards of the bridge," Lieutenant Dolan recalled, "the Germans opened up with mortar fire on the bridge. Major Kellam was killed and Captain [Royden] was rendered unconscious from the concussion. He died later that day."

Heim and Peterson did not realize any of this. They just knew they needed ammo. "Peterson asked me to go back across the road to see if Bolderson had any extra rockets. I ran across the road and with all the crossfire I still find it hard to believe I made it to the other side in one piece. When I got to the other side I found one dead soldier and Bolderson and Pryne were gone. Their bazooka was lying on the ground." Private Heim found some rockets and made it across the road to rejoin Peterson, just in time to see the 57mm blow up the last enemy tank.

The enemy attack had been blunted. The surviving Germans withdrew and contented themselves with long-range fire. Dolan and his men went to ground and hoped for the best. "We had almost a 560 degree perimeter defense. The rest of the day we were under heavy mortar fire and machine gun fire. The mortar fire was very effective . . . against the two forward platoons because of tree bursts."[22]

On high ground above La Fière, General Gavin watched A Company's determined stand. His instincts told him that even though the German attack had been defeated, they would be back. This was when he sent the officer down to Chef-du-Pont ordering Maloney's troops to reinforce La Fière. Gavin was a splendid commander, but he was wrong. The Germans were not coming back, at least not tonight. The eastern end of La Fière causeway remained in American hands.

The 101st had two basic missions: secure control of the four causeways that led inland from Utah beach and seize and hold the Douve bridges and locks that comprised the southern flank of the Cotentin. The purpose of the first mission was to safeguard the Utah beach landings. The Germans had flooded the flat tidal basin that lay just inland from Utah. The 4th Division needed the four causeways in order to move men and vehicles off the beach at necessary speed. The Germans, of course, knew of the importance of the causeways and placed heavy guns to cover each one. The Screaming Eagles were supposed to find and destroy those guns. The Douve crossings needed to be taken for the same reasons the 82nd needed to take the Merderet crossings—to prevent movement of German reinforcements and provide a springboard for the American invasion forces to advance deeper into Normandy.

The two northern causeways, Exits 3 and 4, were located near the towns of St-Martin-de-Varreville and Audoville-la-Hubert. The 502nd Parachute Infantry drew the mission of securing these beach exits along with their accompanying towns. Captain Lillyman and his pathfinders, fresh from their nocturnal activities on the fringes of the regiment's drop zone, began scouting for the guns that covered the two exits. These were 122mm Soviet guns that the Germans had captured on the Eastern Front. The Germans had placed them about two miles west of Utah beach. Lillyman and his men found the bunkers housing the guns. Royal Air Force bombers had pasted the site on May 29 and again on June 5 right before the paratroopers went into Normandy (in so doing these bombers demonstrated how effective a more extensive bombing campaign of German Cotentin defenses could have been). Lillyman discovered that the bombers had collapsed one bunker, destroying the gun within. The Germans had then removed the other three guns to points unknown. In addition to the wrecked bunker Lillyman's men found only torn ammo crates, a flipped-over Renault tank, and discarded enemy equipment at the site.

The pathfinder captain soon made contact with Lieutenant Colonel Patrick Cassidy and Lieutenant Colonel Steve Chappuis, commanders of the 1st and 2nd Battalions respectively. Lillyman passed along the news that the guns had been neutralized. Cassidy and Chappuis breathed a big sigh of relief. Both of them knew that the guns could have caused real problems for the 4th Divison troops who would soon storm Utah beach. They now turned their attention to organizing the random groups of troopers drifting into the area so that they could secure the western ends of the beach exits. This happened swiftly. The Americans were in perfect position when the Germans began retreating, at 0930, from the 4th Division amphibious assault forces. The 502nd troopers cornered between fifty and seventy-five enemy soldiers and annihilated them.[23]

Other troopers went about securing various towns and secondary objectives near the northern beach exits. Private Burgett, following his precarious descent, far away from his intended drop zone, met up with several other troopers by employing his toy cricket[24] for recognition in the dark. They wandered in the darkness trying to get their bearings. At dawn, they finally met up with one of their officers, Lieutenant William Muir, another Michigan native. The group now numbered eleven soldiers, one or two of whom were 82nd Airborne troopers. Muir declared an intention to capture the nearest town, whatever it may be. He posted two of Burgett's buddies as scouts, and they led the small group slowly west along a country road. Burgett trailed, just ahead of the main group, roughly a quarter of a mile behind the two scouts.

They walked without incident for half a mile or so, until they arrived at a bend in the road and Burgett lost sight of the scouts. The two men had disappeared. Burgett halted the column and told Lieutenant Muir what had happened. In search of the two lost men, Burgett and the lieutenant plunged into the surrounding foliage. Burgett felt terribly uneasy, as if he was being watched by enemy soldiers hidden behind a nearby hedgerow. Then he saw something that made his heart catch. "I saw . . . two rifles and packs lying on the ground. The sick feeling came deep inside my stomach, for this was the equipment of our two scouts and here I was standing in an open field." Burgett found out after the war that one of the scouts was captured by a German patrol. The other scout is still missing in action.

But at this moment, as Burgett now assumed the role of lead scout, the whereabouts of the two men remained a mystery. Burgett, feeling quite lonely and frightened, led his small group another few hundred yards down the spooky country lane. Soon they came to a collection of houses and barns. The private knew that there could be enemy soldiers hiding in the buildings so he called a halt. As he did so, three French girls, about his age, emerged from a doorway and ran toward him: "Vive les Américains!"

They offered him wine, but he refused. "Not that I don't like wine, but I just didn't feel like being poisoned, and at this time I didn't trust anyone." Lieutenant Muir asked the girls if anyone in town spoke English. They directed him to the home of a woman who taught English. She told the lieutenant that he was on the outskirts of Ravenoville. He folded up his map and told his men to keep moving. They found several Americans lying in a ditch, not doing much of anything. These soldiers told the lieutenant that anything farther forward was in enemy hands. Muir rounded them up, attached them to his own group, and gave the word to attack.

Beyond the ditches they could see Ravenoville, a collection of stone houses and barns at the other end of open fields. With great impetuosity and aplomb, they spread out and charged across the field, Muir in the lead. "We all jumped up and followed him, yelling and screaming at the top of our lungs." They fired as they ran. "I saw my first Kraut running through the trees on an angle toward our right flank. I stopped, took a good sight on him and squeezed the trigger. The rifle bucked against my shoulder. The German spun sideways and fell face first out of sight in the grass. Another Kraut stepped around the corner of a building, stopped and just stood there looking down at the spot where the first soldier fell. He was facing me. I had a good straight-on shot at his chest and took careful aim. Again the rifle bucked against my shoulder, and he too fell face forward."

Burgett had no time to contemplate the fact that he had, for the first time, killed fellow human beings. Caught up in the frenzy of combat, he ran forward. "Fighting was at a fever pitch now. All around, men were running between buildings, through yards and over fences. Four troopers ran through a gate in a hedge surrounding a house and almost immediately there came a long ripping burst of a Kraut machine gun. The four Americans died in the weed-choked front yard." The gun was firing from a window in an adjacent house. Other troopers shunned the yard and moved down a hedge "until they were in throwing distance of the house, and grenaded it. One trooper leaped through a side window, fired several rounds from his M-1, then stepped to the front door and motioned that it was all clear."

About thirty Germans had been killed and another seventy-five taken prisoner. The rest, remnants of an entire company, retreated. Burgett and his buddies inspected the buildings and were amazed at how easily the Germans had yielded. "The walls were all of stone and two feet thick, with small rifle apertures to fire out from, and many of the rooms were filled with food, ammo and weapons." A German-speaking GI asked the prisoners why their comrades had left. "They said that when we came running at them yelling ... and shooting across the open fields, they figured the whole invasion was directed right at them." A tiny American force of about twenty men had routed an entire German company from stone fortifications.

Lieutenant Muir spread his tiny garrison around Ravenoville to defend against an inevitable counterattack. Burgett and a buddy got assigned to the road leading into the town. They mined the road, hunkered down in a ditch, and fortified themselves with captured enemy grenades, in addition to K-ration breakfast meals.

A few hours later, they spotted a German crawling along the road. Burgett raised his rifle. "It was an easy shot, I saw the dust fly from his jacket as I squeezed the trigger and he dropped straight down." A machine gun opened up on them. An instant later, "the whole world seemed to explode in flame" as a German attack began in earnest.

The two sides shot at each other from either side of the narrow blacktop road. "Action became automatic, firing at fleeting shapes, crawling to different positions and firing, reloading and firing again and again." The fighting took place at extremely close quarters. "The Germans were in the ditch on one side of the road while we were in the ditch on this side. A distance of not more than fifteen yards separated us. At times, just as I slipped my rifle through the foliage to fire, I could feel the muzzle blasts from the enemy rifles as they fired toward us. We were so close together that our faces were being blackened by the enemy's muzzle blasts. The smell of powder burned deep into our nostrils." It left their throats dry and parched, almost with a powdery sort of copper taste. The Americans fought hard and warded off the German attack. Ravenoville remained American territory.[25]

As D-Day unfolded, Lieutenant Colonel Cassidy continued his attempt to forge some order out of the chaos of the misdrop. Even as he sent men to keep Exits 3 and 4 under control, he sought to consolidate the western and northern edges of his area. Small groups of troopers set up roadblocks around Foucarville. Cassidy dispatched a small patrol, under the command of Staff Sergeant Harrison Summers, B Company, 502nd, on a special mission. The little hamlet of Mesieres was nothing more than a tiny collection of stone buildings at a crossroads, but it housed the German artillerymen who manned the missing guns of Exits 3 and 4. Located a kilometer west of St-Martin-de-Varreville and several hundred yards west of the abandoned bunkers, the Americans called Mesieres "Objective WXYZ."

Cassidy's battalion had been given the mission of taking WXYZ. At 0830 Cassidy sent Summers (who was about to become an airborne legend) and his odd collection of men to capture

WXYZ. It wasn't exactly a formidable force. Summers had only fifteen men, most of whom he did not know, but it was the best Cassidy could muster at this early stage of Overlord. The sergeant and his hodgepodge patrol moved carefully along a hedgerow-lined dirt road leading to Mesieres.

At 0900 they arrived at the first building in Mesieres and immediately took cover in roadside ditches as German sniper fire spewed forth from the building. Summers mulled over his next move. One glance at the prone, frightened men around him told him that they were reluctant to leave the ditch. If he gave the order to assault the building, would they obey? He did not know. He glanced at two men who seemed more eager than the others. One of those men was Private John Camien. Summers ordered Camien and another trooper, probably from the 506th, to check out the building while the rest of the group laid down fire for them.

Much to Summers's relief, they obeyed. The two men sprinted to the back door of the building, kicked it in, and entered. They saw the Germans shooting through firing ports. "The two of us killed three Germans in the first house." From there, Camien and the other man ran across the street to clear out a cluster of three buildings. At the second house, they "received no fire but took two prisoners and killed four sleeping Germans with two hand grenades. The following house was empty, so we went on to the next, where I went upstairs and the boy from the 506th took downstairs. I killed one German and at the same time I heard someone running up the attic stairs. I went up after him and took prisoner this German officer. While I was upstairs . . . the 506th boy killed a German soldier and was killed himself by a round from a P-38. Their shots must have been simultaneous."

Private Camien, catching his breath, now found himself joined by several other soldiers—Lieutenant Elmer Brandenburger, a B Company, 502nd, officer who had been fighting on the fringes of Mesieres all morning; an anonymous tall 82nd Airborne captain; Private William Burt; and Sergeant Summers. In front of them, the fifth building beckoned. To get there, they had to charge across the road.

The 82nd Airborne captain took a bullet through the heart and fell dead close to the road. Summers and Camien, lugging tommy guns, remained unscathed. They were sprinting now for the front door of the building. Burt was carrying a light machine gun. He found some cover in a ditch and laid down fire. Some of the other members of the patrol drifted into the ditch around Burt and provided additional fire.

Brandenburger got sidetracked. "As I left the house, I heard someone shouting that there was a machine gun firing from a stone building at the far end of the village." Brandenburger called for two men to grab a bazooka and follow him. He glanced to his right and saw Burt. "I still remember [him] with his machine gun alongside the road covering for us." Brandenburger ran across the road and dived over a hedgerow adjacent to the road. Machine-gun bullets clipped the foliage around him. "Where in hell is that bazooka team?" he wondered. He shouted for them, but they were nowhere to be found. Suddenly he heard a thud. "A couple of potato masher grenades landed nearly beside me. They didn't go off. I can remember my feeling of fright when I saw them hit the ground so close to me that I could have spit on them if I had any spit left." He kept working his way in the direction of the machine gun and eventually got hit in the left arm. He staggered into the safety of a ditch where medics later found him.

Meanwhile, Summers and Camien kicked open the door of the fifth building in the WXYZ complex. "A French girl told us that there were five Germans hiding in the closet," Camien recalled. "I put a burst of tommy-gun fire into the door, heard a scream, the door flew open and one German soldier fell dead onto the floor. Another attempted to run up the stairs. Sgt. Summers shot him and killed him." They searched the house room by room. Summers shot several other enemy, and three Germans surrendered. The fifth building was clear.

Once again Summers and Camien caught their breath and prepared to move on. The next three buildings were arranged in a sort of triangle just to the north of the road and west of the fifth building. Supported by Burt's machine gun, Summers and Camien now turned into a two-man wrecking crew. Adrenaline was pumping through their veins. It was as if nothing existed except the next building, the next group of Germans. They had fallen sway to the kind of violent tunnel vision so necessary to survive in close combat.

As Burt covered them with his machine gun, Summers and Camien cleared out all three buildings, room by room, taking some time to rest between buildings. The Germans in those buildings could not get a good look at their two assailants because Burt provided such effective suppressive fire on their firing ports. Before they knew it, Sergeant Summers and Private Camien burst into each building, spraying the walls and halls with .45-caliber slugs from their tommy guns. In all, the two Americans killed about ten enemy soldiers and took another seven prisoner.

Summers and Camien were nearing exhaustion now, and they had seen and experienced many horrible things—the surprised, agonized looks of other men as they died at close range; the uniquely thick, pungent smell of their blood as it flowed from their wounds and onto the floor; the rot, decay, and degradation of violence. Camien turned to the sergeant and asked, "Why are you doing it?"

"I can't tell you," Summers replied.

"What about the others?" Camien asked.

The sergeant shrugged. "They don't seem to want to fight, and I can't make them. So I've got to finish it."

"OK, I'm with you."

Their next objective, a well-built long two-story château with dormer windows, was about a quarter-mile to the west. To get there, Camien and Summers hugged the inside edge of a low embankment that ran west along the road. Behind the two attackers, Burt and a growing number of supporting troops displaced and followed. Many of these newcomers had no idea what was happening ahead of them. They only knew that something was going on and that they were supposed to lend fire support.

Summers led the charge into this ninth building, which turned out to be a mess hall. He kicked in the door, turned left, and began searching rooms. The first two rooms he searched were empty, but not the third room. At the third room, Summers was greeted with a surreal sight. Fifteen German artillerymen were sitting at a long table, eating breakfast, completely oblivious to the battle around them. Summers could hardly believe his eyes. The Germans attempted to scramble out of their chairs and grab their weapons, but it was far too late. Summers sprayed the room with his tommy gun, emptying a full clip of twenty rounds. At such point-blank range, the weapon was devastating. The bullets tore through bodies and plates alike. The enemy soldiers fell all over themselves, all of them dead or gravely wounded. Summers never understood why they had put themselves in such a vulnerable position. He later referred to them as the "fifteen biggest chowhounds in the German Army."

It was late afternoon now. The last building, the main barracks, beckoned from atop a gentle rise some fifty yards to the west. The barracks was another sturdy two-story structure. There was no covered approach, from any direction, to the place. Summers and company took shelter behind hedges at the end of the road, rested, and contemplated the best way to attack.

As they did so, other Americans were closing in on this last piece of the WXYZ puzzle. Cassidy had been sending troops to WXYZ for several hours. A group of these reinforcements was now moving through an orchard, just across the road from Summers's patrol. Another airborne force, consisting mainly of the 502nd regimental headquarters, was approaching from the west and a 4th Division reconnaissance force from the east.

From somewhere behind, an enemy sniper opened up on the paratroopers in the orchard, killing three of them in quick succession. In an attempt to get away from the sniper, the surviving Americans crashed through the orchard along with a line of hedges. This put them right in front of the barracks. German soldiers in the barracks shot them to pieces, killing four and wounding a like number. In an attempt to shield the pinned-down Americans, who were bleeding and dying on the grass in front of the barracks, Summers and his people blazed away at the barracks. Private Burt saw a haystack near a shed that stood adjacent to the barracks. He shot up the haystack with tracer rounds, starting a fire that spread to the shed, which went up like a Roman candle. The Germans had ammunition stored there and a whole platoon inside guarding it. These unfortunate enemy soldiers now had to choose between two apocalyptic options: fire or American bullets. They chose the latter. Basically this amounted to a choice in favor of death by violent gunshot wounds rather than incineration. American small-arms fire and grenades devastated the hapless Germans, killing every single one of them. In a matter of moments, thirty German soldiers lay dead. To the Americans they looked like shredded, bloody rag dolls.

The fire in the shed did nothing to dislodge the main group in the barracks, though. Staff Sergeant Roy Nickrent, a garrulous Chicagoan, had lugged a bazooka all the way through the orchard, in the process surviving the sniper and the fire originating from the German barracks. Now, nestled behind a hedgerow to the north of Summers's position, Nickrent leveled his weapon and took aim at the enemy-held building. "I fired two rounds to adjust my range. The first one fell short while the second hit the stone wall of the building near its base. I continued to adjust my aim until the seventh round went through the roof. Black smoke began to pour through the hole."

Nickrent's bazooka had set fire to the roof. The fire soon spread throughout the barracks. This larger group of Germans now faced the same dilemma their comrades in the shed had faced moments before. This group chose to flee north through an open field. In so doing, they put themselves right in the path of the 502nd headquarters troopers in one direction and the 4th Division men in the other. Once again, the Americans shot the Germans to pieces. They killed about fifty enemy and accepted the surrender of another thirty-one.

When the carnage finally ended, Summers and his patrol members relaxed and lit up cigarettes. The sergeant was bruised all over from bumping into walls and kicking in doors all day. "How do you feel?" someone asked him.

"Not very good," he responded. "It was all kind of crazy. I'm sure I'd never do anything like that again."[26]

The battle had taken nearly the entire day. Incredibly, a platoon-sized group of Americans, mostly strangers to one another, had captured nearly a dozen stone-reinforced, fortified buildings. In so doing they defeated a German artillery company of about two hundred men. Exits 3 and 4 were wide open.

As it turned out, Exits 1 and 2, farther to the south, ended up being more important for the safety of the invasion. As will be recounted in a later chapter, the first assault waves at Utah beach landed about a mile south of their intended invasion beach. This made them heavily dependent on Exits 1 and 2. The 506th had the task of capturing these exits. Most of the regiment's men had been scattered all over the Cotentin. All night long, they had wandered the fields, hedges, and lanes of Normandy, like so many other troopers, searching for friendly faces.

By daylight, some of them had succeeded. One group, under the command of Lieutenant Winters, the legendary commander of E Company, performed a herculean task that probably saved many lives on Utah beach. Winters had been misdropped and had lost all of his weapons and ammo except for a knife. In spite of this, he gathered a small force together, met up with Lieutenant Colonel Cole (502nd) and his mixed group of troopers, and moved east toward the beaches. Along the way, this force cornered a small German supply column, killing several enemy soldiers and capturing others. When the sun rose, the men from different units went their separate ways. Winters and about a dozen E Company soldiers headed south, in search of their unit's objective at Le Grand Chemin, near Exit 2. They reached the town and found many 2nd Battalion soldiers, along with several staff officers.

Two of those officers, Captain Clarence Hester (battalion S-3) and Lieutenant Lewis Nixon (battalion S-2) briefed Winters. These men were good friends. They had worked together for two years, living through the hell of airborne training. The battalion commander, Lieutenant Colonel Robert Strayer, barely had enough men to cover all the jobs that needed to be done. He needed Winters to take his dozen representatives of E Company and capture a four-gun battery of 105mm guns that menaced Exit 2. The enemy had dug the guns into a field at the Brecourt family farm, close by Le Grand Chemin. Mysteriously, these guns had not yet begun firing at the beaches, but that might change at any moment. Approximately fifty German infantrymen defended the guns. They were dug in behind hedgerows, with interlocking trenches, fortified with machine guns and mortars. Winters had the equivalent of a squad—one 60mm mortar, two light machine guns, two tommy guns, and five rifles.[27]

On the face of it, this sounded like a suicide mission, but the skill and bravery of Winters and his men made it otherwise. Winters devised an audacious but simple plan. He knew that the angle of the hedgerows lining the field made it possible for his men to approach from several directions. As his training had taught him, he planned to lay down a strong base of fire while his men maneuvered along the flanks of the enemy force, eventually moving close enough to destroy the guns and kill the crews.

Winters faced his men and calmly outlined his plan. "First thing I did was have everybody drop all equipment except ammunition and grenades for that's all we'd need. Then I placed two of my machine guns in a position where [they] could give us a little covering fire as we went . . . into position. Next, I divided the group into two units. One went with Lt. [Buck] Compton, the other with myself. He took one hedge, I another."[28] Compton had Sergeants Don Malarkey and Bill Guarnere with him. Winters ordered Sergeant Carwood Lipton (the man who landed at Ste-

Mère-Eglise) to take Sergeant Mike Ranney and move to the right flank. They were to provide supporting fire and then bring up TNT when it came time to destroy the guns.

Everyone was in place now. Winters saw a German helmet moving along the lip of one of the trenches. He fired two shots and the helmet went down (later he found a pool of blood in that spot). The three riflemen with Winters and one of the machine-gun crews fired more rounds in the direction of the first German gun. This functioned as cover fire for Compton's group. Compton, Malarkey, and Guarnere were crawling under cover provided by the hedges around the field. Ever so steadily, they neared the first gun.

Over on the right, Lipton and Ranney discovered that thick foliage prevented them from seeing the German positions. Lipton glanced around, looking for a tree to climb. "There were no . . . trees with a large single trunk that I could climb . . . and position myself behind the trunk to fire. There were smaller trees, smaller trunks, and I found that in climbing up into these smaller trees, I had to settle myself down among the branches on the front side in order to be able to see in the direction of the enemy. It gave me a ringside seat, looking right down into the German positions that were only seventy-five yards away." Using a carbine, Lipton added his fire to that of Winters's group. "I fired at a German in a prone position. When I fired, he dropped his head down to the ground and made no other movement." Lipton continued firing unopposed. For the moment, the Germans were fixated on the fire coming from Winters. Out of the corner of his eye Sergeant Lipton saw Compton, Malarkey, and Guarnere preparing to throw grenades.[29]

In one flurry of motion, the three of them hurled their grenades in the direction of the German gun. Following the explosions, Compton led them through the hedge, straight at the enemy gun position. The Germans were taken by surprise. They had been so fixated on the threat originating from Winters, to their front, that they had not noticed Compton's group. In an instant, Compton jumped into the German trench that led into the gun pit. Sergeant Malarkey was right behind him. "As he dropped into the trench, a German was standing about fifteen feet from him. He pulled his Tommy gun and fired at him, and the gun jammed and misfired. In the meantime, the German ran down the trench, and Compton turned and waved us all across."[30]

Lying in his firing position at the first hedge, Winters saw Compton and knew it was time to move. He leaped to his feet and shouted, "Let's go! Follow me!" Firing and running, Winters and his three men quickly made it to Compton. The German gun crew, along with their accompanying infantry, was fleeing. Compton, Malarkey, Guarnere, Winters, and the others pitched grenades at them as they ran. One of those grenades hit a German in the head and exploded.

The trench system snaked forward in the direction of the guns. From those positions German crews shot at the Americans with small-arms fire. Across the open field, at the opposite side of Brecourt, several German machine guns kept up an insane chatter. Winters now took his first casualty. "One man, [Popeye] Wynn of West Virginia, was hit in the butt and fell down in the trench hollering, 'I'm sorry, Lieutenant. I goofed off, I goofed off, I'm sorry,' over and over again. At the same time a Jerry potato masher sailed into the middle of us."[31]

They hit the dirt as far away from the grenade as possible, but Corporal Joe Toye, a twenty-five-year-old coal miner from Pittston, Pennsylvania, never saw it. All he heard was a scream from Winters: "Joe, look out!"

Toye barely had time to react. "All I did was flip to get the hell out of the way, and that goddamn thing went off." Whatever Toye did, it was enough to avoid injury. The grenade exploded between his legs, but in spite of that, the fortunate Toye was not hit. "I flipped, and it . . . took a chunk out of my rifle. I never saw it! If it wasn't for Winters . . . I'd be singing high soprano in some church choir."

Shaking off the cobwebs, Toye glanced down the trench to his left and got a glimpse of the enemy soldiers who had thrown the grenade. "I took a couple pot shots at them. I got up enough nerve to crawl down in the trench, and I saw them easily. These guys must have been only 17 or something. They had been hit, and they were sitting there, and so I started searching them."[32]

In the meantime, Winters led Guarnere and Private Andrew Lorraine on a ruthless surge for the first gun. They pitched grenades in front of themselves as they went. This flushed out three German soldiers, who took off running across the field. The three Americans raised their weapons and fired. "Loraine [*sic*] hit his man with the first burst," Winters recalled. "I squeezed off a shot that took my man through the head. Guarnere missed his man who turned and started back for the gun, but he'd only taken about two steps when I put one in his back and knocked him down, then Guarnere . . . pumped him full of lead with his tommy gun. This fellow kept yelling, 'Help, help' for about five minutes."

Lieutenant Winters saw a fourth German about one hundred yards away. "I . . . had the presence of mind to lie down and make it a good shot. All of this must have taken about 15 to 20 seconds since we rushed the position." Winters took a moment to rest and assess the situation. "Jesus Christ," he thought, "somebody will cut loose in a minute from further up the trench." To prevent this from happening, the lieutenant flopped down and peered into the next enemy position just in time to see two Germans setting up a machine gun. He took aim and fired. "I . . . hit the gunner in the hip. The second [shot] caught the other boy in the shoulder."

Now Guarnere, Lorraine, Toye, Malarkey, and the others joined Winters. With the first gun captured, Winters went back to check on Wynn, "who was still sorry he goofed off." Winters inspected Wynn's wound, determined it wasn't too bad, and told him to crawl back to an aid station.[33]

As Wynn made his way back, crawling cautiously along the ground, Sergeant Lipton saw him and provided some first aid. From his perch in the slender birch tree Lipton had traded shots with the Germans for a few minutes but then thought better of it. Enemy bullets were clipping branches and leaves all around him. The sergeant knew it was time to leave. "That's the fastest I ever came out of a tree and when I got to about a dozen feet off the ground, I just dropped the rest of the distance." When he got to Wynn, he poured some sulfa powder in the wound and dressed it. "I had to bandage Wynn's butt!"

Lipton found Winters, who had drifted back to the captured gun position. "[He] wanted to disable the gun." Only then did Lipton realize that he had left his musette bag and demolitions kit back at the road, where they had staged this attack. "I told him I would go back for it, and I crawled back and started back up with the musette bag and the demolitions."

German machine-gun fire was heavy, zinging mere inches over his head. Lipton became aware of someone crawling next to him. It was Warrant Officer Andrew Hill of regimental headquarters. "Hey, Sarge, where's battalion headquarters?" he asked.

Lipton wondered what Hill was doing out here. He pointed toward the rear. "Back that way." Hill chanced a look in the direction

Lipton was pointing. Just then, a German bullet hit him in the forehead and exited through his ear, killing him instantly. "He was the first American that I saw actually killed," Lipton said.[34]

Sergeant Malarkey, normally a levelheaded, excellent soldier, now did something very foolish. Believing that one of the dead Germans in the field was wearing a holster containing a Luger pistol, Malarkey left the cover of the trench and braved withering enemy fire in search of the Luger. As he inspected the holster (which, ironically, was empty), the enemy fire tapered off. Observing Malarkey from their positions at the opposite end of this Brecourt farm field, they apparently thought he was a medic. Winters saw what Malarkey had done and screamed in disgust, "You idiot! Get the hell out of there! The place is crawling with Germans."

Malarkey, chagrined, realized that Winters was absolutely right. "When Winters yelled, I jumped up and started running back to the first gun where I had come from, and as soon as I jumped up . . . four or five German machine guns started firing at me, and the bullets were kicking up the ground all around me . . . but nothing hit me. I dove under the gun. I lay there, face up as they kept firing into the gun itself, and the fragments of bullets were dropped into my face and burning me. I was stuck there until it all ended."[35]

Farther up the trench, Winters ordered his men to capture the second gun. Throwing grenades and hollering as they ran along the trench, they took the gun easily. They also captured the two wounded machine gunners Winters had shot a few minutes earlier. The lieutenant knew his tiny assault force was low on ammo and overextended. He paused to regroup and sent back word for his two machine-gun teams to come forward. This took about half an hour, after which the group captured the third gun against little opposition. In the meantime, Winters had found, in the second gun position, some excellent enemy maps that delineated artillery positions all over the Cotentin.

All this time he was still waiting for Lipton and his TNT to disable the guns. Sergeant Guarnere attempted unsuccessfully to destroy them with some improvisation. "I tried to disable them by dropping grenades down the barrels, but it wasn't really working." Fortunately, Captain Hester soon arrived with several blocks of TNT and some white phosphorous grenades. Guarnere and the others destroyed three of the guns, blowing their breeches out and curling the barrels (giving them, according to the participants, the appearance of half-peeled bananas). Lipton was disappointed when he finally came back with his demolitions kit and found the guns already disabled. With this vital job done, Guarnere gave way to exhaustion. "The adrenaline I had been running on just left me. I was so tired that I remember looking over the top of a hedge with a pair of field glasses to see if there were any more Germans around, and I fell sound asleep. Joe Toye came up behind me and tapped me on the shoulder, and I think I jumped 10 feet. The 10 seconds I slept were like 10 hours."[36]

There was one last gun to go. Reinforcements arrived and took it. Lieutenant Ronald Spiers, D Company, 506th, led a wild one-man charge at the final position. He jumped into the gun pit, spraying the crew with tommy-gun fire. "Look at that crazy motherfucker go!" several men exclaimed. Spiers shot up the crew and nearly was killed by one of their grenades. In the attack, he lost two men killed.

In a matter of three hours, all four vital guns had been destroyed, by the equivalent of an overstrength American squad. The machine guns at the other end of the field were still going strong, though, and Winters knew that it was time to withdraw. The mission had been accomplished. There was no point in losing anyone to the German machine-gun fire. He ordered his men to withdraw back to Le Grand Chemin. They did so with methodical precision. Winters was the last one out. "As I was leaving I took a final look down the trench and here was this one wounded Jerry we were leaving behind trying to put this machine gun on us again so I drilled him clean through the head . . . and pulled out." About an hour later, Winters guided several Sherman tanks—just in from the beaches—to Brecourt. Making liberal use of their cannons and coaxial machine guns, the tanks cleaned out the enemy machine-gun positions.

Lieutenant Winters had lost four killed and two wounded. The Germans had lost fifteen killed, several more wounded, and twelve captured. Thanks to the success of the American attack at Brecourt, the 4th Division GIs at Exit 2 would not have to worry about artillery fire coming from the direction of Le Grand Chemin. Historian Stephen Ambrose succinctly summarized a major reason for the success of the tiny but effective American assault force that day. "From the supreme commander in Berchtesgaden on down to the field officers in France to the local commanders in Normandy to the men in the barracks . . . [the German Army] was an army inferior in all respects (except for weaponry) to its Allied opponents."[37]

Even as Winters and his tiny "band of brothers" destroyed German artillery positions opposite Exit 2, a mixed group of 502nd and 506th troopers did the same for Exit 1. Allied intelligence knew all about the guns threatening Exits 2, 3, and 4, but they had no idea of the existence of a battery of four 105mm guns dug in along a field north of Holdy, a tiny hamlet near Ste-Marie-du-Mont. These guns were a dire threat to Exit 1.

In the early moments of the night drop, an unfortunate stick from the 502nd had landed in tall trees adjacent to the sixty German artillerymen manning these guns. The Germans slaughtered many of these troopers in their harnesses and captured the rest. Some Americans later claimed that the Germans slowly, sadistically, executed these men by attaching thermite grenades to their legs. When activated, the thermite grenades (designed to wreck the breech of an artillery piece) generated intense heat. Troopers who landed near Holdy told of hearing agonized screams coming from the vicinity of the artillery position. Not long after D-Day, Private Burgett was in the area and said he saw several dead Americans, lying faceup, shoulder to shoulder, with their "manhood cut or shot completely away, leaving nothing but blood-caked, gaping wounds in their crotches." An American battalion surgeon, Captain George Lage, who supervised an aid station in Holdy, beheld many of the same things and later wrote to his wife: "Some of the cruel, cold blooded things that some of the Germans did made us all see red. From that time on, we decided if they wanted to fight dirty, we could too. We took very few prisoners compared to the number we could have for just that reason. This war business . . . can be terribly horrible."[38]

Lieutenant McKearney, the platoon leader in E Company, 502nd, landed near Holdy. He wandered the area, collecting ultimately a fighting force of about sixty men. His first order of business was to determine his whereabouts. He soon found himself in contact with Lage. "We came to a little village. As it was surrounded by a stone wall, I decided to move in. As we approached it we were challenged in English. Inside was a medic captain from our own battalion—Captain George Lage . . . and three aid men." Dr. Lage told them that they were in Holdy. "We set up a perimeter defense around the village, and remained tight until dawn." McKearney soon found out that he was almost right on top of the enemy battery. "With typical Irish luck, I had stopped just short of a battery of . . . German field pieces."

McKearney's men quickly sealed off every route from the field. The Germans were now in quite a fix. They could not use their 105mm guns on the Americans at such close range, nor could they escape. They could only engage the Yanks in a small-arms fight that was not to their advantage. The two sides traded shots for nearly two hours. "They were just as amazed to see us as we were to see them," McKearney believed. "We were so close that they could not deflect their fixed field positions to hit us. They tried to dislodge us in a half-hearted manner. The morning wore on. The wounded were staggering in. At one time, 'Doc' Lage had forty or more wounded men. The dirty bedroom he had as an operating room was sticky with blood. The wounded were laid in the town court. It seemed fantastic. It was like a scene from a film."

As McKearney's people battled the German artillerymen, Colonel Bob Sink, commander of the 506th Parachute Infantry, was sitting in a jeep, risking life and limb on a reckless reconnaissance ride. He and the men with him encountered many Germans but managed to survive unscathed. While on this journey, Sink spoke with a runner who told him about the action around Holdy and the surprise battery of 105s. Sink sent reinforcements, about seventy-five in all, to Holdy.

This force, under the ambiguous joint command of Captains Knut Raudstein and Lloyd Patch, arrived at McKearney's position at 1000. The officers were working out an intricate plan for a double envelopment of the enemy force when one of McKearney's bazooka men decided the whole issue. He shouldered his weapon, closed to within thirty yards of the enemy, and fired. The bazooka round tore into a group of enemy soldiers in a ditch behind one of the guns. He resolutely loaded and fired four more times. Two of his shots scored direct hits on ammunition dumps, blowing them sky-high. This collapsed German resistance, and the bazooka man knew it. "Come on! All you got to do is kill the rest of them!" he screamed at his buddies. They tore into the field and shot up the Germans. The fight lasted only a few more minutes.

When it was over, Lieutenant McKearney gazed upon the sickening detritus of the battle. "What a scene of carnage! This was my first . . . association with violent death. A man at one hundred yards seemed so impersonal." By contrast, this was very personal. He and several of his men found the troopers who had been killed in their harnesses. "Most of these men were slashed about the face and body. Our men said nothing. Words are so useless at a time like this." Somberly they cut the dead troopers down, wrapped them in their chutes, and prepared to bury them. "I tried to think of a suitable prayer. All I could think of was my Mass prayers in Latin. This broke the tension."[39]

Patch's force moved on to nearby Ste-Marie-du-Mont and met strong German forces. Some of the Americans boresighted one of the 105s and fired a couple of shots into the steeple of Ste-Marie-du-Mont's church. As it turned out, most of the town was in German hands except the steeple, that GIs were using for sniping and observation. McKearney and another officer, Lieutenant Raymond Hunter, became very worried about a German counterattack to recapture the guns. All day long they were under sniper and mortar fire and they grew increasingly nervous with each ricochet or explosion. They decided to destroy the guns.

This was a mistake. Colonel Sink knew that the 377th Parachute Artillery Battalion had been badly scattered—this unit probably endured the worst drop of any unit on D-Day—and he coveted the four German guns for the artillery support they could provide. Sink sent a detail to tow the guns to his CP, but by the time they arrived, McKearney and Hunter had destroyed three of the guns. Only one undamaged gun was turned over to the 377th.[40]

General Taylor landed all alone in a cow pasture near Holdy. He struggled to free himself of his chute, fully expecting to see several of his soldiers at his side. "But looking around I saw not a single soldier, only a circle of curious Norman cows, who eyed me, disapprovingly I thought, as if resenting this intrusion into their pasture." On the upside, the presence of these cows told him that the pasture was not mined. He cut his way out of his chute and made off into the night, in search of other Americans. The first trooper he met was Staff Sergeant Ed Haun. The general was so happy to see Haun that he hugged him.

Within half an hour Taylor and Haun made contact with several other soldiers from the 101st, including General Anthony McAuliffe, the division artillery commander; Lieutenant Colonel Julian Ewell, commander of the 3rd Battalion, 501st; Major Lawrence Legere, assistant operations officer of the division; and Colonel Gerald Higgins, Taylor's chief of staff. By daylight the force was larger but still dominated by headquarters staff and officers. They could see the church steeple at Ste-Marie-du-Mont, a landmark quite familiar to them from their pre-invasion briefings. Thanks to that knowledge, and conversations with locals, the Americans now knew exactly where they were.

Taylor had a brass-heavy force of about eighty-five men. He decided that they would go due east and open up Exit 1 at the town of Pouppeville. In the master plan, this mission was supposed to be accomplished by two battalions of the 506th, but Taylor, like so many other airborne commanders that morning, had to get by with what he had. With a famous wisecrack ("Never have so few been led by so many"), Taylor told his men to get moving along the dirt road that led to Pouppeville. Farther ahead in the column, Private First Class Bill Kopp also could not help but notice all the officers doing jobs normally reserved for enlisted men like himself. "There were so many officers and so few enlisted men . . . that even lieutenants were assigned as riflemen."[41]

As the Americans approached the beach exit road, they saw figures approaching in the distance. Another group of soldiers, platoon-sized, was coming from the vicinity of Pouppeville, heading straight for Taylor's force. It was a German patrol! Both sides saw each other at the same time. No one opened fire. Instead, the Americans and Germans both dived for the cover of roadside ditches.

At the front of the American column, one officer, Captain Vernon Kraeger, quickly tired of the standoff. Kraeger, the commander of G Company, 501st, was spoiling for a fight. He had seen two planeloads of his men shot down several hours ago, during the jump. All at once, Kraeger hopped onto the road and started walking in the direction of the Germans. The captain's bravery inspired one his men, Corporal Virgil Danforth, to follow him. "Captain Kraeger insisted on walking down the center of the road toward the town carrying his carbine which was almost as big as he was." Another soldier from G Company joined them and they began shooting at the Germans. "Sergeant Lionel Cole was on the right trying to kill all the Germans in the ditch and the hedges on that side while I was on the left side doing the same thing. We kept telling the Captain to get back where he belonged but he kept telling us to mind our business. He had almost lost his whole company . . . and he was just plain mad."

They were taking fire from enemy soldiers in Pouppeville, but most of the Germans in the ditches cowered passively while the three Americans raked them over. Danforth, a sniper, was trying to manipulate his bolt-action Springfield rifle. "I was having a rough time feeding the bullets into the gun one at a time and at the same time out ran the Captain and killed a number of Germans on my side of the road. I shot eleven in one group in the ditch—all in the head. That was the only part I could see sticking out above the ground so it wasn't much of a trick."

In fact, Danforth's fire was devastating. The Springfield, like any sniper rifle, excelled at long-range, accurate shots. At close range, it packed an even deadlier wallop. Each round from Danforth's rifle made a clanking sort of metallic sound (roughly akin to that of a steel mallet rapping against a girder) as it pierced the helmets and skulls of the German soldiers.

The German patrol was, for all intents and purposes, eliminated. Led by Kraeger, Danforth, and a few others, the Americans now left their ditches and approached Pouppeville. As they did so, they began taking fire from the outlying buildings of the town. Once again, they dived for the cover of the ditches. Sixty Germans from the 91st Division (a well-trained and -equipped unit) defended the town. They shot at the Americans from second-story windows.

Lying in a gully near the front of the American column, on the south side of the road, T/5 George Koskimaki, the Michigander who served as General Taylor's radioman, was crouched low, trying to make himself as small a target as possible. Koskimaki's company commander, lying on the other side of the road, spotted the young radioman. The captain wondered how many other signalmen were with this assault group. He ordered Koskimaki to leave the ditch, walk down the road, and count the number of signals people. "Encumbered with my radio equipment and other gear, my movement was rather sluggish as I got up and started toward the rear. A concealed German . . . opened fire at me and with bullets whanging off the road surface, I dived back into the ditch. The shooting stopped. After waiting a bit, the Captain suggested I go back to do the checking." The same thing happened again. Luckily for Koskimaki, the captain decided to forget about this silly order.

Scouts along the flanks of the American force began shooting at the German-held buildings in Pouppeville. As they did so, the troopers in the ditches crawled forward. By now, Koskimaki, exhausted, had fallen asleep. "Someone behind me was nudging and shaking my foot to urge me forward." Koskimaki started to move, "but the person in front of me was still lying there. I reached forward to shake his leg, assuming he had dozed off like I did." He hadn't. He was a dead German.

Some of the Americans were out of the ditches now, rushing toward Pouppeville. Koskimaki could see Major Legere at the head of a small group of soldiers, looking for all the world like just another squad leader. "He moved past me and up the center of the road about twenty yards to my front. A shot rang out and he was down writhing in the road, brought down by a sniper's bullet. The call 'Medic' immediately went down the column." A young trooper, with Red Cross bands clearly displayed on either arm, hoisted himself from the ditch and ran to the fallen major. This young medic, T/5 Edwin Hohl, knelt beside Legere and fumbled with his first-aid kit. Koskimaki watched in horror as "the unseen sniper fired again. Hohl was killed instantly with a bullet in the chest."

Private Bill Kopp, a machine gunner whom Colonel Ewell had placed at an intersection a little farther up the road, looked back in time to see Hohl's death. "I saw him topple on top of the major after being shot. I can still picture his face."

One of the scouts spotted the German sniper and unleashed a volley of fire that silenced the enemy rifleman. Legere was gravely wounded; most of his thigh had been shot away by the sniper's dum-dum bullet (a wooden projectile outlawed by the Geneva Convention). Someone pulled Legere into the ditch and another medic worked on him. Eventually Legere had to be shipped back to the States for a long recovery.

Ewell split the assault force into two groups and ordered them to envelop the town from the north and south. From both directions they moved into Pouppeville for a house-to-house assault. Koskimaki, trailing right behind the lead riflemen, paused to look at Hohl's body. The tragedy of the youthful medic's death struck home to the radioman. "He was just a kid."

Hurling grenades and firing into windows, the Americans cleared out the first few houses, driving the remaining Germans to a large schoolhouse that served as their main headquarters. At one point during this melee, a trooper came unexpectedly face-to-face with a German in a doorway. The American had a bayonet fixed to his M-1 Garand. Reacting more than thinking, he thrust the bayonet under the German's chin, straight through his head, and out the back of his skull. The man extracted the bloody, gore-stained bayonet, took it off his rifle, and never used it again.

Ewell was with the lead troops, right at the cutting edge. At one point, he peeked around the corner of a house. A sniper's bullet glanced off his helmet, leaving only a dent. Others were not so lucky. Private First Class Fred Orlowsky, like so many others with Ewell, was running toward the schoolhouse, dodging German fire. "I saw Lieutenant Nathan Marks get shot in the forehead while peering around the corner of a small building towards the larger house where the Germans were holed up. Sergeant Tom Criswell and PFC Bob Richards were shot within a few yards of me as they were running toward the big house in the height of the attack."

The sight of these men getting hit temporarily slowed the American advance. Corporal Danforth crouched in a doorway and watched as a medic tried to help Sergeant Criswell, who was bleeding badly. German fire kept driving the medic back to cover. Danforth, a very brave man, moved from his doorway into the line of sight of the Germans. "I . . . tried to draw their fire so [the medic] could get to the downed men but they put a bullet in me too. It hit the ring of my helmet and split in two and half of it went into my skull and I still have the headaches to prove it. Captain Kraeger then got hit in the arm with a wooden bullet. About all this did was make him madder."

The Americans brought up a bazooka and fired a few rounds into the German headquarters. The German commander emerged from the house. Ewell took a few ineffective shots at him with his pistol, until it became clear that the enemy officer wanted to surrender. Thirty-eight Germans emerged from the building with arms raised. They had lost twenty-five dead and wounded.

With Pouppeville now in his grasp, General Taylor sought to make contact with 4th Division troops coming up from Utah beach. He sent Second Lieutenant Eugene Brierre, an airborne military policeman in charge of security for division headquarters, on a search for friendly amphibious forces. Brierre went down to the beach, found some Americans under the command of Captain George Mabry, and brought them back to Taylor's CP at Pouppeville. Brierre also found time to minister to a dying German in one of the houses. "He signaled to me to hand him something; I saw that he was pointing toward a rosary. I . . . picked up the rosary and handed it to him. He had a look of deep appreciation in his eyes and he began to pray, passing the beads through his fingers. He died shortly thereafter."

Later in the day, T/5 Koskimaki excitedly watched as tanks rumbled up from Utah beach. "I remember how elated I felt when the first tanks poked their way through the streets. One paratrooper rushed forward and planted a kiss on the first tank."[42]

Thanks to the aggressive efforts of small groups of determined troopers, the 101st Airborne successfully captured the four beach exits and the guns that menaced them. But the other half of the division's mission did not go nearly as well. Troopers from the 501st and 506th Parachute Infantry Regiments were to capture St-Côme-du-Mont, a key town three miles north of Carentan on the N-13, along with the five Douve River crossings that comprised the southern flank of the entire VII Corps front on the Contentin. Misdrops and tough German resistance thwarted them. These Americans achieved only mixed success by the end of D-Day.

Colonel Howard "Skeets" Johnson, commander of the 501st, was a hard-driving, hard-assed, almost fanatical officer. During his invasion eve speech to his troopers, he brandished his fighting knife and promised to plunge it into the heart of a "Nazi bastard" before another setting of the sun. Actually, Johnson had to rely on something more modern—his pistol—to do away with the first enemy soldier he encountered. Johnson landed directly opposite the front gate of Château le Bel Enault, a beautiful three-story mansion that served as a German CP. A German sentry raised his rifle and shot at Johnson as he was struggling free of his harness. Luckily for Johnson, the sentry missed. This gave Johnson the chance to draw his .45-caliber pistol and shoot the sentry.

One of the men in Johnson's stick had landed in a sequoia tree at the south edge of the mansion. He freed himself and came running toward the sound of the shots. Unfortunately, Germans were emerging from the building at the same moment. They shot and killed the trooper. Two other men in the colonel's stick landed on the roof, crashed through the windows, and cleared le Bel Enault room by room.[43]

Meanwhile, Johnson drifted away in search of his objective—the La Barquette locks and the two highway bridges near St-Côme-du-Mont. The colonel succeeded in collecting about 150 men. This force quickly captured the locks. These locks controlled the flow of seawater in and out of the Cotentin. The Germans had used them to flood the Douve and Merderet river basins. Control of the locks could give the Americans a way to impede the flow of German reinforcements into the peninsula.

Johnson was so pleased with the easy seizure of the locks that he ordered part of his force to detach and push on to his other major objective, the two highway bridges south of St-Côme-du-Mont. Those troopers who remained at the locks came under German artillery fire all day long, but the enemy did not mount any serious D-Day counterattack to win back the locks.

Johnson soon found out that German resistance was much more formidable elsewhere. The only other cohesive groups of Americans in the area were busy dealing with strong German opposition north of La Barquette locks, in and around St-Côme-du-Mont. In effect, this small town served as a kind of barricade to the bridges.

All day long, fighting raged in and around St-Côme-du-Mont. Radioman Joe Beyrle of I Company, 506th, landed on the roof of the church at St-Côme-du-Mont and quickly found that he was in unfriendly territory. "Taking fire from [the] church steeple, [I] slid down and made my way through a cemetery surrounding a church, over a wall and headed toward our objective which was the two wooden bridges over the Douve River." When Beyrle left town, he went in the wrong direction (west) but did not realize it until he came upon the Carentan–Cherbourg railroad line. He reversed himself and went back to St-Côme-du-Mont, where he used his gammon grenade to blow up a power station. Once again, he left town. This time he moved south on N-13. "As I was trying to make my way to the bridges, I crawled over a hedgerow and landed in a German machine gun position manned by 10–12 Germans and was captured."

The German soldiers were paratroopers just like Beyrle. They marveled at his equipment. "We had a mutual admiration society. That probably helped me survive." Guards took him to an underground headquarters in an apple orchard near St-Côme-du-Mont. An English-speaking intelligence officer interrogated Beyrle. "I would give only my name, rank and serial number." That was standard, but there was something quite unusual about this particular interrogation. "There was a young blond woman setting on the corner of the officer's desk." Beyrle could not escape the feeling that he knew her from somewhere. "She proceeded to tell me that she had been in Ramsbury and had danced with . . . many of my buddies and officers." She could even identify these men by name. Beyrle ended up in a POW camp in Germany but was later liberated by the Soviets and fought alongside them for several months in the last months of the war. As if that were not bizarre enough, his parents received a telegram stating that he had been killed. One of Beyrle's captors took his dog tags, later tried to infiltrate American lines in Normandy, and was killed. The body of this German was mistakenly buried, under Beyrle's name, in an American cemetery. After the war, Beyrle had the strange, perhaps unnerving experience of visiting his own grave.[44]

Another 506th trooper, Private Bill Oatman, also got captured that day near St-Côme-du-Mont. Following a narrow escape from his burning C-47, Oatman had another close call. He landed in a minefield. Oblivious to the deadly peril all around him, Oatman crawled out of the field without tripping a mine. He met up with a couple of other troopers and roamed the environs of St-Côme-du-Mont looking to make trouble or find their unit, whichever came first. "While we were lying in a gully figuring which way to go to meet up with our company, we heard some noise and about eight or ten Krauts came running towards our gully. When they got to the gully, they split up and ran up both sides. We had pulled the pins in our grenades so we just waited till they got pretty well past us. Then, we threw the grenades and took off in the other direction. I know we got a few of them because of all the screaming and hollering."

They had a few more brief firefights until they found a French farmhouse. Several French children brought them wine and bread. They showed the kids their maps and they pointed out where they were, but for some reason Private Oatman and the others did not trust them, so they headed in the opposite direction. This was a mistake. They ran right into a large German unit. "We had quite a battle until we ran out of ammunition. We were taken prisoner and they stripped us of everything. They took us to a farmhouse where we saw some other wounded paratroopers and also some of our boys hanging in the trees, still in their chutes, with their privates cut off."[45]

Throughout D-Day, the Americans tried several unsuccessful, uncoordinated attacks on St-Côme-du-Mont. Captain Sam Gibbons, a staff officer in the 501st (and a future congressman), led a group of fifty men on one such attack. He had landed near Carquebut to the north. Now, as the sun rose, his platoon-sized group cautiously made its way south along the N-13, closing in on St-Côme-du-Mont. "The flankers to the east and west and all of the riflemen were walking in the fields and having to cross hedgerows and . . . some of those hedgerows were six feet high and were a solid combination of stone, dirt and bushes, vines and trees [a foreshadowing of the geographical challenge that would soon impede the Americans in Normandy]. Of course, before each hedgerow was crossed it was necessary to make sure no one was ready to surprise you on the other side."

Shortly after a break (in which Gibbons shared two cans of Schlitz beer with several other men), the point man found evidence that the Germans were near. "In the west ditch was a wounded German soldier. The German had been hit in the stomach area and was in bad shape. He had already turned rather gray-looking and seemed to be rather incoherent." They moved on and left the wounded man where he lay. "He was a pitiful sight, so all alone, so badly injured, and so near death."

They closed to within 300 yards of St-Côme-du-Mont. From here they could see the buildings. Nothing looked untoward. The windows and shutters were all closed. Nothing stirred. The place looked like several other towns they had passed along the way. Gibbons ordered his men forward. He heard the clacking of a bolt nearby, glanced to his right, and saw the muzzle of a machine gun poking out of a hedge, right at him. He dived for a ditch and "all hell broke loose! We had been ambushed. Instantaneously, shots started coming from the buildings in St-Côme-du-Mont and from the hedges that stretched out to the east and west, just outside of the town."

Captain Gibbons was pinned down. He could hear one of his fellow officers fifty yards away, shouting orders, even as the machine gun continued to chatter in the next hedge. Gibbons knew he had to eliminate that machine gunner. If Gibbons didn't, he would remain pinned down while German snipers in St-Côme-du-Mont picked him off. "I took a grenade out of my pocket, pulled the safety pin, and lobbed it over the hedge. After it went off, I heard no more firing from his position and assumed that that problem was out of the way for awhile."

With the help of supporting fire from other troopers, Gibbons made it to better cover. He consulted with his second in command

and his sergeants. "It was obvious that we were badly outnumbered. So there we were—200–300 yards north of St. Côme du Mont meeting superior fire from a major force. We had no automatic weapons, no radios—only our semi-automatic rifles and a few pistols. We hardly knew each other, but we were getting well acquainted." Gibbons decided to break off the fight.[46]

At the tiny village of Les Droueries, scarcely a kilometer to the east of where Gibbons and his patrol were fighting, another mixed group was also encountering strong resistance. The commander of this force, Lieutenant Colonel Robert Ballard, Commanding Officer of the 2nd Battalion, 501st, actually had a good drop. From the start he knew he was in the right spot, just to the east of Les Droueries. He gathered together the typical mixed force of troopers, and as the sun rose, the force numbered some seventy men moving west, straight at Les Droueries. One of Ballard's scouts reported seeing a German going into a building in Les Droueries. The colonel concluded that the Germans defended the town in strength and decided to attack them. He was tempted to bypass Les Droueries and move on to St-Côme-du-Mont (not to mention his objective, the highway bridges), but he knew he could not. If he did, he might leave an enemy force of unknown size in his rear, so Les Droueries had to be taken.

Ballard divided his men into two platoon-sized companies. At 0530 they approached Les Droueries in two parallel columns, hugging hedgerows along the two roads that led into town. In one awful instant, the town came to life with German small-arms and mortar fire. The roads leading into town were no more than 200 yards apart from each other. At the easterly road, where F Company steadily worked its way toward the town, a young lieutenant, Leo Malek, led the way. Clutching his carbine, keeping his men under cover, he made sure to keep sight of the terrain ahead. "In front of us was an open pasture and a farmstead from which we were receiving enemy fire. We set up a mortar and scored several hits on the buildings. Enemy fire persisted. We tried to advance along a lane running perpendicular to our hedgerow. More enemy fire." German machine-gun fire swept everywhere. One hundred yards or so in front of Lieutenant Malek, his point man, Private Jack Schaffer, took cover from the enemy machine-gun fire. He hugged the ground for a while, hoping not to get hit, and then found himself in a very lonely position. "I realized that I was left alone. The others had gone back." He eventually tried to make his way back to where he thought the others had retreated. "I was pinned down for about a half hour before I started my return trip. I continued on back and met a patrol of Americans and got directions to where the others were located."

A few hundred yards away, the other prong of Ballard's attack, E Company, also got pinned down. German mortar fire inflicted several casualties. By 0700 Ballard had lost about fifteen men. He repeatedly tried to attack the town but failed. At one point, he was reinforced by a twenty-man patrol that executed a wide flanking maneuver and captured one of the buildings in Les Droueries, but this was not decisive. All day long, Ballard and his men were stymied at Les Droueries, far away from the highway bridges.[47]

No Allied airborne unit had a bloodier drop than Lieutenant Colonel Wolverton's 3rd Battalion, 506th. When he led his men in such soulful prayer at Exeter on D-Day eve, Wolverton could not have known the terrible fate in store for him and many of his troopers. The transport crews dropped the battalion fairly accurately on their intended zones south and east of St-Côme-du-Mont, but this was not a good thing. The Germans regarded this area as ideal for paratroopers and defended it accordingly. At the eastern edge of the drop zone, they had doused a barn with oil. Now they set it afire when they saw Wolverton's troopers descending. This lit up the area and made the paratroopers quite vulnerable on their descent. Many were killed before they ever hit the ground. Others landed right in the midst of the Germans and were killed or captured in seconds. Out of 723 troopers, only 130 made it to the battalion's intended objective, the wooden bridges that forded the Douve at Brevands.

Wolverton himself got hung up in an apple tree east of St-Côme-du-Mont. German soldiers cornered him and shot him to death, right in his harness. The same thing happened to Wolverton's executive officer. Corporal Ray Calandrella, aboard Wolverton's plane, landed nearby but managed to avoid this fate. He hit in a field all by himself and assembled with several other troopers. Germans were everywhere. Calandrella could hear their machine guns ripping and he could see tracer rounds slashing through the night sky. The fire from the barn lit up the whole area, almost like daylight in spots.

Calandrella was leading a small patrol of six men when he heard a Teutonic-sounding voice yelling "for me to surrender or halt. Instead of doing that, I turned and beat it back about 30 yards. The

Jerry fired a shot close but missed." Calandrella and the others got away and found a hiding place when the sun rose. All day long, they could hear the Germans around them. Finally, the inevitable happened. The Germans detected their presence and cornered them with a superior force. "One of our men yelled that he was hit in the leg. One was captured and two were either killed or wounded." A German soldier was so close that Calandrella could have "reached out and grabbed him." Eventually, the enemy soldiers rooted them out. Calandrella and several others got captured.[48]

As Wolverton's headquarters group struggled for survival, one of his staff officers, Captain Charles Shettle, managed to assemble two officers and thirteen enlisted men. They headed straight for the Douve bridges. On the way, they cut one of Carentan's main power lines. They also were reinforced by eighteen more troopers. At 0430 Shettle's group reached the bridges. The two structures were located within half a mile of each other. One of them was a footbridge and the other a vehicle bridge. The Americans took cover behind an embankment that paralleled the Douve River. Shettle studied the bridges and pondered his best course of action. He knew full well the importance of these objectives. Control of the bridges meant control of the entire southern flank of the Cotentin. Any German reinforcements moving toward Utah beach in this area needed these bridges.

As Shettle studied the bridges, twenty more American soldiers filtered into his position. They were wet and tired from crossing drainage ditches and eluding Germans. In the memory of one of these men, Shettle immediately spread them out along his tenuous line. "The bridges were nearly half a mile apart so our line was stretched very thin. Across the river was a small hill defended by a fairly large force [of Germans]. There was a levee running along the river so we dug in along this levee and prepared to defend these bridges." German small-arms and mortar fire peppered the area. "The snipers killed several men, but the mortars . . . did practically no damage. Only a few men were slightly injured from them."[49] The mortar fire, however, grew steadily more effective.

In spite of the German presence across the river, Shettle wanted complete possession of the bridges. For this to happen, he needed men to cross the bridges under fire and establish a lodgment on the east bank. He asked for volunteers to cross the footbridge. Two men stepped forward—Private First Class Donald Zahn and Sergeant George Montilio. Armed with only a tommy gun, Private First Class

Zahn stooped and ran across the bridge, avoiding German machine-gun fire. Zahn made it across and ran to a point about eighty yards beyond the bridge. There he scouted a wooded area and found signs of German positions. Deciding it was time to leave, he made his way back to the bridge, where he met Montilio, who was just crossing. They took cover and talked over their next move. Ten troopers joined up with them. Because it was now full daylight and German fire had zeroed in on the bridge, these men had crossed the bridge by means of the girders on the underside of the bridge (similar to climbing a ladder horizontally).

As the Americans wondered what to do next, a German pistol shot rang out from a nearby hedgerow. A bullet tore through Private First Class Hank DiCarlo's back and exited near his right breast. Zahn sprayed the hedge with his tommy gun, killing the German who had pulled the trigger. The Americans heard screaming from the other side of the hedge and the German fire intensified. Zahn and several others pitched grenades, fired a few clips, and took off for the bridge. When they reached it, they recrossed it on the girders. As they crossed, this patrol noticed American demolition specialists, in scalp locks and war paint, wiring the bridge for destruction. Shettle was hedging his bets. If he could not have the bridges, he wanted to make sure that the Germans could not, either. His men at the footbridge settled into an uneasy stalemate that would last all day long.

Meanwhile, at the vehicle bridge, the situation was the same. The Germans on the east bank, controlling the high ground and outnumbering the Americans, were nonetheless content to stay at a distance and trade shots. For their part, the Americans were not strong enough to push across to the east side of the Douve. They found this out when a small force under the command of Lieutenant Turner Chambliss, an idealistic West Pointer, ran into heavy enemy fire at the bridge. One of Chambliss's men, Private First Class C. A. Spiller, got wounded during their wary approach to the objective. "As we neared the bridge, the Germans opened fire. I was in a ditch with other fellows. The Germans zeroed in our position with artillery. The first shot hit long, the second was short, and the third hit within eight feet of me. The man ahead of me was killed and I got hit in the side."

Crossing the bridge was out of the question. Private First Class James "Pee Wee" Martin, like all the other soldiers, had taken cover and waited for the killer artillery and mortar to abate. He saw Lieutenant Chambliss, his platoon leader in G Company, 506th, stand up suddenly. "He . . . was shot twice through the mouth." Someone pulled the lieutenant to the cover of a ditch, but he was dying. Martin was deeply saddened. He could not stop thinking about an incident that had taken place just before the invasion. Martin and the other men were consistently amazed at how idealistic and moral the lieutenant was. "He was . . . very G.I., very strict, but fair. He never drank or ran around and all the other officers must have been a little envious because they pumped the men for lapses which they might use to needle him. There were none."

The lieutenant was so intensely proud of West Point that Martin wondered if the 2nd Platoon should be known as an entity belonging to the Army or West Point. "I stenciled 'West Point' over the breast pocket of all of our combat jump suits." Martin and the rest of the platoon showed up in formation the next day with their new adornments, but the lieutenant never seemed to notice, then or after. Deflated, the men jumped into Normandy with their apparently unnoticed West Point stencils.

Now, as Lieutenant Chambliss's young life neared an end, he demonstrated quite clearly that he had noticed the stencils. An H Company sergeant was cradling his head. Chambliss asked him if any 2nd Platoon men were around. They weren't. According to Martin, Chambliss told the sergeant that he "wondered why we put 'West Point' on our jackets. He wondered if we were mocking his background." This hit Martin like a thunderbolt. "I cried tears of shock and frustration and shame as his body was carried past my position. I keep wondering how he could have failed to perceive the great pride and affection we had for him."

Shettle and his men held on to the western approaches to the Douve bridges, but they could not establish bridgeheads on the other side. They did not know it, but their ordeal was just beginning. For the next two days they held out and waited for reinforcements. As the captain remembered it, their existence consisted of "very little sleep, worry about our exposed position, lack of ammunition, and only hard chocolate bars [D-bars] for food."[50]

The airborne troopers jumped into Normandy believing they would fight two or three days and then be relieved. But, for many of them, the fight was only beginning.

CHAPTER TEN

THE AIR COVER

Allied airmen had spent more than two years making Overlord possible. While the ground troops trained, the aviators fought. Ever so steadily, they pummeled the Luftwaffe into submission. The veritable destruction of the once formidable enemy air force served as a kind of gateway back to the continent. To the airmen, Overlord represented a new and welcome phase in the war, one in which the Germans were on the defensive, one that foresaw the end of the war, one that meant that the airmen could now look forward to the day when the Europe below them was no longer an unfriendly maw of perilous, enemy-controlled territory that promised only captivity to the downed airman.

The bomber crewmen and fighter pilots of the U.S. Army Air Force in England were tingling with pre-invasion anticipation and excitement. They had felt this way for weeks, ever since they began carrying out the transportation plan, an offensive whose obvious purpose was to prepare the way for invasion. It is fair to say that the aviators had worked themselves to a fever pitch; they were keenly waiting for the special day.

In the declining hours of June 5, teletype machines clacked at American bomber and fighter bases in England. The awkward machines—so reminiscent of the stock market tickers of an earlier era—spit out the fragmentary orders that eventually set the Air Force into motion. Tonight, at Grafton Underwood (American crewmen liked to call it Grafton Undermud for obvious reasons), Colonel Dale Smith of the 384th Bomb Group sat in his tiny office in the group's operations shack. He heard the teletype machine chattering in the main room outside his office. A few seconds after the teletype went silent, Smith's operations officer, Major Tom Beckett, stepped into the little office and solemnly handed him a piece of paper. Beckett rarely, if ever, gave the colonel copies of the fragmentary order ("frag order"). Usually, Beckett orally conveyed the orders while they waited for the formal, more complete field orders that followed. Not this time, though, and that could only mean one thing. Colonel Smith felt a nervous surge of anticipation. "My hand trembled a little as I held the yellow paper. I had a good idea what it contained: the long anticipated invasion." The 384th was ordered to bomb enemy positions near Caen in the morning. "I told Tom to call a meeting immediately of all senior staff officers, squadron commanders, and Company commanders, and to have them assemble at the Senior Officers' Quarters. We had a lot to do."[1]

At nearly the same time at Ashford, home of the 406th Fighter Group, Captain William Dunn, the ace and Eagle Squadron veteran, was awakened by the sound of hundreds of aircraft engines. He lay in his cot and listened for a moment. What was this all about? he wondered. He decided to go to the operations shack to find out. When he arrived, the invasion frag order was just coming over the teletype. "What's going on, guys?" Dunn asked.

"Those birds you hear overhead are . . . C-47s . . . hauling paratroopers," an operations officer responded. He proceeded to tell Dunn about the invasion along with the missions his group would fly. Someone else handed Dunn a copy of Eisenhower's "Great Crusade" pamphlet, the one that had so turned off paratrooper Private Webster just a few hours before. Dunn read it and had a completely different reaction. He was impressed with the seriousness of the supreme commander's resolve. Captain Dunn and the other officers immediately set to work preparing for their mission. "We haven't got too much time before we all become heroes," one of them breezily observed.[2]

Lieutenant Jack Havener, a B-26 copilot in the 344th Bomb Group, did not see his group's orders, but he and the rest of the combat crewmen sensed the imminence of the invasion when they were alerted for an 0200 briefing. "Some celebrated, some prayed, some wrote a letter home and some withdrew into themselves and wouldn't speak." Havener thought the occasion called for some comic relief. Several weeks earlier, he had found a British bowler hat. He wrote "D-Day" on a three-by-five-inch card, stuck it in the hatband, and propped the hat on his head. Then he fashioned a similarly ridiculous-looking outfit. "I cut out a huge handlebar moustache from black art paper and stuck it under my nose. Over my underwear I wrapped my light tan trench coat, hooked on my pistol belt, holster and gas mask and strode out barelegged in my G.I. shoes." Toting an umbrella in one hand and a pistol in the other, he walked from Nissen hut to Nissen hut proclaiming, "This is it, men!" He got the response he was hoping for. "Even though there were some pretty serious countenances on some members of the huts I visited, not one remained that way after they'd seen Havener making an ass of himself. I know it certainly eased my tensions!"[3]

Not long after Havener's impromptu comedy routine, it was time for the pre-mission briefings. All over England, combat aviators trooped into briefing halls, or tents, and listened, with rapt attention, as intelligence officers explained their respective roles in this historic event. A palpable sense of excitement—almost electrical in its intensity—pervaded the briefings. When Lieutenant Mac Meconis, a pilot in the 466th Bomb Group, entered his unit's briefing room at Attlebridge, he was amazed by all the security and intelligence activity. He had to give a password and be checked off a list before actually entering the room. "S2 men were all over the place, refusing to answer our leading questions, guarding the large war map. When finally all flying personnel had crowded into the room and settled down to a tense silence, Col. Pierce [the group commander] was the first to rise. A blind man could see he was nervous. His hands shook as he handled papers and I saw him wet his lips before [he] read."[4]

When bombardier Al Corry of the 387th Bomb Group strode into the briefing room at his unit's base at Chipping Ongar, he knew this was it. A day before, he had been recalled from leave in London. Then, earlier tonight, he had noticed ground crewmen painting white stripes on the group's B-26 medium bombers. At the briefing he crammed into an uncomfortable wooden chair and waited for his colonel to speak. Corry was wearing most of his flight gear—flak vest, leather jacket, two shirts, and fur-lined boots.

When the colonel saw that everyone was in place and the doors to the room had been closed, he stood up. He wore his cap at the jaunty angle that was so popular among airmen and he chomped on an unlit, stubby cigar. "Hey, guys, good morning, good morning, good morning! Well, here we are. This is it. This is the big day we've been waiting for. That's what we all came here for.

We're going to France at six—as air support for the Allied forces invading the Normandy coast. This is to be the invasion."

For a couple of seconds the men absorbed what he had just told them, but the silence did not last long. "The quiet erupted into a big roar. We were all pretty excited."[5]

At a fighter base in Thruxton, twenty-two-year-old Lieutenant Quentin Aanenson, freshly arrived from his pilot training in the States, donned his flight gear and settled in for his briefing. The Minnesotan was so new to his unit, the 366th Fighter Group, that he had not yet officially joined a squadron. New or not, he could sense the unearthly tension. "It was almost deadly still. We glanced at each other knowingly, but no one spoke. A Lieutenant Colonel moved up to the map in the front of the room, faced us for a moment in silence—and then said rather softly, 'Gentlemen, this is it. The invasion of France is beginning.' "

The room erupted in jubilation and cheers. In the middle of the mayhem, Lieutenant Aanenson sat there and thought, "I can't believe I'm here." He knew that this was a moment in history "that would never be forgotten."[6]

For many of the youthful American aviators the ecstasy soon gave way to sober reflection on the dangers that lay ahead. First Lieutenant Chet Pietrzak, a native of Erie, Pennsylvania, was just as excited as everyone else at briefing when the commanding officer of his 388th Bomb Group broke the news of the invasion. But Pietzak, a bombardier, had managed to survive twenty-two missions; he knew what combat was all about. The same was true for many others in the briefing room. Some aviators worried that the recent absence of the Luftwaffe meant that the Germans were husbanding their planes for a maximum effort to disrupt the invasion. These veterans feared that D-Day would be a bloodbath.

No sooner had the 388th crewmen settled down and the colonel relayed the basics of the mission than Pietrzak and the other aviators began a spontaneous prayer. "I'll never forget this as long as I live. The whole group got off their chairs and knelt down as one person. No one said a thing. They just did it. And they prayed. There was a whole different atmosphere right then, and to this day I still feel it. It's like nothing else I ever felt. Now we had something to fight for—those guys who would be underneath us."[7]

At the briefings, the crewmen learned the information they would need to know on D-Day. Bomber crews were briefed on formations, rally points, bomb loads, targets, altitude, weather, flak, and the like. Fighter pilots studied reconnaissance photographs of their patrol areas, flak concentrations, and German fighter bases. They learned which units had responsibility for combat air patrol in which areas; they learned how they were expected to communicate, and they learned what kind of strafing targets they might find in which sectors of Normandy.

As the sun gracefully rose in the eastern sky on this momentous morning, the great aerial armada droned inexorably toward the coast of France. The men in these planes, especially in the tightly packed bomber formations, had to be very alert. Roughly eleven thousand planes were in the air over southern England. The cloudy weather, a remnant of the recent storms, made the going that much tougher. Some bombed choke points and troop concentrations at Caen or St-Lô. A few American bombers supported the British landings, hitting such targets as Ouistreham, where British and French commandos would soon go ashore.

At Omaha beach, some twelve hundred bombers of the 8th Air Force prepared to bomb enemy emplacements, pillboxes, bunkers, troop concentrations, and supply depots at or near the beach. The bomber crewmen could not even begin to see the beaches below. In order to make sure they did not bomb their fellow Americans in the landing craft and ships below, they held their bombs or waited another half-minute or so before they dropped their bombs.

The majority, like Sergeant Edwin Ehret's B-17 crew, opted to do the latter. Seated at his modest little desk in the neck of the plane, right behind the flight deck, the radioman had a "million-dollar seat high . . . above the screaming and pounding of our bombs." He was awed by the whole spectacle. "Fortresses filled the sky ahead . . . behind . . . below . . . to the sides . . . they're everywhere. Impressive isn't the word for it as hundreds of forts go over their respective targets each dropping its load of destruction from their yawning bomb bays. Down the bombs tumble through the soft clouds, like ears of corn falling out of a bushel basket." Ehret felt the bombs release from his own plane. He left his station to check that all bombs had released. They had. As his B-17 turned west and then headed for home, he muttered a quiet "prayer for the boys down there. They'll be pushing open the very jaws of hell."[8]

Unfortunately for those about to push open "the very jaws of hell," Ehret and the other heavy-bomb crewmen did them no good. Most of the bombs from this enormous aerial armada fell harmlessly inland, behind German beach defenses and away from German reinforcements. The heavies at Omaha dropped close to 3,000 tons of bombs that detonated anywhere from 300 yards to three miles behind the beaches. These bombs killed plenty of Norman cows in pastures and fields but precious few Germans.

The ineffectiveness of the bombing at Omaha was a bad harbinger. Realizing that the hilly, ridge-pocked shoreline of Omaha would probably be the toughest to assault, the planners had invested a lot of hopes in the bombing, at the expense of naval bombardment. In retrospect, this was foolish. In this war, heavy bombers had not yet proven their usefulness as a tactical support weapon for ground troops, nor would they. Shellfire from the Navy's destroyers and cruisers proved to be the best weapons for destroying the enemy's extensive concrete-reinforced beach defenses. The Allies would have been much better served to employ more of these ships in pre-invasion bombardment and invasion support, but they did not. Senior commanders like Eisenhower, Bradley, and Montgomery needed only to study the lessons learned in the Pacific at places like Tarawa and Kwajalein to understand the need for a more overwhelming, efficient naval bombardment. But, strangely, they turned a blind eye to these lessons. For instance, at Kwajalein the 7th Infantry Division received more direct support from more battleships, cruisers, and destroyers than directly supported all of the American assault troops at both Utah and Omaha beach. In the view of one Pacific-experienced officer, the SHAEF senior commanders (especially Bradley) thought of operations in the Pacific as "strictly bush league stuff." The assault troops at Omaha beach paid the price for such inexcusable prejudices.[9]

The medium bombers, flying below the clouds, at altitudes between 3,500 and 7,000 feet, achieved much better results at Utah beach. Beginning at 0515, an hour and a half before H-Hour, a force of about four hundred B-26s hit German positions on the beaches and immediately inland. Approximately 43 percent of their bombs hit within 300 feet of their targets.[10]

When the crews learned they were bombing at such low altitudes, they were fearful. "Many of us were reminded," Lieutenant Allen Stephens explained, "of the first B-26 low-level missions against German submarine pens earlier that year, on which all ten of the attacking ships were lost."

Fearful or not, they went ahead and did their job. Stephens piloted one of the first planes to bomb the Utah beach area. "Our targets were coastal guns and blockhouses along the beach." As his B-26 closed in on the target, Lieutenant Stephens saw the immense fleet below. Viewing this awesome sight, he felt a great sense of pride at being part of something that would reshape world history. The closer his plane got to the target, the more excited he became, but enemy fire soon quelled the excitement. "We went through the heaviest concentration of antiaircraft fire I had yet seen. Tracers and flak explosions were so thick that it looked impossible to get through without being hit." They dropped their bombs, turned away, and flew safely home to their base at Rivenhall.[11]

Elsewhere in the formation, Lieutenant William Redmond and his 387th Bomb Group skimmed along the coast, closing in on the German beach defenses they were slated to bomb. They were flying at 4,000 feet. From his bombardier's perch Redmond could see for miles. Somewhere near St-Vaast, about seven miles from the target, Redmond spotted four German flak boats. "[They] opened fire with deadly tracers." Lieutenant Redmond saw the tracers score hits on several planes from another group. "One disintegrated in a ball of flame, apparently its bombs exploded. I became very mad at the Germans." He yelled to his gunners to return fire, and they did so.

In minutes they were over the target. Redmond could see the invasion fleet and the German response. "All along the coast naval guns blinked at our destroyers and landing barges." The lieutenant concentrated on his bomb site and, at the correct moment, let his bombs fly. He could see them striking home. "Our bombs knocked out the machine gun and mortar nests in the target area."[12]

In another plane near Redmond's, fellow bombardier Al Corry hunched over his site. "I set my inter valometer so that every two seconds a bomb would release. I also had a manual trip switch, so I'd drop a couple using my foot as the aiming point." He salvoed the bombs and saw them fall to earth, explode, and "make good foxholes for some of those guys coming ashore. I could see Germans on the far side running . . . away from the front."[13]

The 344th Bomb Group was one of the last in the formation. The men in this unit dropped their bombs on Beau Guillot, La Madeleine, and St-Martin-de-Varreville, about twenty minutes before the first wave of 4th Division troops hit the beach. Second Lieutenant George Eldridge was the deputy lead bombardier of this group's eighteen-plane formation. His plane was so low— 5,000 feet—that he did not even need oxygen. He could see enemy batteries hurling shells at the ships offshore. Any second, he figured, those German guns would turn on his formation. "Our target was right on the beach and we paralleled the beach on the bomb run. Bomb bay doors were open now and we were on the run. It seemed an eternity but only a minute or less and bombs were away. I . . . released on the leader. We were carrying sixteen 250-pound GP [General Purpose] bombs. Our gunners were cutting loose at anything they could see. Tracers could be seen going in all directions. Our bombs hit on the beach and near the target area." The aviators were amazed at the destruction their bombs wrought. "The bombs, carpeting the target, are bursting like . . . bubbles in a vat of nitric acid," one of them said. "There are spouts of flame and belching smoke which seem to leap at us like some angry monster writhing horribly. It is terrible in sheer destruction." With bombs away, they executed some evasive maneuvers, turned right over the peninsula, and flew home.[14]

As Eldridge feared, the Germans did swing their guns upward in an effort to target the low-flying B-26s. One of the planes farther back in the formation came close to being shot down. In that plane, Sergeant Ralph Nunley, the tail gunner, was watching his group's bombs explode when he heard someone on the intercom say, "We've taken a hit!" Flak had battered their right engine. The pilot feathered the propeller and shut down the engine. Now they had to make it home on only one engine. To make it, they would have to jettison some weight. That meant throwing away some of their equipment and all of their ammunition. "We were to take the ammunition and dump it out of the bomb bay. We were being shot at and there was quite a bit of apprehension. I was pretty sure that . . . we would not have time to bail out at that altitude we were flying."

Soon they were over the ocean, heading back to England. Sergeant Nunley heard a terrible banging sound coming from somewhere in the middle of the plane. "I thought the front of the plane had been blown off." He took a closer look and discovered "a big hole in the belly of the ship." Someone had been dumping ammunition out of this hole. A belt had gotten caught and "was hung up in the hole and flapping. Soon after that . . . it fell." Tense moment followed tense moment. Finally they made it to an emergency landing strip in southern England. "It was a successful landing without accident and we got out of the plane and we walked . . . until we got a place where we could sit." Nunley's knees were trembling; they barely functioned, from either fatigue or fear. He was never completely sure.[15]

Other B-26s had similarly close calls. "Our ship was full of small holes, but no one was wounded," Lieutenant Clyde Funk of the 386th Bomb Group related. The Germans shot down three medium bombers at Utah beach.[16] Considering the dangerously low altitudes from which the B-26s bombed, it is remarkable that they did not suffer greater losses. Most likely, this is because the Germans had to divide their fire. They had so many targets in front of them—naval and aerial—in such a concentrated area that they could not spew forth enough effective fire at any of those targets without concentrating on one at the expense of the other.

Among the vast majority of the medium-bomber crewmen who made it safely back to England, many were debriefed, ate a hot meal, and then loaded up for another mission or even two. First Lieutenant Robert Hobbs, an Arkansas native and bombardier/navigator on an A-20 medium bomber, flew a mission in the early afternoon of D-Day to destroy rail-yard oil storage tanks near Carentan. His flight of forty-five A-20s made landfall twenty miles east of Carentan, turned right, and flew straight toward their target. "Concentrating on keeping exactly on-course and locating the target through my Norden bomb sight, I had little time to look around. The rail yard oil storage area in Carentan was easily picked up at our low altitude of three thousand feet, and we made a direct hit." He saw all six of his 500-pound bombs salvo and descend straight on-target. "Keeping my eye in the bomb sight, I could see boxcars flying in the air, and big explosions from the oil storage area."[17]

Hobbs and the other medium-bomber crewmen could enjoy such unmolested victories because of the efforts of the Air Force's most glamorous branch—fighters. On D-Day the fighters covered everyone—the Navy, the C-47s, the gliders, the heavies, and the mediums—and added much of their own firepower to the mission of reducing German resistance.

The number one mission of the fighters was to safeguard the invasion fleet, a necessary but bitterly disappointing assignment for the cocky fighter jocks, who yearned to strike a killing blow to the Luftwaffe (actually, they already had). The fighter pilots took off from their bases in southern England and spent hours patrolling above the fleet. Many of the American fighter planes flying naval cover that day were P-38s. Naval gunners could easily recognize these fork-tailed twin-engine planes. Plus, the P-38 excelled at air-to-air combat but not necessarily at strafing.

One of those P-38 pilots flying top cover for the fleet was Lieutenant Edward Giller of the 55th Fighter Group. Giller, the son of a Jacksonville, Illinois, farmer, had a degree in chemical engineering from the University of Illinois. In 1941, after a mundane year of work as a chemical engineer with the Sinclair Oil Company, he got interested in aviation. He entered a civilian pilot training program and grew so enamored of flying that he decided to join the Air Force. Now, three years later, on D-Day, he sat in the cramped cockpit of his P-38, high above the fleet, and searched for enemy aircraft. "We were so high that we were disconnected ... from the activity on the ground." The whole mission seemed unreal somehow, perhaps because he felt "no sense of personal involvement."

The air controllers, back in England studying their radar sets, had almost no enemy aircraft to report. On the few occasions they did, Giller and his colleagues eagerly pointed their planes in the direction of the reported enemy. "Fighter pilots being fighter pilots, all wanted to have a chance to chase a German, and the biggest hazard was when you arrived in the sector given by the control radar from England. You would find 300 other Americans in there, which made flying more hazardous." Each report turned out to be a false alarm.

Giller spent three hours on-station and then went back to his base in Wormingford. He and the other pilots landed, refueled, ate, and went up for another uneventful mission. "[We] spent a couple of hours circling quietly. There was little activity ... and finally we were released ... and started back for England."[18]

Other fighter pilots who flew cover for the Navy also spent quiet hours circling and circling, heads on a swivel, looking for trouble that never came. Strapped into a rugged P-47 Thunderbolt, Francis Gabreski, a famous ace in the 56th Fighter Group, flew four of these missions, mostly in an area between Boulogne and the Seine, on D-Day. It ended up being one of the quietest days he ever spent in combat. His 56th had arguably done more than any other unit to make this day so quiet. For months they had engaged German fighters and swept them from the skies, earning the sobriquet Zemke's Wolfpack from an adoring press, who lionized the group's commander, Hubert "Hub" Zemke.

After crossing the Channel, Gabreski enjoyed a breathtaking view of the fleet, but that was the most exciting moment of his day. "We would go out and patrol our area as best we could until we were about out of fuel. Then we'd come home, load up again, and go back out. We flew between layers of clouds. Sometimes I could barely make out the ground through light spots in the overcast, but that was all."[19]

Farther to the west, near the Brest peninsula, Lieutenant W. A. Simkins and his 405th Fighter Group hunted for German submarines that might attempt to harass the Allied fleet. "Occasionally we'd hear that someone thought they had sighted a submarine, or that they thought a ship was trying to get out of a harbor, but it was mostly a boring patrol. We were given an area to patrol from point A to point B. You did as you were told because you knew that you were performing a specific function."

Simkins never saw any enemy ships, but another man in his unit, Lieutenant Ralph Jenkins, did. He thought he spotted something below. "I descended from twenty thousand feet to ten thousand to have a better look, and suddenly the sky was filled with antiaircraft fire coming from this ship. I reported this to headquarters. I suspect it was a German ship heading for the invasion area."[20]

Unlike Jenkins, most of the pilots who flew antisubmarine patrols found nothing. Like idle bodyguards, they flew for hours, staying alert for a threat that never materialized. The hours went by, and for some, like Lieutenant Leonard Schallehn, another pilot in the 405th, bladders filled to the breaking point. "I did have to go to the john awful bad, and we went back and forth, back and forth in an area we were assigned. I finally said, 'To heck with it.'" He unhooked his seat belt, found the remarkably impractical gyrating relief tube in the cockpit, and let nature take its course. "Just in the middle of it, we [bounced] down and I lost a lot of my relief tube [contents], emptying into the cockpit all over my legs." That was all Schallehn remembered of D-Day.[21]

Some units, like Lieutenant Robert O'Neill's 406th Fighter Group (same outfit as Bill Dunn), flew cover missions for the beaches. O'Neill, the New Orleans native, could not help but look down at the drama unfolding thousands of feet below. "We . . . could see the large Warships open up with everything they had at the shore installations. When they would fire their guns, it would appear that the whole ship exploded. Then, we could see the flashes from the big guns of the Germans." But O'Neill and his squadron mates knew that they could not afford to stare at the spectacle below. Their job was to deal with enemy planes, not spectate. "We had to keep our necks on a continual swivel in anticipation of something."

The only excitement came when an air controller, code-named Snack Bar, vectored them to intercept some enemy planes. "But before we could execute, we received word from 'Snackbar' that the British Aerial Cover had taken care of that situation. It was utterly frustrating to be waiting for something that didn't appear, and not being able to do anything to help the men who were fighting and dying below us!" Only three German fighters challenged the landings during the daylight hours. In the evening, twenty-two more enemy planes used the cover of darkness to attack the ships, but they did almost no damage.[22]

As O'Neill indicated, the fighter pilots were itching to do anything they could to help the assault troops. Some of the fighter pilots, upon completing their patrols, went down to the deck to empty their guns into any targets of opportunity. When Major Enoch Stephenson's squadron finished patrolling north of the Channel Islands, he led his pilots on a strafing sweep near Caen. "We found a German convoy of about a dozen trucks . . . headed toward the beachhead. We could see swastikas on the hoods of the trucks. We peeled off and got into trail, one behind the other. Since I was the leader, I was in front. When the Germans heard us coming they stopped in the middle of the road, got out of the trucks, and ran for the ditches. We destroyed the convoy, then headed back to our base in England."[23]

Normally, fighter pilots preferred aerial combat with enemy planes to the strafing of ground targets. But on this day those who were assigned strafing missions, like Lieutenant Aanenson, were delighted. Flying at 2,000 feet, in a P-47 somewhere near the rear of his squadron's formation, Aanenson could not get over the number of ships and planes around him. He and his fellow pilots were nearing Pointe-du-Hoc, soon to be the target of the 2nd Rangers. Ships and landing craft choked the waters below. Planes buzzed everywhere. In seconds, Aanenson zoomed over Pointe-du-Hoc, headed for German artillery positions a mile or two inland. The leaders, many planes ahead of Aanenson in the formation, visually verified the target, in order to make sure they did not mistakenly hit any American paratroopers who might be in the area. Two by two, the P-47s overflew the target, dropped their bombs, and strafed anything that moved. "Our mission was over in a few minutes. Things happened so fast that it was difficult for us new combat pilots to judge the results. In about 40 minutes we were back on the ground in England—no planes lost, three or four with flak damage."[24]

At nearly the same time, several miles west of Aanenson, the 365th Fighter Group closed in on its target—a railroad underpass in the central Cotentin. They were flying so low—50 to 100 feet—that they had to watch carefully for trees and power lines. In one of those P-47s, twenty-one-year-old Second Lieutenant William McChesney, from Pittsburgh, prepared to jettison his bombs. "We went in . . . right up the railroad, dropped two 1,000-pound, eleven-second delayed action bombs, and continued to orbit the target area, which was absolutely obliviated. You can imagine sixteen aircraft (thirty-two 1,000-pound bombs) hitting a small railroad. We then returned to base. It was just a madhouse. Everybody was on everybody's airplane asking us what we saw, what it was like, and so forth." Like many other fighter pilots, McChesney flew a second mission later in the day. "We bombed an ammunition dump with terrific success. We strafed everything that moved in gray-green . . . and every vehicle moving anywhere, leading to, or retreating from Omaha Beach."[25]

A few miles beyond the beaches, Lieutenant Norman "Bud" Fortier, a twenty-year-old New Hampshire native, flew below 2,000 feet, along a tree-lined road, looking for targets. He had been flying combat missions with the 355th Fighter Group since the previous September. This morning he was leading half his squadron. "Suddenly we were directly over a column of about twelve

German tanks heading north. Caught by surprise, [they] scattered off the road into the wooded area on each side."

As Fortier led the way, the American planes dived for the deck. The tanks made it to the cover of the woods, but Fortier and his pilots simply strafed the whole wooded area. "There was plenty of return fire." At treetop level, Fortier dropped both of his 250-pound bombs. "I pulled into a steep climbing turn and looked back. Twin geysers of red-orange flame sprouted from the woods, and a few seconds later I felt rather than heard the explosion." Fortier saw oily smoke rising from the woods, so he knew he and his men had scored some hits.

They reorganized, kept flying, and found "a freight train in a marshaling yard." Once again, they turned sharply, descended, and began strafing runs. Their bullets peppered the boxcars and blew up the locomotive. "We were getting shot at but couldn't see where it was coming from. Low on ammunition, we headed home." Later in the day, Lieutenant Fortier flew another mission. On this one, he cornered a German Stuka dive-bomber and shot it down.

Other fighter-bombers destroyed bridges at Etienville, shot up more convoys all over Normandy, harassed German reinforcements, and generally made life miserable for the enemy. The Allies sortied nearly 13,000 aircraft on June 6. The Luftwaffe, almost completely invisible, did not shoot even one of them down. Flak batteries or ground fire shot down 113 aircraft, the majority of which were transport planes.

In the final analysis, the aerial bombardment was a mixed success. The heavies were almost totally ineffective; they were ill suited for ground support. The mediums did significant damage at Utah beach and elsewhere. The fighters deterred a cowed enemy fighter force, in addition to contributing plenty of mayhem of their own. The ubiquitous nature of Allied aircraft over the skies of Normandy certainly contributed to Allied morale and broke the will of many Germans to resist. The official U.S. Army Air Force historian asserted that the success of Overlord "was possible only because of the absolute air domination won by the AAF and RAF in the months before D-Day." This was absolutely true. Domination of the air undeniably made Overlord feasible, but so did something else—domination of the sea.[26]

CHAPTER ELEVEN

THE NAVAL BOMBARDMENT

A t Omaha beach, the shooting started shortly after 0530, about twenty minutes before sunrise. By now the sailors had fed the assault troops (at least those who could eat) and the soldiers had boarded their landing craft. The troops bobbed around miserably, sickeningly, on the various types of craft that slowly churned their way through the surf, toward the foreboding beach.

As they did so, a German battery, located somewhere near Port-en-Bessin, just east of Omaha beach, opened up on the battleship USS *Arkansas*. The venerable battlewagon replied in kind, as did the rest of the bombardment group, consisting of two battleships, four cruisers (three British and one French), and twelve destroyers. About one thousand yards from the beach, aboard PC-553, a small patrol craft, Ensign Ernest Carrere was supervising the firing of his boat's main weapon, a three-inch deck gun. "Our target was a pillbox." Carrere had been furnished clear and accurate photographs of the pillbox. As he concentrated on finding the pillbox, he glanced out to sea. He had a perfect view of the *Arkansas*. "Our magnificent vantage point permitted us to see the *Arkansas* firing its main battery of 14 inch shells. You could trace the course of the shells." They looked like "small planes headed . . . towards the beach."

These high-velocity shells whizzed back and forth as the German heavy guns, many of which were dug into cliffs and ridges along the expanse of Omaha, traded shots with the Allied ships. The noise and the concussion from the blasts bordered on intolerable. As their guns belched, flashing in the pre-dawn half-darkness, the battleships and cruisers rocked backward, their heavy anchors holding them in place. Each time they fired, concussion and shock waves rippled across the water.

The USS *Texas* concentrated on targets at the western end of Omaha beach. Firing from about five miles offshore, the battleship hurled fourteen-inch shells from its main guns at German pillboxes and gun emplacements along the Vierville draw. Soon after, she turned her attention to Pointe-du-Hoc. The Royal Air Force had bombed the Pointe during the night, leaving humongous craters pockmarking the muddy, grassy landscape around the German bunkers that honeycombed the place. Aided by a spotter plane circling above the chaos of the bombardment, the *Texas* now added its own firepower, blasting and pockmarking the Pointe that much more. Aboard the *Texas*, Dorr Hampton, a gunner's mate on one of the battleship's three-inch mounts, helped load and fire the gun while he strained to see what they were shooting at. "I think we fired for one hour with the fourteen-inch guns. It seemed there was quite a few shell splashes out there. At one time we must have hit an ammunition dump. A big mushroom went up in the air." Aside from the ammunition dump explosion he could not see much through the smoke and dust except "concrete and stuff . . . blowing up from shelling . . . just like a jackhammer busting up concrete." Smoke and dust from the explosions reached hundreds of feet into the air.[1]

While the battleships and cruisers raked over the cliffs and beach draws, the destroyers—beautiful, swift, and sleek—sliced through the water, closing to within one or two miles of the coast. Their job was to serve as mobile artillery, pinpointing targets and eliminating them with precision shots. They performed magnificently on D-Day. As the day unfolded, they proved to be the most effective ships at providing close, devastating support for the ground troops. Now the destroyers fired at prearranged targets up and down Omaha beach.

Cruising through the waters immediately east of the Vierville draw, the USS *McCook* blasted pillboxes and antitank guns. Aboard the *McCook*, Martin Somers, a war correspondent well known for his willingness to face danger, stood on the bridge, right next to the skipper, Lieutenant Commander Ralph "Rebel" Ramey. Somers observed as the destroyer spit shell after shell from its five-inch guns. "Within a few short minutes, on automatic fire, we get our second target and attempt our third. This one is a battery cunningly concealed behind a stone wall down a gulch curving

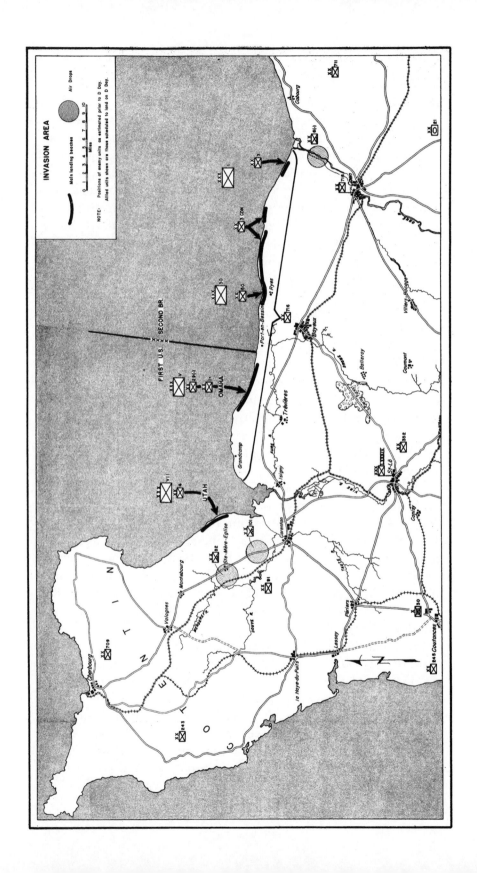

away from the sea. A salvo below, a salvo above, a salvo to the left—this fellow is really stubborn. The next salvo smashes the gun and sends it down the gulch, starting a minor avalanche."

Within half an hour, the *McCook* had fired 250 shells at its preassigned targets. It switched to targets of opportunity. "We cruise backward and forward along the shore, searching for targets. There are large splashes off the starboard bow, and a lookout shouts that we are being bracketed by big guns ashore. But the splashes are not repeated, and we never know whether we've been aimed at."[2]

A bit farther down the coast, the USS *Harding*, under the tutelage of Commander George Palmer, prowled its patrol area, near the 1st Division's Easy Red sector. Like every other American destroyer, the *Harding* was looking to inflict maximum damage on the Germans ashore. Similar to every other crew in the Allied fleet, the *Harding*'s crew had secured the destroyer for action. "The ship's compartments and living spaces are isolated by having all water-tight doors and hatches closed," Lieutenant Ken Shifter, the ship's chief engineer, explained. "All ventilation ducting is isolated and secured and all water lines and electrical circuits are closed off at the sources so in case of rupture they do not contribute to flooding or starting fire by electrical arcs from damaged cables. We fed the crew by using the Repair Parties to deliver 'C' or 'K' rations. Short breaks were authorized from time to time during lulls so people could use the head facilities a few at a time."[3]

Thus prepared, the *Harding* went to work. On the bridge, Palmer's executive officer and navigator, Lieutenant William Gentry, concentrated on navigating as the crew sprang to action. "Five-inch guns were shooting fast and I suppose accurately; within thirty seconds the shore disappeared in clouds of smoke, dust, and debris. My landmarks disappeared, but we still were able to navigate, now by radar. The racket . . . kept on and on—we could see [flashes] from the German guns ashore and hear the whine and scream of the shells as they passed overhead and astern of us." German flat trajectory shells screamed by at low levels. "Some members of the crew were sure a couple of shells went between our stacks."

Topside, at one of the ship's 20mm gun mounts, Seaman James Jones could barely see anything as he shot at the shore. "Shells were bursting ahead of us and then short and then over us. I thought they would hit us for sure, but they did not. We shelled our assigned position."

In forty-five minutes, the *Harding* fired about four hundred rounds at targets from Port-en-Bessin to Colleville. In the process it destroyed two fortified houses and silenced several enemy batteries, forcing their crews to take cover in the bluffs.[4]

The naval bombardment at Omaha beach climaxed at 0630, right before the first troops went ashore. For thirty-five to forty-five minutes, ships like the *Texas* and *Harding* did the best they could to eliminate resistance. Their ordnance, combined with that of the Air Force, detonated thousands of mines that otherwise might have maimed the foot soldiers.[5] At the same time, smaller ships like the destroyer escort USS *Amesbury* patrolled the flanks. Aboard the *Amesbury*, twenty-one-year-old signalman James Long went to battle stations with the rest of the crew. "Our job was strictly to screen the transports and the heavy bombardment group. We were just moving up and down, checking for submarines, downed planes, bodies, anything that happened to come our way."

Long lifted a pair of binoculars to his eyes and watched an LST pass, on its way to the beach. "She was about five hundred yards past us when an explosion stopped her dead in the water. She had evidently run into a mine." The explosion "just tore up through the inside of the ship." Long was part of the fire and rescue team on his crew. He and several other men boarded a launch that took them to the stricken, sinking LST. Long went to the bridge, gathered up anything of importance, put it in a weighted sack, and threw it over the side. He had just finished this when he saw something outside the bridge that stopped him short. "There was a young fellow laying there with half his head blown away. We rolled him into a stokes litter and covered him over and carried him over the rail and passed him over to our ship. We got off any wounded and anyone else that was there that we could get to." Many others were trapped beneath the twisted, jumbled metal that had once comprised the anatomy of the destroyed LST. Long's party could not do anything for them. They went back to their ship, did what they could for the wounded, and resumed patrolling.[6]

Patrol craft like the *Amesbury* were mainly concerned with the possibility of attacks from German submarines or E-boats (torpedo boats similar to American PT boats). Submarines did not threaten the landings at all, but once Admiral Theodor Krancke, the

German naval commander in France, realized, at about 0300, that the invasion was happening, he dispatched some of his E-boats. The only serious E-boat attack occurred east of the American landing beaches, at Le Havre. A torpedo hit the Norwegian destroyer *Svenner*, cracked it in half, and sank it. A British battleship, HMS *Warspite*, quickly sank one of the E-boats and sent the others retreating back to Le Havre. The *Svenner* was the only Allied ship the German Navy succeeded in sinking on D-Day. Otherwise, the Kreigsmarine was almost as big of a no-show as the Luftwaffe.[7]

Allied sailors had more to fear from mines than enemy ships or planes. This was especially true at Utah beach, where Force U had a tougher time than Force O (where German shore batteries did not score even one hit on any of the bombardment ships). This was somewhat ironic, since the actual landings were exactly opposite—the troops going ashore at Utah had a far simpler task than those going ashore at Omaha.

As at Omaha, the lead assault troops began boarding their landing craft in the last hour of darkness. On the deck of the USS *Bayfield*, Lieutenant Cyrus Aydlett, the ship's coding officer, saw many of those soldiers get ready to go. The *Bayfield*, a Coast Guard attack transport, served as the flagship for Admiral Don Moon, commander of the U Force, as well as headquarters for General Barton and his immediate superior, General Joseph Collins, commander of the VII Corps.

Laden down with weapons and equipment, the troops climbed over the side of the ship and gingerly descended down rope nets to their bobbing Higgins boats. Aydlett circulated among those who were waiting to go over the side. He wondered how many of these men would soon be dead. "I was suddenly filled with emotion. I could not restrain this inevitable feeling of being completely choked up with compassion for these bronzed and drill hardened soldiers—standing there tense with painful uncertainty nervously adjusting their packs . . . puffing on cigarettes as if that would be their last." No one spoke except for the loading officer who called each man by name, like a grim reaper, "signifying his turn to go over the side." Aydlett had no idea what to say to any of these men. He contented himself with moving among them, providing whatever moral support he could.[8]

The only real support the sailors could provide was fire support, over the heads of the soldiers in their beach-bound landing craft. The shooting at Utah began at 0505, half an hour earlier than at Omaha. German observers spotted and opened fire on the destroyers *Corry* and *Fitch*. Not long after that, a large-caliber battery at St-Vaast shot at several minesweepers as they skimmed along the coast. The HMS *Black Prince,* a cruiser, immediately engaged the St-Vaast battery, bravely distracting the enemy gunners from the little sweepers.

Aboard the USS *Tuscaloosa,* Admiral Deyo, commander of the bombardment group, could see enemy shells splashing uncomfortably close to *Black Prince.* "Tall splashes spring up and subside first and then beyond her. Now [USS] *Quincy* is getting attention, medium-calibre shells, perhaps 170s. Some ships ask permission to reply. Permission is not granted." Deyo wanted to wait just a bit longer until his spotting planes got into position. Minute by minute, the enemy fire grew more accurate. He knew he had no choice but to open fire. At 0536, he relayed the order: "Commence counterbattery bombardment."

In no time, he could hear an eight-inch shell being dropped into a loading tray, inside Number Two turret, just beyond the bridge. The guns of this turret and the other two swung to port, facing the target. "Nine long, graceful 8-inch rifles rise as one to the correct elevation. Two buzzes, 'Stand by,' one buzz! Flash; jar; lurch; acrid smoke passes my face." The *Tuscaloosa*'s rounds had no sooner gone out than incoming shells splashed close by. "Geysers of water with black, ugly centers lead up as high as our mastheads. On the open bridge, ears plugged with cotton, helmet straps buckled, we look and listen, bracing our feet as the 10,000-ton cruiser jumps and lurches to the blast of her guns."[9]

Even though the paratroopers had neutralized many guns inland, the Germans still had about 110 guns, deployed in twenty-eight batteries, along the Cotentin coast. Deyo had one American battleship, the *Nevada,* under his command. Anchored five miles from the coast, this powerful ship hurled fourteen-inch shells at many of those batteries. On the signal bridge of the *Nevada,* Electrician's Mate First Class Ross Olsen and a group of sailors gazed at the coast, just as the enemy shooting began. "We could see the beach and . . . houses on the beach. We could see shells landing in the water around us. The early shelling seemed to be concentrating on us, as we were the largest ship."

They were impatient to return fire. When Deyo gave the word, the *Nevada* became a cauldron of noise and fury. The booming of the main guns was overwhelming. Olsen could feel the sound waves and concussion slam into his chest. In spite of this, he felt much better now that his ship was shooting back at the enemy. Soon German shells hit even closer than before. "Some of the shells were landing so close to the ship that they splashed water up onto the deck and got the men manning the 2m guns wet." The ship's port side was parallel to the coast. Shells splashed on the starboard side, prompting Olsen to wonder how they "managed to get through the superstructure above us without hitting something up there."

In the meantime, spotter planes relayed target information to the command center of the *Nevada*, aiding with the plotting of targets, range, and identification. "They gave the ships corrections when needed to concentrate our fire." The *Nevada* fired so continuously and so violently that the paint peeled off its overheated guns, leaving only blue steel showing. There were so many shell casings littering the deck that they had to pause to sweep them overboard. The concussion from the fourteen-inch guns even slightly damaged the ship, destroying a lifeboat, knocking off the door to the mess hall, peeling off insulation material, and breaking lightbulbs.[10]

A few hundred yards to the north of the *Nevada*, the USS *Quincy* blazed away at enemy positions along the beach—machine-gun holes, bunkers, pillboxes, and dug-in tank turrets all came under fire. In his sky control perch on the *Quincy*, Lieutenant John Blackburn, a gunnery officer, helped spot targets, using information relayed from a spotter pilot circling over the beach in a Spitfire. Blackburn looked down just in time to see his cruiser's main guns fire. "The belch of nitrous brown smoke and yellow flames from the . . . two forward turrets gave us the reassuring feeling that at last we were in the fray." He could also see German shells splashing harmlessly somewhere to the right. "We must have been at the extreme range for the shore batteries."

For several minutes the *Quincy* fired counterbattery salvos at the German guns that were firing ineffectively at the anchored bombardment ships. Then she turned her attention to her predetermined target, machine-gun emplacements right in the middle of Utah beach. A destroyer had already been shelling that area. "Bomb clouds and rubble obscured the beach, but I could see where the salvos from the tin can were landing. Since she was much closer and better able to see what she was shooting at, we would just plunk ours in nearby—one four-gun salvo every fifteen seconds. I watched them landing and called in the spots to our plotting room people."

Next, he turned his attention to a "small white blockhouse" on the beach. Lieutenant Blackburn could tell that the shots were ineffective. He spoke with the spotter and the plotting people in an effort to correct the accuracy. "We were apparently looking at different targets without realizing it. Eventually, we realized the problem and got things worked out. Just in time, too, because the shells were walking toward a French farmhouse."[11]

As at Omaha, the destroyers provided the most effective fire of all. Some of them sailed so close to the coast that they risked running aground. This was a real peril. If they ran aground, they would be sitting ducks for German artillery, not to mention the kind of damage they would do to their screws and rudders.

At the northern edge of the landing force, north of Ravenoville, a mere three or four miles from the enemy guns at St-Vaast, the destroyer USS *Fitch* closed in on the beach at top speed. "My ship's job was to move...near the proposed landing area, turn right and proceed along the beach in the direction of Cherbourg firing at certain designated targets and anything else that looked suspicious or that opened fire on us," Ensign Richard Bowman later wrote.

As they sped along the coast, Bowman heard the telltale sound of enemy guns. "ZING! Two 155 millimeter...shells hit in the water 100 yds. off our starboard bow. About 20 more hit all around us—in our wake—off our beam—off our bow—and some of the fellows standing amidships swear that two screamed right between our stacks before hitting the water 50 yds. away." The *Fitch* fired back and kept moving.[12]

Since they operated in such close proximity to the enemy, destroyers like the *Fitch* had the most dangerous job of any ships in the bombardment group, especially after the sun rose at 0600. In an effort to provide some degree of protection, support planes laid down smoke screens between the coast and the destroyers. But one of those planes, supporting the USS *Corry*, got shot down before it could release its protective smoke. Aboard the USS *Butler*, a destroyer that was screening the cruisers and the *Nevada*, Petty Officer Felix Podolak glanced up at the skies and saw the *Corry*'s spotter plane get hit. "The plane was coming along...and the German shore batteries just blew it out of the sky. All you could see was a big ball of fire. The plane just dropped, burning on the water off the shoreline."[13]

With no smoke screen, the *Corry* was naked. Most of the German artillery observers, struggling to identify targets through smoke, debris, and flashes, could only see the *Corry*. Every functioning enemy battery in the area zeroed in on the unfortunate destroyer. The *Corry* had been firing at a furious pace, particularly at one enemy casemate, which, after about one hundred shots from the *Corry*'s five-inch guns, had been blasted into flaming, smoking ruins. The guns on deck were so hot that the sailors were hosing them down when enemy salvos began to hit perilously close.

The skipper, thirty-three-year-old Lieutenant Commander George Hoffman, realized the mortal danger he and his crew now faced. He decided to retreat. Radioman Third Class Bennie Glisson, sitting in the *Corry*'s radio shack, felt the ship make an abrupt turn. "We swung around, and showed them our fantail like an old maid to a Marine." Standing at his battle station on the flying bridge (just above the main bridge where Hoffman was situated), Ensign Jacob Henson, an Ohio State University graduate, also felt the ship change course. "The captain ordered full speed forward and then suddenly full speed astern. He was desperately trying to throw the shore batteries off their distance calculations." They sped out of there at twenty-eight knots. The waters ahead were full of reefs. Hoffman had to do some fancy sailing, dodging the reefs and the German shells at the same time. He ordered a zigzag course—hard left and right rudder at short intervals. Just when it seemed the *Corry* might make it, the ship ran squarely into a new peril—a submerged mine.

The explosion from the mine lifted the ship sideways and out of the water. Before he knew it, Ensign Henson was lifted off his feet. "I was propelled into the air about 5 feet, coming down on the nearby voice tube, used for communication when necessary. I was bruised and injured on my tailbone and received some scratches on my legs but otherwise I was OK."

Lieutenant (jg) Howard Andersen, the ship's medical officer, was belowdecks, in the wardroom, treating a sailor with a minor shrapnel wound, when the "explosion occurred below us in the forward fire and engine rooms. I was blown to the opposite side of the wardroom and landed on my backside but was not hurt because of good padding." The power cut off immediately. Andersen took a few moments to come to his senses and then went to the deck, where he set up an impromptu aid station. He found two of his corpsmen and went to work doing whatever he could for the wounded. "The three of us applied splints on men who had fractures (one with fractures of both lower legs, one with a fractured leg and thigh). Several men had burns from swimming in burning oil or were scalded by hot steam escaping from ruptured boilers." As he worked, Andersen felt no fear, only indignation that the Germans had hurt his friends.

Meanwhile, the *Corry* was dying. "The ship broke in two, almost at once," one of the *Corry's* officers recalled. "The forward fireroom, forward engine room and after fireroom flooded immediately, keel was broken, main deck was severed causing a large fissure that crossed the main deck and around the hull." Within minutes "the water was up over the main deck and we gave word to prepare to abandon ship."[14]

In spite of the fact that the ship had lost power, some of the gunners were still shooting, using manual power. The twisted wreck of this once sleek destroyer mushed and thrashed about one thousand yards before coming to a dead stop. Belowdecks, in the forward engine room, Chief Machinist's Mate Grant Gullickson and his terrified crew had no idea what was going on. The lights went out; the floor plates in their cramped engine room were coming loose; steam was everywhere. The men coughed in the hot, choking environment. Gullickson was sure he was about to die a terrible, claustrophobic death beneath the sea. The steam dissipated and the room cooled off, but only because water was beginning to fill up the compartment. It gushed in everywhere, steadily rising to waist level. He and the other sailors struggled to open the hatch that might liberate them from this confined space. The hatch opened and they made their way onto the main deck. Water was quickly inundating the deck.

The explosion had ripped Gullickson's life belt away. He knew he had to find some kind of flotation device and get off the ship immediately. The *Corry* was a clay pigeon now. German gunners could not help but hit the sinking wreck as it lay dead in the water. "The shells were hitting near and some were hitting the ship." He found a life belt and heard Hoffman's order to abandon ship. "We didn't jump off the ship or anything. We literally floated off the ship because the ship was underwater." Gullickson swam to a floater net, "a lifesaving device," and managed to grab hold of it. "Shells continued to burst in the water around us and each time one would hit, it really felt like someone was . . . trying to force a seabag up your rectum."[15]

Aboard the *Butler*, Chief Machinist's Mate Vincent Ohlman saw the *Corry* slipping below the waves. "Her top part [was] sticking out of the water, just a little over her boat deck because there was quite a lot of stack sticking out and most of the bridge." His ship headed for the *Corry* to pick up survivors and engage the enemy batteries that had finished off the sunken ship. "We picked up 32 men." Some of them were in the water close to two hours. "They were so stiff they could hardly move."[16]

In sky control aboard the *Quincy*, Lieutenant Blackburn saw the *Corry* go down and disgorge survivors into the water. Blackburn could see them swimming around, hanging on to debris and safety nets or climbing into lifeboats. Splashes around them testified to the accuracy of the enemy's continued bombardment. "As we were watching this drama unfold, the *Quincy* was ordered to use five-inch projectiles to lay a smoke screen on the landward side." It took them a while to do this because they had to empty high-explosive shells from their ammo hoists and replace them with white phosphorous smoke shells. "Finally after the seeming passage of hours, our smoke began drifting between the *Corry* and the shore battery."[17]

Somewhere below the smoke screen, Grant Gullickson bobbed in the water for two hours, clinging to the floater net, before finally getting picked up by a lifeboat from the *Fitch*. "By this time we were almost incapacitated due to the coldness of the water. Our hands were so numb that they were unable to grasp and hold a line to pull us out of the water. The *Fitch* people reached over the side and some literally came down and drug [*sic*] us out of the water and brought us aboard *Fitch*. They gave us coffee, heavily laced with alcohol. They opened their lockers to provide us with dry clothes and [they] prepared food and gave us medical help. You name it, they gave it to us."

Ensign Henson, protected by both Mae West and waist-belt life vests, slipped into the water and bobbed around for several minutes, until he came to a life raft "already well loaded with other people so I hung onto the raft by hand. I saw a seaman sitting in the raft with his right shoulder ripped open about 12 inches long and about 1 inch deep. It must have been terribly painful if the salt water got to it." The *Fitch* also rescued his group. "We were given medical treatment and stimulants for being in the cold water for more than 2 hours."

When Chief Machinist's Mate Gullickson felt better, he began looking for other survivors from his ship. He was saddened to find one his buddies lying dead in a bunk. Another had been killed by an exploding shell in the water. Still another "had steam burns over ninety-nine percent of his body. We tended to him and he could talk a little, but the burns were too much. He passed away the next day." Out of 294 men who made up the *Corry*'s crew, 13 were dead or missing and another 33 were wounded. The *Corry* was the largest ship the U.S. Navy lost on D-Day.[18]

In the short time—less than an hour—the bombardment forces had to soften up targets for the assault forces, the Navy did the best that it could. Shells from battleships, cruisers, and destroyers inflicted considerable damage on the German defenses, but it was not enough. The bombardment was too brief; nor was it effective enough to clear the way for Overlord. The need for operational surprise necessitated this short bombardment, and the success of the elaborate Allied deception plan undoubtedly saved many lives, so perhaps a balance was struck. But there is little question that Overlord planners failed to earmark anywhere near enough naval firepower to soften up the beaches, especially Omaha.

As the clock ticked inevitably toward H-Hour, the naval fire slacked off. The preparation was finally over. Now it was time for the ground troops, the main actors in this theater of violence, to take the stage. After four years of absence from the European continent, the Allies were about to fight their way back onto it. The fate of the whole enterprise now rested upon the sturdy shoulders of several thousand soldiers, many of whom were still in high school the last time Allied soldiers trod the soil of France.

CHAPTER TWELVE

SANDY UTAH

The Army's amphibious duplex drive (DD) tanks were supposed to go in first, followed by boat teams from the 8th Infantry Regiment. Within five minutes they would be followed by more tanks (landed on the beach from LCTs) along with tank dozers and engineers. The target for all of these assaulting units was a strip of beach at Les Dunes de Varreville between Exits 3 and 4.

Already by 0630, even as the bombardment ships ceased fire and specially fitted rocket-firing LCTs disgorged their ineffective projectiles, the plan was going awry. A combination of southerly winds, southerly tides, thick smoke, sandy debris, nervous confusion, and underwater mines upset the precise schedule and led the invasion force to the wrong beach. This turned out to be fortunate, but only because American leaders reacted well to the unforeseen change of plan.

One of the Landing Craft Control (LCC) vessels responsible for leading the way into the beach fouled its screw on a dan buoy. Two more LCCs struck mines, blew up, and sank (the survivors hung on to debris and desperately called for help from other ships passing by). Then a nearby LCT, carrying four DD tanks, hit another mine. The skipper of this craft, LCT-607, had frozen when the order came to line up and head for the beach. His second in command, Ensign Sam Grundfast, a graduate of New York University, assumed control. His stint as skipper did not last long—the ship hit the mine only minutes after Grundfast took over.

The force of the mine lifted the LCT-607 out of the water, shredded it, and turned it over. Tank crewman Carl Rambo, on a nearby LCT, saw the whole ghastly spectacle. "I saw tanks blown fifty to a hundred feet in the air. They tumbled as if they were flipped matchboxes. The LCT was broken in two."

Ensign Grundfast was one of the lucky few who were thrown clear of the boat. "The next thing I knew, I was underwater. I opened my eyes, I looked up, and I saw the surface of the water somewhere above my head." He paddled as fast he could to the surface. "Were it not for the Mae West life jackets that I had everybody wear and tie up tight, I don't think I would be here today." He and another man from his crew took refuge on the overturned wreck of what had once been LCT-607. An LCM came along later and picked them up. Grundfast was badly wounded. He had a lacerated face, a displaced nose, and considerably torn up legs (requiring skin grafts later on), but he was fortunate. Only he and two other men survived.[1]

The death of LCT-607 added to an already confusing situation. Neighboring LCTs circled in the water, their skippers not quite sure what to do next. Aboard the remaining control craft, LCC-60, Lieutenants Howard Vander Beek and Sims Gauthier decided to take the initiative and lead the way into Utah beach. When the LCT-607 struck the mine, the tiny (fifty-six-foot-long) LCC-60 had actually been lifted out of the water. "A shock wave came through that vessel," Gauthier related. "I was sitting at the navigator's position charting our course. I had to grab on to keep from falling off of the stool."

Having seen the kind of damage mines could do, Vander Beek and Gauthier wanted to make sure that the confused LCTs around them did not wander away from mine-swept lanes as they sought to find their bearings. As LCC-60 circled the LCTs, Vander Beek brandished a bullhorn and shouted orders to follow him. The tiny LCC now led the way into the wrong beach, at La Madeleine, near Exit 2, roughly a mile south of the intended beach. The LCT skippers disgorged their DD tanks 3,000 yards from the shore. These specially fitted amphibious monsters swam their way in. Four had gone down with Grundfast's LCT. The other twenty-eight made it.[2]

As the tanks lumbered in, the LCVPs (Higgins boats) containing the assault waves of the 1st and 2nd Battalions, 8th Infantry, sped past them and hit the beach. Now it was time for these soldiers of the 4th Infantry Division to make good on two years of training.

The first unit to make it to the beach was E Company. Aboard one of those boats, Private First Class John Pfister, a twenty-five-year-old native of Erie, Pennsylvania, struggled under the weight of eighty pounds of equipment. In addition to his gas-impregnated fatigues and invasion vest he was lugging a bazooka (with five rounds), a carbine, and a box of .30-caliber ammunition for his crew's machine gun. Pfister was a member of the weapons platoon.

German artillery shells exploded in the water and along the beach just ahead. The coxswain of Pfister's Higgins boat came to a stop and dropped the ramp about one hundred yards from the beach. Private First Class Pfister and his buddies had no idea of the water's depth, so they inflated their Mae West life vests. "The water was chest high. I went under at first and was lucky enough to be able to walk in." They slowly waded to the flat, sandy beach. "There was nowhere to hide. I could see machine gun fire on the beach." Ahead, nestled against sand dunes, Pfister could see a three-foot-high seawall the Germans had recently built. "We could see pillboxes about 25 to 50 yards back."[3]

The other companies of the 8th Infantry's two assault battalions were not far behind E Company. In scattered formations, they bore down on Utah beach. German small-arms fire was sporadic, but artillery fire, mainly coming from several miles north, was accurate and terrifying. The enemy scored several hits on landing craft, including the one radioman Bruce Bradley was riding. Bradley was part of a forward observer team attached to the lead waves. "Geysers of seawater were coming from shellfire aimed at us. The noise of the shelling and counterfire was much louder now; then a deafening blast, and we were thrown down and knocked sideways. We had been hit by a shell. The coxswain was gone, the ramp was down, the boat was sinking sideways. I was lucky to inflate my Mae West. Most of the guys in the boat drowned." Bradley dog-paddled his way ashore and then staggered to the seawall, plopping down right next to a dead GI.[4]

Private Fred Crum's Higgins boat passed right by one of the sunken LCCs. "There were five survivors clinging to it, all apparently uninjured. Then we saw . . . dead guys floating around suspended in water by their life jackets. All feeling of exhilaration and adventure left us." Previously his infantry boat team, loaded down with demolitions, had been keyed up and ready for a fight. Now most of them felt sick and not just from the sight of the dead. "About half the guys got really seasick. With . . . the tossing

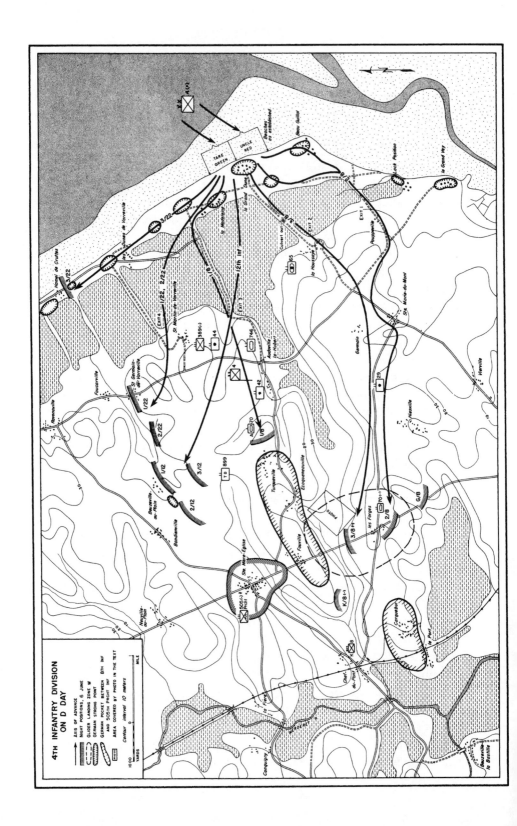

4TH INFANTRY DIVISION ON D DAY

AXIS OF ADVANCE
NIGHT POSITIONS, 6 JUNE
GLIDER LANDING ZONE W
GERMAN STRONG POINT
GERMAN POCKET BETWEEN 8TH INF
AND 505TH PRCHT INF
AREA COVERED BY PHOTO IN THE TEXT

Contour interval 10 meters

YARDS
1000   0   MILE

boat, with its limited space, everything was a mess." Men vomited in their helmets, in the boat, and even on one another.

Thoroughly miserable and weakened, the men yearned to get off this wretched boat, even if that meant facing enemy fire. Just before they got to the beach, Private Crum looked up and saw a lone fighter plane flying at low level along the beach, laying down a smoke screen. "By the time he covered the full length of the beach and began pulling up he had absorbed so much enemy fire that the plane disintegrated in one big flash and shower of flames and smoke."

Crum heard the ramp of the Higgins boat slam into water. In one motion, he and the other soldiers gathered their loads and staggered into the water. "We moved off as quickly as the weight we carried permitted." They waded through thigh-high water. "Each step seemed as though a ball and chain had been tied to our ankles. We didn't care much whether we got hit or not, in fact we didn't think about it." They reached the seawall, where they unloaded their bangalore torpedoes, satchel charges, and heavy weapons. Crum and the others were fairly safe here. They rested and waited for orders.[5]

Private Bill Gay, a BAR man in C Company, 8th Infantry, landed close by (very near the present-day Utah beach museum at La Madeleine). "I hit the solid ground running as fast as I could with all that weight on. I had gone about 50 or 60 feet when something knocked me about three feet to the right and 'arse over tea-kettle.' I knew I was not hurt and when I came up on my feet again, I moved into high gear and really turned on the speed looking for cover. Later on I started to take a drink of water but there was no water in my canteen. It had been punctured by a bullet." That night he took off his pack and found that it had been severed by more enemy bullets. "So I guess that is what knocked me down."

Most of the enemy defenders on this beach had been demoralized or stunned by the naval and aerial bombardment. Once the Americans made it safely ashore, dodged mines or obstacles, and reorganized at the seawall, they began to deal with enemy soldiers. Here and there, just beyond the seawall, pillboxes dotted the beach, as did fortified houses. Even before Bill Conrad of F Company jumped off his Higgins boat, he noticed "a two story white house standing by itself. We waded through three feet of water and charged the house firing through the door. We heard shouts and one of our platoon soldiers kicked in the door so that I could throw a grenade inside. Ten to fifteen Germans came out with hands up to become prisoners."

Not far away, the soldiers of G Company landed in the vicinity of a cluster of pillboxes. One boat from this company hung up on a sandbar. "The front ramp dropped and we went out into water up to our armpits," Irv Bradbury recalled. "Dry land was just ahead. Yeh, 800 yards ahead. The water was cold, but one paid it no mind. We had been getting sprayed with salt water for the past several hours."

As they neared the beach, small-arms fire and shrapnel hit several men. The beach was getting crowded with vehicles, some of which were on fire. The unwounded kept moving past the carnage, all the way to the seawall. Here they regrouped, moved to the left (south), and found a pillbox. Private James Conway laid down cover fire while a flamethrower team approached the pillbox. "We got on the blind side since [the enemy] could only fire towards the Channel." The flamethrower team got on with their grisly task. "It was awful, a burning inferno." The Americans could smell burning flesh and hair. They came to another pillbox. This one "had a tank turret mounted on top of a track. Two tanks came up behind us, a soldier fired a smoke grenade, and one of the tanks fired. The turret went straight up in the air, and fell to one side. A white flag went up."

Radioman R. A. Mann saw men in German uniforms, with terrified looks on their faces, emerge from the pillbox. "I was surprised to see that some of the prisoners that came from the pillbox had Oriental features." These men were Mongolians, *Osttruppen* or "Ossies," whom the Germans had captured on the Eastern Front. They preferred service in the German Army to certain death in Nazi POW or slave labor camps. A substantial component, perhaps as much as one-third, of the German Army defenders at Utah beach were Ossies.[6]

Roughly one hundred yards away, Private Harper Coleman, the H Company machine gunner, struggled ashore under the weight of his gun. "We went in . . . water somewhat more than waist deep and a good distance from dry land." The young private made it to the beach and then saw something that made him do a double take. "We had a greeter. How he got there I do not know . . . but Brig. Gen. Theodore Roosevelt was standing there waving his cane and giving out instructions as only he could do. I went right past him as he was directing everyone to keep going and get off the beach."[7]

Roosevelt, eldest son of the colorful president by the same name, got here by lobbying fiercely. Theodore "Ted" Roosevelt was one of the best, most courageous senior officers in the U.S. Army. He was universally respected among the dogface soldiers of the 4th Division as well as his peers in the upper echelons of the Army. He had served as Terry de la Mesa Allen's assistant division commander in the Big Red One in the Mediterranean. Now the fifty-seven-year-old Roosevelt, heart condition and all, was General Barton's number two man in the Ivy Division.

Roosevelt splashed ashore with E Company. He was one of the first men to touch French soil. When Roosevelt told Barton of his desire to go in with the first wave, Barton at first refused, but Roosevelt, undeterred, persuaded him that his presence would be good for morale of the troops. "They'll figure that if a general is going in, it can't be that rough." Fully expecting Roosevelt to get killed, General Barton reluctantly assented. This was probably his best pre-invasion decision. Roosevelt's presence on the beach that morning was priceless.

When he got to the seawall, he immediately realized that the first wave had landed in the wrong place. In an effort to determine exactly where the first waves had landed, he scouted the terrain that lay just in from the beach. He went back to the beach and, for several minutes, directed traffic, imploring the soldiers to get off the beach. This was when Private Coleman saw him. From time to time German mortar shells landed near the general, showering him with sand. Unperturbed, he strode up and down the water's edge, an otherworldly figure in his olive drab sweater and knit cap, armed only with his cane and his resolve. A flurry of energy, he moved on to a shell hole that the Navy's beach control officer was using as a temporary headquarters. Lieutenant Colonels Conrad Simmons and Carlton MacNeely, commanders, respectively, of the 1st and 2nd Battalions, 8th Infantry, joined him, as did their commanding officer, Colonel James Van Fleet.

They had an important decision to make. Roosevelt figured that they were a mile south of their intended beach, the one that straddled Exits 3 and 4. This was actually a stroke of luck. Neither the aerial nor the naval bombardment had succeeded in taking out a battery of large-caliber guns that could have wreaked havoc on the assault troops at Les Dunes de Varreville. The landings here at La Madeleine were going well. Clearly, the Germans had been taken by surprise. They were lobbing artillery on the beach from long range, but most of the Germans holding this beach had little desire to resist. That was great, but there was a problem. Roosevelt could see that already traffic was building up here in front of Exit 2. Should he order the follow-up waves—30,000 men and 3,500 vehicles—to land here or should he divert the landings to the original beach a mile to the north? If they landed here, they would heavily depend on Exit 2, leading to the possibility of a massive logjam, whereas the beach to the north offered the possibility of capturing Exits 3 and 4 (a major reason why it had been chosen).

Ironically, Van Fleet had always been in favor of landing at La Madeleine, but the Navy had told him that the waters were too shallow. His opinion was unambiguous. "Go straight inland. We've caught the enemy at a weak point, so let's take advantage of it."

Roosevelt agreed. He knew that he had the initiative; far better to exploit it and risk logistical difficulties rather than rigidly adhere to a plan that had been made irrelevant by the course of events. Moreover, if he experienced problems moving inland from Exit 2, his troops could probably push south and capture Exit 1 and Pouppeville, thus alleviating the traffic buildup at Exit 2. He made the decision: "We'll start the war from right here."[8] It was a sound, flexible, intelligent decision, and it made all the difference at Utah beach that morning.

Small groups of infantrymen, like Private Crum's, began picking their way beyond the seawall. "Our gang finally got off the beach going inland about 500 yards to dig in." As Crum negotiated the seawall, he saw General Roosevelt "collaring anybody he thought looked like an engineer and ordering them to get some mines cleared out somewhere. He made a conspicuous figure standing up on the wall and it's a wonder he didn't get bumped off."[9]

As Crum indicated, army engineers and naval demolition teams were ashore now. The Navy's job was to clear underwater obstacles, while the Army handled everything on land. These teams began clearing paths through the numerous minefields and obstacles (steel piling, hedgehogs, barbed wire, concrete cones, and the like) that infested the beach. They also went about blowing gaps through the seawall. If they did not do their job, then vehicles, supplies, and equipment would never get off the beach. This was why Roosevelt took a personal interest in the mine and obstacle–clearing operations of the engineers and demolitions teams.

When they landed, they found that the beach obstacles and minefields were more dispersed than expected (probably a result of landing on the wrong beach). This made their work easier, but it was still a tough, dangerous job, done under constant enemy shell fire. Private Sam Ricker, the 4th Engineer Combat Battalion soldier who had comforted himself with Psalms 23 on the trip across the Channel, landed and immediately went to work disarming mines he found in the sand. "Some of the mines . . . were relatively new to us. There was one . . . antipersonnel mine . . . that could be detonated by stepping on it with your foot . . . and you could trip what we called a 'bouncing betty.' It would jump up in the air about waist and shoulder high and it exploded. It was loaded with ball bearings."[10]

While Ricker and his buddies ferreted out mines, engineers of the 237th Engineer Combat Battalion wired beach obstacles for demolition. They scurried around, some on hands and knees, tying satchel charges to obstacles. Sergeant Al Pikasiewicz of B Company tied all the charges together with primer cord and ran it out to his lieutenant. "When the lieutenant would pull the fuse, the timing cord would take so many seconds to burn before it blew the . . . primer cord, which gave us just that many seconds to get the hell out of the way."

Pikasiewicz ran to the seawall and yelled to his lieutenant that everything was ready. The lieutenant threw a smoke grenade (a visual warning to others of the impending explosion) and yelled, "Fire in the hole!" Everyone crouched against the wall, waiting for the impact. Sergeant Pikasiewicz looked out to sea and saw infantrymen from a follow-up wave leaving their landing craft, heading straight for the demolitions. He and several other soldiers screamed a warning at them. The infantryman reacted by taking cover—right against the obstacles.

Pikasiewicz turned to his unit's medic and said, "Look what's happening. My God, they're laying in on the explosives." In an instant, the sergeant got up, left the protection of the wall, and grabbed several of the infantrymen by their packs. "Get the hell out of here. This is ready to blow!" The infantrymen scrambled away, and Pikasiewicz ran for the wall. "When I was fifteen to twenty feet from it, [everything] blew and a piece of shrapnel hit me in the helmet."

Richard Cassaday in C Company had barely made it to the beach when he was hit by shrapnel. His unit's medic got to him and administered first aid. Cassaday lay there and watched as his buddies blew a gap through the seawall. "Someone came along and took one of my satchel charges. They laid seven hundred pounds of explosives, Composition C-2, on the seawall." Someone shouted "Fire in the hole!" and, in seconds, an entire section of the wall disintegrated.[11]

Once the engineers had blown gaps in the seawall, some of them helped clear mines along the causeway that comprised Exit 2. Private Jack McQuiston, a nineteen-year-old from the 1st Engineer Special Brigade, crouched gingerly and probed for mines among the sand dunes near Exit 2. The night before, the Cleveland-born McQuiston had gambled with his buddies to calm his nervous stomach. More than the gambling, the Navy's pre-invasion meal of steak, mashed potatoes, green beans, apple pie, and ice cream soothed his stomach. Once he boarded his Higgins boat and rode into the beach, he even managed to keep the meal down. The LCVP dumped him about one hundred yards offshore, and he waded to the beach. Along the way, he saved one of his buddies who had stumbled into water over his head. "All I could see was his arms. I went back and pulled him out. He almost drowned."

Now McQuiston and his comrades concentrated on the dangerous task at hand. German artillery shells exploded randomly up and down the expanse of the beach. "We heard a voice and saw a soldier coming toward us waving a handkerchief with arms raised. He was dressed in a U.S. paratrooper uniform. We dropped to the ground with rifles pointed at him. He explained he was with the 101st Airborne and had overshot his mark when bailing out." The paratrooper worked alongside them. "We continued to remove mines, hedgehogs, obstacles, and barbed wire. In one hour we had opened the first road and causeway off the beach."[12]

The man exercising informal command of the engineers on the beach, Major Robert Tabb, executive officer of the 237th, was proud of what his men accomplished in such a short period of time. Tabb was a native of tiny Dover, Missouri, and a 1942 graduate of West Point. On the trip over, he had slipped on the deck of his LCT and badly sprained his ankle. It swelled up terribly, but

Tabb told a medic to tape it up. "I was determined to get on that beach and not be left behind." He and his commanding officer, Major Herschel Lynn, planned to direct engineering operations from their amphibious M-29 vehicles (the soldiers called the M-29 the Weasel). But when Major Tabb's M-29 left the LCT it promptly sank. He had to abandon everything except for a radio, a map case, and his musette bag. When he finally staggered ashore, Tabb saw General Roosevelt, who promptly told him that Lynn had been wounded and had also lost his M-29.

Limping on his gimpy ankle and popping plenty of aspirin, Tabb circulated among the men as they cleared the beach and the area beyond. "The clearance of obstacles in the planned lanes on the beaches proceeded pretty much according to plan. Hand-placed explosives were used primarily. Later . . . tank dozers . . . were extremely helpful." By noon they had cleared Utah beach and opened up Exit 2 for vehicle traffic. "Gaps had been blown in the seawall, and lanes had been cleared and bulldozed through the dune line to vehicle holding areas. The beach obstacle task force was in effect dissolved." Some engineers remained on the beach to improve it further and build POW enclosures, but many others dispersed among the various infantry and armored units pushing inland.[13] By and large, the engineers did an outstanding job at Utah beach.

For the first hour or so, the tankers, whose weapons were such an integral part of the initial assault plan, occupied themselves mostly with blasting holes in the seawall or firing on pillboxes. The tankers landed later than expected and found little room to maneuver on the crowded, mined beach. DD tanks had gotten ashore and could maneuver a bit, but not tanks landed from LCTs. More than anything, the tanks had to sit tight and wait for the engineers to create openings for them to get off the beach. Once the engineers cleared the way for them, the tanks of the combat-experienced 70th Tank Battalion took a leading role.

The tank crewmen looked for gaps in the seawalls. Sergeant Rambo safely got his DD tank ashore. He followed his company commander's tank toward a hole in the wall. "We went over chunks of concrete in the hole and onto a causeway that went through a flooded swamp." They crossed a little culvert and his commander got hung up for a moment but soon freed himself.

Meanwhile, Rambo was experiencing engine trouble. "We could barely move in low gear." In spite of elaborate waterproofing, water had infiltrated their engine. "We couldn't spot the trouble and tried turning the engine over, but there was nothing we could do."

He was holding up traffic on the narrow causeway (Exit 2). Other vehicles were bunching up behind his tank. "Some engineer came by and said to get that tank out of here, but I said it won't move." The engineer brought up a bulldozer and pushed Rambo's tank into the swamp. "That took me out of action."[14]

Farther inland on the causeway, teams of tankers and infantrymen of the newly landed 3rd Battalion, 8th Infantry, worked their way inland in the direction of the village of Houdienville. Swampy water was all around these men. The causeway was little more than a narrow ridge jutting a few feet upward. Drainage ditches and canals were everywhere. Private William Jones, the I Company soldier from Tennessee, was walking slowly behind a Sherman tank. The tank was grinding its gears, trying to cross a small ditch. All at once, the tank exploded. "It hit a mine and it blew it up, caught on fire, and killed everybody on the thing. One of the crew was hanging outside the hatch door, dead."

Jones and the other infantrymen passed the tank, waded through the ditches, and made it to Houdienville. The people of this tiny village stared stonily at the Americans. "They didn't really know how to take us, I guess." The mood was tense. The American soldiers were worried that the Germans might be in the buildings. Suddenly one of the Frenchmen took off running. "We hollered for him to halt. He didn't halt, and one of our men shot him and left him there."

Private Jones turned away from this sad spectacle and began to search a house. He and two other men hollered for anyone inside to come out. "We didn't know any French. Nobody came out." They knocked in the door with their rifle butts. "I threw a grenade in the door, stepped back, and waited until it exploded. Then we went on in. There was a man, three or four women, and two or three kids in that room. The only damage that was done was the old man had a cut on his cheek. It was just . . . luck that they didn't all get killed."

Immediately outside of town, the infantrymen contacted half a dozen paratroopers who were taking sniper fire from a brick farmhouse. Jones's squad went to clean out the farmhouse. "They were firing from the upstairs windows. We were slipping up on them, crawling down this ditch." They crawled past a dead German soldier, into a thicket, and charged the farmhouse. "Mortar shells from our own outfit began falling around us." They took the farmhouse easily. Their biggest peril was their own mortar shells.

The 3rd Battalion, and its accompanying tanks, made it all the way across the causeway (partially thanks to Major Tabb's engineers who forded a stream for them) and, by nightfall, reached Les Forges, the high ground south of Ste-Mère-Eglise. One platoon from K Company even made contact with Captain Creek's embattled paratroopers at Chef-du-Pont.[15]

To the south, the 8th Infantry's 2nd Battalion, and plenty of 70th Tank Battalion helpers, pushed west along Exit 1 and adjacent dirt paths. In the meantime, Captain John Ahearn, commander of 70th Tank Battalion's C Company, led seven tanks through the seawall and onto Exit 1. Ahearn could see American infantry walking along the road. They did not seem to notice a concrete pillbox on their flank, but Ahearn could see it clearly. "I ordered my tanks to fire on it. As we fired, a number of German soldiers came out with their hands up. They turned out to be . . . East Europeans. They were not about to stand and fight for the fuhrer. They quickly surrendered."

The captain got out of his tank to take them prisoner, but they waved their arms and screamed, "Achtung, Minen!" Grateful, Ahearn scrambled back to his tank and waved them forward. They made it safely to the infantry, who shepherded them back to the beach. The column of tanks resumed its advance. They were heading south now. The road narrowed to little more than a dirt path. The tanks could barely fit between the hedgerows on either side. This was not good. Tankers like Ahearn did not like confined areas, because such places negated the tank's advantage of maneuverability, firepower, and intimidation. The closer enemy soldiers could get, the more damage they could do. There was also the possibility of mines.

All at once, Ahearn heard the dull thud of an explosion. A mine had blown off a bogie wheel in his left tread. "We were inoperative."

Ahearn's driver, Sergeant Tony Zampiello, got out of the tank and inspected the damage. "I saw that the left side of the tank was gone. I started to cry."

After comforting Zampiello, Ahearn got in touch with Lieutenant Thomas Tighe and told him to take five tanks and head for Pouppeville. Ahearn's crew, with another tank, stayed put. They brewed some coffee, cracked open some rations, and ate their first meal in close to ten hours.

Ahearn hopped off his tank and scouted the area on foot. Cautiously he had covered about one hundred yards when he heard someone yelling for help. "I looked out in a field and saw two or three infantrymen, [most] likely they were paratroopers." Captain Ahearn climbed over a large, thick hedgerow and approached them. "I knew there were mines. I knew it was dangerous. In my attempt to get as close to them as possible, I gingerly stepped over a small hedgerow. I was standing there, wondering what the hell I was going to do . . . and Puff!"

He had stepped on a German Schu mine. "I was knocked unconscious and rolled up against the hedgerow. I don't know how long I was there, but as soon as I was conscious I started yelling for help."

Back at the tank, Zampiello heard the muffled explosion and Ahearn's stricken call for help. "I heard him calling, 'Zamp! Zamp!'" Zampiello and the gunner, Felix Beard, ran toward the sound of their captain's voice. They could easily have tripped off more mines, but they never thought of that. They only knew that Ahearn, a first-class combat leader, needed help. When they reached him, Zampiello could see he was in bad shape. "Both his feet were blown apart."

Ahearn was a big man, so Zampiello and Beard had an extremely difficult time picking him up. They were also worried about whatever mines might be lurking between Ahearn and them. They went back to the tank, got a rope, and threw it to Ahearn. In this way, they managed to drag their heavy captain over to them. Somehow they lifted him up. "We carried him to the tank, and I was surprised we didn't get blown up. There must have been mines all over the place. We radioed the medics, but none came for two or three hours."

When the medics finally came, they evacuated Ahearn to the beach. Engineers had built a hasty field hospital near the beach for the 261st Medical Battalion. Doctors from this battalion operated on Ahearn. Later the captain and other badly wounded soldiers were loaded aboard an LCT bound for England. "I was on deck, and all I had on me were my dogtags, a dirty t-shirt, and a pair of shorts. Everything had been hazy as I was in shock, but now I realized I had lost both my legs. It was a very traumatic moment, and I began to cry. I was soothed by a navy corpsman." For his bravery in attempting to rescue the wounded paratroopers, in addition to his role in protecting the left flank of the entire 4th Infantry Division, Ahearn earned the Distinguished Service Cross.[16]

Farther to the east of the area where Ahearn tripped the mine that cost him his legs, Lieutenant Colonel MacNeely was maneuvering his 2nd Battalion through swamps and along the Exit 1 road that led to Pouppeville. "We . . . followed a path along the beach with swamps on our right side," Private Coleman of H Company remembered: "This must have been a mile or so before we came to a path that was built up through the swamp and led into the town of Pouppeville."[17]

Before long, G Company became trapped in a minefield. Three men set off mines. Captain George Mabry, MacNeely's operations officer, led them out of the minefield and along Exit 1 until they linked up with Tighe's tanks. They assaulted a pillbox, moved on, captured a small group of Germans, and advanced, unimpeded, on Pouppeville.

At the edge of the swamps, along the eastern approaches to the town, they halted. Mabry knew that the invasion plan called for the 101st Airborne to capture Pouppeville by now, but he could not be sure that that had happened. One of Mabry's scouts, Sergeant Malvin Pike of E Company, could clearly see Pouppeville from his concealed position at the edge of the swamp. "We could see bushes and a few trees where the causeway ended, and then I saw a helmet and then it disappeared." The helmet belonged to an American paratrooper.

Tighe's lead tank rumbled up the road, right past Pike. From Pouppeville's eastern edges American paratroopers from Julian Ewell's 3rd Battalion, 501st, warily watched the tank, not sure if it was German or American. Lieutenant Luther Knowlton was crouched under cover, along the road. "Nothing was moving on the causeway until a tank came grinding around the bend about 250 yards beyond [Pouppeville]. The tank approached slowly up the narrow road. One of our men fired his machine gun from the shelter of [a] stone wall. The bullets ricocheted off the heavy armor plating."

The tank ground to a halt. One of the crewmen, while keeping himself hidden behind an armored hatch cover, displayed an orange identification panel. Knowlton knew now that he was looking at a friend, not a foe. "I tossed an orange smoke grenade into the road from my place of cover." Mabry's men broke from cover, walked forward, and shook hands with Knowlton's paratroopers. Mabry met with General Taylor and briefed him on the progress of the invasion. The linkup at Exit 1 was now complete. From here, the 2nd Battalion advanced farther west, north of Ste-Marie-du-Mont, all the way to Les Forges, where they stopped for the night. To the north, the 1st Battalion captured Exit 3 and made it as far as Turqueville.[18]

It was early afternoon now. Back at the beach, the follow-up waves of the 4th Division were pouring ashore. The Germans were still shelling the beach, but the biggest problem for these follow-up waves was congestion. Most vehicles had to use Exit 2. Exit 1 was too far away from the landing spot, and Exit 3 was too close to German artillery positions to the north. General Roosevelt could not afford to jam up his precious beach exits with thousands of infantrymen. Consequently, the follow-up waves of the 22nd and 12th Infantry Regiments had to wade through the inundated areas if they hoped to reach their D-Day objectives.

The 22nd headed north toward Exit 4. The regiment's 3rd Battalion landed and turned sharply to the right. These soldiers worked their way along the seawall up the beach, destroying any remaining beach defenses from behind. They made it past Les Dunes de Varreville, all the way to Hamel de Crutes. The other two battalions plunged straight into the swamps. They waded through water that mostly ranged anywhere from knee- to chin-high. Some sections of the swamps were so deep that the men could only cross by clinging to ropes they had strung across the deep areas. "It was a good thing that we had five foot long Toggle Ropes with handles on both ends," Staff Sergeant Angelo Bavosa of B Company later wrote. "As one soldier got across the deep ditches, he pulled the following soldier across."[19]

Slowly, almost arduously, they worked their way inland. Sam Jacks, a nineteen-year-old rifleman from North Carolina, was soaked, just like every other man in his unit. At one point, he found a foxhole and jumped into it. He was surprised to find a badly wounded 101st Airborne paratrooper already occupying the hole. "He was laying there and his guts were half . . . blown out, his arm was all mangled and he was sitting there crying and calling

Judy. I never will forget that. He was saying, 'Judy, Judy, Judy.' Then he called mama." Completely unnerved, Jacks left the hole and sloshed through a nearby drainage ditch. A German sniper shot at him. Jacks peered over the ditch and was surprised to find that he could see the German perfectly. "I kneeled down there and I blew a hole in that sucker."[20]

The 22nd Infantrymen skirted past St-Martin-de-Varreville and made it as far as St-Germain-de-Varreville by nightfall. Along the way, they fought stubborn groups of Germans who shot at them from buildings, ditches, or high ground. Each time, the Americans shot back, closed with them, and overran them. Private First Class Bob Meyer, a BAR man in G Company, was temporarily pinned down when Germans opened fire on his unit. Bullets were flying everywhere. In the middle of this confused fight, one of the other G Company soldiers stood up and said, quite matter-of-factly, "To hell with this." He turned around and walked, completely unscathed, to the rear. Amazingly, this was the first time Meyer had ever heard this man speak. "[He] was more animallike than anyone I had ever seen before. When he stood, his arms and hands stretched down past his knees. I never heard him speak. If he had to respond, a sort of grunt was all you would get. There'd been several attempts to get him out of the army on a Section 8, but our captain was convinced he was faking." Meyer was amazed that the strange man did not get hit on his stroll away from the combat zone. "God must have been watching over him. We were sure that back on the beach he was seen for what he was, a Section 8, and sent home."

The unit eventually routed the Germans, but one of their die-hard officers emptied a machine gun into G Company's commander, Captain Robert Russell, a graduate of Virginia Military Institute. The bullets practically sawed the captain in half. The enemy officer then threw down his gun and tried to surrender. All the while he was laughing. "Our executive officer Joe Jackson, who weighed 240 pounds with no fat, stuck him with a bayonet and pitched him like a bundle of grain."[21]

The 12th Infantry Regiment, under the earthy Colonel Red Reeder, was the last infantry unit of the 4th Division to come ashore on D-Day (one regiment from the 90th Infantry Division, the 359th Infantry Regiment, landed a bit later). "Our boat grated on the sand. Its iron gate dropped. I felt as if I were in the kickoff of some terrible football game," Reeder later wrote. "German artillery cracked over our heads. We ran about 200 yards to the top of the dunes. Along the dunes we found small white signs with a death's head in black and the black letters: **MINEN!**"

Reeder studied the terrain around him. He could tell immediately that something was wrong. He turned to his aide, Lieutenant Bill Mills, a man who excelled in map reading. "Mills, things don't look right to me. Where the hell are we?"

Mills correctly surmised that they had been landed too far south. Reeder did not hesitate for a moment. He knew exactly what to do. "It don't matter. We know where to go!" He told Mills to spread the word about what had happened and decided that his men would have to move through the swamps to get to their objectives.

Along came General Roosevelt, who was seemingly everywhere that morning. "Red, the causeways leading inland are all clogged up. Look at it! A procession of jeeps and not a wheel turning."

Reeder followed Roosevelt's gaze. Jeeps, trucks, and other vehicles were lined up bumper-to-bumper on Exit 2, none of them going anywhere anytime soon. This only confirmed for the colonel what he had already decided: His soldiers were going to get wet.

"We are going through the flooded area!" Reeder yelled as loud as he could. The 12th Infantry Regiment prepared to move out. "I gave an arm signal, and 3,000 heavily burdened infantrymen walked in the manmade lake. We waded through the water . . . which varied in depth from waist to arm pit and in a few spots . . . over our heads. We had the non-swimmers paired with the swimmers, and . . . I was proud of the non-swimmers around me who were holding onto their weapons."[22]

One of the men struggling to keep his weapon dry was Private Darel Parker, a twenty-three-year-old draftee from Belmore, Ohio, who served with a bazooka team in C Company. "The water was only knee-deep or a little less, but every so many yards [there were] ditches and I don't know how deep they were, but they were over my head. We had been given a long and pretty strong rope, so the tallest man in the group made his way across the ditch with the rope, and the rest of us made our way across on the rope with the aid of someone holding it on our side. The last man was on his own to get across."[23]

At the head of I Company, First Lieutenant Bob Kay, the company's commander, discovered the same flooded ditches. In the distance he could hear artillery rumbling. Now and again he heard the chillingly distinctive ripping sound of German machine guns. "The wadeable ridges often ended in eight to ten foot deep water troughs, necessitating use of our toggle ropes and inflatable life-belts to swim our troops across. It was a slow, physically exhausting requirement that eventually took almost three hours to negotiate."[24]

They waded safely for about a mile until the water finally dissipated near St-Martin-de-Varreville. In the town, Colonel Reeder reorganized them and sent his first two battalions in a northwesterly direction, through hedgerows and orchards that eventually led to Ste-Mère-Eglise. At one point, Reeder noticed that forward movement had stopped. He walked up to the two front scouts and asked, "What's the trouble?"

One of the scouts replied, "All you have to do is walk up that little bank and get fired on."

"How many Germans do you think there are?" Reeder asked the scout.

"Two."

"Where are they?"

"I don't know. You can't tell, sir."

"Three thousand men are behind you and two Germans are holding us all up," Reeder patiently explained. "Any suggestions?"

The scout did not respond. Reeder told him to sideslip these two Germans and keep moving. They did. Later in the afternoon, they ran into real resistance near Beuzeville-au-Plain. Once again, Reeder's leadership made a positive difference. "From company to company, squad to squad, 'Red' Reeder raced back and forth pointing out weak spots in the enemy positions, targets of opportunity, and urged the men on," one officer remembered. "Enemy machine-guns and riflemen were posted at strategic points along the hedgerows and on high spots of ground. Each of these rattlesnake nests had to be painfully exterminated before the advance could continue. Grenades and bayonets solved this problem."

Reeder also made liberal use of several batteries of artillery that had landed by now and set up at the beach. "Late in the afternoon we were in a battle with the Germans a hedgerow away—about two hundred yards—both sides kneeling like minutemen at Lexington. Bullets were whip-cracking overhead. I radioed for artillery help. In a few minutes it crashed down just behind the Germans with an unbelievable roar, and a splendid

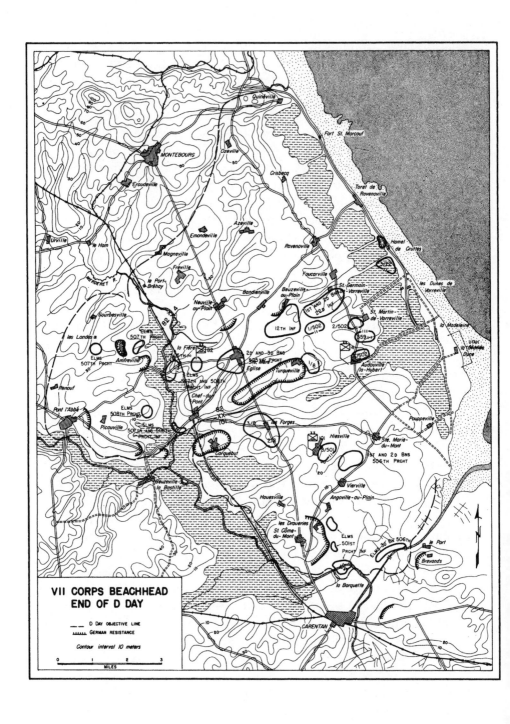

VII CORPS BEACHHEAD
END OF D DAY

- - - D DAY OBJECTIVE LINE

⊥⊥⊥⊥⊥⊥ GERMAN RESISTANCE

Contour interval 10 meters

0   1   2   3

MILES

barn with a red tile roof went up in smoke. It was a close-up of the awful waste of war."

By the time the sun set, the 12th Infantry had linked up with the 82nd Airborne. The whole regiment had made it safely across the inundated area and was hunkered down in positions roughly one mile east of Ste-Mère-Eglise. Many of the gliders from the evening missions landed right in the midst of the 12th Infantry. Reeder's men had won a solid foothold in France.[25]

The same could be said for the entire Utah beach invasion force, as General Collins found out. He spent the day aboard the *Bayfield*. During the early-morning hours, as the assault on Utah beach unfolded, he had been worried, mainly because of a lack of information. Now, in the evening, he knew that his VII Corps had succeeded in its mission of establishing a serious lodgment in France. Lieutenant John Brawley, a communications officer on the general's staff, could see the worry melt away from his boss's countenance. "General Collins was pleased. Gone were the early morning tensions. He could talk with his commanders ashore from the radio room of the *Bayfield* and things were going exceptionally well for VII Corps."[26]

Indeed they were. The airborne units, in spite of adversity, had captured many of their objectives and had generally caused major problems for the Germans in the Cotentin. A total of 20,000 troops (including the entire 4th Division) and 1,700 vehicles were ashore. At the cost of 197 casualties, the invasion forces had attained nearly all their D-Day objectives. Their advance was only stopped by strong pockets of German resistance north and south of Ste-Mère-Eglise, as well as in the Foucarville area. The landings could hardly have been expected to go any better.[27]

General Roosevelt deserved great credit for his excellent, decisive, effective leadership (he later was awarded the Medal of Honor for his exploits on D-Day). But, in an even larger sense, the credit for the success of the Utah landings belonged to the assault troops who exploited German surprise, dealt with the adversity of a blown plan, and rapidly moved inland to link up with the paratroopers. From an American perspective, the Utah beach landings proved to be the only bright spot on an otherwise traumatic, bloody day.

CHAPTER THIRTEEN

THE RANGERS AT POINTE-DU-HOC

At the extreme western edge of the Omaha beach sector, the rocky, imposing facade of Pointe-du-Hoc beckoned beneath a hushed, smoky stillness. Several miles offshore, ten British-made Higgins boats, jammed full with soldiers of the U.S. 2nd Ranger Battalion, plodded through the treacherous, raging waters of the Channel. The British called these boats LCAs (Landing Craft Assault). They were similar to the American-made LCVPs, but the British had added a bit more armor, making the boats more secure but also heavier and lower in the water. Each LCA contained, on average, twenty-five soldiers. Every boat bucked and crashed against the relentless waves. Most of the Rangers were wet, miserable, and cold. Some were seasick.

The sea was so rough that it threatened to overwhelm the boats. In fact, one of the 2nd Rangers' supply craft had already sunk, drowning four men. At nearly the same time, Captain Harold "Duke" Slater and his boat team from D Company realized they were in deep trouble. Four-foot waves inundated their boat, LCA-860. The men took off their helmets and frantically bailed water, but it was not enough. Their boat went down. Four of Slater's men drowned in the cold Channel. Rescue boats picked up Slater and the rest, gave them dry clothes, and returned them to England, over Slater's vigorous protests. "We gotta get back!" he hollered. But he and his men were suffering from hypothermia and exhaustion. They were in no shape to participate in the assault on the Pointe. They did not return to the unit until almost three weeks later.

Aboard nearby LCA-668, First Sergeant Len Lomell and the

rest of his D Company boat team actually cheered as they watched Slater's craft go down. The company had a standing bet. Whoever took out the guns atop Pointe du Hoc first would win $100 per man. "We had bet hundreds of bucks. We never thought four guys would drown." Lomell and the others only found out about their deaths later. In the meantime, water was building up on the deck of LCA-668. Lomell and his right-hand man, Sergeant Jack Kuhn, ordered everyone to start bailing. "Waves were breaking over our LCA," Lomell recalled, "and the guys had to take their helmets and bail because the pumps on the boat couldn't take the water out of it."

From the moment they had left the safety of their transport ship, Kuhn had been worried about the waves. Now he helped Lomell motivate the men to save themselves. "Nobody had much, if any, sleep the night before. The guys were sick and cold; they turned apathetic. Lomell and I verbally forced them to their feet to keep bailing water."[1]

Other boats were also taking on dangerous amounts of water. Aboard LCA-722, Lieutenant James Eikner, the Mississippian in charge of communications, saw water begin "to leak in through the front ramp which was closed. We had to rip up the floorboards and use our helmets to bail out the water and on top of that some of the fellows were vomiting." On the same boat, not far away from Eikner, Lieutenant G. K. Hodenfield, a reporter from *Stars and Stripes*, threw up on Lou Lisko, one of Eikner's radiomen. The constant bucking of the boat, combined with the motion of bailing, was too much for Hodenfield. Lisko did not have time to recoil before the reporter leaned over and let his breakfast fly. "Though we all had paper bags under our field jackets . . . in case of vomiting, this man did not have time to reach it. He threw up all over my left leg, my carbine and radio equipment. That made me sick, too. I vomited into my paper bag and threw it overboard."[2]

Aboard LCA-888, the commander of this mission, Lieutenant Colonel James Rudder, saw that his craft, like the others, was taking on water. The men around him scooped water with their helmets and poured it over the side. As they did so, they sometimes bumped into each other. No one cared. Rudder, a 1932 graduate of Texas A & M, was the thirty-four-year-old son of a Texas farmer. He had graduated from A & M with a reserve commission in the infantry, but he spent the 1930s coaching football in Texas.

When the war broke out, he went on active duty, attended the infantry school at Fort Benning, and served as a battalion executive officer before joining the Rangers.

Rudder was well qualified to lead this mission, but, in truth, he was a bit surprised to be here. General Huebner, the overall commander of all Omaha beach ground forces, had slated Rudder to lead the entire Ranger force (2nd and 5th Battalions) on D-Day, not just those making the initial assault on Pointe-du-Hoc. For Rudder, that would have meant going ashore with follow-up waves of the 2nd and 5th Rangers whose mission was flexible—depending on the situation at the Pointe, they were to reinforce the Pointe or land on Omaha beach, force their way up the Vierville draw, and work their way west on the coastal road to assault the Pointe from the landward side.

An alcohol-induced meltdown by the 2nd Battalion's commander, who was originally supposed to lead the first wave at Pointe-du-Hoc, changed everything for Lieutenant Colonel Rudder. The incident happened aboard the *Ben Machree* right before the ship left Weymouth. The commander, a Major Lytle, was a recently promoted executive officer. Lytle got drunk and caused a tremendous commotion. One of the battalion's medics, Sergeant Frank South, could hear the major carrying on outside his medical room. South opened the door to see what was going on. "Our newly appointed battalion commander, Major Lytle, had become a bit drunk and . . . was convinced that all the Rangers were being sent on a suicide mission; he was complaining loudly about it." South knew that the major's outburst could destroy the morale of the gung-ho Rangers. He also knew that it would have consequences.

Someone told Rudder about Lytle's histrionics. In response, Rudder immediately transferred over to the *Ben Machree* and relieved Lytle on the spot. When he did so, the major had to be dragged away, kicking and screaming, in the stairwell next to South's medical room. "The process of arresting and leading off the former commander of the operation was a noisy one. I opened the door to find out what was going on, only to see a group of struggling and shouting uniforms, and was immediately ordered back inside by Colonel Rudder." In this struggle, the defrocked major did himself no additional favors when he punched the battalion's respected doctor, Captain Walter Block. "Block was beloved," First Sergeant Lomell explained. "Hitting him was like taking a sock at somebody's mother." The officers finally succeeded in hauling Lytle off the ship.

In spite of what had happened, General Huebner wanted Rudder to appoint someone else to lead the Pointe mission. Rudder refused. "I'm sorry to have to disobey you, sir, but if I don't take it, it may not go." Huebner reluctantly assented.[3]

Now the burly Rudder peered in the direction of the coast, hoping to get his bearings. Finally, through mist and sea spray, he saw something—a neck of rocky coastline he recognized as Pointe-de-la-Percée. He knew right then that something was wrong. He should not be able to see Pointe-de-la-Percée, the objective of C Company, 2nd Rangers. This could only mean that his nine boats were at least two miles too far to the east.

Aboard LCA-668, First Sergeant Lomell noticed the same thing. He turned to Sergeant Kuhn and said, "Hey, Jack! Look at this. That's not the Pointe. That's C Company's target." Kuhn concurred.

On LCA-888, Rudder's craft, the British coxswain was not so sure. He briefly argued with Rudder before realizing that, somehow, they had gotten off-course. Lieutenant Eikner watched Rudder persuade him. "[He] . . . convinced [the coxswain] that he was in error and made him flank right and then we had to parallel the coastline for a couple of miles and we were within small-arms range and I can remember the first small arms hit our boat. We had been standing up except for those who were bailing water, so we all ducked down."

The error meant two things, neither of them good: First, as Eikner indicated, the nine surviving LCAs had to sail parallel to the coast, under German guns, as they made their way west to Pointe-du-Hoc; second, their timetable was now blown. The naval bombardment had lifted at 0630, and thanks to the navigational error, the Rangers would not land until at least 0700. This gave the enemy time to recover from the bombardment and prepare for the assault. Perhaps even worse, it meant that the follow-up forces did not receive in time the prearranged signal to reinforce the Pointe. Instead, they pursued the alternative plan of landing at Omaha beach. Companies D, E, and F, 2nd Rangers, were on their own at Pointe-du-Hoc.[4]

For nearly half an hour Rudder's boats ran a minigauntlet of German fire along the coast. Corporal Lisko's LCA-722 took plenty of the fire. "A Ranger [Private First Class John Sillman] who was sitting across from me was hit by a bullet in the upper left chest. He lost a considerable amount of blood and started groaning and moaning from the pain. Bullets from machine guns and rifles were flying from the top of the Hoc, and nobody dared move to help him."[5]

Contrary to the original plan (which called for D Company to assault the western facade of the Pointe), all of the boats landed on the eastern side of the Pointe, along a 500-yard front that stretched from the tip of the Pointe all the way to a gentle cove. The 30-yard strip of rocky beach had been heavily cratered by the naval and aerial bombardment. Most of the craters were filled with water. The bombardment had also pockmarked the cliffs, in places letting loose mounds of earth and rock that tumbled into muddy clumps on the beach or along the facade of the cliffs.

Fittingly, Rudder's LCA-888 landed first. He and the rest of the boat team struggled out of the craft and into the water. Lieutenant Eikner was the last to leave the boat. He was hauling a load of 60mm mortar shells. "I ran down the ramp and in the water about up to my knees and headed on across what I thought was the beach and stepped into a shell hole that was covered with water. I went down over my head and of course we were under fire." A few German soldiers chucked grenades over the cliff or took potshots with their rifles. But the biggest threat came from a 20mm gun and a machine-gun position on the left flank. "Some of our people were getting hit and I remember one young man that was hit three times on the landing craft and twice more on the beach. Believe it or not, that young man survived."[6]

Aboard LCA-858, in the middle of the formation, Lieutenant George Kerchner, a platoon leader in D Company, could not shake the feeling that the delay had caused the mission to go terribly wrong. "This whole thing is a big mistake," he thought, "none of us will ever get up that cliff because we are so vulnerable." In spite of this gloomy assessment, he knew there was nothing he could do about it now. There was only one way to go—forward. His British coxswain had promised a dry landing. But now the boat ground to a halt, the ramp went down, and Kerchner saw "fifteen or twenty feet of water, a muddy dirty gray stretch." The whole beach was marred with craters. The edge of one such crater had grounded LCA-858. "Everybody out!" the British coxswain commanded.

Kerchner disgustedly surveyed the water. He figured it was

about a foot deep. So much for that dry landing. "Come on, let's go!" he yelled above the din of machine-gun and 20mm fire coming from somewhere to his left. He no sooner stepped off the ramp when he fell into water over his head. "When I came to the surface, I started to doggie-paddle keeping my head above water while I tried to reach the beach." Kerchner was in the middle of a shell crater. The men of his boat team, seeing what had happened to him, wisely stepped to either side of the crater. In the process they barely got their feet wet. Kerchner finally made it out of the flooded crater and onto the rocky beach. "I looked around for someone to help me cuss out the British Navy for dumping me in eight feet of water, but there was nobody to sympathize with me. They were all busily engaged." The machine gun on the left had hit three men. Kerchner fought the impulse to go after the machine gun. He knew his mission was to get up the cliff and neutralize the guns.[7]

Immediately to the right, in LCA-668, the rest of D Company struggled ashore. Private Sigurd Sundby was supposed to be the first off this boat, but his lieutenant decided to go ahead of him. Sundby saw him plunge into shoulder-deep water, so he decided to jump in the opposite direction. "I jumped way out there . . . and I went way over my head." Like so many other Rangers, he was in a flooded shell crater. "I had the trigger of my Mae West in one hand, my rifle in the other hand (it was still covered)." As his feet touched the bottom of the crater. Sundby activated the Mae West. It worked perfectly. "I came sailing out of that water right out of that crater . . . into shallow water." He made his way to the face of the cliff.[8]

A few yards away, First Sergeant Lomell also landed in deep water. Thoroughly soaked, he turned around to see how the rest of his boat team was doing. As he did so, a bullet from the German machine gun hit him in the fleshy part of his chest, barely missing his ribs. "I felt a burning sensation in my right side. I spun around and didn't know where the shot came from." Lomell was not seriously wounded, but he was stunned and confused. His eyes rested on Harry Fate, a man with whom he had had a nasty confrontation a few days before when Lomell had taken Fate's sergeant's stripes. "I didn't think he was hacking it the way he should. He had been angry ever since." Fate had even made a veiled threat to shoot Lomell once they got into combat.

Because of this threat, Lomell was now convinced that Fate

shot him. "[He] was about fifty feet away and in position where he could have fired the bullet." Enraged, Lomell strode toward Fate. "You son of a bitch!"

Fate protested his innocence, "Honestly, Len, I didn't do it."

A medic assured Lomell that Fate was telling the truth. This brought the first sergeant to his senses. "The wound wasn't bad; [the bullet] had just gone through the muscle on my right side. We couldn't waste time to sort this out—later Fate got his stripes back and we became very good friends."[9]

The main thing now for all of the Rangers was to get up the cliffs. To help them do so, they had an ingenious array of equipment—rocket-fired ropes with grappling hooks, rope ladders, even machine-gun-laden ladders provided by the London Fire Department. As each boat closed to within twenty or twenty-five yards of the coast, the Rangers fired the rocket charges—the things made an awful racket—that shot their ropes to the top of the Pointe. Most of the grappling hooks caught firmly. The biggest problem was that the ropes were wet from the heavy seas. The cliffs themselves were also slippery from rain, sea spray, and the fresh clay that had been unloosed by the bombardment. Plus there was the little matter of enemy soldiers pitching grenades, cutting ropes, and firing their weapons at the Rangers!

All of the Rangers were accomplished climbers. They had been trained extensively at this sort of thing. If anyone could overcome this adversity, it was them. They had been taught to fight in small groups. Each boat team was like a mini–combat team. They did not worry about forming up with the other boat teams. Instead they independently set about the task of climbing the cliffs and accomplishing the mission—hopefully in conjunction with others but alone if necessary.

Some of the Rangers, like Private Sundby, experienced problems with the wet ropes. "I went up about . . . forty, fifty feet. I got just about there and the rope was wet and it was kind of muddy. My hands couldn't hold. I couldn't hold anything; they were just like grease, and I came sliding back down." He landed right next to Staff Sergeant Melvin Sweany, who had little sympathy for the private's predicament. "What's the matter, Sundby, chicken? I'll show you how to climb." With Sweany in the lead, the two of them made it to the top.[10]

Sundby was not chicken, nor was his experience unique. Many other Rangers had problems with the muddy, wet ropes. Even

Sergeant Bill "L-Rod" Petty, one of the battalion's toughest, most aggressive soldiers, struggled to climb the cliff. Medic Frank South saw Petty at the western edge of the landing zone, in F Company's sector. South was attending to wounded men when he noticed Petty "standing and cursing at the bottom of [a] rope. The rope was slippery, muddy, and wet."

South's boss, Captain Block (the battalion surgeon whom Major Lytle punched), saw Petty standing next to the rope. Block walked over to him and said, "Soldier, stop fooling around and get up that rope to the top of the cliff!"

South watched as Petty turned on the doctor and bellowed in his Georgia drawl, "I've been trying to get up the goddamned rope for five minutes and if you think you can do any better, you can fucking well do it yourself!"

South knew that Dr. Block had a temper of his own, but this time he restrained himself. "Block, furious and red-faced, returned the stare, looked at me, shook his head, and turned away." South could not help but chuckle at the two of them.[11]

In spite of the problems, most of the Rangers made it up the cliffs within fifteen minutes of landing. Private Salva Maimone of E Company free-climbed. "The Germans were throwing grenades down the cliff." Not far away, Staff Sergeant Gene Elder of F Company also free-climbed. "Germans were shooting, bullets were flying, and as the men came up to join me, I told them, 'Boys, keep your heads down. Headquarters has fouled up again and issued the enemy live ammunition!' "[12]

Sergeant Kuhn found that as he ascended the cliff, he could protect himself from the fire thanks to cover that had been created by the bombardment. "It was possible to get some cover by climbing behind chunks of cliff dislodged by the shelling." Very close by, First Sergeant Lomell was clinging to a rope, straining to reach the summit. "Concentrating on what I had to do and climbing the slippery rope was exhausting. Next to me was Sergeant Robert Fruhling, our radio man, struggling with his . . . radio set with a big antenna on it. We were approaching the top, and I was running out of strength."

Lomell heard Fruhling cry for help, "Len, help me! I'm losing my strength."

"Hold on! I can't help you. I've got all I can do to get myself up," Lomell replied. Lomell quickly looked around and saw Sergeant Leonard Rubin, "a born athlete, a very powerful man." He told Rubin to help the stricken radioman. "He just reached over, grabbed Bob by the back of the neck and swung him over. Bob went tumbling and the antenna was whipping around, and I was worried that it was going to draw fire. When I went over the top, I tumbled into a shell crater."[13]

At the cost of fifteen casualties (one dead and fourteen wounded), the Rangers had scaled the imposing cliffs. How did they do it? Ten years after the event, Colonel Rudder visited the Pointe and wondered the same thing. "Can you imagine anybody going up that thing?" he asked his ten-year-old son.

"It's twice as high as I thought," the boy responded.

Rudder shook his head in amazement and rhetorically asked, "Will you tell me how we did this? Anybody would be a fool to try this. It was crazy then, and it's crazy now."[14]

Maybe so, but they did it all the same. Obviously, the rigorous training and the personal courage of the Rangers had a lot to do with their successful ascent of the cliff. The element of surprise helped a bit; the Germans expected any potential attack on the Pointe to come from the landward side. One or two BAR men helped drive some Germans from the edge of the cliff. So did pieces of fuse the Rangers had tied to their grappling hooks—the Germans saw the fuses and thought they might be attached to explosive charges. More than any other factor, though, naval gunfire proved to be decisive for the Rangers during their climb (and partially thereafter). Two destroyers, the USS *Satterlee* and the HMS *Talybont*, closed to within 1,500 yards of Pointe-du-Hoc and unleashed a terrific volume of fire on the Germans near the cliffs. This made them retreat to the safety of their bunkers and trenches, allowing the Rangers to climb the cliffs, mostly unmolested. This was the time when they were at their most vulnerable, and the destroyer fire made sure that the Germans could not take advantage of the Rangers' vulnerability.

Like Lomell, most everyone else plopped into shell holes when they made it to the top. Pointe-du-Hoc looked like the surface of the moon. Deep craters had been gouged everywhere by the naval and aerial bombardment. Ten kilotons of explosives had been dropped on the place. The immense destruction provided excellent cover for the assaulting Rangers, but it also made it difficult for them to see anything beyond the next shell hole. Sergeant

Kuhn took one look around and found himself a bit disoriented. "I was shocked to find nothing that resembled the mock-ups and overlays we had studied prior to D-Day. The terrain was in complete disarray."[15]

Most of the Rangers saw no Germans moving around the Pointe's uneven landscape. Nor could they see one another. They paused for a few moments to rest. One man immediately dropped his trousers and defecated. With such personal issues resolved, small groups of men, most of whom had ascended the cliffs together, began to move toward their objectives.

Sporadic enemy fire harassed them, but the most vigorous resistance came at the very tip of the Pointe. Here the Germans had built a formidable concrete observation post (OP) that afforded them a panoramic view of both Utah and Omaha beaches. Several groups of Rangers repeatedly attacked the OP. From the seaward side Staff Sergeant Charles Denbo and Private Harry Williams crawled, under machine-gun fire, into a trench that zigzagged in front of the OP. The two men saw German guns poking through gun slits. They threw four grenades at the slits, three of which flew through and exploded. The machine gun stopped firing, but Sergeant Denbo was wounded by a rifle bullet.

Moments later, Lieutenant Ted Lapres, an E Company officer whose LCA-861 landed right at the tip of the Pointe, arrived with several other soldiers. They set up a bazooka and fired two shots. One hit the edge of a firing slit; the other sailed right through. Lapres and a few others worked their way around the OP only to find Corporal Victor Aguzzi working over the landward side of the OP. Lapres and his men had had no idea of Aguzzi's presence. They cut some wires they found outside the OP, destroyed the bunker's antenna, and kept a close watch on the OP. They could only do so much, though, because they had no demolitions. The stalemate at the OP lasted the better part of a day. The Rangers did not capture the bunker until well into the afternoon of June 7, but that did not really matter. They had neutralized the OP's ability to communicate with German artillery batteries, negating the possibility that the enemy could use the Pointe's ideal location to direct their fire onto the landing beaches.[16]

Meanwhile, other groups of Rangers discovered that the 155mm guns they had been sent to destroy were missing. Salva Maimone, and many other E Company Rangers, headed for Gun Position 3. "When we got there, there were no guns in the domes [casemates]." He and a few others kept moving inland, searching for the guns. "We had to work our way by crawling from one crater to another, and there was machine-gun fire on both ends of the cliff." Thirty yards to the west, Private Sundby and a gaggle of D Company soldiers captured what should have been Gun Position 4. They found nothing in the casemate. "On the edge of the concrete I saw that it was hollow." Sundby saw some wires and cut them. He and his sergeant caught a glimpse of two Germans on the horizon. They shot at them but could not tell if they hit them.[17]

When First Sergeant Lomell struggled to the top and tumbled into his shell crater, he encountered Captain Gilbert Baugh, commander of E Company. "He had a .45 in his hand, and a bullet had gone through the back of his hand into the magazine in the grip of the .45. He was in shock and bleeding badly, and there was nothing we could do other than give him morphine." Lomell, Fruhling, and Rubin left Baugh for the medics and moved on to another shell hole where they found about a dozen D Company men. "We made a move to jump to the next crater for the move toward 4, 5 and 6 gun emplacements. The Germans opened fire on us as we started out, and we jumped back to avoid the fire."[18]

As they stumbled back into their crater, one man accidentally stabbed another through the thigh with his bayonet. Lomell gave him first aid, told him he had to move on, and left for another try at the gun positions. "We made our way . . . to gun positions 4, 5 and 6. There were no guns there, and we thought, 'What the hell? What's happened here?' "

In response to pre-invasion air raids on Pointe-du-Hoc, the Germans had towed the guns away from the Pointe. In the event of an invasion, the Germans planned to move them into place. In the meantime, they placed telephone poles in the casemates. These poles completely fooled Allied photo intelligence analysts. All over the Pointe, the Rangers made this discovery.

The Rangers understood that the key now was to move inland, search for the guns, and accomplish their second mission—the cutting of the coastal road that led to Omaha beach. Even as Lieutenant Colonel Rudder set up his command post at the edge of the cliffs and small clumps of Rangers fought several bloody, confusing engagements against German soldiers who seemed to pop up everywhere, other Rangers, totaling some forty-seven men, began to move inland at various intervals along a mile-long front.

First Sergeant Lomell led the most notable force. After finding the vacated casemates at Gun Positions Four, Five, and Six, his group walked quickly inland, along a dirt road that led to the paved coastal road (called GC 32 in 1944, nowadays known as D-514). They had no idea what might be ahead of them. Visibility was limited by vegetation on either side of the road. Still, Lomell did not see their actions as particularly brave. "I want to point out that this was not inherently heroic. This was just plain common sense and good rangering. As we left the group at the Pointe, the Germans opened up with 88mm guns, laying in crawling fire. What they were trying to do was start at the edge of the cliffs, knowing that we were trying to get inland. Of course, that makes you move faster, because it's crawling up your back."

In addition to the artillery fire, German soldiers, holed up in barns or hedgerows, shot at Lomell's men as they advanced. "The Germans would fire on us, and then we'd go for them, but we knew we couldn't take the time to get into sustained firefights. Our orders were to get the guns as quickly as possible." They gave first aid to the wounded and moved on.

Sergeant Kuhn, moving alone along the road just behind Lomell's force, spotted them, made contact, and joined them. They paused for a few moments and then resumed their advance with Kuhn and Lomell in the lead. The two men kept pace with each other, on either side of the road, eyes searching the surrounding hedgerows for any sign of trouble. Just ahead to the right was an old stone barn. Suddenly Kuhn felt someone grab him and throw him into the doorway of the barn. "Lomell . . . threw both of us through the doorway." Kuhn was nonplussed. He had no idea why Lomell had done that.

Lomell looked at him in amazement. "Didn't you see that Jerry kneeling in the road aiming at us?" Kuhn hadn't. He peeked around the doorway for a look. As he did so, the German fired two shots that barely missed Kuhn. Lomell went into the barn and tried firing at the German through a window. Kuhn chanced another look and saw the German running away. "I stepped out to cut him down, but the tommy gun would not fire. My clip had been hit right where it inserts into the gun." The German got away and Kuhn went back to the Pointe to find another tommy gun.

By the time Kuhn returned, Lomell had reached the coastal road and deployed his men in blocking positions along either side of it. The push inland had cost Lomell about ten casualties. He was now down to anywhere between thirteen and twenty men (accounts differ). Sergeant Kuhn settled into a rain ditch along the road with Staff Sergeant Larry Johnson. A hedge afforded them nice concealment and a fine view of the approaches. Lomell set up on the opposite side of the road. Kuhn heard movement from behind a stone fence that paralleled the road. "A German soldier appeared . . . looking up and down the highway. Seeing it apparently clear, he came through the wall and ran across the road right up to me. I saw a . . . burp gun slung across his chest. I jumped up and fired point-blank, hitting him in the chest. My slugs must have cut the strap on his weapon, for it fell to the ground about three feet in front of me. The German ran a few steps, then dropped."

Johnson asked Kuhn to retrieve the dead German's weapon. As Kuhn leaned out to grab the burp gun, he saw another German drawing a bead on him. "I had no way to protect myself and felt I was about to be shot. Len saw it all and gunned the German just as he shot at me." A bullet struck the road next to Kuhn but missed. "For the second time on D-Day, Lomell had saved my life."[19]

Lomell now decided to resume the search for the missing guns. He detached himself and Kuhn for a reconnaissance patrol. Warily they hopped onto the paved road and investigated a farm lane that led to the south. "You could have hid a column of tanks in it, that's how wide and deep the road was. It was a sunken road with very high hedgerows." They noticed some markings in the dirt of the farm lane. Lomell thought that the markings indicated the presence of something heavy—maybe a farm wagon or, perhaps, the guns? They edged their way down the darkened road. "We decided to leap frog. Jack covered me, and I went forward. When I got a few feet forward, I covered him."

In this manner, they proceeded for about two hundred yards, until Lomell found a camouflaged draw near a hedgerow. He peeked over the hedgerow and into an apple orchard. "Sticking out of this apple orchard were these long gun barrels with netting over the top with fake leaves on [them]." There, right in front of Lomell, were the missing guns of Pointe-du-Hoc. "The wheels went up over our heads. Their muzzles went way the hell into the air, above our reach. They were all sitting in proper firing condition, with ammunition piled up neatly, everything at the ready, but they were pointed at Utah Beach, not Omaha. There was nobody at the emplacement."

Lomell could hardly believe his luck. The Germans had inexplicably left these five guns unguarded (the sixth was missing and never accounted for). He wondered where the enemy artillerymen could be. In another second he had an answer. "Another hundred yards off, in a field, were about 75 Germans forming up, putting on their jackets, starting their vehicles. They were being talked to by some officer standing in his vehicle."

Lomell knew he had to work fast. He turned to Kuhn and pointed at the German artillerymen. "Jack, keep your eyes on them, and if one starts toward here, get him."

Both Lomell and Kuhn were carrying a thermite grenade. Lomell took both grenades and put them in the traversing and elevation mechanisms of two of the guns. The heavy foliage around the guns concealed Lomell from the Germans. In seconds, the grenades detonated. "They made a light popping noise that couldn't be heard by the enemy but destroyed" the guns, mainly by melting the mechanisms. "It put the guns in a firm inoperable weldlike position. I took my tommy gun, wrapped it in my field jacket, and smashed the sights on all five guns."

He and Kuhn ran back to the roadblock to retrieve more thermite grenades from the other Rangers. They returned to the guns, completely undetected, and Lomell destroyed the remaining three while Kuhn impatiently covered him. "Hurry up. Hurry up. Let's get the hell out of here," Kuhn urged, in a low voice.

Lomell worked as fast as he could. "I don't think I spent ten minutes, all told, destroying those guns. We didn't waste a second."

They did a magnificent job. In a matter of minutes, two Rangers, without firing a shot, accomplished the vital mission that drew Companies D, E, and F of the 2nd Ranger Battalion to the Pointe that morning. At the very same time, Sergeant Frank Rupinski, from E Company, was leading a reconnaissance patrol. Unbeknownst to Kuhn and Lomell, Rupinski's people were no more than 200 yards away, closing in on the guns from the opposite direction. Rupinski's patrol did not find the guns, though. Instead, they discovered the main cache of ammunition that went with the guns. The sergeant found some demolitions, wired up the ammo, and blew it sky-high.

At that exact moment, Lomell and Kuhn were climbing over a hedgerow, making their way back to their roadblock. "There was a tremendous roar," Lomell recalled, "like the whole world had blown up. There was a shower of dirt, metal, ramrods. It deafened us; we couldn't hear each other talk for awhile. Jack and I scurried back to our roadblock like scared rabbits." Lomell and Kuhn thought that a short round from the USS *Texas* had caused the blast. Only years later, at a reunion, did they find out the truth.

As they manned their roadblock on D-Day, Lomell, Kuhn, and the other Rangers puzzled over the lackadaisical German attitude toward the security of their guns. Historians have been just as puzzled. The answer to the mystery probably has to do with E Company's small engagement back at the OP, over a mile away. By neutralizing the OP, the Rangers paralyzed the entire battery of German artillerymen. Lomell, in retrospect, certainly thought so. "I believe the reason they couldn't fire was because E Company had taken out their observation post at the Pointe. They had no directions to fire with no firing orders. Their lines of communication had been cut off. I don't think those Germans knew there were any Rangers or American soldiers within a mile of them. They were so nonchalant about walking around, acting as if there were no enemy about. They weren't in a hurry to do anything."

The guns were destroyed by 0830. Adrenaline still pumping, Lomell dispatched two volunteers (Sergeant Gordon Luning and, ironically enough, Harry Fate) to get word of this to Rudder. Employing different routes, they made their way through a maze of trenches, minefields, and firefights along the Pointe and back to Rudder's CP at the edge of the cliff. The CP was under sniper fire. The Rangers, spread out in thin perimeters around the Pointe, were fighting confusing, costly battles against Germans who would pop out of their trenches, open fire, and then melt away. Other Rangers fended off counterattacks coming from both flanks.

Fate and Luning both arrived at the CP at 0900. Luning found Lieutenant Eikner and told him the good news about the destroyed guns. Elated, Eikner tracked down Rudder and told him. Rudder ordered the lieutenant to pass the word to the fleet. Since Eikner did not have any working radios, he sent the coded message via a signal lamp he had set up at the foot of the cliff. "I sent the message, *'Praise the Lord,'* a code phrase" that meant the guns had been taken out. He also dispatched a carrier pigeon with this message and signaled, with the lamp, a request for resupply and reinforcements. An hour later, the USS *Satterlee* sent back a return message from General Huebner: "No reinforcements available—all Rangers have landed at Omaha." Eikner crawled over to the colonel and passed along the message. The burly Rudder nodded. He wasn't surprised at all. Ever since the tardy landing, he knew that his three companies of Rangers would have to fight it out on their own, for as long as it took. They were doing a fine job. The guns were destroyed. The roadblocks were deployed. Rudder's Rangers had accomplished their mission for Uncle Sam. Now they were fighting for their own lives. Rudder glanced to the east, in the direction of Omaha beach. The Germans, he knew, would soon counterattack and attempt to annihilate his force. He and his men would fight them with everything at their disposal, but ultimately, their survival depended on those landings at Omaha. He wondered, idly, how they were going. Forty-eight hours later, he was still wondering the same thing.[20]

CHAPTER FOURTEEN

BLOODY OMAHA

I f Rudder could have seen Omaha beach from his perilous perch on the cliffs of Pointe-du-Hoc, he would have been greatly dismayed by what he saw. Even as Rudder's Rangers hung on desperately at the Pointe, the initial waves of the Omaha assault force fought a grim battle for survival. All along the invasion coast, landing craft headed for the beach. From the beginning, the American landings at Omaha flirted with disaster. No Allied soldiers had a tougher mission on D-Day than those Americans who drew the assignment of invading Omaha, a three-mile stretch of thin, rocky beach nestled between Pointe-de-la-Percée in the west and Port-en-Bessin in the east.

The terrain here was ideal for defenders. High ground—cliffs, bluffs, ridges, or gentle, sloping hills—dominated most of the beach. Most of the beaches were narrow, about thirty to fifty yards of rocky sand that rose slightly to a shingle embankment and, in some places, a seawall. Thousands of years of erosion had created four deep gullies at various intervals along the beach. These gullies, or exits, as the Americans called them, provided the only way vehicles could get off the beach. From west to east, the exits were D-1 at Vierville, D-3 at Les Moulins (often simply called the Les Moulins exit), E-1 at St-Laurent, and E-3 at Colleville. The success or failure of the American landings at Omaha hinged on the capture of these beach exits. Failure to capture the beach exits meant no vehicles, no armor, no supplies, and, ultimately, no beachhead.

The Germans naturally recognized the intrinsic defensive advantages of Omaha as well as the importance of its exits. They fortified the place extensively. They defended the exits with thirty-five pillboxes, eight bunkers housing 75mm guns, and eighty-five separate machine-gun posts (sometimes called murder holes by the Americans). Along the rest of the beach the Germans had eighteen antitank positions, six Nebelwerfer (screaming mee-mie) mortar pits, thirty-eight rocket batteries, and four artillery positions. Trenches linked all these positions to one another. The Germans constructed and sited their bunkers quite ingeniously, in such a way that they enfiladed the beach. This meant two things: First, they could lay down effective fire on the flanks of attacking troops. Second, their embrasures faced the beach, not the sea, making it difficult for naval bombardment to hit anything but their reinforced concrete facades. Some of the positions were even dug into the cliffs.

Then there were the mines and obstacles, thousands of them. At the waterline the Germans placed wooden posts. On top of most of these posts they fastened deadly Teller mines. Steel gird-ers bristled everywhere. The girders were designed to rip open a Higgins boat and sink it. There were plenty of Belgian gates, too. Behind this first belt of deadly obstacles they strung barbed wire and sowed thousands of mines.

The aerial and naval bombardment was supposed to take care of most of these defenses, but it didn't. The beach was largely untouched. As H-Hour approached, only the ground troops, es-pecially the infantry, could win Omaha beach for the Allies. The opposition was so intense, the beach so cluttered with mines, ob-stacles, and destroyed vehicles, that the battle boiled down to small, isolated fights, usually for the beach exits, between clusters of infantrymen (by trade or circumstances). In the apt description of one officer who was there, the fighting at Omaha beach con-sisted of "violent swirls of death and destruction with areas of quiet in between."[1] Rarely in American military history have American soldiers faced deadlier circumstances or greater adversity than at Omaha beach on D-Day morning.

Nowhere was this more true than at Dog Green beach at the D-1 exit on the extreme western edge of Omaha. The men of Company A, 116th Infantry, 29th Infantry Division, were packed aboard six LCAs, heading for the beach. Two of the LCAs promptly sank in the choppy Channel. Some of the men drowned; others bobbed around until rescue craft could pick them up. The four other LCAs, full of thoroughly wet, miserable, and seasick

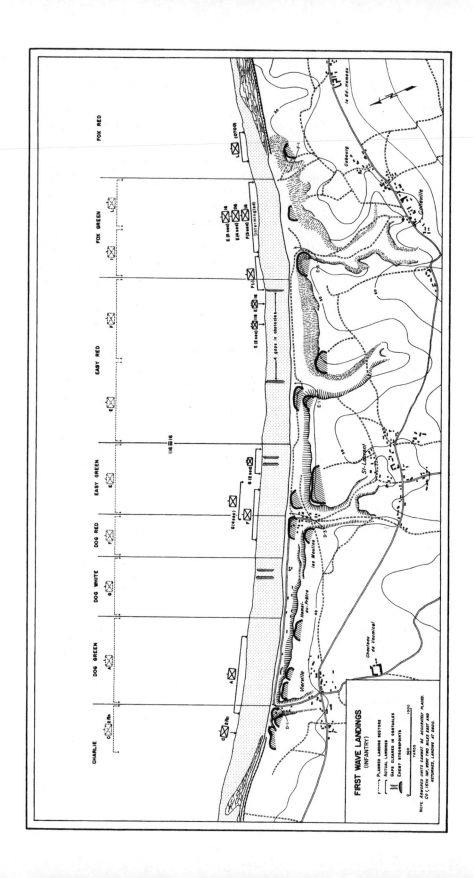

FIRST WAVE LANDINGS
(INFANTRY)

soldiers, proceeded on. Aboard one of those boats, bespectacled Private First Class Gilbert Murdoch watched one of his buddies nod off, in spite of the circumstances. The man had taken so many Dramamine (antiseasickness) pills that he could hardly keep his eyes open. Murdoch's thoughts returned to a few hours before when they all had gathered on the deck of their transport. Many of the men had solemnly shaken hands with one another. He and his friend Private First Class George Roach, a diminutive flame-thrower man, had smiled at each other; nothing more than that, but it was a moment of fellowship that Murdoch could not forget. Murdoch snapped out of his reverie. They were getting closer to the beach now. Cold, misty sea spray drenched Murdoch and he shivered.

The landing craft ground to a halt. The British coxswain lowered the ramp. For a brief moment there was silence, and then the first two men, standing in front of Murdoch, charged off the LCA. "[Dominguez] . . . ran off at the right side and he was immediately cut in half by machine-gun fire. At the same time that [he] jumped, I jumped from the left side . . . of the ramp and found myself in about nine feet of water." The landing craft had hit a sandbar. Murdoch inflated his Mae West life vest, grabbed onto a landing craft, and rode it into the beach.

Company A ran into a literal wall of enemy fire—machine guns, rifles, mortars, and artillery. The Americans didn't have a chance. From the advantage of the high ground overlooking this section of beach the Germans poured fire on their helpless adversaries. Sergeant Thomas Valance staggered out of the same boat as Murdoch. Valance crouched over and waded through knee-high water. As he did so, he could see tracer bullets coming from a massive concrete bunker that enfiladed the whole beach. He could also see a few houses farther up the draw. Bullets and shrapnel were buzzing everywhere. He heard the sickening thud of enemy metal tearing through the bodies of his men. He fell to the ground, and the incoming tide washed around him. "I remember floundering in the water with my hand up in the air . . . trying to get my balance, when I was shot . . . through the left hand and suffered from a broken knuckle. And I was shot through the palm of my hand."

The wound didn't really hurt; it just stung. Valance looked to his right. Private Henry Witt was crawling toward him. Witt looked at Valance and screamed, "Sergeant, they're leaving us here to die like rats!"

Valance turned away and crawled up the beach. He found a carbine and squeezed off a couple of ineffective rounds in the direction of the bunker. "There was no way I was going to knock out a German concrete emplacement with a thirty-caliber rifle." Firing the ineffective carbine at the bunker was a mistake. The enemy machine gunners turned their attention to Valance. "I was hit several times, once in the left thigh, which broke a hipbone. I remember being hit in the pack a couple of times, feeling a tug, and my chin strap . . . was severed by a bullet. I worked my way up onto the beach and staggered up against a [sea]wall." All day long he lay there wounded, watching the bodies of his friends, "in many cases, severely blown to pieces," wash up with the rising tide.[2]

Within ten minutes, all but two of of A Company's officers were killed. Those two were Lieutenant Edward Gearing and Lieutenant Elijah "Ray" Nance, who was hit in the heel as he exited his landing craft. A machine-gun bullet hit another officer, Lieutenant Alfred Anderson, in the throat as he left his boat. He collapsed into the shallow water, thrashed around, and tried to speak, all with blood gushing from his slashed throat. "Advance with the wire cutters," he gasped. More machine-gun bullets sliced Anderson in half. Every man on LCA-1015 was killed, including the company commander, Captain Taylor Fellers, who had foreseen this disaster. Most of their thirty-two bodies washed onto the beach in the course of the day. They might have hit a mine, or perhaps they were raked over by German machine guns, mortars, and artillery. No one ever knew for sure.[3]

The entire scene was absolutely ghastly, far beyond the power of any words to describe it. Not far away from where Valance encountered Witt, Private First Class Dom Bart could not even make it beyond the waterline. "With a stream of lead coming towards us, we were at the mercy of the Germans." Bart put his head down and played dead. "I floated around in the water for about one hour and was more dead than alive. Tried to land at several places, but always had to withdraw. It was impossible to get ashore. I lost all hopes and said my last prayer to the Good Lord."[4]

Behind Bart, farther out to sea, Private First Class Murdoch was making his way forward, creeping and crawling as the tide steadily washed over him. "My glasses were coated with salt water and were spotted." He had trouble seeing anything with any clarity, but he noticed his boat's 60mm mortar team twenty yards ahead. Murdoch called out to them. "They cried that they were hit and they . . . couldn't fire their mortar even though it was set up to fire." Murdoch made it to them and fired a few mortar rounds that didn't explode. "Murdoch, you dumb bastard, you're not pulling the firing pins," the mortar sergeant said. Chastened, Murdoch fired a few more rounds, but he couldn't see if they were doing any good.

He moved on. His rifle jammed, so he acquired a new one from a wounded man to whom he gave a shot of morphine. Murdoch turned around and saw a DD tank from the 743rd Tank Battalion emerging from the water. "It . . . immediately was holed on the right side, by an 88, and promptly blew up." When this and other tanks landed, they spread out as best they could at the waterline and opened fire at any target the crews could make out through the smoke and haze. As Murdoch indicated, many of them got picked off before they could do much of anything.

Not only did the tankers have to watch out for enemy antitank fire; they also had to proceed very carefully along the beach. Very close to where Murdoch saw the tank knocked out, George Johnson, holed up in a tank dozer (designed to help clear debris and provide fire support), peered through his periscope. Through the periscope's rectangular prism he saw obstacles and prone men (dead and alive). All at once, his tank's dozer blade collided with a Teller mine. The explosion put his tank out of action, but Johnson survived with nothing more than a muddy uniform. Company B of the 743rd lost eight of its sixteen tanks in front of the Vierville exit.[5]

Private First Class Murdoch skittered past the destroyed tank and came upon Roach. His friend still had his flamethrower tank strapped to his back. "What happened with you?" Murdoch wondered.

Roach told him that his lieutenant and noncoms were all dead or wounded. The two friends were lying behind a beach obstacle as they talked. They noticed tracers whizzing over their heads, glanced up, and saw a Teller mine on the tip of the obstacle. The German gunner was trying to hit the mine. At almost the same time, Murdoch noticed he had been shot in the ankle. He and Roach ended up retreating from the beach and swimming out to a destroyed tank that was stuck in about four feet of water. When they got there, they found the tank's wounded crew. "We could see three heads bobbing up and down . . . their faces all powderburnt. The tank commander, a buck sergeant, was sitting behind the turret with his left leg off at the knee and the bone in the water and the artery in the water."

The sergeant was angry at his crewmen because they would not respond to his orders. He asked Murdoch to give him a morphine shot, so Murdoch crawled into the turret and found a first-aid kit. "I gave him a shot." The tank commander was convinced that the beach was safer than his stranded tank. Emboldened by the morphine, he finally convinced his wounded crewmen to head for the beach. Murdoch and Roach tried to talk them out of it, but they went anyway. "As they got closer to the beach, a long shore current [swept] them to the left. The last I saw they were kicking and trying to make the beach."

Roach moved on and Murdoch stayed put. Enemy machine gunners must have run out of targets on the beach, because they started getting interested in Murdoch. Tracers were shooting past him. "I got so damned angry that I stood on the turret and fired the fifty-caliber machine gun until there were no rounds left. Whether I hit anything, I don't know; I could hardly see beach. My glasses were so fogged over with salt spray and I had nothing really to clean and dry them with." The rising tide eventually swept Murdoch off the turret. Using an empty jerrican as a flotation device, he floated in the water until a British patrol craft picked him up. He knew that his company had been decimated. Of the 200 men in the company, only about 50 survived and almost all of them were wounded. Among the Bedford contingent, 19 were killed.[6]

Immediately to the right of A Company, indeed almost intermixed with them, C Company of the 2nd Rangers experienced the same kind of nightmare. Their mission was to push through Exit D-1 and secure Pointe-de-la-Percée (the bluffs that Rudder's force originally mistook for Pointe-du-Hoc). In so doing, C Company would secure the western flank of Omaha beach. Numbering only sixty-eight men, C Company rode in two LCAs. In one of the boats, the company commander, Captain Ralph Goranson, joined in as his men sang to Sergeant Walter Geldon, "because June 6 was his 3rd wedding anniversary."[7]

In the other boat, Lieutenant Sidney Saloman, leader of the 2nd Platoon, stood in the bow of the landing craft, directly behind the steel ramp. He saw cliffs coming into focus. Artillery rumbled in the distance, but here in the boat everything was quiet. He looked at Captain Goranson's LCA, plodding along right next to his. The two boats looked so forlorn, so lonesome, out here in the Channel. Still, they were intact and moving and that counted for something. "So far, so good," Saloman thought to himself.

He turned and gave a reassuring look to his men, most of whom were several years younger than the thirty-year-old lieutenant. "There was a wooden bench on either side of the craft. The men sat on either side facing into the center. Then, in the center of the boat, there was also a bench that went from bow to stern. The men straddled it facing forward. Some were brown-bagging it, nausea had taken over, and brown paper bags . . . were being filled. From some it was mainly the dry heaves. They had been too nervous and tense to eat the early morning breakfast served on board the Prince Charles. There were a few forced chuckles, as the platoon chowhound not only filled his brown bag, but also his steel helmet."

They were close enough now that shells began exploding around their craft. Bullets pinged off the armor of the LCA. "I crouched a little lower behind . . . the ramp, still peering over it."[8]

The two Ranger boats landed simultaneously just east of the Vierville draw, directly across the draw from where A Company was landing. British crewmen lowered the ramps and the Rangers scrambled to get out, plunging into chest-high water. At that exact moment, the Germans poured a staggering volume of fire on the exiting Rangers—machine guns, rifles, mortars, even artillery. Mortar shells rained down on Captain Goranson's boat, blowing off the ramp. Several of his men were already in the water, but others got hit. His radioman, Sergeant Donald Scribner, was struggling against the weight of his equipment (a heavy radio, rifle, grenades, ammunition, bedroll, and pack). A mortar shell exploded. Fragments tore through a nearby Ranger. "The young man . . . never knew what hit him," Scribner said. "The LCA started filling up with lots of blood. It was just as red as anything could be." The boat was sinking. Scribner finally got out and plunged into the Channel. He began sinking. "I didn't think I was going to stop going down." Luckily the water wasn't very deep. He somehow made it to the beach.[9]

Others were doing the same. When Lieutenant Saloman and his men left their landing craft, German machine-gun fire swept through them. Several men were hit. A few fell into the water and died. Others tried to make it to the beach. Right behind Saloman, Sergeant Oliver Reed grunted as a bullet smashed into his stomach. Before he could fall, Saloman grabbed him and pulled him to the water's edge. The lieutenant wanted to do all he could for Reed but knew he had to keep going. "Sergeant, this as far as I can take you. I have to get along."

Saloman turned and ran onto the beach. He was trying to make it to the comparative shelter of Pointe-de-la-Percée's bluff. "A mortar shell landed right behind me and killed or wounded all of my mortar section. I got some of the shrapnel—it hit my back and I landed right on my face. I fell down in the sand and thought I was dead." Shocked, Saloman reached inside his field jacket pocket for his maps. His platoon sergeant ran up to him. "Am I hit?" Saloman asked.

"Yes."

Saloman thought he was dying. "You got to take my maps."

Before he could hand them over, machine-gun bullets started kicking up sand around them. This angered the irrepressible Saloman. "I said to myself that I wasn't going to die. This was no place to be lying, so I took my maps, got up and ran toward the overhang of the cliffs." A medic made it to him and dug some of the shrapnel out of his back. He poured some sulfa on the wounds and bandaged them up. "Take care of the rest of the guys," Saloman ordered.[10]

At nearly the same moment, Captain Goranson was on the beach, trying to make it to the bluff where Saloman and a few others had taken cover. Goranson wanted to make it across the 300-yard expanse of beach and to the bluff more than he had ever wanted anything in his life. "Going across the beach was like a dream. All the movement of my body and mind were just on automatic drive. As I went across, I saw men falling down. Every man in the company was trained to achieve the company objective, so no matter who fell, the job would get done! As I came across, I fell down on the beach once, and machine gun fire started raising sand up all around me. Immediately I got up and made it the rest of the way."[11]

By now, those who were still able-bodied, thirty-one in all, had made it to the bluff. Many of the wounded were lying on the beach in various stages of despair or shock. They pleaded for help or tried to make it to the bluff. Sergeant Scribner, in spite of his heavy radio, made it to the bluff. He looked back and saw Sergeant Geldon, "lying out on the beach with his hand raised up asking for help." Moments before, they had all been singing to Geldon to commemorate his anniversary. Now he was lying on an anonymous beach, badly wounded, scared, hoping someone could save him, hoping against hope that he could live to see his wife again.

Scribner started back to help Geldon. Along the way he saw Sergeant Reed "sitting up tight . . . along the cliffs. He was kind of rolled up into a knot. He looked like his face was all swelled up, he was kind of shivering, and I could tell he was hit." Scribner put his hand on Reed's shoulder and told him he would get help. He ran across the open beach looking for some medical supplies. German fire whizzed everywhere, but somehow Scribner survived. During his frantic search, he could not help noticing the remnants of A Company, 116th. Many of the soldiers from this company were "lying there, blown to bits." Scribner found some medical supplies and made it back to the cliff, but Reed was gone. He glanced back and saw Geldon lying in the same place. This time he was lying still. "Walter didn't make it. He was dead."[12]

The surviving Rangers under the cliff were not exactly immune to enemy fire. The Germans knew they were there and started dropping grenades down the cliff. Goranson first realized they were doing this when he heard one of his men, Mike Gargas, hollering, "Mashed potatoes! Mashed potatoes!" Goranson didn't know what Gargas was talking about until "I looked back and there was a German potato masher grenade smoking away." The grenade exploded, but nobody was hurt. On such a grim day, this incident passed for humor.

The captain surveyed the situation. In a matter of minutes he had lost over half his company. His survivors were pinned down under this overhang, but they were still full of fight (they were Rangers, after all!). His mission was to capture the Vierville draw (D-1) and move west onto Pointe-de-la-Percée, but an enemy bunker in the middle of the exit negated any thought of doing that. This was the same bunker that was giving A Company so much trouble. If the Rangers tried to destroy it head-on, they would all be slaughtered. Goranson quickly determined that the cliffs of Pointe-de-la-Percée offered the only way out of their predicament. "I signaled Lieutenant [Bill] Moody with 2 fingers pointed up to undertake plan 2."

Plan 2 meant scaling the cliff. Once at the top, they would

destroy enemy defenses and try to open up the exit from the western side. Moody and three other men, Sergeants Julius Belcher and Richard Garrett and Private First Class Otto Stephens, led the way. They were expert climbers. The four men free-climbed the 100-foot cliff as their comrades gave them cover fire. "The last 10 or 15 feet they chinned themselves up with their trench knives and secured a series of toggle ropes from the barbed wire emplacement up there so the rest of us could immediately . . . climb up the cliff."

At the top Moody's group moved quickly. On some high ground to their left a stone house dominated the landscape and the Vierville draw. Naval gunfire had battered the house. Trenches and pillboxes zigzagged the area around the house. The Rangers figured that the house must be fortified. Covering one another as they ran, they attacked the place. Moody kicked in the door and shot a German officer. There were no other living Germans in the house. Most of the Germans had taken cover in their trenches or pillboxes. Moody spread his men out into small patrols, hunting for enemy troops in the maze of positions (quite similar to the fighting at Pointe-du-Hoc).

Down at the base of the cliff, Lieutenant Saloman prepared to reinforce Moody. Saloman had nine men left now. One by one, they grabbed the toggle ropes and started climbing. Just as Saloman was about to go up, he glanced at the beach and took in the awful sight of the remnants of his men. "Bodies lay still, where they had fallen, trickles of blood reddening the sand. Some of the wounded were crawling as best they were able, some with a look of despair and bewilderment on their tortured and pain-racked faces. Others, with a determination to reach the cover of the cliff, tried to get back up on their feet, only to be hit again by the enemy firepower. Bodies rolled back and forth at the water's edge. With a slight shudder, I turned to start my climb, hand over hand and up the ropes, feet searching for the toe holds."

At the top, Saloman spotted a shell hole and took cover. There he found Moody. The two officers peered over the edge of the hole. They were studying the terrain, discussing what to do, when Saloman felt Moody fall onto his shoulder. "He had been killed by a bullet hole through his eyes. I grabbed the man next to me and said, 'Let's go!' "

Saloman had three men with him. They ran ahead and jumped into a trench. After a short time, they found a dugout. "I tossed a white phosphorous grenade into the dugout. We waited several seconds, then blasted away with Tommy guns and rifles." The Germans, who had emerged from the position screaming in agony as the white phosphorous burned into their skin, collapsed in a lifeless heap. "Further down the trench, and around a curve, we came upon a German mortar crew in a fixed gun position. Some more grenades, more rifle and Tommy gun fire, as the three of us continued through the trenches." They searched the mortar position, ignoring the torn, dead bodies of the enemy crew. "Painted on the walls of the mortar area were targets for stakes that were in the ground for positions up around the beach at Vierville." They now understood quite well why the enemy mortar fire had been so frighteningly accurate.

By 0750, Goranson's small group of Rangers cleared out parts of Pointe-de-la-Percée, but at best, the area was only under their loose control. All day long, they fought small battles against infiltrating groups of German soldiers. The Rangers inflicted terrible damage on them. According to Goranson, they found sixty-nine dead German soldiers in the area. His unit lost twenty-three killed and over twenty wounded, most of them on the beach. They did not accomplish their mission of capturing Exit D-1, but they did make it possible for others to do so. Plus, they demonstrated incredible resilience in the face of awful circumstances. Their grueling Ranger training paid great dividends. Without it, they would not have been able to ascend the cliff or fight as effectively as they did.[13]

To some extent, A Company of the 116th and C Company of the 2nd Rangers experienced their difficulties because the three other assault companies of the first wave landed too far away. Company G of the 116th was supposed to land immediately to the left of A Company. Instead they landed about one thousand yards too far to the east. Company E was completely lost. The men of this outfit landed more than a mile to the east in the 1st Division's sector. Only Company F landed in the exact right place, in front of D-3 at Les Moulins, but too far away to do A Company any good. Effectively, these mislandings meant that the German defenders of Exit D-1 could entirely concentrate their fire on A Company and the Rangers.

Of course, their misfortune was G Company's good fortune.

The six boats carrying this company landed safely east of Les Moulins under the cover of smoke billowing from grass fires on the bluffs overlooking the beach. The soldiers disembarked in knee-deep water, waded ashore, and made it across the beach to a shingle embankment. Private Frank Simeone was huddling under cover waiting for orders. Germans mortar shells exploded inaccurately. "Some of it was going overhead and some falling short of us." The German spotters could not see through the smoke. The officers of G Company soon discovered that they were in the wrong place. Word came down that they would have to move 1,000 yards to the west. Simeone and the other soldiers began walking west. "It was a complete shambles and disorganized." Indeed it was. Some members of the company ran into deadly machine-gun fire at areas not shrouded by smoke. Others filtered inland. Still others found hiding places and stayed put. The rest broke off into small groups and made their way to the Vierville exit.[14]

Meanwhile, F Company was landing right in front of Les Moulins (D-3) exit. Some of the boat teams were lucky enough to land in spots that were obscured by smoke. The men quickly disgorged from their craft, raced across the beach, and took cover along the shingle embankment directly in front of the exit. Many of them were exhausted and still fighting vestiges of seasickness. Moreover, they understood that German fire beyond the shingle was intense.

Other F Company soldiers, like Staff Sergeant Harry Bare, were not so lucky. A native of Philadelphia, the thirty-year-old squad leader had two years of college at Villanova under his belt when the war came along and he enlisted. At H-Hour, his boat landed right in front of the draw, directly in the line of sight of German defenders. The ramp went down and the first man off, Bare's lieutenant, instantaneously got shot in the throat. "Fire rained down on us, machine-gun, rifle, rockets from the bunkers on top of the cliff. The men went over the sides of the boats to avoid the fire."

Some of the others froze in place on the landing craft. Sergeant Bare tried to get them moving. He pushed them forward onto the beach. "My radioman had his head blown off three yards from me. The beach was covered with bodies, men with no legs, no arms— God, it was awful. It was absolutely terrible." Bare and a few others made it to the embankment. "I could feel the cold fingers of fear grip me." He sat there shivering and soaking wet, wondering what to do.

As a mortar man, Private First Class John Robertson was one of the last men out of his landing craft. He watched in horror as his boat team leader got killed. The men in front of Robertson were jumping into shoulder-high water. One of them, carrying a flamethrower, jumped in and took a shot in his flamethrower tank. He exploded in a fiery mass. Robertson was terrified. He was lugging sixty pounds of mortar rounds and other equipment. When his turn came, he jumped into the water and waded slowly through it. Machine-gun bullets zipped around him. "I struggled up to where the water was about a foot deep, and I just lay there wondering what I was going to do. A shell landed nearby, turning me over and causing a bitter taste in my mouth."

Robertson heard engine noise behind him. He turned around. A DD tank was rumbling in his direction. That motivated Robertson to brave the terrible fire sweeping the beach. He made it to the shingle.

Rocco Russo, an assistant bazooka man, was having a very rough time. On the boat ride in, he had managed to stave off seasickness until someone puked all over him. "That caused me to throw up also." By the time the ramp dropped, Russo was so sick he almost wanted to die. He made it part of the way up the beach, where he and his bazooka gunner plopped down and attempted to spot pillboxes up the draw. "The German defenses were high up on the cliffs, completely concealed but with a premier view of the beach. We . . . fired two rounds from the Bazooka. But this was accomplishing nothing and merely set us up as targets."

They packed up and moved on, all the way to the shingle. Even here they were not completely safe, though. A mortar shell landed near Russo. "I looked down and saw a big chunk of bloody meat in my lap. It had hit the top part of my assault jacket and fallen into my lap so I had blood from . . . my jacket to my lap. I was shook up." At first Russo wondered if he had been horribly wounded, but he quickly saw that the body part came from someone else. "One of the guys had lost a leg and it was in my lap."

Gradually, after fifteen or twenty minutes of the initial shock of the traumatic landing, the F Company soldiers began to work on the German defenses in the draw. Staff Sergeant Bare and a few other soldiers slithered over the embankment and found a road that led inland. "A burst of machine-gun fire made us duck behind [a] ridge." He saw that the fire came from two bunkers, about twenty yards farther up the road. "I crawled forward, circled wide, and came down between the bunkers, and destroyed both with grenades in the gun slots. I was very lucky. My canteen was torn to pieces by at least six rounds. Why I wasn't hit, God only knows."

Sergeant Warner Hamlett helped go after several other pill-boxes when he got tired of seeing his comrades slaughtered on the beach. While he was crawling on the beach, trying to advance, a private fell beside him, "white with fear. He seemed to be beg-ging for help with his eyes." Seconds later, a shell screamed in and exploded nearby. Hamlett buried his face in the sand, but the private wasn't quite quick enough. "Shrapnel rose over my head and . . . took [his] chin off, including the bone, except for a small piece of flesh. He tried to hold his chin in place as he ran" for cover. A little later, Hamlett was waiting for wire cutters to ma-terialize and lead the way up the draw. A lieutenant was supervis-ing their work. "A bullet hit him in the forehead. He continued to instruct his men until he sat down and held his head in the palm of his hand before falling over dead."

When Hamlett and the others made it over the wire, they took fire from several pillboxes. The Americans took cover in gullies or behind bushes. At first they tried to use long poles to push TNT charges into the pillboxes, but the Germans shot down the men carrying the poles. When this failed, Hamlett's group infiltrated the trenches that connected the pillboxes. They "slipped behind the pillboxes, and threw grenades into them. After the explosion, we ran into the boxes to kill any that survived the grenade."[15]

In spite of these small victories, the surviving members of the first wave of 116th Regiment assault troops, strung out along a mile of deadly beach, were mostly pinned down, soaked, terrified, and ineffective. In this sector, the invasion so far was a disaster.

By 0700 the follow-up waves started coming in. At Les Moulins, Major Sidney Bingham, the commander of the 2nd Battalion, 116th, along with his headquarters group and much of H Com-pany, came in right on top of F Company. Unfortunately for this second wave, the smoke over the beach had cleared somewhat, so the Germans had a nice view of these attackers as they stepped off their landing craft. Within a matter of minutes, seven of H Company's nine boats had been hit by artillery fire. An 88mm shell scored a direct hit on one boat, killing or wounding twenty-six men as they stepped off the ramp. The boat immediately caught fire and sank. The six unwounded survivors plodded ashore as best they could.

Machine-gun and artillery fire swept the beach. Private First Class John Amendola made it off his boat, only to be pinned down on the beach. He raised his head from the sand and looked around. "Two men from my section got down behind a tetrahedron to escape the bullets. An artillery shell hit the tetrahedron and drove the steel back into their bodies." Amendola crawled over to help them. "I tried to pry the steel loose from the men but couldn't do it. Then I figured they were dead anyway." The advancing tide immersed Amendola as he lay prone beside his two dead friends. The tide brought with it the bodies of many of those who had been killed leaving their boats. Private First Class Amendola was surprised at how quickly the color had drained from their faces. This entire experience seemed unreal somehow. "They looked just like . . . wax. I felt like I was seeing some kind of show. I felt this really can't be happening."[16]

Unfortunately, it was all too real. Even as H Company was fighting to get ashore, K Company was doing the same a couple hundred yards away at the other side of the draw. Felix Branham, the patriotic Virginia farm boy who had joined the unit in 1938, made it off his boat with no problem. On the beach he saw the regimental commander, Colonel Charles Canham, urging men to get off the beach and inland. Canham was an exacting commander. He had trained the 116th mercilessly, and Branham hated him for it. But now, amid the maelstrom of Omaha beach, Branham had to admit that perhaps Canham wasn't so bad after all. The colonel had been shot in the wrist, but that hardly slowed him. He walked around with his arm in a sling, shouting orders and encouragement.

Unconsciously imitating the colonel, Sergeant Branham turned to his buddy Gino Ferrari and said, "Let's move up, Gino." Before they could go two steps, Branham felt "something splattered all over the side of my face. He'd been hit in the face and his brains splattered all over my face and my stuff." That night, as Branham dug in at a position inland, he cried tears of grief and frustration. Back in England, Branham had chided his buddy Ferrari for

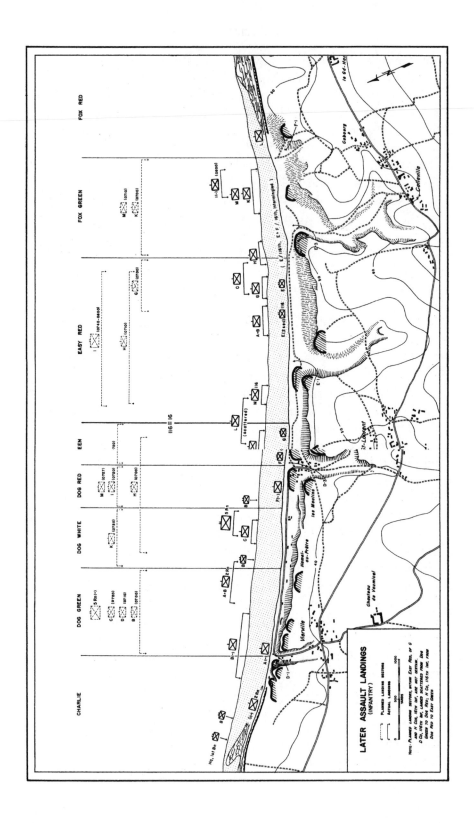

LATER ASSAULT LANDINGS
(INFANTRY)

carrying so much money in his wallet. He joked that the minute Ferrari got hit on the beach, he would loot his wallet. But Branham didn't touch Ferrari's wallet. In fact, he couldn't even bring himself to look at Ferrari's body.[17]

Slightly to the west of where Ferrari was killed, Major Bingham (USMA Class of 1940) landed. Plumes of smoke obscured Bingham's view of the beach, and at first he thought all was well. "I noticed explosions and thought that they were from the engineers blowing up the beach obstacles." Bingham soon learned otherwise when he stopped to rest beside a tetrahedron and noticed sand kicking up at his feet. "It then occurred to me that . . . MG bullets were kicking up that sand. From then on there was no doubt in my mind. I was scared, exhausted. I finally crossed the beach and got to the shingle . . . where about 100 men from F company were seeking what little shelter that . . . afforded." As he took cover, Bingham was lying right in front of the major geographical feature at Les Moulins, a three-story stone house that had been battered by naval gunfire. The major noticed that men were having trouble firing their rifles because they were clogged with sand. He had his men strip the rifles down and clean them. Then he led a push for the house. They made it unscathed and Bingham set up his CP in the house. But he could not establish radio communication with anyone else. "I might just as well have been in the States for all the good I did the outfit that day," Bingham modestly wrote. "Everything . . . was done by small groups, led by the real heroes of any war. Very few were decorated chiefly because no one was left to tell about what they did."

Bingham was correct in his recognition of the real heroes of Omaha beach, but he understated his own role. All day long, he organized small groups of men from his 2nd Battalion and the adjacent 3rd and led them inland, in essence flanking the German defenses at Les Moulins draw from the east.

Captain Cawthon, commanding Bingham's headquarters company, saw the major all over the place on D-Day morning. Cawthon landed near the three-story house, almost right in front of the draw. As he trotted up the beach, Cawthon heard a bloodcurdling scream: "I'm hit!" Cawthon looked around. "The white face, staring eyes, and open mouth of the first soldier I witnessed struck in battle remains with me. The image of no one . . . remains more vivid." Cawthon shouted for a medic and moved on to the shingle. He peeked over it and saw the house. A mortar shell landed nearby. Fragments slightly wounded Cawthon in the face.

He decided to press inland. As he did so, he saw Bingham rounding up men. "This is a debacle," Bingham declared.

Cawthon could not disagree. "He did not seem to be brooding about it. He told me to sort out the boat teams and round up some firepower, and then he left on the run down the embankment to look for a way up the bluffs."

As Cawthon wandered around carrying out Bingham's orders, he was wounded a second time. "This time, I did not hear the explosion or see the flash, but there was another jar to the side of the face . . . and again I started leaking blood. My injuries, though much less serious than most at Les Moulins, were spectacularly visible." A medic treated him and told him that "here was a rare case of a shot having gone clearly through one cheek and out the other without damage to teeth or tongue." Cawthon's lucky wound served as quite a curiosity for many of the soldiers around him— the captain did not welcome the attention—but after a brief rest he went looking for Bingham. Cawthon found him on a country lane that led to St-Laurent, leading a mixed group to the outskirts of the town. The Germans stopped them there, but they had penetrated the enemy's beach defenses and had flanked Les Moulins draw (Exit D-3).[18]

Some two thousand yards to the east, at Dog Green, where two companies of American soldiers had been decimated at the D-1 exit, follow-up waves experienced the same kind of nightmare. With the exception of the positions the Rangers had destroyed atop Pointe-de-la-Percée, German strong points in this vicinity had not been reduced much. Thanks to the virtual destruction of the first wave, the intact German defenders trained their weapons on the reinforcing companies at Dog Green—A and B Companies, 2nd Rangers, along with B and D Companies, 116th Infantry. They suffered terrible casualties.

Starting at 0700, the men of these assault companies began hitting the beach. Private First Class Robert Sales served as the radioman for B Company's commander, Captain Ettore Zappacosta, a highly respected leader. As their Higgins boat approached the beach, the two men peered through a slit at Dog Green beach.

"Captain, there's something wrong," Private First Class Sales hollered. "There's men laying everywhere on the beach!"

"They shouldn't be on the beach." Captain Zappacosta replied.

The ramp went down and the captain led his men into the surf. Sales heard a machine gun chattering and saw bullets riddle his captain in the legs and shoulder. "It didn't kill him instantly, but he was hollering at me. The only thing that saved me, I stumbled and went off the side of that ramp." Sales plunged into the cold water. When he surfaced he saw Zappacosta just ahead of him. The captain called out, "I'm hit!" From the boat a medic, T/5 Thomas Kenser, answered, "Try to make it in!" A bullet tore into the medic and he fell dead into the water. Zappocosta went under the waves, never to be seen again. Other men, filing off the Higgins boat behind the medic, got torn apart by machine-gun fire. Every single one of them got hit.

Shivering and soaked but still unwounded, Sales got rid of his radio and some of his other equipment. A mortar shell nearly killed him, but he grabbed onto a floating log that had a mine on the bottom (probably an uprooted obstacle with a Teller mine). "I pushed that log in front of me real close and made my way to the beach. It took me a long time." When he reached the beach, he saw the company communications sergeant. The sergeant was lying under cover, but he raised himself up to say something to Sales. "A sniper . . . hit him in the head. It looked like his head exploded. He dropped his face right back in the sand. I knew he was done for. If you moved, you were dead. I realized then how tough things were."

Private Harold Baumgarten realized how tough things were the second he exited his LCA. A Bronx kid and former high school football star of Jewish ancestry, the nineteen-year-old Baumgarten had completed a year of pre-med studies at New York University before being drafted in 1943. As a token of ethnic and regional pride he had drawn a Star of David on the back of his field jacket and written: "The Bronx, New York."

He hopped off the ramp of his LCA and began wading toward the beach. A machine-gun bullet went through the top of his helmet. Another one smashed into his M-1 Garand. "The water was being shot up all around me, and many a bullet ricocheted off the water top at me." Men were falling all around him. One of them, Private Robert Ditmar, took a round in the chest. He yelled, "I'm hit!" and tried to make it to the beach. He tripped over a tank obstacle, twirled around and fell, his body sprawled over the sand.

He rolled around on the sand and yelled, "Mother! Mom!"

It got worse. Baumgarten made it to the waterline, but he and many others were right in the killing zone of the now infamous Vierville exit bunker (the Germans had built it right into a hillside, where it still rests). Baumgarten saw his platoon sergeant walking around aimlessly. He had a "gaping wound in the upper right corner of his forehead. Then I saw him get down on his knees and start praying with his rosary beads. At this moment, the Germans cut him in half with their deadly crossfire."

Private Baumgarten tried to fight back. "I saw the reflection from the helmet of one of the snipers and took aim and later on, I found out, I got a bull's eye on him." Baumgarten's rifle was too damaged to shoot anymore, so he broke it in half and threw it away. Machine-gun bullets ripped up the sand around him. He was pinned down and frustrated. "I raised my head up to curse the Germans." An 88 shell exploded just ahead. "Fragments . . . hit me in the left cheek. It felt like being hit with a baseball bat, only the results were much worse. My upper jaw was shattered, the left cheek blown open. My upper lip was cut in half. The roof of my mouth was cut up, and teeth and gums were laying all over my mouth. Blood poured freely from the gaping wound." He washed his face in the dirty Channel water, played dead, floated with the rising tide to the seawall, and got treated by a medic. Private Baumgarten looked back in the direction of the waterline. "I saw the bodies of my buddies who had tried in vain to clear the beach. It looked like the beach was littered with the refuse of a wrecked ship." Baumgarten was hit five more times that day before finally being evacuated.[19]

Approximately fifty yards to the left of where Baumgarten got hit, Sergeant Bob Slaughter, a twenty-year-old Roanoke, Virginia, native and member of D Company, 116th, was lying at the waterline, hoping to survive. He saw the landing craft from which he had just debarked get hit and sink. Men around him were hit and bleeding. "There were dead men floating in the water and there were live men acting dead, letting the tide take them in." A soldier ran past him, got shot, stumbled, fell, and screamed for a medic. A medic ran over to him, got shot, and pitched over. "I will never forget seeing that medic lying next to that wounded GI and both of them screaming. They died in minutes."

Mortar shells started falling around Slaughter and the men near him. "Getting across the beach became an obsession. We decided we'd better get across [the beach] or we were going to get killed out there on the edge of the water." Slaughter was the leader of a machine-gun section. He and his machine gunners ran as fast as they could, zigzagging their way up the beach, playing a deadly game of cat and mouse with German machine gunners. One man fell dead in a pool of water (his blood quickly turned the water red), but the rest of the section made it to the seawall.[20]

The Rangers of A and B Companies, 2nd Battalion, were landing at almost the same deadly place—and with the same results— as Slaughter's outfit. The seemingly simple act of making it ashore was a major challenge for these well-honed, psyched-up soldiers. As the landing craft carrying the Rangers approached Dog Green, German artillery and mortars zeroed in on them. Staff Sergeant Ray Alm was in charge of a mortar crew in B Company. His LCA had closed to within 200 feet of the beach "when a shell blew off the front of our landing craft, destroying the ramp. My two best buddies were right in front of me, and they were both killed." Alm and the rest of the boat team jumped over the sides and into water over their heads. Only by letting go of most of his equipment, including a bazooka, could Sergeant Alm make it to the beach, where he took cover behind an obstacle. The bodies of dead first-wave troops floated past him. "There was blood in the water—it was just dark."

Several yards away, Edward Gurney bumped into dead bodies as he painstakingly splashed his way out of the water. "Any man standing was a German sniper's target. So I retrogressed back to the days of my childhood and 'mud-crawled' my way to the shore. I had to stop to catch my breath three times while crossing the sandy area. Each time I knelt down to take a breath, two mortar shells landed near me." He made it to the pile of stones that constituted the shingle in this section of the beach. "A German machine gunner took an intense interest in me. He tried to use his gun to cut away the stones protecting me." The stones stayed in place. Gurney took a look around and was surprised to see that he was alone. No wonder the German gunner was so interested in him! For some reason that Gurney never understood, the enemy gunner ceased firing. That allowed Gurney to make it to the seawall.

A Ranger officer, Lieutenant Gerald Heaney, soon joined him at the seawall. Heaney was an Irish-American lawyer and fiercely proud of his heritage. He was twenty-six, a bit on the old side for a Ranger. He came from Goodhue, Minnesota, and had earned his law degree from the University of Minnesota. Heaney's LCA was bracketed by enemy mortar and machine-gun fire. Like so many others, he jumped over the side into deep water. He and a sergeant "worked our way towards shore, doing our best to keep our weapons dry. All around me men were being killed and wounded." They made it to the beach. "I remember being so exhausted when I reached the shore that I had all I could do to make it the short distance from the shore to the seawall." He and the sergeant made it, but enemy mortar shells harassed them. The shells exploded along the shingle, mixing deadly rock fragments together with the copious amounts of Krupp steel flying through the air.[21]

The Rangers and 29'ers who made it as far as the shingle or the seawall mixed together with the few survivors from the first wave. In wet, inert clumps, they huddled under cover and waited—for what they did not exactly know. They were in shock, and that shock created a kind of collective inertia.

Behind them, all along the beach, the engineers (both army and navy) struggled to clear gaps so that more vehicles and tanks could be landed. Like everyone else, they were just trying to make it ashore and survive. Garwood Bacon of the 7th Naval Beach Battalion jumped from his burning, sinking LCI and made it to the edge of the water. He could hardly believe the chaos his eyes beheld. The beach was littered with the dead and dying. Off to his left, a DD tank, with its treads in the water, was firing machine-gun bursts at a German pillbox dug into the side of a hill. "Destruction and chaos engulfed the entire area. It was even tougher than we anticipated. All this took just a matter of seconds to observe."

Bacon spent most of his time back at his sinking LCI trying to help the wounded make it to the beach. "One staggered drunkly [*sic*] to his feet with a stunned expression and then gave a hysterical scream, grabbed frantically at his face as blood spurted and poured down his face and the front of his jacket from a head wound. The complexity of mingled expressions of surprise, pain, fear and bewilderment he showed were indescribable." Not until later in the afternoon did Bacon and his team even begin to clear obstacles.[22]

The story was much the same for Fritz Weinshank's 6th Engineer Special Brigade. Weinshank was born in Germany. His father fought in World War I. Two of his uncles were killed in that war. Young Fritz grew up under French occupation in the Rhineland. He was a patriotic German until the Nazis took over. Since the Weinshanks were Jewish, they decided to immigrate to the United States. Fritz went to high school in Brooklyn and got drafted in 1942.

Now, on the morning of D-Day, he was a radioman sitting in the hold of an LCI heading for Dog Green. The LCI hit a mine. "Our hold started to fill with . . . acrid smoke, and the pipes were coming off the wall." He and many others made it off the LCI and into the water. Weinshank did the backstroke all the way to the beach, landing right at the Vierville draw. "I was half-drowned, and I saw nothing but dead Americans." He also saw a knocked-out tank from the 743rd. He crawled under the tank until someone told him that the Germans had it zeroed in. Somewhere nearby, a medic was patching up a wounded man. The man was pale and "he was smoking and his guts and everything was just wide open."

A sergeant from Weinshank's unit found a radio and gave it to him, but Weinshank could not get it to work. "There was a blue haze over the dials and it had burned out. I couldn't do my job." Most of the other engineers on the beach felt the same way.[23]

So did artillerymen, most of whom were circling in landing craft offshore looking for an opening on the crowded beach. Since the engineers could not clear many gaps through the beach obstacles, very few reinforcing vehicles or artillery pieces could be landed. Indeed, it was even difficult for landing craft to find any openings along the beach. An LCT carrying M-7 self-propelled guns ("priests") from the 58th Armored Field Artillery Battalion tried four separate times to land, only to back off and circle some more. Each time this happened, Master Sergeant Raymond Summers took in the ghastly sight of Dog Green beach. "I could see countless figures sprawled on the beach. Machine gun fire was coming from several points over the beach. Mortars and shells began bursting on the beach and on the edge of the water. The men weren't getting off the beach as planned."[24]

By 0830, so few gaps had been cleared and the beaches were so jammed with destroyed vehicles and landing craft that the commander of the 7th Naval Beach Battalion, the unit responsible for traffic control, suspended the landing of all vehicles.

The best way to alleviate this critical traffic problem was to capture the beach exists. At Vierville, small groups of Rangers, like one led by Lieutenant Heaney, ventured over the seawall. "[We]

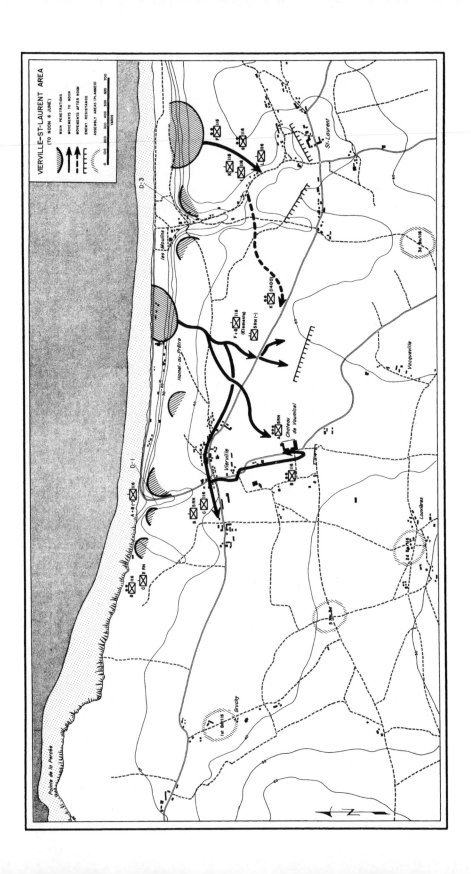

VIERVILLE-ST-LAURENT AREA
(TO NOON 6 JUNE)

MAIN PENETRATIONS
MOVEMENTS TO NOON
MOVEMENTS AFTER NOON
ENEMY RESISTANCE
ASSEMBLY AREAS (PLANNED)

0   100 200 300 400 500 600 700
YARDS

went over the seawall and ran as hard as we could across the road to the cover of the houses that lay in the foothills. Slowly, but surely, we then began to work our way up the hill."[25]

Accurate, aimed fire from surviving tanks of the 743rd (mostly at the seawall or the waterline, since they could not yet get off the crowded beach) helped men like Heaney infiltrate the Vierville draw. Naval gunfire provided even more help. Aboard the USS *Texas*, Rear Admiral Carleton Bryant, commander of the Omaha beach bombardment force, ordered his ships to do anything they could to help the stricken troops destroy enemy resistance. "Get on them, men! Get on them! They are raising hell with the men on the beach, and we can't have any more of that!"

The destroyer *McCook* closed to within 1,300 yards of the beach. It had to in order for its spotter, Seaman Second Class Gerald Grove, to see any targets through the confusing maw of smoke and haze that hung over the beach. Correspondent Martin Somers watched as Grove scanned the beach with high-powered binoculars. "He sees a few faint flashes from a stone house tucked away up the gulch within range of the vital road from the beach, and these flashes coincide with the explosion of shells setting our beach-bound tanks ablaze. Range is established, and our guns go to work." They blasted the enemy guns into submission. The *McCook* fired close to 1,000 rounds in the course of the day.

Cruising close by, the *Carmick* also did terrific damage to enemy defenses. It established intermittent communications with First Sergeant Bill Pressley of B Company, 116th, who found a radio belonging to naval forward observers who had been killed. Sergeant Slaughter watched as Pressley, totally unschooled in gunnery observation, communicated with the destroyer. A battery of Nebelwerfers, housed in a pillbox, was raking the beach. Pressley told the destroyer that he did not know his position "except he was to the left of the Vierville draw and . . . he was trying to knock out a mortar emplacement." The radio operator on the *Carmick* asked Pressley to fire one mortar round of his own. He did so and the ship fired a round. First Sergeant Pressley then directed their next few rounds until he thought they were right on-target. "Okay . . . fire for effect." The destroyer knocked out the Nebelwerfer.

Most of the time the *Carmick* did not enjoy such communication. It had to search for targets on its own. Its spotter figured out where to fire by watching where American tanks and infantry were shooting. The captain of the *Carmick*, Commander O. R. Beer, got the ship to within 900 yards of the beach—so close that her keel almost scraped the bottom—in order to have the best view possible. Several times, the *Carmick* shot at targets, saw explosions, and noticed troops advancing.

Corporal Bill Preston was part of a tank crew in the 743rd. He and his crew members were ensconced in their tank, moving slowly along the beach, shooting at anything that looked suspicious in the hills, when naval fire began sailing over their heads. "There were some 88's in open emplacements which could have ruined us, but shortly after they started to fire a shot from a destroyer put the one near us out of action. I cannot say enough for the Navy, for the way they brought us in, for the firepower they brought to bear on the beach, for the coordination between us. Whenever any of us fired a burst of tracer at a target, the destroyers, standing in so close they were almost ashore, fired a shot immediately after us each time hitting what we were firing at on the nose the first shot. It was amazing and plenty encouraging." The *Carmick* fired 1,127 rounds in support of the troops at Dog Green.[26]

The support of ships like the *McCook* and *Carmick* was excellent, but it wasn't quite enough to propel the soldiers all the way up the draw. The German defenses were too strong for such a frontal attack. The best way to take the D-1 exit was from behind. As Major Bingham had demonstrated at Les Moulins, the best way to infiltrate inland was not through the exits but on their flanks, up the scraggly bluffs and hills. This was tougher terrain to negotiate, but it was not as heavily defended.

Company C of the 116th Infantry was scheduled to reinforce Dog Green fifty minutes after H-Hour. They landed almost precisely on time, but not at Dog Green. The naval coxswains controlling the boats that were ferrying C Company took one look at Dog Green and decided they wanted no part of it. One of the coxswains, George Thomas Poe, saw purple smoke boiling up from Dog Green. To Poe this meant that demolition teams were still trying to clear underwater obstacles that could "rip the bottom of the boat. I signaled to my wave commander, pointing out the purple smoke. He signaled for us to land on Dog White beach that was a little to the left."

Poe complied. He heard plenty of explosions and shooting from the direction of Dog Green. Keyed up and frightened, he wanted to get as far away from that danger as he could. That morning, right before leaving the USS *Charles Carroll*, someone had given him several shots of whiskey from a bottle they had stolen from somewhere on the ship. The whiskey had warmed him up, especially on an empty and nervous stomach. Right now, he was running on alcohol and adrenaline.

He saw a sandbar and gunned his engines, barely making it over and onto the beach. "It took me a few minutes to get all the troops out of the boat. I think a few of them had ideas of digging a foxhole in the boat." Once the troops debarked, Poe saw them make it safely across the beach and to the seawall about one hundred yards away. He closed his ramp, turned around, and headed back for the *Charles Carroll*.

On the way there, the whiskey caught up with him. He was as drunk as could be. While waiting to have his Higgins boat hoisted back onto the mother ship, he rammed another boat. Then, when his boat was back aboard, "I stepped out of the boat and fell flat on my face." The crewmen of the *Charles Carroll* thought he was wounded and sent him to sick bay. "They stripped me of my clothes and that's when the doctor examined me and rolled me off the operating table, saying, 'Get this drunk son of a bitch out of here.' The good doctor put me on report for being drunk." Poe was reduced in rank from petty officer third class to seaman first class.[27]

Twenty minutes after C Company detoured safely to Dog White, Lieutenant Colonel Max Schneider did the same. His plans had already changed once this morning; now they were going to change again. After he had been diverted from Pointe-du-Hoc, his orders were to land at Dog Green. But as he stood at the bow of his LCA and studied Dog Green from a distance of a couple hundred yards out to sea, those orders made little sense. Schneider was combat-experienced. Through bravery and skill in battle he had worked his way up from Ranger company commander in North Africa to battalion commander now (in truth, he was none too thrilled to accept the older combat-inexperienced Rudder as his superior officer). Schneider knew when to improvise.

Herb Epstein, Schneider's intelligence sergeant, was standing right next to him, watching the horror of Dog Green unfold. "The fire was so intense and Colonel Schneider was observing this fire. We were in the lead boat. As we got close to shore, Schneider commanded the boat flotilla captain to swing the whole group left, parallel to the beach. As we were going parallel to the beach, Schneider saw an area that wasn't too hot and ordered the flotilla commander 'to get us in and get us in fast.' We turned again another 90 degrees and they got us to water that wasn't very deep." The British coxswains did a fantastic job of negotiating the obstacles in this sector and beaching the Rangers in the shallow water Epstein mentioned.

Schneider's Rangers landed at Dog White beach, clambered out of their boats, and quickly made it across the beach to the seawall. One of the boats swamped, but an LCT picked up its occupants and later returned them to the beach. Of the 450 Rangers in Schneider's force who hit the beach, 6 became casualties. Clearly, Schneider made the right decision and saved many lives in the process. In the estimation of one Ranger historian, Schneider's improvisation "was one of the key tactical decisions of the invasion. It would place the right unit at the right place at the right time."[28]

The Rangers took cover behind the seawall, sometimes sharing places with the C Company, 116th, soldiers who had gotten there a few minutes before. "The wall was crowded," Lieutenant Francis Dawson, a Ranger platoon leader in D Company, recalled. "The men from the 29th Division were there, and you just had to push in for space. The wall was probably four feet high, made of wood. Being six-foot-four, I had to keep my head down."[29] Many of the troops were exhausted and seasick from spending several hours bobbing around in their landing craft.

At almost the same time, Brigadier General Norman "Dutch" Cota was landing nearby with the headquarters group from the 116th Infantry. Cota was second in command in the 29th Division, and he was every bit a fighting general. As Cota waded into the beach, the man standing next to him, Major John Sours (regimental S-4 of the 116th), caught a burst of machine gun fire and keeled over dead. For a few moments, Cota was pinned down at the waterline. Even there he could see that clumps of American soldiers were huddling behind the seawall, doing nothing but existing. Here and there German shells exploded along the beach. Cota knew that, given more time, the German gunners would zero in on the huddled masses at the seawall. He knew he had to get them off their backsides and inland.

He made it across the beach and starting walking up and down the expanse of the seawall, urging soldiers to get off the beach.

"Every time I'd look up," one soldier recalled, "I'd see Gen. Cota walking along that beach urging people to move."

Cota circulated among the Rangers. "What outfit is this?" Private Mike Rehm heard him ask.

"Rangers," someone responded.

"Well, goddamn it, if you're Rangers get up and lead the way!"

Cota now knew that the 5th Rangers had landed at Dog White, so he began searching for Schneider. Private Donald Nelson, an E Company Ranger, was lying behind the wall, fighting seasickness and the weight of his seventy-two-pound pack, when he saw General Cota. "Mortars were landing between us and the water which was only 175 or 150 feet. General Cota came trotting down the beach behind us. He asked us, 'Where's your commanding officer?' We pointed to the right, and said, 'Down there.' "[30]

Cota headed in that direction. As he searched for Schneider, Cota encouraged whatever junior officers he encountered to get their men moving. One of them was First Lieutenant Jay Mehaffey, a platoon leader in C Company. The general plopped down next to Mehaffey. "How many Rangers got in?"

"We got about two companies here," Mehaffey replied. "I don't know about the rest."

"Get 'em up the cliffs," Cota urged. "It's suicide to stay here."

Another Ranger officer, John Raaen, offered to help Cota find Schneider. Cota knew Raaen because his son had attended West Point with him. "No, you stay here with your troops," he told Raaen. The general turned and looked at the enlisted Rangers who were squatting near the seawall. In Raaen's memory, these men "were hanging on [Cota's] every word and gesture." Cota said to them, "You men are Rangers! I know you won't let me down!"[31]

He left and soon found Schneider and his command group. The colonel was lying on the sand, but when he saw Cota approaching at a leisurely walk, stood up, braving the shell fire, and they conferred. Rather than move left or right in the direction of D-3 or D-1, the two senior officers decided to attack straight up the bluffs. If they could make it to Vierville, they could use the coastal road to cut off the exits.

Sergeant Epstein heard Cota say, "Colonel, we are counting on the Rangers to lead the way." Sergeant Victor Fast, Schneider's interpreter, thought he heard the general say, "I'm expecting the Rangers to lead the way." Schneider's assistant operations officer, Lieutenant Stan Askin, lying just a few feet away, heard Cota say,

"Well, it looks like the Rangers are going to have to get us off the beach." Whatever the precise wording of Cota's statement (in all likelihood he said all of the things attributed to him that morning), the general's visit helped galvanize the Americans into action at Dog White. Many C Company, 116th, soldiers were already making their way over the seawall, and the Rangers were planning to do the same. Cota validated this approach.[32]

The Rangers, together with their 29th Division comrades, moved over the seawall and set about breaching the German defenses behind it. Beyond the seawall was a paved road whose seaward side was strung with barbed wire. German fire covered the approaches to the wire. Beyond the wire was a flat stretch of about 150 yards that gradually rose into bluffs containing German trenches and dugouts.

As their comrades lent fire support from behind the wall, groups of 29'ers and Rangers blew gaps through the wire. In one spot, a C Company, 116th, soldier slipped a bangalore torpedo under the wire and blew it. Another soldier got up and ran through the newly created gap. Suddenly a German machine gun opened up on him. He fell, screamed for a medic, and called out, "Mama!" In seconds he died. From behind the wall Cota was watching the whole scene. He leaped to his feet and ran across the road and through the gap, pausing only to order others to follow. Several men did so and made it without getting hit by the machine-gun fire. Dozens more followed them. They crawled through the field, using its tall grass for concealment. At the end of the field they found German trenches and eagerly dived into them. The trenches led to the top of the bluffs, parts of which were mined. Cota was right there with the attackers, dodging mines and Germans. He led a group that included Private Russo, the F Company soldier who had had a severed leg fall in his lap earlier that morning. "We were really surprised to see a general there but very pleased. He laughed and said that it seemed like he would make a good squad leader."[33]

At the same time, the Rangers were blowing several of their own gaps through the wire. At one of those gaps, Private Ellis "Bill" Reed worked with one of his buddies to assemble the multisectioned bangalore torpedo. "Woody [Dorman] and I had to assemble each piece of the torpedo, get up from behind the seawall, push the bangalore torpedo across the road on top of the bluff and put it under the concertina wire." In spite of enemy machine-gun fire, they got the bangalore in place and blew it.

Lieutenant Dawson was one of the first soldiers through the newly blown gap. "On the double I went through the dust and a path the explosives had torn through the wire." Dawson ran and took cover, got up and ran again, then took cover, just as he had been taught in training. He found a footpath leading up the hill and noticed, on his right, a sign that read: "Achtung, Minen!" Avoiding that area, he climbed the hill using the footpath until he reached the crest of the hill. "There I found myself among Germans. The ones I did dispose of quickly caused the others to surrender. I was . . . alone, as I must have outdistanced my platoon in climbing."

The bangalore explosions set the grass on the hillsides afire. Smoke infested the whole area, so much so that many Rangers, including Lieutenant Askin, put on their gas masks. "Acrid, choking clouds of smoke . . . forced some of us to don gas masks as we struggled toward the crest. In this confusion men were losing contact with one another—entire platoons became separated."

In spite of this, Lieutenant Dawson soon met up with his platoon. A machine-gun position was holding up the Ranger advance and firing on the beach, too. Dawson saw the position and motioned for his BAR man, Private First Class Harry Bolton, to come up to him. The BAR man came forward, but "the machine gunner . . . turned the machine gun and killed" Bolton. "I then retrieved the BAR, and opened fire on the Germans, killing them as they retreated."

By 0900 the Rangers and 29'ers had ascended the bluffs and cleared out most of the Germans from their trenches. Most of them turned west and tried to capture Vierville. Many got pinned down by German machine-gun fire on the edges of town. The Rangers were hoping to fulfill their mission of relieving Rudder. "We were . . . still intent on getting through or around the town, so we could strike out for Pointe du Hoc," Lieutenant Askin wrote, "but the enemy had their own priorities and were taking their toll from concealed emplacements dug into hedgerows. As we eliminated one gun position after another, the Germans quickly brought up replacements." Most of the Rangers did not go much farther than Vierville. "Most of the rest of the day we spent rooting out snipers or looking for artillery observers," Corporal Gale Beccue of E Company recalled. "I was still wet from the soaking I had had on the beach, so when I found some German officer's clothing in a billet, I changed into German socks, underwear, and a heavy turtleneck sweater under my own uniform."

The snipers were, at times, deadly. Lieutenant Charles Parker of A Company was only a few feet away when snipers got his runner and another officer. "A bullet hit [William] Fox in the shoulder, leaving a small blue hole, and then angled down. Another one struck the lieutenant in the side of his head, blowing out a piece of his skull, leaving his brains partly exposed."

General Cota and a few men from the 116th found a dirt track road into Vierville. They marched through part of the town and kept moving until they reached the D-1 exit. Gingerly they descended the draw. By now the USS *Texas* was pounding the bunker that had slaughtered so many Americans in the course of the morning. Lieutenant Jack Shea, Cota's aide, was impressed with the power of the battleship's guns. "The concussion from the bursts of these guns seemed to make the pavement of the street in Vierville actually rise beneath our feet in a 'bucking' sensation." They made it down the draw, all the way to the beach, where Cota told several pinned-down men that the draw was open. He also cajoled an engineer to hop aboard a bulldozer and blow a hole in the seawall. This was the first mission the engineers needed to accomplish before vehicles could use the D-1 exit. Several more hours would pass before that happened, but it was a start. The 116th Regiment, the Rangers, the engineers, and everyone else in the 29th Division's sector of Omaha beach had experienced a hellish morning, but enough men survived to get off the beach and make the invasion an ultimate success. Cota's leadership helped motivate them and point them in the right direction. He meant every bit as much to the 29th Division that morning as Ted Roosevelt did to the 4th at Utah beach.[34]

At the eastern end of Omaha, at beaches code-named Easy Red, Fox Green, and Fox Red, the veteran 1st Division ran into just as much adversity. The first wave here consisted of DD tanks from the 741st Tank Battalion, four assault companies from the 16th Infantry, and attached engineers whose job, of course, was to clear the beach for vehicles and follow-up waves of infantry.

As H-Hour approached, rough seas and an eastward current

caused all sort of problems. When the DD tanks were launched from 6,000 yards offshore, most of them experienced immediate problems. The waves damaged their struts and tore the canvas that provided flotation, leading to flooding of crew and engine compartments. In short order, the "swimming" tanks began to sink, one after the other.

P. L. Fitts was a bow gunner and assistant driver on one of the tanks in C Company. The moment the ramp of his LCT went down, he knew the seas were too rough. They were "rougher than anything we'd ever practiced in." He thought it would be foolish to launch in such conditions. "But it wasn't my decision. The orders came back. We were going to launch."

Fitts's tank was the second one off his LCT. "The tank ahead of me went off and disappeared into the Channel and was gone, sunk." In spite of the sinking of the first tank, the orders didn't change. They drove off the ramp. They did not sink at first, but twenty minutes later they had taken on so much water that they could not continue. The tank commander gave orders to launch their life raft. "I was the last one to step off of the tank rail into the raft. The tank disappeared from under my foot into a swirl of water, gone. This was 5,000 yards offshore." Most of the other DD crews of the 741st suffered the same fate. Of the thirty-two tanks that were launched, only five made it to the beach and three of those were brought in by an LCT and immediately disabled by German antitank fire.[35]

This happened to a load of tanks brought in by Lieutenant H. R. Cluster, skipper of LCT(A)-2008. Cluster took his tanks all the way in to Fox Green. "I ordered the ramp dropped and signaled to the tank officer to take his tanks ashore. They immediately came under fire from . . . German 88s. We learned later that the Germans had gridded and ranged the entire beach. All three of our tanks were hit by 88s almost as soon as they rolled onto the beach."[36]

When the infantry and engineers hit the beach, they had no semblance of order. A strong current landed most of the soldiers too far to the east, stacked up on Fox Green. Only four boat teams, totaling some one hundred men, landed in the first wave at Easy Red, the broadest expanse of beach in the whole Omaha sector. Two of those boat teams came from E Company of the 116th! They had been mislanded by over a mile.

These problems, combined with beach obstacles and intense

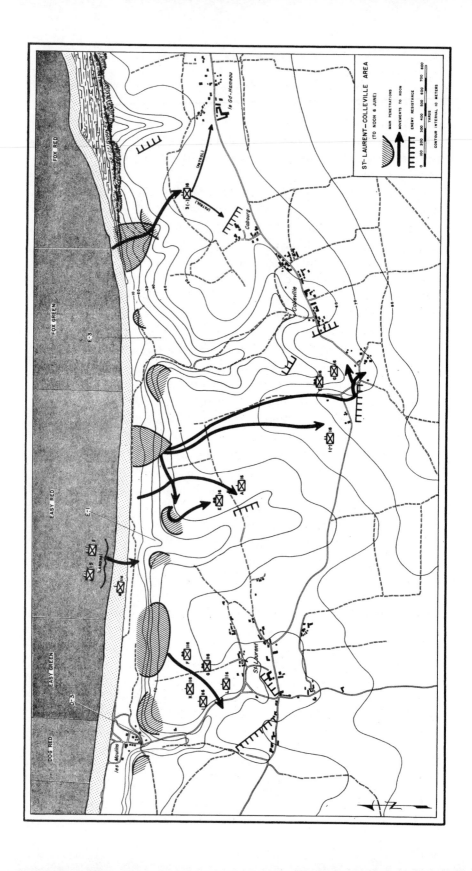

ST-LAURENT—COLLEVILLE AREA
(TO NOON 6 JUNE)

MAIN PENETRATIONS TO NOON

MOVEMENTS TO NOON

ENEMY RESISTANCE

0 100 200 300 400 500 600 700 800
YARDS

CONTOUR INTERVAL 10 METERS

FOX RED

FOX GREEN

EASY RED

EASY GREEN

DOG RED

E-3

E-1

D-3

la Gd-Hameau

Cabourg

Colleville

St Laurent

les Moulins

enemy opposition, guaranteed a nightmarish experience for the first wave. Harry Kennedy, a young coast guard coxswain on an LCVP, warily avoided any obstacles he saw on the path to the beach. "There was nothing to do but weave our way shoreward and pray. We were lucky and reached the shore. As we lowered our ramp and the soldiers started to charge, they were met with streams of machine gun bullets which brutally mowed down some soldiers." Sniper fire and 88mm shells raked the beach from every direction. Having disgorged his troops, Kennedy quickly raised his ramp and got out of there. Another coast guard coxswain drove his boat through waters that were "boiling with bullets from hidden shore emplacements, like a mud puddle in a hailstorm. It seemed impossible that we could make it in without being riddled." Amazingly, most of them did.[37]

Conditions being what they were, the engineers could not begin to clear the kind of gaps needed to facilitate succeeding waves of vehicles. Captain Charles Murphy, the veteran 1st Engineer Combat Battalion officer who busted two of his sergeants back in England for going AWOL, got hit the moment he set foot on the beach. A mortar shell exploded a few feet away. "My radio operator and my runner [his former first sergeant] were killed. I felt like I'd been kicked by a mule and I just went out. I came to with the water rushing the back of my neck and I couldn't move my left arm and my left leg." Shrapnel had hit his field glasses, ricocheted, and broke a rib on his left side. "Initially I was scared to death. I was afraid to reach and feel how big a hole was back there." He managed to crawl to the shingle and recover well enough to remain in command of his company.[38]

On the way into the beach, Sergeant Frank Chesney of the 37th Engineers was so seasick and so nervous that he sought some kind—any kind—of distraction. He and another man of Polish extraction sang in Polish until the ramp dropped at Easy Red. So much enemy fire greeted them that they raced for any cover they could find. Chesney looked around and saw his battalion commander get killed. "He happened to be lying on the dune line looking over with a pair of binoculars to see where the fire was coming from, and . . . he got hit. I could see blood gush from his head and just down he went. He was killed almost instantly." Sergeant Chesney went over the dunes and cleared what mines he could. Eventually he got wounded by a mine.[39]

As at Utah beach, the Navy's job was to clear the underwater obstacles. Seaman second Class John Talton was part of Naval Combat Demolition Unit 44. LCMs (rhino ferries) towed rubber boats containing the NCDU teams. Not far from where Chesney landed, Talton and his team struggled just to make it out of their boat and get ashore. "The machine gun fire . . . resembled rain drops on a mill pond. Raymor had a triangular hole in his helmet and was bleeding down the front of his face. Mitcher's right eye was hanging [in] his socket and he was addled."

Talton made it to the waterline and fired his carbine at any flashes he saw. He threw the carbine aside and wandered around the beach looking for a more powerful weapon, finally settling on a tommy gun he took off a dead man. In the process Talton witnessed a mind-numbing series of horrors. "The man I relieved of his tommy gun had lost the area of face from nose to chin. Just below me [a] driver of a half track had lost the top of his head as neatly as if it had been removed surgically. Behind me legs were sticking up in the water like a pitiful V for victory." Talton never got to do his job. When he wasn't pinned down, he spent the day helping wounded men.[40]

Chuck Hurlbut and his 299th Engineer Combat Battalion were supposed to land at Easy Red, but the current took them a few hundred yards to the east to Fox Green, right in front of strong German positions defending Exit E-3. Hurlbut hopped off his landing craft and started wading in. Behind him he pulled a raft containing his boat team's demolition explosives. "All of a sudden, BOOM! A mortar came over and it hit the raft, and it just went all over. It hit all our demolition stuff. I was knocked head over heels. I guess I blacked out. When I came to, I was on my hands and knees. I was spitting blood."

Hurlbut was lucky to be alive. The raft was gone, as were the three men who had been riding it. When Hurlbut regained his senses he stumbled to the waterline, right into a wounded buddy. "I could see his legs had really got it. I could see the raw bone through the flesh." Hurlbut, a small man, tried everything he could to move the larger man. By planting his feet in the wet sand and pulling him by the armpits Hurlbut moved him a little ways, but it was exhausting. Finally, a tank driver stopped, dismounted from his tank, and helped carry the wounded man to a dune where Hurlbut gave him first aid. The agony and tragedy of the whole scene got to Hurlbut. "Just pure chaos . . . all these dead guys, buddies. That's hard to cope with. It hurts. It gets you."

Earlier that morning, back on their ship, he and a buddy in his unit said their good-byes. As they did, Hurlbut's friend showed him a special flourish he had added to his uniform—"the ugliest, gaudiest, and most outlandish necktie I ever saw in my life." The two friends had had quite a laugh over the silly-looking tie. Now, as Hurlbut stared at the unfolding horror that was Fox Green beach, he noticed someone walking toward him. "About 60 yards away comes a guy staggering along the beach. His backpack is tattered, his clothes are in shreds. One arm is dangling. He turns and half his head is blown away. And something told me I know that guy, something about his stature, his walk. And he turned toward me and looked at me, and through all that gore . . . I saw the tie. I wanted to cry out to him; I couldn't. I didn't have any voice. He just staggered away" and died.[41]

The problems experienced by the tanks and the engineers made the assault that much more difficult for the four infantry companies of the first wave, as well as the five others that followed in the next two hours. In spite of this adversity, the infantry found ways to get off the beach.

Veteran platoon sergeant Mike McKinney's L Company landed too far east, at Fox Red, the extreme eastern edge of Omaha beach. He had made two invasions and not gotten sick. Today he was sick. "I heaved right on my feet." When the ramp went down, he splashed into shoulder-high water, held his rifle high, and was the first to make it to the beach. German machine guns, guarding a small gully known as Exit F-1, swept the whole beach. "I could see little puffs coming out of the sand. Other guys got hit going through the water."

The beach was narrow, leading to bluffs that actually offered nice cover for anyone who could make it that far. "We were moving laterally on the beach looking for an area . . . [in which] we could move off the beach," Steve Kellman, another L Company man, recalled. As he did so, mortar fragments hit him in the right leg. "After falling down twice, I looked at my leg and saw that there was blood coming through the legging. I crawled against the bluff and tried to put a bandage on to cover the wound." He lay on the beach all day long, until, that night, a litter team found him and took him to an LST where a doctor operated on his leg.

The minute Sergeant McKinney landed, he noticed a pillbox nestled in the gully. He helped organize the survivors into a cohesive attacking force. About 125 men out of 200 had made it across the beach. There were a few men from M Company as well as several E Company, 116th, soldiers who were totally lost. Wet and frightened, they all huddled under the cliff. Within half an hour, they were attacking. "We finally get a firing line going. We get the guys started up the hill. They get the bangalore torpedoes under the wire; they blow the wire. The flamethrower gets in there. The guys go up with satchel charges, they blow the apertures off." The surviving Germans retreated quickly from the pillbox. McKinney found a mortar team from M Company and laid some fire on the retreating Germans as they took shelter in a grove of trees farther up the bluff. In this manner, L Company and its partners advanced inland. Later in the day, McKinney led a patrol that established contact with the British, who were advancing south and west from Gold beach.[42]

Farther to the west, where Fox Green met Easy Red, the situation was awful. Jumbles of American soldiers, from a mélange of 16th Infantry companies, were pinned down behind obstacles at the waterline. Most of them, like Private David Snoke, were lucky to make it that far. "I was first in line to get off our boat . . . and just as the ramp was going down, 3 shells (88's) hit on our port side about 10 ft. out. Right after that I hit the water. I glanced behind me in time to see the lieutenant get hit in the head with an 88. That was when I first started to get scared. He was only 5 ft. behind me." Seconds later, a mortar shell exploded seven feet away. "I got a hunk of shrapnel in the hand, two hunks in the arm, and one hunk in the side. I thought sure I was dead. Not even a minute after that, I saw Cpl. Armstrong get hit in the head and shoulders by machine gun fire. That's when I got really mad and forgot (almost) about getting hit." He dropped his equipment, found a firing position on the beach, and shot two clips of ammo in the direction of the Germans. Later he dug a hole with his fighting knife.[43]

Not more than 100 yards away from Snoke, Sergeant Harley Reynolds, a North Africa and Sicily veteran, was about as scared as he had ever been. He had landed in an area that was covered by an awesome-looking concrete bunker that spit forth a frightening volume of fire. He didn't know it, but he was in front of Exit E-1. He was cowering behind a hedgehog, thinking. "What does it feel like to get hit? Too many bullets flying not to get hit." Machine-gun bullets were coming so close that they made a hissing sound as they passed by. "I spotted the shingle [embankment], a sort of raised road bed running parallel to the beach. Many men were lying behind it." He took off for the shingle. "I felt tugs at my pants leg—several times." Later he found that bullets and shrapnel had torn his pants up. One of Reynolds's men plopped down beside him. With a bewildered, exasperated expression he asked, "Sarge, how long do we have to put up with this shit?" Reynolds could only laugh at the silly question.[44]

Farther down the beach, Colonel George Taylor, commander of the 16th Infantry, was actually wondering the same thing. In spite of the murderous enemy fire, Taylor was walking up and down the beach, urging men to get inland. Like Cota in the 29th Division sector, Taylor understood that the shingle embankment, dunes, obstacles, and bluffs offered temporary shelter from small-arms fire, but soon the Germans would zero in on them with artillery and mortars. The greatest danger, he knew, was here on the beach, not, ironically enough, inland in the direction of the Germans. As the colonel trekked along the beach, he disseminated his message to hundreds of pinned-down men. One of them was Private Ira Berkowitz, a nineteen-year-old rifleman replacement in K Company. "We were running out of space as each succeeding wave came in." The tide was rising quickly. "We now had no more than three feet of dry beach, in some spots, to take shelter." Colonel Taylor approached his pinned-down group: "You have to get off this beach. Only the dead or the dying are going to be here." Not far away, Sergeant Warren Rulien saw Colonel Taylor point to the high ground and heard him tell several officers, "If we're going to die, let's die up there."[45]

In their hearts, men like Berkowitz and Rulien knew the truth of Taylor's words even before he strode the beach uttering his famous lines. Senior officers like Taylor helped reinforce the latent desire, somewhere in each frightened man, to get the hell off Omaha beach as quickly as possible. Within two hours after the 1st Division troops went into Omaha, groups of soldiers began to successfully fight their way off the beach. The most famous examples were patrols led by junior officers like Lieutenant John Spaulding and Captain Joseph Dawson, whose men pierced German defenses and ascended the bluffs, pushing inland toward Colleville and Cabourg.[46]

But other more or less anonymous soldiers were fighting inland, too. Near the eastern edge of Easy Red near Exit E-3, Fred Erben and several other C Company soldiers had to destroy two pillboxes in order to have any chance of getting off the beach. The pillboxes had interlocking fields of fire. They also were protected by barbed wire and land mines. Somebody brought bangalore torpedoes up. "They were assembled under fire, one by one, with three-foot lengths of tubing pressed into one another until they formed a long pole that could be passed through the barbed wire." Erben picked up a satchel charge and prepared himself to run at the pillbox.

Someone yelled, "Fire in the hole!" and blew the bangalore, ripping a gap in the wire and exploding many of the mines. Private Buddy Mazzara, with an eighty-two-pound flamethrower strapped to his back, trotted into the gap. "I went up with the flamethrower to button up the aperture of the pillbox and Fred Erben came in with his dynamite charge." The combination of Mazzara's flames and Erben's TNT persuaded the surviving enemy soldiers to surrender. "Some soldiers came out of the pillbox with their hands up saying, 'No shoot. Me Pole.'"

The Americans waved them back to the beach and moved inland as quickly as they could. "Everyone rushed through the wire and started running for the bluffs," Private Theodore Aufort remembered. "There was a good path to climb. I looked back momentarily and it was unbelievable, the amount of fellows that were killed and wounded."[47]

The most vital breakthrough occurred at Exit E-1, in the middle of Easy Red beach. Sergeant John Ellery of B Company landed about fifty yards east of the exit and made it across the beach in spite of the "greatest concentration of mortar, machine-gun, and artillery fire that I have ever seen. I was aware of men falling around me, but it was not until I reached the base of the bluff that things began to come into focus."

The bluff under which he took cover was just opposite the beach exit and its strong defenses (most notably the reinforced concrete bunker that was exacting a huge toll all along the beach). Ellery never saw Colonel Taylor, nor did he need any senior officers to inspire him. He saw a couple of lieutenants, a captain, and many fellow sergeants demonstrating great courage and knew what had to be done. "Several men collected around me . . . and I told them that we had to get off the beach, and that I'd lead the way." A German machine-gun team was somewhere over their heads, beyond the bluff, shooting down at the beach. "I started up the bluff, with four or five men behind me." When they were about halfway up the bluff, the machine gun opened up "from the right front. Everyone hugged the ground. I scurried and scratched along until I got within ten meters of the gun position. Then I unloaded all four of my fragmentation grenades, and when the last one went off, I made a dash for the top. Those kids were right behind me, and we all made it." The enemy gun stopped shooting. The crew probably retreated. Sergeant Ellery and his squad did not make it as far as Trevieres, their D-Day objective, but they advanced about one thousand meters before setting up positions in a ditch beside a hedgerow.[48]

Very close to where Ellery's squad made it over the bluff, Sergeant Reynolds and another group prepared to make a run over the shingle in hopes of blasting their way through German defenses just east of Exit E-1. German artillery shells landed on the beach behind them, close enough to cause alarm but not injury. Sergeant Reynolds cautiously peeked at what lay ahead. "I could see a narrow pond ahead with marsh grass." Between Reynolds and the pond, barbed wire, augmented with a trip wire, was strung along a narrow roadbed. Beyond the pond there was a minefield, which gave way to a steep hill that edged to the left of the gully that comprised Exit E-1. German fire from pillboxes in the gully had slacked off somewhat, and Reynolds felt it would be "just a short dash across the pond, thru a little flanking fire from our right; to put us beyond the pillboxes."

The plan made sense, but first a gap needed to be blown in the barbed wire. All of a sudden, Reynolds saw a little man carrying a fully assembled bangalore torpedo. "I don't know where he came from. He exposed himself to put the first section under the wire. Then he very carefully inserted the fuselighter, turned his head to the left in my direction and looked back. He pulled the string to the fuselighter and pushed himself backward." The fuse didn't light, so the man calmly crawled forward and relit it, successfully this time. "He turned his head in my direction . . . made only one or two movements backward when he flinched, looked in my direction and closed his eyes looking into mine. Death was so fast for him. His eyes seemed to have a question or pleading look in them. His head was maybe three feet from the explosion, but it didn't damage him."

Reynolds and his men moved like lightning through the blown wire, over the road, past the pond, and into the minefield. The grass in this field had died, exposing many of the mines but not all. "I was leading and had gone maybe fifty yards when a man I didn't know rushed by. He tripped a mine hanging about waist high on a fence post. It blew him in half and splattered me. I was sick every time I thought about it for days." Another man tripped a mine that blew off his heel. Reynolds paused his squad until they could find a way out of the minefield. As he did so, he looked back to where the bangalore man was lying dead and saw reinforcements "pouring thru the blown wire." Then he heard a second bangalore torpedo blow up about three hundred yards away. Another gap had been blown in the wire, ushering more American troops over the bluffs, outflanking E-1. Reynolds's squad gingerly found a way out of the minefield and fought isolated groups of Germans in their trenches and dugouts along the gully. He never knew the name of the little bangalore man. Nor did he know if the man ever received a medal for his bravery.[49]

Back at Easy Red beach, the engineers, still under heavy fire, succeeded in blowing a gap in the obstacle belt that commanded the approach to E-1. Leonard Wilmont, a crew leader in Naval Combat Demolition Unit 26, helped wire up several obstacles. "Each one of us had forty-two pounds of explosives on our backs. We put a three-pound block of tetratol on the concrete; we'd lay a little E-cord on the mine. We kept moving and machine-gun bullets were hitting everywhere. Eighty-eights were landing all over the beach. Finally we got our whole 100-yard gap charged." They blew the wired obstacles, creating a yawning 100-yard gap along the beach, more than adequate to accommodate vehicles. The gap would need to be smoothed out and improved into a road of sorts by other engineers with bulldozers, but it was a start.[50]

Before any vehicles could use the gap, though, the Germans needed to be driven from the hills overlooking the west side of E-1. The key to their entire position was the bunker that had wreaked havoc all morning. Like so many other German bunkers, this one was constructed in such a way that it faced toward the beach and away from the sea. As of late morning, it was still killing and maiming, immobilizing large groups along Easy Red, preventing vehicles from using the exit.

One of those immobilized men was James Knight, a member of the 299th Engineer Combat Battalion. He and his demolition team could not venture onto the beach to blow a gap in their assigned obstacles because the obstacles were right in the bunker's kill zone. They took cover under the bluffs, not far from where

Sergeant Ellery had been. Knight was looking out to sea, watching the crowded, chaotic scene of stricken, burning landing craft. All at once, he saw a destroyer closing in on the beach, seemingly headed right for him. "She started to turn right and, before she completed the turn to be parallel to the beach, all her guns opened fire. Shells landed . . . above my rock cover."

Knight did not know it until years later, but he was watching the USS *Frankford*, a destroyer that, like so many others, comprised the best direct-fire support American troops enjoyed on D-Day. On the *Frankford*'s bridge, the skipper, Lieutenant Commander James Semmes, had decided (after being unable to establish communications with the ship's shore party) to close to within several hundred yards of the beach, thus courting the risk of running aground and making his ship a stationary target for German heavy artillery. Lieutenant Owen Keeler was the gunnery officer aboard the *Frankford*. "Navigating by fathometer and seaman's eye, he took us in close enough to put our optical rangefinder, ranging on the bluff above the beach, against the stops, 300–400 yards away."

Spotters on the *Frankford* searched for targets but came up with nothing to relay to Lieutenant Keeler. "The camouflage on the beach was still good. We could not spot a target—and frankly we did not know how far our troops had advanced." This was a valid concern. There were several instances on D-Day of destroyers, in their eagerness to provide direct support, mistakenly firing on American troops. "Then one of our light tanks that was sitting at the water's edge with a broken track, fired at something on the hill. We immediately followed up with a five-inch salvo. The tank gunner flipped open his hatch, waved, dropped back in the tank, and fired at another target. For the next few minutes, he was our fire-control party. Our rangefinder optics could examine the spots where his shells hit."

In this way, the *Frankford* pinpointed the bunker and began to hammer it. This took many shots. "You could see every shell burst into a large cloud of dust as they struck their target," one soldier related, "but no other visible damage. From our vantage point, the projectile [from the destroyer] appeared to be about the size of a domestic water heater. Every round fired struck the target, but the shore battery continued to fire."

The bunker was protected by layered walls of concrete four feet thick. At last, several five-inch rounds from the *Frankford* went right through the bunker's embrasure. The wounded Captain Murphy watched this happen. "We saw them go right in there. Boy, that was the end. I loved the Navy from then on." So did Sergeant Christopher Cornazzani. "About five rounds . . . blew part of the roof off. There was no more enemy fire from it." Back on the *Frankford*, Lieutenant Keeler's spotter could see enemy soldiers emerging from the bunker. "We did have the satisfaction of seeing our soldiers take some prisoners out of . . . [the bunker]." The navy men could also see troops beginning to move up the crest of E-1.

Engineers like Knight could now do their jobs. "I truly believe that in the absence of the damage [the *Frankford*] inflicted . . . the only way any GI was going to leave Omaha was in a mattress cover or as a prisoner of war." Captain Murphy's engineers hopped aboard their bulldozers and smoothed out a section of the beach. In the course of the day Exit E-1 served as the main egress route for the Americans at Omaha beach. Trucks, tanks, half-tracks, jeeps, supplies, and reinforcements from the follow-up regiments (the 115th, the 18th, and the 26th) all poured through there and moved inland to various D-Day evening positions. From his perch overlooking Easy Red, Sergeant Reynolds could see the whole Exit E-1 gully. "It was filled with vehicles and troops. The troops were streaming inland." The beach was still a very dangerous place because it was under German artillery fire, but the Americans at Easy Red had at least established a lodgment from which to expand when and if German resistance could be overcome.[51]

Medical units were coming ashore now at Easy Red, including Dr. Richard Fahey's 60th Medical Battalion. He and the other medics found the detritus of battle. "There were many wounded and dead. I saw one man whose remains consisted only of a sheet of skin flattened on the sand. There was a circular place in the middle of the skin apparently where the explosion occurred. The only part of his body that remained were his hands, the calvarium of his skull, and his feet."

Major Charles Tegtmeyer, the 16th Infantry's regimental surgeon, landed with the second wave. He could hardly do anything for the wounded until later in the day. "At the water's edge floating face downward with arched back were innumerable human forms eddying to and fro with each incoming wave, the water above them a muddy pink in color. Everywhere, the frantic cry, 'Medics, hey, Medics,' could be heard above the horrible din."

Tegtmeyer did the best he could to treat the wounded and evac-
uate them safely in landing craft waiting at the water's edge. "I
examined scores . . . telling the men who to dress and who not to
bother with." Meanwhile, Dr. Fahey "wandered up and down the
sand pulling the wounded to safety, or what was relative safety,
behind disabled . . . vehicles, or sometimes into little foxholes that
were dug out."[52]

The doctors and their aidmen did the best they could, but the
carnage was overwhelming, dispiriting, irretrievably tragic. Some
of the wounded could not be evacuated in time to save them.
Many others made it to LSTs or LCTs only to wait several hours
for treatment. Under the trying circumstances of bloody Omaha
beach, this was all that could be done.

Miles offshore, aboard the cruiser USS *Augusta,* at 1330, General
Omar Bradley heaved a huge sigh of relief as he received his first
good news of the day. All morning long his mood had darkened
as he received fragmentary reports that indicated disaster. "Our
communications with the forces assaulting Omaha Beach were thin
to nonexistent. From the few radio messages that we overheard
and the firsthand reports of observers in small craft reconnoitering
close to shore, I gained the impression that our forces had suffered
an irreversible catastrophe, that there was little hope we could
force the beach." For a time, he was so desperate that he considered pulling the plug on Omaha beach, evacuating whoever could
get out, and sending follow-up waves to Utah or the British
beaches. "I agonized over the withdrawal decision, praying that
our men could hang on."

Now an aide handed him a message from General Gerow:
"Troops formerly pinned down on beaches . . . advancing up
heights behind beaches." Bradley felt like the weight of the world
was off his shoulders. "Thank God," he thought. In order to make
sure the report was accurate, he sent two members of his staff to
the beach to take a look. When they came back, "their report was
more optimistic than I dared hope for. Our troops had forced one
or two of the draws and were inching inland. I gave up any thought
of abandoning Omaha Beach."

Bradley knew that the enemy would not push American forces
into the sea—at least not on this day. "By nightfall, the situation
had swung in our favor. Personal heroism and the U.S. Navy had

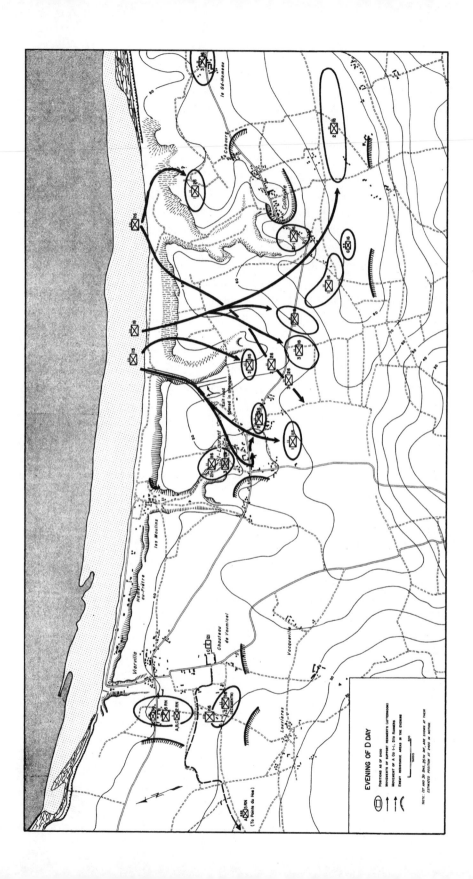

EVENING OF D DAY

carried the day. We had by then landed close to 35,000 men and held a sliver of corpse-littered beach five miles long and about one and a half miles deep. To wrest that sliver from the enemy had cost us possibly 2,500 casualties."[53]

The assault was over. In the face of terrible adversity, American troops at Omaha beach had managed to win a costly victory, one that was, for most of them, simply a matter of personal survival more than anything else, but one that will most likely stand forever as a seminal moment in the history of American soldiers. At the Utah beach exits, American troops and vehicles were pouring inland. Throughout the Cotentin, U.S. paratroopers held many of their objectives and, in general, were fighting tenaciously. In the skies above the U.S. beaches, American planes reigned supreme, and offshore the U.S. Navy was doing its part to ensure Allied naval supremacy. On this day, American soldiers, sailors, and airmen had contributed much—at tragic cost—to Allied success. The Allies were firmly ashore and the Americans, alongside their British, Canadian, and French allies, had helped make that happen.

It was the end of the beginning.

The second volume of this history,
The Americans at Normandy
(to be published November 2004)
will describe the fighting after D-Day.

NOTES

Prologue

1. The most prominent proponents of German tactical and soldierly superiority are Martin van Creveld in his *Fighting Power: German and U.S. Army Performance, 1939–1945* (Westport, CT: Greenwood Press, 1982); Basil Liddell Hart in *The German Generals Talk* (New York: William Morrow, 1948); Max Hastings in *Overlord: D-Day and the Battle for Normandy* (New York: Simon and Schuster, 1984); and Trevor Dupuy in *A Genius for War: The German Army and General Staff, 1807–1945* (Englewood Cliffs, NJ: Prentice Hall, 1977). I am by no means alone in making the case that American soldiers fought with great resilience and distinction at Normandy. Other books, of varying scope, have begun to shed light on this issue, such as Stephen Ambrose, *D-Day: The Climactic Battle of World War II* (New York: Simon and Schuster, 1994); Michael Doubler, *Closing with the Enemy: How G.I.'s Fought the War in Europe, 1944–1945* (Lawrence: University Press of Kansas, 1994); Joseph Balkoski, *Beyond the Beachhead: The 29th Infantry Division in Normandy* (Harrisburg, PA: Stackpole Books, 1989); and Peter Mansoor, *The G.I. Offensive in Europe: The Triumph of American Infantry Divisions* (Lawrence: University Press of Kansas, 1999).

Introduction: February 1944

1. I have relied on numerous sources in the preparation of this chapter: Stephen Ambrose, *The Supreme Commander: The War Years of General Dwight D. Eisenhower* (Garden City, NY: Doubleday, 1970), pp. 334–376; Alfred Chandler, editor, *The Papers of Dwight David*

Eisenhower: The War Years, volume 5 (Baltimore: Johns Hopkins Press, 1970), pp. 144–145; Dwight D. Eisenhower, *Crusade in Europe* (New York: Doubleday, 1948), pp. 220–244; Geoffrey Perret, *Eisenhower* (Holbrook, MA: Adams Media Corporation, 1999), pp. 256–275; David Eisenhower, *Eisenhower at War, 1943–1945* (New York: Vintage Books, 1986), pp. 97–141; Carlo D'Este, *Eisenhower: A Soldier's Life* (New York: Henry Holt, 2002), pp. 477–491; Forrest Pogue, *The United States Army in World War II: The Supreme Command, the European Theater of Operations* (Washington, DC: Center of Military History, United States Army, 1996), pp. 36–65; Gordon Harrison, *The United States Army in World War II: Cross Channel Attack* (Washington, DC: Office of the Chief of Military History, United States Army, 1951), p. 159; Merle Miller, *Ike the Soldier, As They Knew Him* (New York: G. P. Putnam's Sons, 1987), pp. 582–596; Harry C. Butcher, *My Three Years with Eisenhower: The Personal Diary of Captain Harry C. Butcher* (New York: Simon and Schuster, 1946), pp. 4–7, 454–492. The entire text of the CCS directive is reprinted in *Report by the Supreme Commander to the Combined Chiefs of Staff on the Operations in Europe of the Allied Expeditionary Force* (Washington, DC: Center of Military History, United States Army, 1994), pp. v–vi.

1. The Planning and Preparation

1. Cornelius Ryan, *The Longest Day* (New York: Simon and Schuster, 1959), pp. 27–28.

2. Ambrose, *D-Day,* pp. 109–119; Harrison, *Cross Channel Attack,* pp. 128–157; Ryan, *Longest Day,* pp. 28–31.

3. Roger Hesketh, *Fortitude: The D-Day Deception Campaign* (Woodstock, NY: Overlook Press, 2002); Ambrose, *D-Day,* pp. 80–83; Eldredge Wentworth, "Biggest Hoax of the War: Operation Fortitude, the Allied Deception Plan That Fooled the Germans," *Air Power History,* Fall 1990, pp. 15–22; Stephen Ambrose, "Eisenhower, the Intelligence Community, and the D-Day Invasion," *Wisconsin Magazine of History,* Summer 1981, pp. 261–270.

4. Harrison, *Cross Channel Attack,* pp. 188–190.

5. Ambrose, *D-Day,* pp. 119–124; Harrison, *Cross Channel Attack,* pp. 180–197; Samuel Eliot Morison, *History of United States Naval Operations in World War II: The Invasion of France and Germany, 1944–1945* (Little, Brown, 1957), pp. 27–33.

6. Morison, *Invasion of France and Germany,* p. 51.

7. Balkoski, *Beyond the Beachhead,* pp. 38–43; John "Bob" Slaughter, oral history, Dwight D. Eisenhower Center, University of New Orleans (hereafter referred to as EC).

8. Gerald Astor, *June 6, 1944: The Voices of D-Day* (New York: Dell, 1994), pp. 13–14; Alex Kershaw, *The Bedford Boys: One American Town's Ultimate D-Day Sacrifice* (Cambridge, MA: Da Capo Press, 2003), pp. xi–xii; Felix Branham, oral history, EC; Felix Branham, condensed oral history on Military.com Web site.

9. Charles Cawthon, *Other Clay: A Remembrance of the World War II Infantry* (Boulder: University Press of Colorado, 1990), pp. iii–v.

10. Balkoski, *Beyond the Beachhead,* p. 27; Robert Miller, oral history, EC.

11. Kershaw, *The Bedford Boys,* pp. 74–80. Gilbert Murdoch, oral history, EC.

12. Balkoski, *Beyond the Beachhead,* pp. 44–48.

13. Cawthon, *Other Clay,* pp. 34–35.

14. Balkoski, *Beyond the Beachhead,* p. 48.

15. Franklyn Johnson, *One More Hill* (New York: Bantam Books, 1983), pp. 127–128.

16. Warren Coffman, *I Never Intended to Be a Soldier* (Greensboro, NC: Lifestyles Press, 1999), pp. 1, 51–52.

17. James T. Lingg, unpublished memoir, p. 10, personal Web site.

18. Johnson, *One More Hill,* p. 128; Coffman, *I Never Intended to Be a Soldier,* p. 55.

19. H. R. Knickerbocker et al., *Danger Forward: The Story of the First Division in World War II* (Nashville, TN: Battery Press, 2002, reprint of 1947 edition), pp. 205–206. For an excellent discussion of Huebner's leadership abilities and his tribulations in taking over the 1st, see Adrian Lewis, *Omaha Beach: A Flawed Victory* (Chapel Hill: University of North Carolina Press, 2001), pp. 259–269. Also see Russell Weigley, *Eisenhower's Lieutenants: The Campaign of France and Germany, 1944 and 1945* (Bloomington: Indiana University Press, 1981), pp. 116–117.

20. Johnson, *One More Hill,* p. 129.

21. Valentine Miele, interview with Aaron Elson, 5/19/94, featured at tankbooks.com Web site.

22. Steve Kellman, oral history, Military.com Web site.

23. Mike McKinney, interview with Aaron Elson, 2/5/99, featured at tankbooks.com Web site. One unidentified veteran of the division once told the late Dr. Charles W. Johnson of the University of Tennessee a cryptic story about the way two of his outfit's ser-

geants reacted to the news of the Big Red One's leading role in Overlord. The veteran claimed that not long after they received the news the sergeants went into a deep depression. Both of them chose to commit suicide with their service revolvers. The veteran theorized that the two NCOs could not bear the thought of being responsible for more lives in yet another invasion. Johnson related this story to me in 1993.

24. Omar Bradley, *A Soldier's Story* (New York: Henry Holt, 1951), pp. 154, 236–237.

25. Gerden Johnson, *History of the Twelfth Infantry Regiment in World War II* (Boston: 12th Infantry Regiment Association, 1947), pp. 45–46.

26. Astor, *June 6, 1944*, p. 112; Harper Coleman, unpublished memoir, p. 7, EC.

27. William Jones, oral history, EC.

28. Alton Pearson, unpublished memoir, pp. 3–4, Files of the Center for the Study of War and Society, University of Tennessee (hereafter referred to as CSWS).

29. Red Reeder, *Born at Reveille* (New York: Duell, Sloan and Pearce, 1966), pp. 226–227.

30. Johnson, *History of the Twelfth Regiment*, p. 50.

31. Chandler, *Papers of Dwight Eisenhower*, vol. 5, pp. 143–144; Pearson, unpublished memoir, pp. 2–3, CSWS.

32. Pogue, *Supreme Command*, pp. 118–120; Bradley, *Soldier's Story*, pp. 234–235.

33. Stephen Ambrose, *Band of Brothers* (New York: Simon and Schuster, 1992), pp. 15–18.

34. Donald Burgett, *Currahee! A Screaming Eagle at Normandy* (Novato, CA: Presidio Press, 1999), pp. 3–44.

35. Charles Whiting, *World War II*, Band of Brothers Special Collectors Edition, "Prelude to Invasion: The Screaming Eagles in England," pp. 29–33; Leonard Rapport and Arthur Norwood, *Rendezvous with Destiny: A History of the 101st Airborne Division* (Nashville, TN: Battery Press, 2000; reprint of 1948 edition), pp. 46–50.

36. Rapport and Norwood, *Rendezvous with Destiny*, pp. 41–43, 68–69.

37. Burgett, *Currahee!*, p. 57.

38. Whiting, *World War II*, "Screaming Eagles in England," pp. 29–30.

39. Robert Webb, *Freedom Found* (self-published, 2000), pp. 4–5, 42–45, copy in EC.

40. Jack Isaccs, oral history, EC.

41. Roy Creek, oral history, EC.

42. Dwayne Burns, oral history, EC.

43. Astor, *June 6, 1944*, p. 119.

44. Matthew Ridgway, *Soldier: The Memoirs of Matthew B. Ridgway* (New York: Harper and Brothers, 1956), pp. 99–100.

45. Paul Bouchereau, oral history, EC.

2. The Transportation Plan

1. Pogue, *Supreme Command*, p. 127; Solly Zuckerman, *From Apes to Warlords: The Autobiography (1904–1946) of Solly Zuckerman* (London: Hamish Hamilton, 1978), pp. 232–245.

2. Ambrose, *Supreme Commander*, p. 368.

3. Butcher, *My Three Years with Eisenhower*, pp. 447–448. Spaatz later claimed that Butcher misunderstood him, but President Roosevelt's key adviser Harry Hopkins was also present and corroborated Butcher's version.

4. Richard Davis, *Carl A. Spaatz and the Air War in Europe* (Washington, DC: Center for Air Force History, 1993), pp. 328–329.

5. Chandler, *Papers of Dwight Eisenhower*, vol. 3, pp. 1809–1810.

6. Walter Bedell Smith, *Eisenhower's Six Great Decisions* (New York: Longmans, Green, 1956), pp. 37–38.

7. For a more extensive treatment of the transportation plan controversy, see Pogue, *Supreme Command*, pp. 127–134; Ambrose, *The Supreme Commander*, pp. 363–376; Zuckerman, *Apes to Warlords*, pp. 216–258; Wesley Craven and James Cate, editors, *The Army Air Forces in World War II, Europe: Argument to V-E Day, January 1944 to May 1945* (Washington, DC: Office of Air Force History, 1983, reprint of 1951 edition), pp. 72–83; John Sullivan, *Overlord's Eagles: Operations of the United States Army Air Forces in the Invasion of Normandy in World War II* (Jefferson, NC: McFarland, 1997), pp. 69–82; Harrison, *Cross Channel Attack*, pp. 217–230; Davis, *Carl Spaatz and the Air War in Europe*, pp. 327–408; and D'Este, *Eisenhower*, pp. 496–499, 512–514.

8. Kit Carter and Robert Mueller, editors, *The Army Air Forces in World War II: Combat Chronology, 1941–1945* (Washington, DC: Office of Air Force History, 1973), pp. 327–328; Charles Hudson, diary, April 27, 28, 1944, featured at www.91stbombgroup.com Web site.

9. Carter and Mueller, *Combat Chronology*, p. 339; Frank Vratny, "Bailing Out Behind German Lines," *The Gentlemen from Hell*, com-

pendium of unpublished accounts of the 487th Bomb Group in World War II, Record Group, 403, Box 9.5, Folder 2, Mighty Eighth Air Force Heritage Museum, Archives, Savannah, Georgia (hereafter referred to as Mighty Eighth Library).

10. Carter and Mueller, *Combat Chronology*, p. 341; Allen Stephens, oral history, EC.

11. Carter and Mueller, *Combat Chronology*, pp. 339–355; William Redmond, diary, World War II Veterans Project, Special Collections Library, University of Tennessee, MS 2012, Box 11, Folder 73 (hereafter referred to as SCUTK).

12. Carter and Mueller, *Combat Chronology*, p. 352; Alfred Freiburger, oral history, EC.

13. William Dunn, *Fighter Pilot: The First American Ace of World War II* (Lexington: University Press of Kentucky, 1982), p. 131.

14. Alvin Siegel, "The Wartime Recollections of Lt. Alvin W. Siegel," unpublished memoir, pp. 1, 106–107, EC.

15. Carter and Mueller, *Combat Chronology*, p. 356; Robert O'Neill, unpublished memoir, pp. 1–3, EC.

16. Richard Hallion, *The U.S. Army Air Force in World War II: Air Power over the Normandy Beaches and Beyond*, p. 3, reproduced at www.aero-web.org/history Web site.

17. Quoted in D'Este, *Eisenhower*, p. 512.

18. Sullivan, *Overlord's Eagles*, pp. 93–114; Ambrose, *Supreme Commander*, p. 376; Harrison, *Cross Channel Attack*, p. 230; Pogue, *Supreme Command*, p. 132; Craven and Cate, *Argument to V-E Day*, p. 160.

3. The Brassy Briefing

1. Carlo D'Este, *Decision in Normandy* (Old Saybrook, CT: Konecky and Konecky, 1984), pp. 82–88; D'Este, *Eisenhower*, pp. 500–502; Morison, *Invasion of France and Germany*, pp. 69–70; Eisenhower, *Eisenhower at War*, pp. 230–234; Geoffrey Perret, *Eisenhower* (Holbrook, MA: Adams Media Corporation, 1999), pp. 273–275; Omar Bradley and Clay Blair, *A General's Life: An Autobiography by General of the Army Omar Bradley* (New York: Simon and Schuster, 1983), pp. 232–241.

2. Morison, *Invasion of France and Germany*, p. 70.

3. Perret, *Eisenhower*, p. 274; D'Este, *Decision in Normandy*, p. 83.

4. Morison, *Invasion of France and Germany*, p. 70.

5. D'Este, *Decision in Normandy*, pp. 83–86; Perret, *Eisenhower*, p. 274; D'Este, *Eisenhower*, p. 501.

6. Bradley and Blair, *General's Life*, p. 241; Martin Blumenson, editor, *The Patton Papers, 1940–1945* (Boston: Houghton Mifflin, 1974), p. 456.

7. Bradley and Blair, *General's Life*, p. 241; Bradley, *Soldier's Story*, p. 250; D'Este, *Decision in Normandy*, pp. 86–87.

8. John Ashby Marshall to Daddy, 2/9/45 MS 1881, Box 16, Folder 15, SCUTK.

9. Thomas Alexander Hughes, *Overlord: General Pete Quesada and the Triumph of Tactical Air Power in World War II* (New York: Free Press, 1995), pp. 134–136.

10. D'Este, *Decision in Normandy*, pp. 86–90; Morison, *Invasion of France and Germany*, p. 70; D'Este, *Eisenhower*, pp. 502–503; Butcher, *My Three Years with Eisenhower*, pp. 535, 539; Eisenhower, *Eisenhower at War*, pp. 233–234.

4. From the Sausages to the Ships

1. Johnson, *One More Hill*, pp. 131–133.

2. Chuck Hurlbut, interview with Aaron Elson, 9/26/98, featured at www.tankbooks.com Web site.

3. Edward Jones, oral history, EC; Balkoski, *Beyond the Beachhead*, p. 4.

4. William Jones, oral history, EC.

5. James Eikner, oral history, EC; JoAnna MacDonald, *The Liberation of Pointe du Hoc: The 2nd U.S. Rangers at Normandy, June 6–8, 1944* (Redondo Beach, CA: Rank and File Publications, 2000), p. 45.

6. Gale Beccue, oral history, EC.

7. Branham, oral history, EC.

8. Johnson, *One More Hill*, p. 135.

9. Stan Askin, "Immediate Action Needed," *World War II*, May 1987, p. 34.

10. George "Jeff" Boocks, unpublished memoir, p. 6, MS 1892, Box 2, Folder 13, SCUTK.

11. Marvin Jensen, *Strike Swiftly! The 70th Tank Battalion from North Africa to Normandy to Germany* (Novato, CA: Presidio Press, 1997), p. 125.

12. Reeder, *Born at Reveille*, pp. 241–242.

13. Hurlbut interview, www.tankbooks.com.

14. Vincent Schlotterbeck, letter to friends, 5/22/45, EC.

15. Charles Murphy, interview with Dr. Charles Johnson, 4/13/93, SCUTK.

16. Allen Towne, *Doctor Danger Forward: A World War II Memoir of a Combat Medical Aidman, First Infantry Division* (Jefferson, NC: McFarland, 2000), pp. 94–95.

17. Cawthon, *Other Clay*, p. 44.

18. Jensen, *Strike Swiftly!*, p. 127.

19. Johnson, *One More Hill*, pp. 133–134.

20. Forrest Pogue, *Pogue's War: Diaries of a WWII Combat Historian* (Lexington: University Press of Kentucky, 2001), pp. 39–41.

21. Joseph Bria, oral history, EC; Miller, oral history, EC; Balkoski, *Beyond the Beachhead*, p. 63.

22. Murdoch, oral history, EC. By May, A Company's commander, Captain Taylor Fellers, began to have deep forebodings about his unit's mission. Many of his soldiers who had known him since their civilian days in Bedford felt that his personality began to change at this time. He became morose, introspective, and nervous, as if he knew he and his men were being sent to a certain death. This is discussed in Kershaw, *The Bedford Boys*, pp. 92, 105, 111.

23. Owen Brown, oral history, EC.

24. Boocks, unpublished memoir, p. 7, SCUTK.

25. Jay Mehaffey, oral history, EC.

26. Jones, oral history, EC.

27. Paul Massa, oral history, EC.

28. Webster, *Parachute Infantry*, pp. 6–7; Rapport and Northwood, *Rendezvous with Destiny*, pp. 71–72.

29. James Gavin, *On to Berlin: A Fighting General's True Story of Airborne Combat in World War II* (New York: Bantam Books, 1978), pp. 106–107; Harrison, *Cross Channel Attack*, pp. 278–284.

30. Bradley Biggs, *Gavin* (Hamden, CT: Archon Books, 1980), pp. 19–36; T. Michael Booth and Duncan Spencer, *Paratrooper: The Life of Gen. James M. Gavin* (New York: Simon and Schuster, 1994), pp. 163–171.

31. Burns, oral history, EC.

32. Burgett, *Currahee!*, pp. 69–70.

33. Chandler, *Papers of Dwight D. Eisenhower*, vol. 3, p. 1903.

34. Ibid, pp. 1848–1850; Pogue, *Supreme Command*, pp. 163–164; D'Este, *Eisenhower*, p. 487.

35. Ryan, *Longest Day*, pp. 47–49; Thomas Allen, "Untold Stories of D-Day," *National Geographic*, June 2002, p. 15. Ike had to deal

with yet another scare on June 4 when a teletype clerk in the Associated Press bureau inadvertently transmitted what was meant to be a practice message. It read: "Eisenhower's forces have landed in France." Soviet, German, and U.S. media all picked up on the false story. Eisenhower's public relations staff quickly shot the false story down, but it caused the supreme commander plenty of worry.

36. Butcher, *Three Years with Eisenhower*, pp. 555–557; Eisenhower, *Crusade in Europe*, pp. 247–251; Don Cook, "Send Him Back to Algiers—in Chains If Necessary," *Military History Quarterly*, Spring 1994, pp. 34–41. This is an article on the troubles the Anglo-Americans experienced with de Gaulle before and during the campaign in France.

37. Pogue, *Supreme Command*, pp. 168–169; Eisenhower, *Crusade in Europe*, pp. 249–250; D'Este, *Eisenhower*, pp. 518–521; Morison, *Invasion of France and Germany*, p. 80; Butcher, *Three Years with Eisenhower*, pp. 559; Harrison, *Cross Channel Attack*, p. 272.

38. Walter Karig et al., *Battle Report: The Atlantic War* (New York: Rinehart, 1946), pp. 309–311.

39. Morison, *Invasion of France and Germany*, p. 80.

5. Ike's Decision and the Airborne Marshaling Areas

1. Burgett, *Currahee!*, pp. 70–71.

2. Ed Boccafogli, interview with Aaron Elson, 2/19/94, reproduced at www.tankbooks.com Web site.

3. Webster, *Parachute Infantry*, p. 16.

4. Ryan, *The Longest Day*, p. 61.

5. Pogue, *Supreme Command*, pp. 169–170; D'Este, *Eisenhower*, pp. 525–526; Smith, *Six Great Decisions*, p. 55; Harrison, *Cross Channel Attack*, p. 274; Ambrose, *D-Day*, pp. 188–189.

6. Webster, *Parachute Infantry*, p. 17.

7. Tom Porcella, oral history, EC.

8. George Koskimaki, *D-Day with the Screaming Eagles* (Medalia, MN: House of Print, 1970), pp. 30–31.

9. Burns, oral history, EC.

10. Robert Brewer to Dad, 6/5/44, Collection Number 68, Box 3, Folder 319, Western Historical Manuscript Collection, University of Missouri–Columbia, World War II Letters (hereafter referred to as WHMC).

11. Boccafogli interview with Elson, www.tankbooks.com.

12. Porcella, oral history, EC.
13. Webster, *Parachute Infantry*, pp. 17–21; Rapport and Northwood, *Rendezvous with Destiny*, pp. 79–80.
14. Creek, oral history, EC.
15. Charles Lieberth, oral history, EC.
16. Koskimaki, *D-Day with the Screaming Eagles*, pp. 34–35; Webb, *Freedom Found*, pp. 51–52; Anonymous paratrooper ("Charlie") to Marion, 7/7/44, Box 38, Folder 3265, WHMC.
17. Eisenhower, *Crusade in Europe*, pp. 251–252; Butcher, *My Three Years with Eisenhower*, pp. 650–653; Koskimaki, *D-Day with the Screaming Eagles*, pp. 33–34; Ambrose, *D-Day*, pp. 193–194; Rapport and Northwood, *Rendezvous with Destiny*, p. 83; Mark Bando, *101st Airborne: The Screaming Eagles at Normandy* (Osceola, WI: Motor Books International, 2001), p. 37.
18. Porcella, oral history, EC.
19. Lieberth, oral history, EC.
20. Edward Barnes, oral history, EC.
21. Burgett, *Currahee!*, pp. 74–77.
22. Ridgway, *Soldier*, pp. 1–3.
23. Martin Wolfe, *Green Light! A Troop Carrier Squadron's War from Normandy to the Rhine* (Washington, DC: Center for Air Force History, 1993), pp. 88–90.
24. Ambrose, *D-Day*, pp. 194–195; Koskimaki, *D-Day with the Screaming Eagles*, pp. 38–39; Maxwell Taylor, *Swords into Plowshares: A Memoir* (New York: DaCapo Press, 1972), pp. 75–76; Perret, *Eisenhower*, p. 282.

6. Crossing the Channel

1. Edward Dunton, oral history, EC.
2. Frank Feduik, oral history, featured at Naval Historical Center home page, www.history.navy.mil.
3. Edward Duffy, oral history, EC.
4. Stanley E. Smith, editor, *The United States Navy in World War II* (New York: Quill, William Morrow, 1966), pp. 589–590.
5. John Blackburn, Michael Brienze, oral histories, EC.
6. James Jones, oral history, EC.
7. Morison, *Invasion of France and Germany*, pp. 85–86.
8. John Talton, unpublished memoir, pp. 8–9. EC.
9. Robert Evans, oral history, EC.
10. Gerald Heaney, oral history, EC.

11. Edward Jones, oral history, EC.
12. August Thomas, condensed oral history on Military.com Web site.
13. Samuel Ricker, oral history, EC; *The Holy Bible: New International Version* (Grand Rapids, MI: Zondervan Bible Publishers, 1978), p. 592.
14. Richard Fahey, oral history, EC.
15. Cawthon, *Other Clay*, p. 47.
16. Richard T. Bowman to parents, 6/6/44, Box 3, Folder 287, WHMC.
17. Harry Bare, oral history, EC.
18. Jack McQuiston, oral history, EC.
19. Buddy Shellenberger, interview with Dr. Ronald Marcello, 5/25/ 00, University of North Texas Oral History Collection, Number 1344, Denton, TX, (hereafter referred to as UNT).
20. Mike McKinney, interview with Elson, www.tankbooks.com.
21. William Jones, oral history, EC.
22. Jensen, *Strike Swiftly!*, p. 133.

7. The Airborne Ride Over

1. Webb, *Freedom Found*, p. 53.
2. Leeper's account is included in John DeLury, unpublished memoir, pp. 44–45, EC.
3. Porcella, oral history, EC.
4. Dwayne Burns, unpublished memoir, p. 72, EC.
5. Charles Bortzfield, oral history, EC.
6. Burgett, *Currahee!*, p. 77.
7. Rapport and Northwood, *Rendezvous with Destiny*, p. 85; Koskimaki, *D-Day with the Screaming Eagles*, pp. 59–61.
8. Joe Bressler, interview with Patrick O'Donnell, featured at www.dropzone.com Web site.
9. Koskimaki, *D-Day with the Screaming Eagles*, p. 65; Ambrose, *Band of Brothers*, p. 65.
10. Clarence Hughart, interview with Patrick O'Donnell, n.d., featured at www.dropzone.com Web site.
11. Bouchereau, oral history, EC.
12. Richard Beranty, "A Screaming Eagle's Journey," *WWII History*, September 2003, p. 64.
13. Rapport and Northwood, *Rendezvous with Destiny*, p. 85.
14. Burns, unpublished memoir, p. 73, EC.
15. Koskimaki, *D-Day with the Screaming Eagles*, p. 62.

16. R. R. Hughart, oral history, EC.
17. Ridgway, *Soldier*, p. 3.
18. Webster, *Parachute Infantry!*, p. 24.
19. Chuck Storeby, oral history, SCUTK.
20. Bressler interview, www.dropzone.com.
21. Porcella, oral history, EC.
22. Roger Airgood, oral history, featured at www.Military.com Web site.
23. Mark Bando, *The 101st Airborne at Normandy* (Osceola, WI: Motor Books International, 1994), pp. 29–30; Milton Dank, *The Glider Gang: An Eyewitness of World War II Glider Combat* (Philadelphia: J. B. Lippincott, 1977), pp. 114–117; Astor, *June 6, 1944*, pp. 190–197; Charles Masters, *Glidermen of Neptune: The American D-Day Glider Attack* (Carbondale: Southern Illinois University Press, 1995), pp. 51–63.

8. The Night Drop

1. Bando, *101st Airborne at Normandy*, p. 27.
2. Ronald Drez, editor, *Voices of D-Day: The Story of the Allied Invasion Told by Those Who Were There* (Baton Rouge: Louisiana State University Press, 1994), pp. 128–129.
3. Koskimaki, *D-Day with the Screaming Eagles*, pp. 45–58; Drez, *Voices of D-Day*, pp. 85–86.
4. Joseph Terebessy, oral history, EC.
5. Wolfe, *Green Light!*, pp. 93–94.
6. Drez, *Voices of D-Day*, pp. 81–82; Koskimaki, *D-Day with the Screaming Eagles*, p. 73. Most likely, Johnson's "naval observer" was an army artillery officer trained to coordinate naval gunfire with ground troops.
7. Astor, *June 6, 1944*, p. 159.
8. Webb, *Freedom Found*, pp. 54–56; Anonymous paratrooper to Marion, 7/7/44, WHMC.
9. Koskimaki, *D-Day with the Screaming Eagles*, pp. 69–70, 75–77; S. L. A. Marshall, Regimental Unit Study, Number 3, "506 Parachute Infantry Regiment in Normandy Drop," Historical Manuscripts Collections, File Number 8–3.1, BB 3, pp. 1–15, U.S. Army Center of Military History, Washington, D.C. (hereafter referred to as CMH).
10. Bill Oatman, oral history, SCUTK, also featured at www.Military.com Web site.

11. Drez, *Voices of D-Day*, p. 136.

12. Astor, *June 6, 1994*, pp. 183–184.

13. Burns, unpublished memoir, pp. 72–76, EC.

14. Ambrose, *D-Day*, p. 214.

15. Ralph DeWeese, unpublished diary, EC.

16. Boccafogli interview. www.tankbooks.com.

17. Webster, *Parachute Infantry*, pp. 29–30.

18. Burgett, *Currahee!*, p. 85.

19. Ambrose, *D-Day*, pp. 198–203, *Band of Brothers*, pp. 66–69; Hastings, *Overlord*, pp. 73–74.

20. Dank, *Glider Gang*, pp. 113–118.

21. Astor, *June 6, 1944*, pp. 191, 197.

22. Dank, *Glider Gang*, p. 118.

23. Koskimaki, *D-Day with the Screaming Eagles*, pp. 320–322.

24. Dank, *Glider Gang*, pp. 119–121; Astor, *June 6, 1944*, pp. 192–196; Koskimaki, *D-Day with the Screaming Eagles*, pp. 324–328; Robert Butler, oral history, EC. Butler was a glider pilot in the formation right behind Murphy. He saw the crash and the remnants.

25. Astor, *June 6, 1944*, pp. 197, 404; Bando, *101st Airborne at Normandy*, p. 30. Lieutenant Thomas Ahmad was the uncle of Diana Ahmad, one of my friends and colleagues at the University of Missouri–Rolla. Diana told me that the family heard from a friend of Thomas's that he got holed up in a church, along with several other Americans, and was killed when the Germans grenaded the church. Morales, however, believes that Ahmad was captured and executed. Morales visited Ahmad's grave immediately after the war. Several townspeople told him that the Germans executed twenty-five Americans and two priests in retaliation for the large number of casualties the die-hard paratroopers had inflicted (presumably the priests were accused of aiding the Americans). Morales immediately drew the conclusion that Ahmad had been one of those executed. Perhaps the Americans made a last stand in the church, the Germans smoked them out, and when the Americans emerged from the church, along with the two priests, the Germans, still seething from their losses, gave in to their emotions and killed them on the spot. Such things happened all too often in World War II. This is, of course, mere speculation. The mystery would only be definitively solved by an exhumation and autopsy of the bodies of Ahmad and the others.

26. Alfred Sapa, oral history, EC.

27. Dank, *Glider Gang*, pp. 121–122.

28. Richard Denison, oral history, EC.

29. Astor, *June 6, 1944*, pp. 197–198; Dank, *Glider Gang*, pp. 123–126. In his book *D-Day*, on page 221, historian Stephen Ambrose listed the 82nd Airborne Division's gliderborne D-Day casualties at 16 percent (25 killed, 118 wounded, and 14 missing out of 957 men). He must have been referring to the combined casualties suffered by the Detroit mission, which went into Normandy at about 0400 on D-Day, and the nighttime resupply mission that went in at about 2100 on the evening of D-Day. There were more planes, and more troops, carrying heavier equipment on the evening mission. Many of the troopers in these gliders landed in enemy-held territory around Ste-Mère-Eglise. The 101st Airborne's evening glider mission also led to serious losses, in the range of 33 percent, as the gliders landed in small fields and shredded themselves on hedgerows and trees. Some also landed in enemy territory. Rapport and Northwood, *Rendezvous with Destiny*, pp. 133–134.

9. The Cutting Edge of Courage: The All-Americans and Screaming Eagles on D-Day

1. U.S. Army, Historical Section Staff, *Utah Beach to Cherbourg* (Washington, DC: Department of the Army, 1947), pp. 30–34.

2. Drez, *Voices of D-Day*, pp. 132–133; Deryk Wills, *Put On Your Boots and Parachutes: Personal Stories of the Veterans of the United States 82nd Airborne Division* (Leicester: AB Printers, 1992), pp. 70–71; Fred Brown, "The Ultimate Sacrifice: D-Day Vet Owes Life to Buddy Who Didn't Make it." *Knoxville News Sentinel* 6/17/01. The man who descended into the burning house was Private First Class Alfred Van Holsbeck.

3. Ray Aeibischer, oral history, EC.

4. Drez, *Voices of D-Day*, pp. 95–97; Koskimaki, *D-Day with the Screaming Eagles*, p. 96.

5. Hughart, oral history, EC.

6. Drez, *Voices of D-Day*, pp. 134–135.

7. Ibid., pp. 89–90, 137, 143; S. L. A. Marshall, *Night Drop: The American Airborne Invasion of Normandy* (Boston: Little, Brown, 1962), pp. 22–25.

8. Hughart, oral history, EC.

9. Marshall, *Night Drop*, pp. 27–28.

10. Ed McCaul, "82nd Airborne Trooper at Normandy," interview with Bill Dunfee, *World War II*, circa 2000.

11. Drez, *Voices of D-Day,* p. 144; William Tucker, *D-Day: Thirty-five Days in Normandy, Reflections of a Paratrooper* (Harwichport, MA: International Airborne Books, 2002), pp. 20–22.

12. Marshall, *Night Drop,* pp. 31–39; Ambrose, *D-Day,* pp. 313–317; Bando, *Screaming Eagles at Normandy,* pp. 142–143, 153–155; Wills, *Put On Your Boots and Parachutes,* pp. 76–78.

13. Charles Sammon to Cornelius Ryan, 3/21/59, copy of the letter in EC.

14. Gavin, *On to Berlin,* pp. 115–117; Booth and Spencer, *Paratrooper,* pp. 174–179.

15. Astor, *June 6, 1944,* p. 168.

16. Gavin, *On to Berlin,* pp. 117–118; Booth and Spencer, *Paratrooper,* pp. 179–181; Astor, *June 6, 1944,* pp. 168–169.

17. Marshall, *Night Drop,* pp. 51–62; John Keegan, *Six Armies in Normandy* (New York: Penguin Books, 1982), pp. 99–102; John Dolan to Lt. General James Gavin, 3/15/59, reproduced at www. dropzone.com Web site.

18. Keegan, *Six Armies in Normandy,* pp. 102–105; David Waters, unpublished memoir, pp. 5–7, EC.

19. Gavin, *On to Berlin,* pp. 118–119; Bouchereau, oral history, EC.

20. U.S. Army, *Utah Beach to Cherbourg,* pp. 39–40; Ambrose, *D-Day,* pp. 310–313; Marshall, *Night Drop,* pp. 75–80; Creek, oral history, EC; Roy Creek, unpublished memoir, featured at www.dropzone. com Web site. Troopers from the 508th helped keep the western approaches to the Chef-du-Pont causeway in American hands, particularly those soldiers who held Hill 30, located to the northwest of Chef-du-Pont. "Debriefing Conference, Operation Neptune," 82nd Airborne Division, EC.

21. Dolan to Gavin, www.dropzone.com.

22. Marshall, *Night Drop,* pp. 81–85; Dolan to Gavin, www. dropzone.com; Marcus Heim, interview with Patrick O'Donnell, featured at www.dropzone.com; U.S. army, *Utah Beach to Cherbourg,* pp. 38–39; "Debriefing Conference," EC.

23. U.S. Army, *Utah Beach to Cherbourg,* pp. 17–20; Rapport and Northwood, *Rendezvous with Destiny,* pp. 103–108; Bando, *101st Airborne at Normandy,* pp. 59–60; Koskimaki, *D-Day with the Screaming Eagles,* pp. 227–235; S. L. A. Marshall, Regimental Unit Study Number 9, "Cassidy's Battalion," Historical Manuscripts Collection, File Number 8-3.1 BA 9, pp. 1–12, CMH.

24. General Gavin claimed that only 101st Airborne troopers used

these toy crickets for recognition, but many 82nd Airborne veterans remember using them.

25. Burgett, *Currahee!*, pp. 91–104; Bando, *101st Airborne at Normandy*, pp. 52–53, *Screaming Eagles at Normandy*, pp. 88–92.

26. For this account of the fighting at WXYZ and the exploits of Staff Sergeant Summers I have relied on several sources: Marshall *Night Drop*, pp. 216–222; Rapport and Northwood, *Rendezvous with Destiny*, pp. 107–109; Ambrose, *D-Day*, pp. 297–299; Bando, *101st Airborne at Normandy*, pp. 60–64; Koskimaki, *D-Day with the Screaming Eagles*, pp. 199–209; and Marshall, "Cassidy's Battalion," pp. 12–18, CMH. Most of the quotes come from Koskimaki's fine oral history. All of these accounts credited Summers with storming every building and fighting as a veritable one-man army. However, new and more complete information has come to light on what happened at WXYZ. Mark Bando related Private Camien's story in his recent book *Screaming Eagles in Normandy*, pp. 69–73. Camien gave his account to an officer who was investigating the fighting to determine what kind of medal Summers should be awarded. Camien probably cared little for medals or recognition. His account indicates that Summers had more help than has previously been thought. This is not to slight the bravery of Summers, who earned the Distinguished Service Cross for his actions, but simply to round out the story of WXYZ and perhaps provide a truer account of the fighting there. Most narrators of WXYZ have stated that Summers carried a tommy gun and Camien a carbine (trading off when necessary as they attacked the buildings). This is unlikely. In fact, they probably both used tommy guns (a brutally effective weapon at close range) for this kind of close combat assault on enemy-held buildings. In relating his story, Camien claimed to use a tommy gun. There is no reason to doubt that he did so. Interestingly enough, the building in which Summers found the fifteen German "chowhounds" was, as of the year 2000, home to the female mayor of St-Martin-de-Varreville.

27. Ambrose, *D-Day*, pp. 303–304, *Band of Brothers*, pp. 77–78.

28. Koskimaki, *D-Day with the Screaming Eagles*, p. 286.

29. Drez, *Voices of D-Day*, p. 190.

30. Ibid., p. 192.

31. Koskimaki, *D-Day with the Screaming Eagles*, p. 286.

32. Stephen Ambrose, interview with Joe Toye, circa 1990, EC.

33. Koskimaki, *D-Day with the Screaming Eagles*, p. 287.

34. Drez, *Voices of D-Day*, p. 191; Koskimaki, *D-Day with the Screaming Eagles*, pp. 284–285; Ambrose, *Band of Brothers*, pp. 80–81.

35. Drez, *Voices of D-Day*, pp. 192–193.

36. Bill Guarnere interview, *World War II: Band of Brothers Collectors Edition*, p. 96.

37. Koskimaki, *D-Day with the Screaming Eagles*, pp. 288–289; Bando, *101st Airborne at Normandy*, pp. 69–70; Ambrose, *Band of Brothers*, pp. 82–84, *D-Day*, pp. 303–304.

38. Bando, *101st Airborne at Normandy*, pp. 77–78; Burgett, *Currahee!*, pp. 115–116; Koskimaki, *D-Day with the Screaming Eagles*, p. 370. These atrocity stories have never been definitively verified, but based on the accounts of many Screaming Eagle veterans, it seems reasonable to conclude that something brutal probably did occur at Holdy.

39. Marshall, *Night Drop*, pp. 287–288; Koskimaki, *D-Day with the Screaming Eagles*, p. 230.

40. Bando, *101st Airborne at Normandy*, pp. 77–78; Marshall, *Night Drop*, pp. 288–289; Rapport and Northwood, *Rendezvous with Destiny*, pp. 129–131.

41. Taylor, *Swords into Plowshares*, pp. 77–81; Koskimaki, *D-Day with the Screaming Eagles*, pp. 164–168.

42. Rapport and Northwood, *Rendezvous with Destiny*, pp. 95–99; Bando, *101st Airborne at Normandy*, pp. 75–76; Taylor, *Swords into Plowshares*, p. 81; Marshall, *Night Drop*, pp. 272–273; Ambrose, *D-Day*, pp. 299–300; Koskimaki, *D-Day with the Screaming Eagles*, pp. 168–175. Corporal Danforth received the Distinguished Service Cross for his bravery at Pouppeville. Captain Kraeger was later killed in action in Holland.

43. Bando, *Screaming Eagles at Normandy*, pp. 41–42.

44. Bando, *101st Airborne at Normandy*, pp. 94, 151; Joseph Beyrle, oral history, featured at www.military.com Web site. Beyrle also had the unique experience of being married in the same church where his funeral mass had been held two years earlier.

45. Oatman oral histories, SCUTK and www.military.com.

46. Sam Gibbons, unpublished memoir, featured at www.military.com Web site.

47. U.S. Army, *Utah Beach to Cherbourg*, pp. 28–29; Rapport and Northwood, *Rendezvous with Destiny*, pp. 115–118; Koskimaki, *D-Day with the Screaming Eagles*, pp. 152–155; S. L. A. Marshall, Regimental Unit Study Number 2, "The Fight at the Locks," Historical Man-

uscripts Collection, File Number 8-3.1 BB 2, pp. 18–31, CMH. Another group had similar experiences at nearby Angoville-au-Plain.

48. Bando, *101st Airborne at Normandy*, pp. 36, 94; Ray Calandrella to parents, 9/2/44, Box 5, Folder 406, WHMC. Calandrella spent two months in captivity. On August 29, he and another man escaped at Chalons-sur-Marne and made contact with American soldiers.

49. Koskimaki, *D-Day with the Screaming Eagles*, p. 299; "Charlie" to Marion, WHMC.

50. Rapport and Northwood, *Rendezvous with Destiny*, pp. 118–121; Bando, *101st Airborne at Normandy*, pp. 105–107; Koskimaki, *D-Day with the Screaming Eagles*, pp. 299–307; Ambrose, *D-Day*, pp. 306–307; Marshall, "506 Parachute Infantry Regiment in Normandy Drop," pp. 15–22; "The Fight at the Lock," pp. 30–45, CMH.

10. The Air Cover

1. Dale Smith, *Screaming Eagle: Memoirs of a B-17 Group Commander* (Chapel Hill, NC: Algonquin Books, 1990), pp. 164–165.

2. Dunn, *Fighter Pilot*, pp. 132–133.

3. Jack Havener, "D-Day: The Shortest Night and the Longest Day," *Officer Review*, May 1994, p. 10.

4. Mac Meconis, "Mission No. 18: 'D' Day Tuesday June 6, 1944," *Second Air Division Association*, n.d.

5. Al Corry, oral history, EC.

6. Quentin Aanenson, "A Fighter Pilot's Story," unpublished memoir/documentary transcript, p. 4, Record Group 403, Box 9, Folder 7, Mighty Eighth Library.

7. Bill Welch, "World War II Stories," featured at www.erieveterans. com.

8. Edwin Ehret, "The Million Dollar Seat," unpublished diary entry, featured at www.91stbombgroup.com Web site.

9. Craven and Cate, *Argument to V-E Day*, pp. 190–193; Sullivan, *Overlord's Eagles*, pp. 117–119; Lewis, *Flawed Victory*, pp. 146–147, 225–231; Lewis, "The Navy Falls Short at Normandy," *United States Naval Institute*, December 1998, pp. 34–39; D'Este, *Eisenhower*, pp. 482–483; Morison, *Invasion of France and Germany*, pp. 333–336; Williamson Murray and Allan Millett, *A War to Be Won: Fighting the Second World War*, p. 419. The officer who made the "bush league" crack was Charles "Pete" Corlett, who had

successfully commanded the 7th Infantry Division in two amphibious invasions in the Pacific, including Kwajalein. Corlett's excellent performance in the Pacific, and extensive amphibious experience, prompted General Marshall to send him to Europe, where he served as commander of Bradley's XIX Corps. When Corlett arrived in England and saw the bombardment plans, he was astonished at their inadequacy. He argued, correctly, as events proved, that more naval gunfire support was desperately needed, as was more ammunition for the push inland. The narrow-minded Bradley completely ignored him. Bradley also flatly turned down the British when they offered him the use of specialized armored vehicles designed to clear paths through minefields and obstacles. As will be seen in a later chapter, mines caused many casualties among the assault waves.

10. Craven and Cate, *Argument to V-E Day*, p. 192; Lewis Brereton, *The Brereton Diaries* (New York: William Morrow, 1946), p. 280.
11. Stephens, oral history, EC.
12. Redmond diary, SCUTK.
13. Corry, oral history, EC.
14. George Eldridge, oral history, EC; Malcolm Edwards, oral history, EC; Carl Christ, oral history, EC.
15. Ralph Nunley, oral history, EC.
16. Clyde Funk, interview with Dr. Ronald Marcello, 2/22/75, UNT; Brereton, *Brereton Diaries*, p. 280.
17. Robert Hobbs, oral history, EC.
18. Edward Giller, oral history, EC.
19. Francis Gabreski, as told to Carl Molesworth, *Gabby: A Fighter Pilot's Life* (New York: Orion Books, 1991), pp. 158–159.
20. Drez, *Voices of D-Day*, pp. 162–164.
21. Leonard Schallehn, oral history, EC.
22. O'Neill, unpublished memoir, pp. 4–5; Craven and Cate, *Argument to V-E Day*, pp. 189–190. The most famous German fighter attack on D-Day is recounted in Ryan's *Longest Day*, pp. 245–248. Colonel Josef Priller led a two-plane attack that strafed the British beaches and the eastern edge of Omaha beach. Priller's strafing run did little damage; he and his wingman escaped unscathed.
23. John Breast, editor, *Missions Remembered: Recollections of the WWII Air War* (Brentwood, TN: J. M. Productions, 1995), pp. 114–116.
24. Aanenson, "Fighter Pilot's Story," p. 4, Mighty Eighth.
25. William McChesney, oral history, EC.
26. Hallion, *Air Power over the Normandy Beaches and Beyond*, p. 6,

www.aeroweb.org/history Web site; Craven and Cate, *Argument to V-E Day*, pp. 189–193; Ambrose, *D-Day*, pp. 251–252; Sullivan, *Overlord's Eagles*, pp. 117–118; Norman "Bud" Fortier, *An Ace of the Eighth: An American Fighter Pilot's Air War in Europe*, (New York: Ballantine Books, Presidio Press, 2003), pp. 193–195. The Americans lost five heavies on D-Day along with twenty-six fighters and three medium bombers.

11. The Naval Bombardment

1. Morison, *Invasion of France and Germany*, pp. 120–122; Ernest Carrere, unpublished memoir, pp. 21–22, EC; Dorr Hampton, oral history, EC.
2. Martin Somers, "The Longest Hour in History: The U.S. Destroyer McCook in the Normandy Invasion,"*Saturday Evening Post*, 7/8/44, p. 98.
3. Ken Shifter to Charles Bowden, 3/1/85, copy of letter at EC.
4. Morison, *Invasion of France and Germany*, pp. 123–124; Ambrose, *D-Day*, pp. 264–265; William Gentry, James Jones, oral histories, EC.
5. Harrison, *Cross Channel Attack*, p. 302.
6. James Long, oral history, EC.
7. Morison, *Invasion of France and Germany*, p. 156; Ambrose, *D-Day*, pp. 265–266.
8. Cyrus Aydlett, diary, pp. 4–5, EC.
9. Morison, *Invasion of France and Germany*, p. 96; Smith, *United States Navy in World War II*, pp. 592–593.
10. Ross Olsen, oral history, EC.
11. Blackburn, oral history, EC.
12. Bowman to parents, WHMC.
13. Felix Podolak, oral history EC.
14. Ryan, *Longest Day*, pp. 207–209; Karig, *Battle Report*, p. 334; Edward Prados, editor, *Neptunus Rex: Naval Stories of the Normandy Invasion, June 6, 1944* (Novato, CA: Presidio Press, 1998), pp. 51–53; Jacob Boyd Henson, unpublished memoir, pp. 6–11, copy in author's possession. I would like to thank Judge Henson for graciously making his account available to me.
15. Grant Gullickson, oral history, EC.
16. Vincent Ohlman to brother, 6/11/44, EC.
17. Blackburn, oral history, EC.
18. Morison, *Invasion of France and Germany*, p. 96; Ryan, *Longest Day*,

pp. 208–209; Gullickson, oral history, EC; Henson, unpublished memoir, pp. 11–12.

12. Sandy Utah

1. U.S. Army, *Utah Beach to Cherbourg*, pp. 43–44; Samuel Grundfast, oral history, featured at www.military.com Web site; Jensen, *Strike Swiftly*, p. 136.
2. Ambrose, *D-Day*, p. 276; Drez, *Voices of D-Day*, 172–177.
3. John Pfister, interview with Bill Welch and John Williams, 3/99, featured at www.erieveterans.com Web site.
4. Drez, *Voices of D-Day*, pp. 183–84.
5. Fred Crum to family, 6/6/45, Box 6, Folder 618, WHMC.
6. *The Ivy Leaves: Official Publication of the National 4th Infantry Division Association*, June 1994, pp. 35–36, 38–39, 41–42, 56–57; Drez, *Voices of D-Day*, pp. 185–186. Some of the Americans mistook the Mongolians for Japanese and spread the rumor that Japanese soldiers were serving with the German Army at Normandy.
7. Coleman, unpublished memoir, p. 8, EC; Harper Coleman to Stephen Ambrose, 1/6/98, EC.
8. Ambrose, *D-Day*, pp. 278–279; Ryan, *Longest Day*, pp. 204–206; H. Paul Jeffers, *Theodore Roosevelt: The Life of a War Hero* (Novato, CA: Presidio Press, 2002), pp. 4–6, 247–252. Roosevelt's famous statement—"we'll start the war from right here"—comes mainly from the recollection of Colonel Eugene Caffy of the 1st Engineer Special Brigade. Van Fleet does not remember Roosevelt saying it. On June 6, 1944, Van Fleet was one of the rising stars in the Army, and it was about time. General Marshall had confused Van Fleet with another officer of the same name whom he knew to be an alcoholic back in his days at the Infantry School at Fort Benning. Van Fleet's career suffered from this unfortunate, and unfair, case of mistaken identity until someone finally pointed out to General Marshall that this Van Fleet was not the same person as the alcoholic he knew at Benning. Quite the contrary, Van Fleet was an energetic, resourceful officer who rose to corps command in World War II and army command in Korea.
9. Crum to family, WHMC.
10. Ricker, oral history, EC.
11. Drez, *Voices of D-Day*, pp. 177–178.
12. McQuiston, oral history, EC.

13. U.S. Army, *Utah Beach to Cherbourg*, pp. 47–50; Robert Tabb III, oral history, featured at www.military.com Web site.

14. Jensen, *Strike Swiftly!*, pp. 139–140.

15. U.S. Army, *Utah Beach to Cherbourg*, pp. 51–53; Jones, oral history, EC.

16. Jensen, *Strike Swiftly!*, pp. 141–144; Ambrose, *D-Day*, pp. 282–283; Graham Cosmas and Albert Cowdrey, *The United States Army in World War II: Medical Service in the European Theater of Operations* (Washington DC: Center of Military History, United States Army, 1992), pp. 203–208. Engineers later told Ahearn that they removed 15,000 mines from the area where he got wounded.

17. Coleman, unpublished memoir, p. 9, EC.

18. Ambrose, *D-Day*, pp. 284–285; Koskimaki, *D-Day with the Screaming Eagles*, pp. 174–175; U.S. Army, *Utah Beach to Cherbourg*, pp. 51–54.

19. *Ivy Leaves*, June 1994, p. 51.

20. Sam Jacks, oral history, featured at www.military.com Web site.

21. Astor, *June 6, 1944*, pp. 273–274.

22. Reeder, *Born at Reveille*, p. 248; Red Reeder, *Assembly: Association of Graduates, United States Military Academy*, May 1994, pp. 8–9.

23. Darel Parker, oral history, EC.

24. Bob Kay, *Ivy Leaves*, June 1994, p. 45.

25. U.S. Army, *Utah Beach to Cherbourg*, p. 54; Reeder, *Born at Reveille*, pp. 248–249; Johnson, *History of the Twelfth Infantry Regiment in World War II*, pp. 61–64. Two other Utah beach incidents are worthy of note. The first Americans soldiers to land on French soil were members of the 4th and 24th Cavalry Squadrons. At 0430 they assaulted the Iles-St-Marcouf, an island just off the coast of Utah beach. Planners feared that the Germans might use the island as an observation post. They didn't, but they did mine the place and that, coupled with long-range artillery, inflicted casualties on the 132-man assault force. The other incident involved B Battery of the 29th Field Artillery Battalion. The LCT carrying this unit struck a mine, killing the majority of B Battery's soldiers before they ever reached the shores of France.

26. John Brawley, *Anyway, We Won: Out of the Ozarks and into the Army in World War Two* (Marceline, MO: Walsworth, 1988), p. 143; J. Lawton Collins, *Lighting Joe: An Autobiography* (Baton Rouge: Louisiana State University Press, 1979), pp. 200–201.

27. U.S. Army, *Utah Beach to Cherbourg*, pp. 55–56; Harrison, *Cross*

Channel Attack, pp. 304–305; Morison, *Invasion of France and Germany,* p. 103.

13. The Rangers at Pointe-du-Hoc

1. Historical Division, Department of the Army, *Small Unit Actions: France, 2d Ranger Battalion at Pointe du Hoc, Saipan, 27th Division at Tanapag Plain, Italy, 351st Infantry at Santa Maria Infante, France, 4th Armored Division at Singling* (Washington, DC: Center of Military History, United States Army, 1982), pp. 5–6; McDonald, *Libertion of Pointe du Hoc,* pp. 71–72; Ambrose, *D-Day,* p. 406; Astor, *June 6, 1944,* pp. 204–206; Michael Frederick and Joseph Masci, "Rangers Take the Pointe," *World War II,* May 2000, pp. 50–51.

2. Lou Lisko, Eikner, oral histories, EC; Astor, *June 6, 1944,* p. 207.

3. Frank South, oral history, EC; Ambrose *D-Day,* p. 405; Astor, *June 6, 1944,* pp. 146–47. Lieutenant Eikner claimed that Lytle was taken to a hospital to dry out.

4. McDonald, *Liberation of Pointe du Hoc,* pp. 72–73; Historical Division, Department of the Army, *Small Unit Actions,* p. 7; Eikner, oral history, EC.

5. Astor, *June 6, 1944,* p. 207.

6. Historical Division, Department of the Army, *Small Unit Actions,* pp. 9–12; Eikner, oral history, EC.

7. Astor, *June 6, 1944,* pp. 213–215; Drez, *Voices of D-Day,* pp. 265–266.

8. Sigurd Sundby, oral history, EC.

9. Astor, *June 6, 1944,* pp. 206–207; Drez, *Voices of D-Day,* p. 269.

10. Sundby, oral history, EC.

11. South, oral history, EC.

12. Salva Maimone, oral history, EC; Drez, *Voices of D-Day,* p. 262.

13. Astor, *June 6, 1944,* p. 209; Masci, "Rangers Take the Pointe," p. 52.

14. W. C. Heinz, "I Took My Son to Omaha Beach," *Collier's,* 6/11/54, pp. 21–25.

15. Astor, *June 6, 1944,* p. 209.

16. Historical Division, Department of the Army, *Small Unit Actions,* pp. 21–23; Robert W. Black, *Rangers in World War II* (New York: Ballantine Books, 1992), pp. 193–196, 366–372. Lapres himself, and several other men, moved inland and helped set up a roadblock along the vital coastal road.

17. Maimone, Sundby, oral histories, EC.

18. Masci, "Rangers Take the Pointe," pp. 52–53.

19. Historical Division, Department of the Army, *Small Unit Actions*, p. 30; McDonald, *Liberation of Pointe du Hoc*, pp. 109–110; Astor, *June 6, 1944*, pp. 210–211; Drez, *Voices of D-Day*, p. 270; Masci, "Rangers Take the Pointe," p. 54.

20. Astor, *June 6, 1944*, pp. 211–213; Drez, *Voices of D-Day*, pp. 269–271; Masci, "Rangers Take the Pointe," pp. 54–56; McDonald, *Liberation of Pointe du Hoc*, pp. 110–115; Black, *Rangers in World War II*, pp. 209–211; Ambrose, *D-Day*, pp. 415–416; Patrick O'Donnell, *Beyond Valor: World War II's Rangers and Airborne Veterans Reveal the Heart of Combat* (New York: Free Press, 2001), pp. 146–148; Historical Division, Department of the Army, *Omaha Beachhead* (Washington DC: Center of Military History United States Army, 1945), pp. 90–91; Eikner, oral history, EC; Heinz, "I Took My Son to Omaha Beach," *Collier's*, pp. 26–27. The authors of *Small Unit Actions* erroneously claim that after Lomell destroyed the first two guns, Sergeant Rupinski's patrol found them and destroyed the other three. The Rangers at Pointe-du-Hoc staved off five counterattacks on D-Day.

14. Bloody Omaha

1. Historical Division, Department of the Army, *Omaha Beachhead*, pp. 20–25; Morison, *Invasion of France and Germany*, pp. 114–116; Robin Neillands and Roderick De Normann, *D-Day 1944: Voices from Normandy* (New York: Orion Books, 1993), pp. 179–180; Cawthon, *Other Clay*, p. 60.

2. Thomas Valance, Murdoch, oral histories, EC; Drez, *Voices of D-Day*, pp. 201–204; Kershaw, *The Bedford Boys*, pp. 125–137.

3. Joseph Ewing, *29 Let's Go! A History of the 29th Infantry Division in World War II* (Washington, DC: Infantry Journal Press, 1948), pp. 40–41; Balkoski, *Beyond the Beachhead*, p. 125; Kershaw, *The Bedford Boys*, pp. 125–132.

4. Andrew Carroll, editor, *War Letters: Extraordinary Correspondence from American Wars* (New York: Scribner, 2001), p. 235.

5. Murdoch, oral history, EC; William Folkestad, *The View from the Turret: The 743rd Tank Battalion During World War II* (Shippensburg, PA: Burd Street Press, 2000), pp. 7–8. Thanks to a decision by a naval officer named Dean Rockwell, the majority of the

743rd's DD tanks made it ashore. Rockwell saw many DD tanks from the 741st sink in the heavy seas, so he decided take the 743rds all the way to shore. About half of the tanks at Omaha beach were not amphibious. These landed from LCTs wherever an opening on the beach could be found.

6. Murdoch, oral history, EC; Drez, *Voices of D-Day*, pp. 202–206; Kershaw, *The Bedford Boys*, pp. 129–137, 239–240; Ambrose, *D-Day*, p. 328.

7. Ralph Goranson, unpublished memoir, p. 9, copy in author's possession.

8. Sidney Saloman, unpublished memoir, pp. 3–5, EC, MS1881, Box 20, Folder 17, SCUTK.

9. Donald Scribner, oral history, EC.

10. O'Donnell, *Beyond Valor*, p. 142; Astor, *June 6, 1944*, p. 219.

11. Goranson, unpublished memoir, p. 9.

12. Scribner, oral history, EC.

13. Saloman, unpublished memoir, pp. 6–8, EC, SCUTK; Goranson, unpublished memoir, p. 10; O'Donnell, *Beyond Valor*, pp. 142–143; Astor, *June 6, 1944*, pp. 219–220; Black, *Rangers in World War II*, pp. 186–190; Ambrose, *D-Day*, pp. 400–405. The movie *Saving Private Ryan* brilliantly portrays C Company of the 2nd Rangers making their assault on Dog Green beach, but it shows the Rangers, mixed together with groups of 116th Infantrymen, moving up the Vierville draw. In fact, the C Company Rangers ascended the cliffs and then turned west. They did not open the draw alone.

14. Historical Division, Department of the Army, *Omaha Beachhead*, pp. 47–48; Balkoski, *Beyond the Beachhead*, pp. 125–127; Drez, *Voices of D-Day*, p. 206.

15. Historical Division, Department of the Army, *Omaha Beachhead*, p. 47; Ewing, *29 Let's Go!*, p. 41; Balkoski, *Beyond the Beachhead*, p. 128; Drez, *Voices of D-Day*, pp. 206–209; Bare, oral history, EC; Rocco Russo, unpublished memoir, pp. 16–18, EC.

16. Ewing, *29 Let's Go,!* pp. 43–44.

17. Branham, oral history, EC; Astor, *June 6, 1944*, p. 230.

18. Balkoski, *Beyond the Beachhead*, pp. 132–133, 140; Cawthon, *Other Clay*, pp. 54–62; Sidney Bingham to Thomas Francis Eagan, 1/11/47, EC. Ernie Pyle mentioned Cawthon's unique wound in his column.

19. Ewing, *29 Let's Go*, p. 43; Drez, *Voices of D-Day*, pp. 213–218; Kershaw, *The Bedford Boys*, pp. 139–145; Neillands and De Normann,

Voices from Normandy, pp. 187–189; Harold Baumgarten, oral history, EC. Baumgarten completed his medical studies after the war and became a practicing physician.

20. Astor, *June 6, 1944*, pp. 225–227; Neillands and De Normann, *Voices from Normandy*, pp. 183–186; Kershaw, *The Bedford Boys*, pp. 146–147; Slaughter, oral history, EC.

21. Black, *Rangers in World War II*, pp. 200–208. Out of a strength of 136 men, A and B Companies of the 2nd Rangers lost thirty-one killed, sixty-six wounded, and five missing at Green beach. O'Donnell, *Beyond Valor*, p. 144; Edward Gurney, unpublished memoir, pp. 3–4, copy in author's possession; Heaney, oral history, EC.

22. Garwood Bacon, oral history, featured at www.military.com Web site.

23. Fritz Weinshank, oral history, featured at www.military.com Web site.

24. Raymond Summers, unpublished memoir, p. 2, Box 59, 3rd Armored Division Archives, University of Illinois, Champaign (hereafter referred to as UI Archives).

25. Historical Division, Department of the Army, *Omaha Beachhead*, pp. 77–78; Heaney, oral history, EC.

26. Morison, *Invasion of France and Germany*, pp. 143–145; Theodore Roscoe, *United States Destroyer Operations in World War II* (Annapolis, MD: Naval Institute Press, 1953), pp. 350–351; Somers, *Saturday Evening Post*, p. 98; Anette Tapert, editor, *Lines of Battle: Letters from American Servicemen, 1941–1945* (New York: Times Books, 1987), pp. 160–161; Slaughter, oral history, EC.

27. George Thomas Poe, oral history, EC.

28. Black, *Rangers in World War II*, pp. 200–201; Herb Epstein, interview with Patrick O'Donnell, n.d., featured at www.dropzone.com Web site; John Reville, oral history, EC.

29. Francis Dawson, oral history, EC; Astor, *June 6, 1944*, p. 251.

30. Black, *Rangers in World War II*, p. 206; Donald Nelson, oral history, EC, Bill McClintock, interview at www.erieveterans.com.

31. O'Donnell, *Beyond Valor*, p. 151; Mehaffey, oral history, EC.

32. Epstein interview, www.dropzone.come; Victor Fast, oral history, EC; Askin, "Immediate Action Needed," *World War II*, May 1987, p. 37. The reason Cota's words have been so closely studied by historians and participants alike is because they led to the enduring Ranger motto, "Rangers Lead the Way." Some bristle at the motto because of its implication that the Rangers alone led the

way off Dog White, Omaha beach. In my opinion, the motto represents no slight against the 29th Division, whose soldiers were also pivotal to the advance off Dog White. General Cota, as he walked along the seawall, was saying and doing anything he could to get the troops moving. For this reason, I believe he said many variations of "Rangers lead the way" in addition to the other imprecations that eyewitnesses claim to have heard him say.

33. Balksoki, *Beyond the Beachhead*, pp. 133–136; Russo, unpublished memoir, p. 19, EC.

34. Historical Division, Department of the Army, *Omaha Beachhead*, pp. 52–53, 58–62; Ewing, *29 Let's Go*, pp. 45–54; Black, *Rangers in World War II*, 205–208; Balkoski, *Beyond the Beachhead*, pp. 135–140; O'Donnell, *Beyond Valor*, pp. 152–153; Astor, *June 6, 1944*, pp. 250–253; Askin, "Immediate Action Needed," *World War II*, May 1987, p. 38; Dawson, oral history, EC; Gale Beccue, oral history, EC.

35. Knickerbocker et al., *Danger Forward*, p. 179; P. L. Fitts, oral history, EC.

36. H. R. Cluster, "D-Day: No Way to Storm a Beach," *United States Naval Institute*, May/June 1994, p. 17.

37. Harry Kennedy, oral history, EC. The Coast Guard role in the invasion is covered magnificently in a paper by Scott T. Price, "The U.S. Coast Guard at Normandy," which can be found at the Coast Guard's Web Site, www.uscg.mil.com.

38. Murphy interview with Johnson, 4/13/93, and interview with Mr. Stan Tinsley, 9/5/90, SCUTK.

39. Frank Chesney, oral history, EC.

40. Talton, unpublished memoir, pp. 10–14, EC.

41. Hurlbut, interview with Elson, www.tankbooks.com. The army engineer and naval demolition teams at Omaha beach suffered roughly 41 percent casualties.

42. Historical Division, Department of the Army, *Omaha Beachhead*, pp. 48–49, 73–75; Kellman, oral history, www.military.com; McKinney, interview with Elson, www.tankbooks.com.

43. David Snoke to parents, 6/6/45, Box 33, Folder 2809, WHMC.

44. Harley Reynolds, unpublished memoir, pp. 12–14, copy in author's possession.

45. Ira Berkowitz, oral history, EC; Drez, *Voices of D-Day*, p. 254.

46. In February, 1945, Lieutenant Spaulding told his story in detail to the great historian Forrest Pogue. Pogue reproduced the interview in Pogue, *Pogue's War*, pp. 64–75. Stephen Ambrose, in

D-Day, pp. 349–352, 442–446, based his superb account of the exploits of Spaulding's platoon on Pogue's interview with Spaulding.

47. Astor, *June 6, 1944*, p. 233–234; Drez, *Voices of D-Day*, p. 241; Buddy Mazzara, oral history, EC. Erben got wounded by mortar fragments later on D-Day. Before Mazzara helped destroy the pillbox, he swam a quarter-mile from his landing craft to shore, all with the flamethrower, plus other equipment, strapped to his back. As he swam he also helped a buddy who couldn't swim make it to the beach. The exploits of Spaulding, Dawson, et al., are described well in Ambrose, *D-Day*, pp. 349–352, 354–356.

48. John Ellery, oral history, EC.

49. Reynolds, unpublished memoir, pp. 14–19.

50. Leonard Wilmont, oral history, EC.

51. Historical Division, Department of the Army, *Omaha Beachhead*, pp. 63–73; Morison, *Invasion of France and Germany*, pp. 143–145; Roscoe, *Destroyer Operations in World War II*, pp. 350–51; Drez, *Voices of D-Day*, p. 251; James Knight, "The DD That Saved the Day," *Proceedings of the United States Naval Institute*, August 1989, pp. 124–126; Murphy interviews, SCUTK; Christopher Cornazzani, oral history, EC; Reynolds, unpublished memoir, p. 20. For a time the *Carmick* also assisted the *Frankford* at Easy Red and may have contributed to the reduction of the bunker at E-1.

52. Cosmas and Cowdrey, *Medical Service in the European Theater of Operations*, pp. 211–213; Fahey, oral history, EC.

53. Bradley, *Soldier's Story*, pp. 270–274; Bradley and Clay, *General's Life*, pp. 251–252. Eisenhower spent the day brooding, smoking, and receiving fragmentary reports. He felt powerless and wished more than anything, that he was closer to the action.

SELECT BIBLIOGRAPHY

Archives and Manuscript Collections

Carlisle, PA. United States Army Military History Institute.

Champaign, IL. University of Illinois Archives.

Columbia, MO. Western Historical Manuscript Collection, University of Missouri, World War II Letters.

Denton, TX. University of North Texas World War II Oral History Collection.

Knoxville, TN, University of Tennessee Special Collection Library, World War II Collection (repository of the Center for the Study of War and Society).

New Orleans, LA. Dwight D. Eisenhower Center.

Savannah, GA. The Mighty Eighth Air Force Heritage Museum Archives.

Books

Ambrose, Stephen. *The Supreme Commander: The War Years of General Dwight D. Eisenhower*. Garden City, NY: Doubleday, 1970.

———. *Band of Brothers*. New York: Simon and Schuster, 1992.

———. *D-Day: The Climactic Battle of World War II*. New York: Simon and Schuster, 1994.

Astor, Gerald. *June 6, 1944: The Voices of D-Day*. New York: Dell Publishing, 1994.

———. *The Mighty Eighth: The Air War in Europe As Told by the Men Who Fought It*. New York: Dell Publishing, 1997.

———. *The Greatest War: Americans in Combat, 1941–1945*. Novato, CA: Presidio Press, 2000.

Balkoski, Joseph. *Beyond the Beachhead: The 29th Infantry Division in Normandy*. Harrisburg, PA: Stackpole Books, 1989.

Bando, Mark. *101st Airborne: The Screaming Eagles at Normandy*. Osceola, WI: Motor Books International, 2001.

———. *The 101st Airborne at Normandy*. Osceola, WI: Motor Books International, 1994.

Baxter, Colin. *The Normandy Campaign, 1944: A Selected Bibliography*. Westport, CT: Greenwood Press, 1992.

Bennett, Ralph. *Ultra in the West: The Normandy Campaign, 1944–1945*. New York: Charles Scribner's Sons, 1979.

Biggs, Bradley. *Gavin*. Hamden, CT: Archon Books, 1980.

Binkoski, Joseph. *The 115th Infantry Regiment in World War II*. Washington, D.C.: Infantry Journal Press, 1948.

Black, Robert. *Rangers in World War II*. New York: Ballantine Books, 1992.

Blair, Clay. *Ridgway's Paratroopers: The American Airborne in World War II*. Garden City, NY: Doubleday, 1985.

Blumenson, Martin, editor. *The Patton Papers, 1940–1945*. Boston: Houghton Mifflin Company, 1974.

———. *Patton: The Man Behind the Legend, 1885–1945*. New York: Berkley Books, 1985.

Booth, Michael and Duncan Spencer. *Paratrooper: The Life of Gen. James M. Gavin*. New York: Simon and Schuster, 1994.

Bradley, Omar. *A Soldier's Story*. New York: Henry Holt, 1951.

———. *A General's Life*. New York: Simon and Schuster, 1983.

Brawley, John. *Anyway We Won: Out of the Ozarks and into the Army in World War Two*. Marceline, MO: Walsworth Publishing, 1988.

Breast, John, editor. *Missions Remembered: Recollections of the WWII Air War*. Brentwood, TN: JM Productions, 1995.

Brereton, Louis. *The Brereton Diaries*. New York: William Morrow, 1946.

Burgett, Donald. *Currahee! A Screaming Eagle at Normandy*. Novato, CA: Presidio Press, 1999.

Butcher, Harry. *My Three Years with Eisenhower*. New York: Simon and Schuster, 1946.

Carrell, Paul. *Invasion: They're Coming*. New York: Bantam Books, 1962.

Carroll, Andrew, editor. *War Letters: Extraordinary Correspondence from American Wars*. New York: Scribner, 2001.

Carter, Kit, and Robert Mueller, editors. *The Army Air Forces in World*

War II: Combat Chronology, 1941–1945. Washington, D.C.: Office of Air Force History, 1973.

Cawthon, Charles. *Other Clay: A Remembrance of the World War II Infantry*. Boulder MO: University Press of Colorado, 1990.

Chandler, Alfred, editor. *The Papers of Dwight David Eisenhower: The War Years*. Volumes, III, IV, and V. Baltimore: Johns Hopkins Press, 1970.

Coffman, Warren. *I Never Intended to Be a Soldier*. Greensboro, NC: Lifestyles Press, 1999.

Collins, J. Lawton. *Lightning Joe: An Autobiography*. Baton Rouge, LA: Louisiana State University Press, 1979.

Cooling, Benjamin. *Case Studies in the Development of Close Air Support*. Washington, D.C.: Office of Air Force History, United States Air Force, 1990.

Cosmas, Graham, and Albert Cowdrey. *The United States Army in World War II: Medical Service in the European Theater of Operations*. Washington, D.C.: Center of Military History, United States Army, 1992.

Cowdrey, Albert. *Fighting for Life: American Military Medicine in World War II*. New York: Free Press, 1994.

Craven, Wesley, and James Cate, editors. *The Army Air Forces in World War II: Europe: Argument to V-E Day, January 1944 to May 1945*. Washington, D.C.: Office of Air Force History, 1951.

Davis, Richard. *Carl A. Spaatz and the Air War in Europe*. Washington, D.C.: Center for Air Force History, 1993.

Dawson, W. Forrest, editor. *Saga of the All American*. Nashville, TN: Battery Press, reprint of 1946 edition.

D'Este, Carlo. *Decision in Normandy*, Old Saybrook, CT: Konecky and Konecky, 1984.

———. *Patton: A Genius for War*. New York: HarperPerenial, 1995.

———. *Eisenhower: A Soldier's Life*. New York: Henry Holt, 2002.

Doubler, Michael. *Closing with the Enemy: How G.I.'s Fought the War in Europe, 1944–1945*. Lawrence: University Press of Kansas, 1994.

Drez, Ronald. *Voices of D-Day*. Baton Rouge: Louisiana State University Press, 1994.

Dunn, William. *Fighter Pilot: The First American Ace of World War II*. Lexington: University Press of Kentucky, 1982.

Dupuy, Trevor. *A Genius for War: The German Army and General Staff, 1807–1945*. Englewood Cliffs, NJ: Prentice-Hall, 1977.

Eisenhower, David. *Eisenhower at War, 1943–1945*. New York: Vintage Books, 1986.

Eisenhower, Dwight. *Crusade in Europe.* New York: Doubleday, 1948.

Eisenhower Foundation. *D-Day: The Normandy Invasion in Retrospect.* Lawrence: University Press of Kansas, 1971.

Ewing, Joseph. *29 Let's Go! A History of the 29th Infantry Division in World War II.* Washington, D.C.: Infantry Journal Press, 1948.

Folkestad, William. *The View from the Turret: The 743rd Tank Battalion During World War II.* Shippensburg, PA: Burd Street Press, 2000.

Fortier, Norman "Bud." *An Ace of the Eighth: An American Fighter Pilot's Air War in Europe.* New York: Ballantine Books, Presidio Press, 2003.

François, Dominique. *507th Parachute Infantry Regiment, 1942–1945.* Bayeux, France: Heimdal, 2000.

Freeman, Roger. *The Mighty Eighth: A History of the U.S. 8th Army Air Force.* Garden City, NY: Doubleday, 1970.

Gabreski, Francis. *Gabby: A Fighter Pilot's Life.* New York: Orion Books, 1991.

Gavin, James. *On to Berlin.* New York: Bantam Books, 1978.

Harrison, Gordon. *The United States Army in World War II: Cross Channel Attack.* Washington, D.C.: Office of the Chief of Military History, United States Army, 1951.

Hastings, Max. *Overlord: D-Day and the Battle for Normandy.* New York: Simon and Schuster, 1984.

Headquarters, First Army, U.S. Army. *Report of Operations, 20 October 1943–1 August 1944.* 7 vols. Carlisle Barracks, PA: United States Army Military History Institute, 1945[?].

Hesketh, Roger. *Fortitude: The D-Day Deception Campaign.* Woodstock, NY: Overlook Press, 2002.

Hirshson, Stanley. *General Patton: A Soldier's Life.* New York: HarperCollins, 2002.

Historical Division, Department of the Army. *Utah Beach to Cherbourg, 6 June–27 June.* Washington, D.C.: Center of Military History, United States Army, 1984.

———. *Omaha Beachhead.* Washington, D.C.: Center of Military History, United States Army, 1945.

———. *Small Unit Actions.* Washington, D.C.: Center of Military History, United States, Army, 1982.

Hughes, Thomas Alexander. *Overlord: General Pete Quesada and the Triumph of Tactical Air Power in World War II.* New York: Free Press, 1995.

Irving, David. *Hitler's War.* New York: Avon Books, 1990.

Jeffers, H. Paul. *Theodore Roosevelt: The Life of a War Hero*. Novato, CA: Presidio Press, 2002.

Jensen, Marvin. *Strike Swiftly! The 70th Tank Battalion from North Africa to Normandy to Germany*. Novato, CA: Presidio Press, 1997.

Johnson, Franklyn. *One More Hill*. New York: Bantam Books, 1983.

Johnson, Gerden. *History of the Twelfth Infantry Regiment in World War II*. Boston: 12th Infantry Regiment Association, 1947.

Karig, Walter, et al. *Battle Report: The Atlantic War*. New York: Rinehart, 1946.

Keegan, John. *Six Armies in Normandy*. New York: Penguin Books, 1982.

Kershaw, Alex. *The Bedford Boys: One American Town's Ultimate D-Day Sacrifice*. Cambridge, MA: DaCapo Press, 2003.

Knickerbocker, H. R. et al. *Danger Forward: The Story of the First Division in World War II*. Nashville, TN: Battery Press, 1947.

Kohn Richard, and Joseph Harahan, editors. *Condensed Analysis of the Ninth Air Force in the European Theater of Operations*. Washington, D.C.: Office of Air Force History, United States Air Force, 1984.

Koskimaki, George. *D-Day with the Screaming Eagles*. Medalia, MN: House of Print, 1970.

Lewis, Adrian. *Omaha Beach: A Flawed Victory*. Chapel Hill: University of North Carolina Press, 2001.

Liddell Hart, Basil. *The German Generals Talk*. New York: William Morrow, 1948.

Litoff, Judy Barrett, and David Smith, editors. *Fighting Fascism in Europe: The World War II Letters of an American Veteran of the Spanish Civil War*. New York: Fordham University Press, 2003.

Luck, Hans von. *Panzer Commander*. New York: Dell Publishing, 1989.

Mansoor, Peter. *The G.I. Offensive in Europe: The Triumph of American Infantry Divisions*, Lawrence: University Press of Kansas, 1999.

Marshall, S.L.A. *Night Drop: The American Airborne Invasion of Normandy*. Boston: Little, Brown, 1962.

Masters, Charles. *Glidermen of Neptune: The American D-Day Glider Attack*. Carbondale: Southern Illinois University Press, 1995.

Mauer, Mauer, editor. *Air Force Combat Units of World War II*. Washington, D.C.: Office of Air Force History, 1983.

McDonald, JoAnna. *The Liberation of Pointe du Hoc: The 2nd U.S. Rangers at Normandy*. Redondo Beach, CA: Rank and File Publications, 2000.

McManus, John C. *The Deadly Brotherhood: The American Combat

Soldier in World War II. Novato, CA: Presidio Press, 1998.

———. *Deadly Sky: The American Combat Airman in World War II.* Novato, CA: Presidio Press, 2000.

Miller, Merle. *Ike the Soldier.* New York: G. P. Putnam's Sons, 1987.

Millet, Allan, and Williamson Murray. *A War to Be Won: Fighting the Second World War.* Cambridge, MA: Harvard University Press, 2000.

Mitchell, George C. *Matthew B. Ridgway: Soldier, Statesman, Scholar, Citizen.* Mechanisburg, PA: Stackpole, 2002.

Morrison, Samuel Eliot. *History of United States Naval Operations in World War II: The Invasion of France and Germany, 1944–1945.* Boston: Little, Brown, 1957.

Murphy, Edward. *Heroes of WWII.* New York: Ballantine Books, 1990.

Neillands, Robin, and Roderick de Normann. *D-Day, 1944: Voices from Normandy.* London: Orion, 1993.

———. *The Battle of Normandy, 1944.* London: Cassell, 2002.

O'Donnell, Patrick. *Beyond Valor: World War II's Ranger and Airborne Veterans Reveal the Heart of Combat.* New York: Free Press, 2001.

Parillo, Mark, editor. *We Were in the Big One: Experiences of the World War II Generation.* Wilmington, DE: Scholarly Resources, 2002.

Perret, Geoffrey. *Eisenhower.* Holbrook, MA: Adams Media Corporation, 1999.

Pogue, Forrest. *The United States Army in World War II: The Supreme Command.* Washington, D.C.: Office of the Chief of Military History, United States Army, 1954.

———. *Pogue's War: Diaries of a WWII Combat Historian.* Lexington: University Press of Kentucky, 2001.

Prados, Edward, editor. *Neptunus Rex: Naval Stories of the Normandy Invasion, June 6, 1944.* Novato, CA: Presidio Press, 1998.

Rapport, Leonard, and Arthur Northwood, Jr. *Rendezvous with Destiny: A History of the 101st Airborne Division.* Nashville, TN: Battery Press, 2000, reprint of 1948 edition.

Reeder, Red. *Born at Reveille.* New York: Duell, Sloane, and Pearce, 1966.

Richlak, Jerry. *Glide to Glory: Unedited Personal Stories from the Airborne Glidermen of World War II.* Chesterland, OH: Cedar House, 2002.

Ridgway, Matthew. *Soldier: The Memoirs of Matthew B. Ridgway.* New York: Harper and Brothers, 1956.

Roscoe, Theodore. *United States Destroyer Operations in World War II.* Annapolis, MD: Naval Institute Press, 1953.

Ruppenthal, Roland. *The United States Army in World War II: European*

Theater of Operations, Logistical Support of the Armies. Washington, D.C.: Center of Military History, United States Army, 1995, Volume 1.

Rust, Kenn. *The 9th Air Force in World War II.* Fallbrook, CA: Aero Publishers, 1967.

Ryan, Cornelius. *The Longest Day.* New York: Simon and Schuster, 1959.

Sefton, G. William. *It Was My War: I'll Remember It the Way I Want To!* Manhattan, KS: Sunflower University Press, 1994.

Smith, Dale. *Screaming Eagle: Memoirs of a B-17 Group Commander.* Chapel Hill, NC: Algonquin Books, 1990.

Smith, S. E., editor. *The United States Navy in World War II.* New York: William Morrow/Quill, 1996.

Smith, Walter Bedell. *Eisenhower's Six Great Decisions: Europe, 1944–1945.* New York: Longmans, Green, 1956.

Sullivan, John. *Overlord's Eagles: Operations of the United States Army Air Forces in the Invasion of Normandy in World War II.* Jefferson, NC: McFarland, 1997.

Tapert, Annette, editor. *Lines of Battle: Letters from American Servicemen, 1941–1945.* New York: Times Books, 1987.

Taylor, Maxwell. *Swords to Plowshares.* New York: DaCapo Press, 1972.

Towne, Allen. *Doctor Danger Forward.* Jefferson, NC: McFarland, 2000.

True, William, and Deryck Tufts True. *The Cow Spoke French: The Story of Sgt. William True, American Paratrooper in World War II.* Bennington, VT: Merriam Press, 2002.

Tucker, William. *D-Day: Thirty-Five Days in Normandy, Reflections of a Paratrooper.* Harwichport, MA: International Airborne Books, 2002.

Tute, Warren, John Costello, and Terry Hughes. *D-Day.* Sidgwick and Jackson, 1974.

United States Army Air Force. *Ultra and the History of the United States Strategic Air Force in Europe vs. the German Air Force.* Frederick, MD: University Publications of America, 1980.

Van Creveld, Martin. *Fighting Power: German and U.S. Army Performance, 1939–1945.* Westport, CT: Greenwood Press, 1982.

Webster, David. *Parachute Infantry: An American Paratrooper's Memoir of D-Day and the Fall of the Third Reich.* Baton Rouge: Louisiana State University Press, 1994.

Weigley, Russell. *Eisenhower's Lieutenants: The Campaign of France and*

Germany, 1944–1945. Bloomington: Indiana University Press, 1981.

Wills, Deryk. *Put on Your Boots and Parachutes: Personal Stories of the Veterans of the United States 82nd Airborne Division.* Leicester: AB Printers Limited, 1997.

Wilmot, Chester. *The Struggle for Europe.* New York: Harper and Brothers, 1952.

Wilson, Theodore, editor. *D-Day 1944.* Lawrence: University Press of Kansas, 1994.

Wolfe, Martin. *Green Light! A Troop Carrier Squadron's War from Normandy to the Rhine.* Washington, D.C.: Center for Air Force History, 1993.

Woodward, Ellis. *Flying School: Combat Hell.* Baltimore: American Literary Press, 1998.

Zuckerman, Solly. *From Apes to Warlords.* London: Hamish Hamilton, 1978.

INDEX